SPACES OF EXISTENCE

VOLUME ONE

UNDERSTANDING LIFE AND LIVING IT

DR. ARNOLD O. THOMPSON

Printed in the United States of America

ISBN 979-8-89114-166-7 (hc)
ISBN 979-8-89114-165-0 (sc)
ISBN 979-8-89114-167-4 (e)

Library of Congress Pre-assigned Control Number: 2025902820

2025.04.04

MainSpring Books
5901 W. Century Blvd
Suite 750
Los Angeles, CA, US, 90045

www.mainspringbooks.com

Other Volumes in the Series:

Also, By Dr. Arnold O. Thompson

The Dark Side of The Gospel

Deliver Us From Evil

The Death of Wisdom The Rise of Folly

Why Do Birds Fly

The Evangelical Church at the Crossroads of Secular Culture and Change

Author's Note

The 85 essays in these volumes are all based on my conceptual model, on page viii, "Spaces of the Universe." My aim was to develop a visual conceptual model that could elucidate the existence of the entire universe, allowing us to comprehend our place within it and navigate its vastness with a clear point of reference.

I completed a double degree program during my undergraduate years. One of my degrees was in Christian Communication with a major in "Evangelism," which focused on the communication of the Gospel from New Testament times. The other degree was in Communication Theory from a State University. I combined these disciplines and created conceptual models that bridged the two areas of study. Each of my books, except "Why Do Birds Fly" (Mainsprings Books, CA, 2023), is based on one of these communication models I developed. Among these models, "Spaces of Existence" is the most comprehensive, addressing all areas of human existence and interaction.

Renowned physicists and scientists have made significant contributions to our understanding of the ecological and physical aspects of the universe. However, as our knowledge of these physical spaces has expanded, the crucial realms beyond our physical space have not received adequate attention. While physical science has excelled in explaining and applying physical spaces, it is by "empirical scientific rules" are limited to address metaphysical spaces. The understanding of the non-physical realm has lagged behind in our times. Consequently, there has been little improvement in our understanding of life beyond the physical. The use of language such as "artificial intelligence," "machine learning," "machine thinking," and similar linguistic constructs, have tended to imitate and confuse, and even limit the essential realm of existence that requires attention in our whole spaces of our universe. These terms cannot truly replicate the complex and unique nature of our world as suggested by humanistic language. Instead, they complicate and obscure the realistic analysis of our evolving world. For instance, the popular saying, "If it looks like a duck, swims like a duck, and quacks like a duck, then it must be a duck," is no longer applicable in a world where any realistic portrayal of duck-like characteristics can be created, concealing a potentially deadly serpent within. Our current era signifies the end of the duck test, leaving us without a suitable replacement to navigate this new universe. These essays aim to offer some guidance in this regard.

In these essays, I recognize the "humanness of humans" and call for the same critical awareness of the "machineness of machines" as the only approach to understanding adequately the spaces of our universe—developing the knowledge, skills, and wisdom to navigate such spaces. The goal would be to know how to navigate a complex world of who we are and who we are becoming and get to who we want to be. Regrettably, we are missing any corresponding development or urgency on the human side of understanding and maintaining humanity. This is in a world heading at quantum speed into a quandary of a universe of machine space.

These extensive essays are meant to help us understand all these spaces inside-out and outside-in, so we never lose who we are, misunderstand who we are becoming, and be sure of who we want to be. These volumes address the entire universe. How can we establish fundamental concepts and structures to comprehend it all? It's a massive endeavor, but that's precisely what these essays aim to accomplish. As science and media advance rapidly, we must strive to understand them even faster. If we fall behind, we lose the game. We need to keep pace with the technology we create, even surpassing the speed of light. We shouldn't embrace the notion that machines can analyze information faster than we can since we are the ones who created them. We are the ones who created the machine speed, the machine "AI" or whatever the machine does. It is folly to lose our humanity and give it to a machine, even in the language we use. For they distort the real issues and machine space compared to ours. If we concede that the machines we create are more powerful than us; we'll soon find ourselves powerless, having fundamentally misunderstood our unique place in the universe. We will suffer not because we made advanced machines but because we gave them who we are. Because we dehumanize ourselves and prioritize the capabilities of machines.

These essays are meant to empower us, to help us recognize and leverage our human potential, and to understand how we have arrived at our current state. If we attribute our existence to a machine or even to a big bang, then those who believe in this will meet their end in the same way. If we subscribe to the belief that anything, like a machine, can perform tasks faster, it's a false equivalence. Just because an eagle soars high, does that make it human? Likewise, other animals with superior senses or physical abilities, such as the bat that can see in the dark, the dog with greater smell than humans, the giraffe, or the lion, should be considered human simply because of their unique qualities? Is this the illogical process in which we subscribe "humanness" to machines?

These volumes address the entire universe. How can we establish fundamental concepts and structures to comprehend it all? It's a massive endeavor, but that's precisely what these essays aim to accomplish. As science and media advance rapidly, we must strive to understand them even faster. If we fall behind, we lose the game. We need to keep pace with the technology we create, even surpassing the speed of light. We shouldn't embrace the notion that machines can analyze information faster than we can, especially since we are the ones who created them. If we concede that the machines we create are more powerful than us, we'll soon find ourselves powerless, having fundamentally misunderstood our unique place in the universe. We suffer when we dehumanize ourselves and prioritize the capabilities of machines. These essays are meant to empower us, to help us recognize and leverage our human potential, and to understand how we have arrived at our current state. If we attribute our existence to a machine or a big bang, then those who believe in this will meet their end similarly. It is a false equivalence if we subscribe to the belief that anything, like a machine, can perform tasks faster. Just because an eagle soars high, does that make it human? Likewise, other animals with superior senses or physical abilities, such as the bat, the dog, the giraffe, or the lion, should not be considered human simply because of their unique qualities.

I want to clarify that I acknowledge that the following statements may seem bold. However, I assure you that they are not exaggerated. The model with the spaces that I will discuss is identified after my "Notes."

Although it is based on various disciplines, all the concepts and spaces I will consider have been carefully examined through the teachings of the Holy Scriptures, which form the foundation of my research on the Spaces of the Universe. I argue that within the sixty-six books of the Bible and in other religious works, there lies the basis for understanding not just the...physical but also the spiritual: Not just how a bird flies or sings, but why. So, although the model is based on the Bible, the essays are written to apply to the one with and without the Bible. These are essays based on more than four decades of research and development into these spaces of the universe in the hope of benefit to all—those who study the universe and those who try to live in it and navigate its spaces.

I make it a point for my personal voice to come through, usually following the introductory words with "I contend." However, even this is rooted in Scripture. The apostles urge Christ's followers to "contend for the faith" (Jude 1:3). This form of contention often serves as a recap or conclusion after presenting the biblical foundation. I would like to make it clear that the additional sub-graphic models and illustrations in this book were not planned in advance. The idea for each came to me in real-time while researching and writing. It was like a burst of inspiration from the Scriptures related to the selected topics. Some are used as a background for a verse, like enhancing a photo of a biblical passage. Others are based on a unique approach I've developed over many years of personal study and meditation in the Scriptures, which I call the "Timothy Trail." This is a systematic approach to research and application. Paul advised young Pastor Timothy, "Study to show yourself approved unto God, rightly dividing the word of truth" (2 Timothy 2:15 emphasis mine). The graphics in this work and the general writing are based on this approach of "rightly dividing" the Scriptures on any given subject to understand the truth as a whole. A list of these "Timothy Trail" is given at the end of this volume.

An audio version lacks photos and graphic illustrations, which are limitations in our modern writing world for writers like me who work in a more expansive communication and artistic space. However, I do not intend to diminish the value of audio literature. Audio offers great timing and practical advantages. Nevertheless, I also enjoy reading Shakespeare and watching performances. Our modern world provides different spaces, so for those who might use this work for teaching, such as a Bible study or personal study, I encourage you to consider adding a hard copy so that the graphic models can also be utilized.

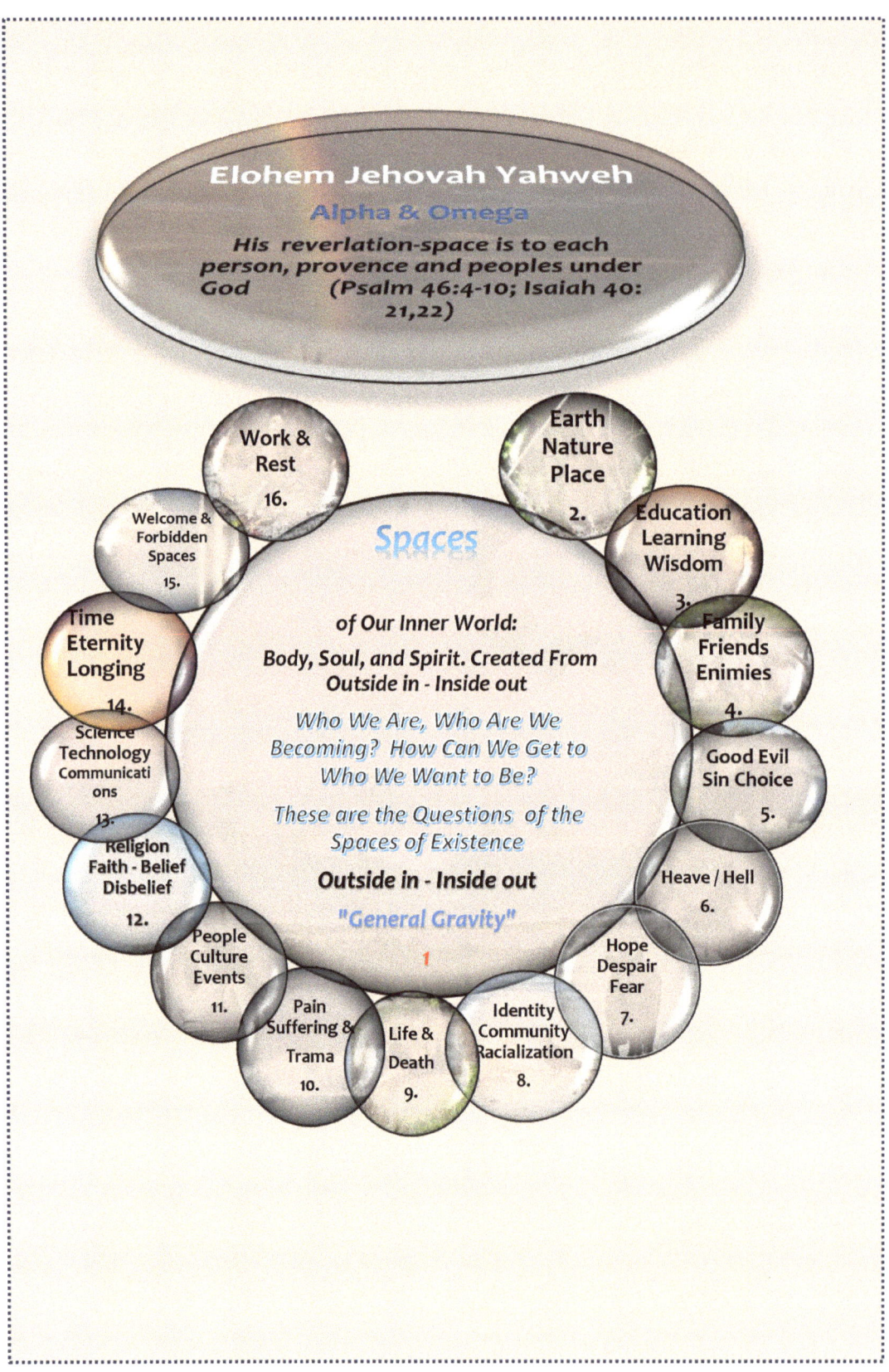

A Model: Spaces of Existence Understanding Who We Are – Getting to Who We Want to Be.

The central large circle in the model represents the space of "us." It delves into the question of who we are within our own skin. The circles surrounding the inner circle denote various critical categories I have chosen to signify the significant influences in our lives. The circle above symbolizes Elohim, God's space, signifying the powerful influence and ability to impact and change us from both within and beyond our physical selves. This concept is based on the Holy Scriptures and seeks to understand the universe's existence and our place within it, guiding us to function in our own spaces of existence effectively (Cf. Numbers 14:21; Jeremiah 23:24; Ephesians 1:23; 4:10; Isaiah 6:3; Psalm 33:5; Habakkuk3:3). If you are seeking a fresh perspective on the universe, these essays are designed to help you find answers.

The essays are rooted in the biblical language of our universe:

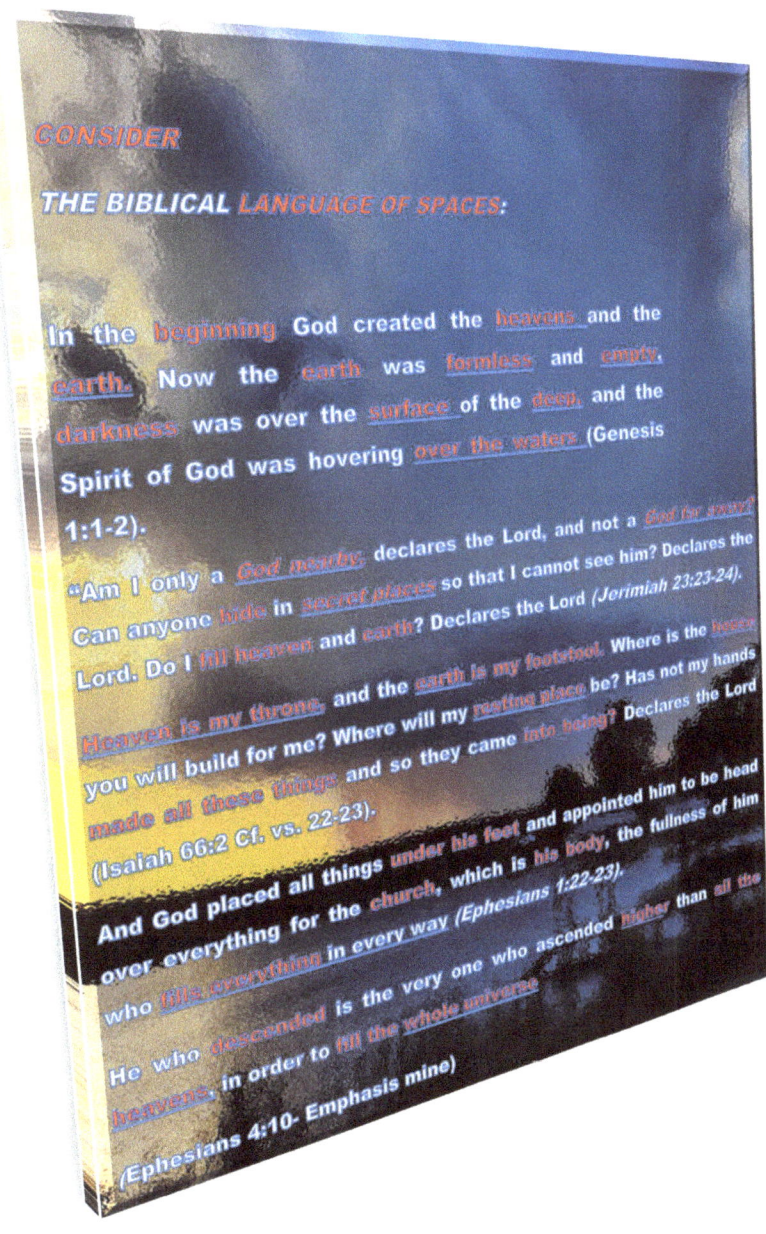

CONTENTS

PART TWO

THE SPACE OF THE CROSS

PART THREE

THE SPACE OF "US"

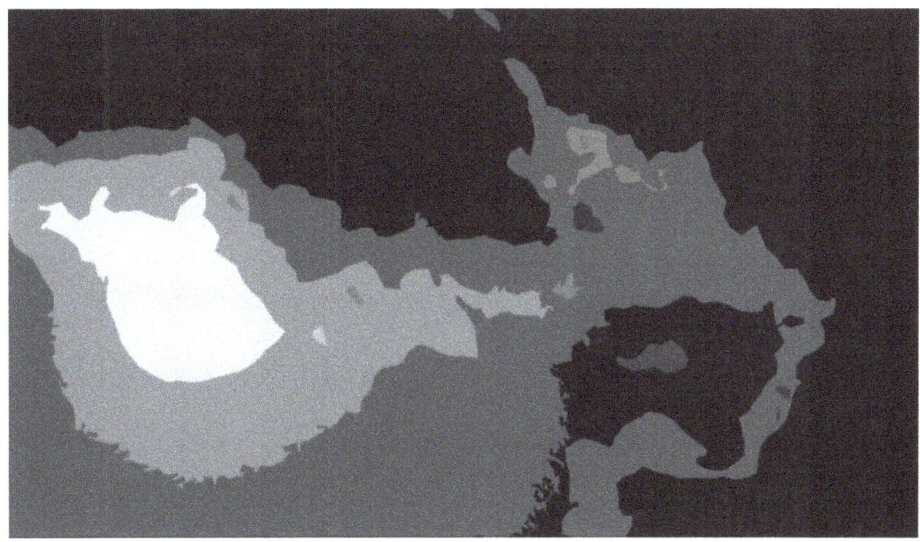

In the Beginning, God Created Spaces...

INTRODUCTION

The Start of Things to Come

The book of Genesis begins by describing the creation of spaces (Genesis 1:1-3). It focuses on the concept of spaces, which will be discussed further throughout the book. Understanding the definitions and applications of spaces is crucial.

In the beginning, God provided the physical space for human existence, meticulously crafting the heavens and the earth. The purposeful and beautiful design of these spaces reflects the craftsmanship of the Almighty. Some spaces are scattered across the earth and even in distant galaxies like divine graffiti, inviting us to marvel at their beauty. Regardless of the various theories about human origins, it's undeniable that human existence would not have been possible without the creation of sustainable and functional ecological spaces.

Theories based on evolutionary processes require more faith to believe in than the creation account in Genesis, which established natural spaces for existence. This includes providing the space for evolutionary development. This book not only explores the existence and influences of physical spaces - if that were the scope, it would be difficult enough. But just as vigorously and boldly, we delve into the complex matters of our inner world of spaces where thoughts are born, feelings cultivated, the will grows strong like the wind or diminishes like the cloud - spaces where overt actions are determined, and even the future is made. I argue that the complexities of human existence looked at from within are far more challenging and mysterious than all the universe's galaxies.

Look at the Book:

Although speaking about evil (which is not our focus here in using this text), the general sentiment of the challenging and complex space of the inner human existence is unmistakable in this Divine narrative:

"The heart is deceitful <u>above all things</u> and beyond cure. <u>Who can understand it? I the Lord search the heart and examine the mind,</u> to reward each person according to their <u>conduct,</u> according to what their deeds deserve" (Jeremiah 17: 9-10 [emphasis mine).

Please remember the following text:

This passage holds the power and authority of the prophet Jeremiah's voice. It carries the weight of God's own voice when He said, "I, the Lord, search the heart...". It reveals that the connection between one's actions, thoughts, and heart is beyond human understanding and only God knows the full extent of it. This passage connects outward behavior with inward thoughts and feelings, highlighting the inseparable link between our outer and inner existence.

It's important to note that this passage does not mean that the inner self cannot be understood. Rather, it emphasizes that true understanding comes from knowing what the Lord reveals about our inner selves. This wisdom and understanding must come from the Creator, who searches the inner workings of each individual.

I want to emphasize that the foundation of this discussion about human existence is rooted in the Holy Scriptures. This is not an anthropological, psychological, or sociological study. Although I have studied these subjects and gained basic understanding, the primary source of understanding human existence comes from studying the Scriptures thoroughly from Genesis to Revelation.

In my in-depth research, I classified each of the sixty-six books of the Bible using a Word Excel program with source notes before writing. While not all information could be included in this book, I found it helpful to create graphic models that arrange research information biblically and dynamically. This book lays the foundation, and the model presented here serves as a blueprint of the various dimensions of human existence, leaving room for further development and understanding.

Where We Start to Determine Where We End

What I am attempting is not isolated in research. Great investigators in the field of science have been swallowed up like a dark hole in so many fields of study. One finds a beautiful thorium of an aspect of the physical universe and proposes to explain the sum of "us" and the universe. Notwithstanding, it is not unusual for another 'genius' to come along later to "poke holes" in the previous one.

I contend, without apology, my simple theorem: *Only one who made it all can explain it all.* And that one claims to exist. Moreover, from the creation of the universe, it has not been silent. He moved like white on rice on His servants through propositional declarations throughout the history of peoples of this world to reveal how it all began and will end. Often, theologians are left out and not taken seriously in the intellectual arena for anything to do with explaining the universe. Regulated as people of "faith" without consideration that "faith without works" is dead (James 2:26). Or, as if faith is devoid of reason, we are left in a world in which we cannot have faith. Yet every scientist must believe in a rational and faithfully designed universe to create any thorium that can explain anything. Without lingering here, I ask: What is more faithful to us than the sun that rises each day, so we do not exist in darkness? How about the moon that rules the night and the water and tides that so many other creatures depend on? What is more faithful than the air, without which we cannot exist? Honestly, I cannot wrap my mind around the genius masterminds who cannot figure these things out. Tell me, who is more qualified to seek a unifying concept of the universe from the finite to the infinite spaces but one who seeks the wisdom of the One Who created it all? Why do we ignore the Prophets who have been the voice of the God who made the universe and spoke through them in the Holy Scriptures as to the spaces of our existence? This is no small question or challenge. If Theology is about studying *God and His works*, where can we end up if we do not start here? I contend we cannot end up with any meaning in finite spaces without an infinite Source space that makes it so.

As a conservative theologian, I do not hesitate to explain the universe and how it works. And as I contend here in this model, it works in spaces of reality. Such a task cannot be left alone to secular humanists who give us a source space of a "Big Bang" developed only by random evolutionary spaces. This approach cannot come even close to explaining the "humanness" of humans that even allow the slightest impetus to try and explain their universe. Why even bother if nothing else exists there but a "big bang? Where does this humanness of humans come from to attempt to explain our spaces of existence? We know we are all going to die. Yet, like a powerful tidal wave of desire, we relentlessly fight to solve all that comes against even shortening it. We fight diseases with a vengeance. Health care is a relentless space that drives us. Survival is not just something we do. It is a space of who we are. Why? Where is desire birth? Can we find love there? Is the humanness of joy, happiness, longing, creativity, moods, reflections, imagination, and other such spaces of existence found there? This is what I mean when I say to every thoughtful person, including the geniuses who try to explain "us" without Him, "What of the *humanness* of humans? How did it get there? How do we explain the complicated, necessary interconnected existence of the spaces in our universe?

But here is how God, in the revelation through Moses, the two significant divides of the universe: (1) Outside in: "In the beginning, God *created the heaven and the earth*" (Genesis 1:1). And (2) inside out that gives us insights into what we all know and experience into the *humanness* of human, Moses wrote: "In the *image of God* he created them" (Genesis 2). I contend there can be no other viable place to begin but here. Spaces of existence that do not start here end with, as the wise King Solomon in his lifelong research concluded, "all is vanity" without an infinite God to finite spaces, many of which yet fascinate, excite, and elude us. Like a Divine spiritual telescope and microscope all in one in the Book, to look to pear relentlessly into these things to find answers to who we are and who we are becoming to figure out who we want to be—that is the rigorous, challenging impetus for this book. Science, through which much pride of knowledge and explanations of our universe have been centered like worshipers of the golden calf, is a small part of the spaces of our vase universe. This work is intended to vastly expand this limiting space of existence. "In the beginning, God created spaces," which in context and substance is precisely how the Bible God's revelation began with all the direct implications of our existence from that propositional statement of Moses. It is the genesis of spaces in this book where I start.

The book is a conservative, Bible-based journey into understanding the spaces of existence. Throughout the panoramic history of literature and revelations, the Bible alone is the source that encompasses all spaces of existence. It informs and demonstrates our fundamental humanness in more straightforward ways than most people think (Hebrews 1:1-3). It tells us who we are and who we are becoming and serves as a guide for all vital choices that are up to us to make in order to become who we want to be (or should be). It is written in a way that allows both those with degrees and the masses without any to be wise in their occupation of our space in His universe, just as Jesus illustrated.

A Challenge of A Lifetime

Exploring the vastness of the universe both internally and externally is a monumental task. Throughout history, brilliant minds have grappled with this challenge, and it remains a complex and formidable undertaking. It is important to remember that human beings, as indicated even in ancient texts, are among the most intricate forms of life on this planet.

Look at the book:

"I praise you because I am fearfully and wonderfully made.

Your works are wonderful, I know that full well"

Psalm 139:14

The Psalmist, in a manner reminiscent of the tranquil inner voice of the soul, eloquently emphasized this concept with the certainty of personal insight and human experience as he added to his praise for his creator: "I know that full well." Each individual person is more intricate than the entirety of the universe. God provided a clue to this comprehension when he declared that he made us in His image. While the universe may exhibit His glory, power, and craftsmanship, it is only through humankind that His unique creative image is revealed, a phenomenon unmatched by anything else. We, as God's creations, are the sole entities capable of occupying a space from which we are able to even endeavor to comprehend this boundless universe. I assert that being "created in the image of God" introduces a level of complexity that no other created beings or entities possess — not even angels, whether good or evil. However, I must quickly affirm that all is not lost. God disclosed that He has thoroughly explored this complexity. He has integrated this enigma into the teachings of His word. Therefore, even though we may never grasp the full extent of our nature or the universe He designed, He has made accessible that which is necessary for our existence, to understand who we are, who we are evolving into, and how we can achieve who we are meant to be (Psalm 119:66; Proverbs 2:6; 15:14; James 1:5; 1 Corinthians 8:2; 13:2). So, we use instruments to observe biotic and abiotic marvels never seen in human existence. Fragile-looking lifeforms exist in ocean pressures that would kill a whale. Lifeforms exist comfortably in their unique spaces where darkness reigns, and technology's eyes have never been seen before in all of human history. However, I contend that the most excellent telescope and microscope of existence still lies within the revelation of God's word that prophets, priests, and people of His word from ancients of time "know that full well." We can know the revelation of God, the revelation of "us," revealing to us in divine propositional actual truth of who we are and who we are becoming and peering into all the possibilities and challenges of who we can be. This is what this book is about.

Moreover, it should not be missed that this created historical process, after all these millenniums, is yet being discovered today, of which the Psalmist never got the opportunity of specific praise. For example, technologies within the last fifty years have allowed us to push into unreachable distance spaces. Move back historical curtains peering into far-off galaxies that only a few men (Enoch, Elijah, and Jesus on His way back home) and traveling angels experienced. And into the ocean's dark debt, observing biotic and abiotic marvels that no previous generations could have followed. Little lifeforms exist in ocean pressures so deep that they would kill a whale. Fragile-looking creations exist comfortably in their unique spaces. Forms that we can "see" now in the darkness of the ocean depth spaces stretched out in existence beyond the mighty reach of our sun, but not the reach of god's creation.

The "humanness" of humans/the Space of Awareness of Awareness

As I ponder like a curious child, I wonder why God has created such vast and unlimited spaces for us. These are spaces that we, as individuals, nations, or civilizations, can never fully reach, regardless of how long we exist on Earth or how advanced our science and technology become. Nevertheless, there is something special within each of us. This essence of humanity, described as being created "in the image of God," provides a space within us that allows us to connect with the past, present, and future. This space is recognized by God and holds significance comparable to anything else He has created. These spaces are pathways of imagination that lead to reality.

Look at the Book:

The Apostle Paul
"None of the rulers of this age understood it.
For if they had, they would not have crucified the Lord of Glory
Rather, as it is written:
"No eyes have seen, no ear has heard, no heart has imagined,
what God has prepared for those who love Him.
But God has revealed it to us by the Spirit.
The Spirit searches all things even **the deep things of God**....*"*

(1 Corinthians 2:9 BSB).

The Unique Space of Imagination

We often take for granted the critical space of our imagination, surrounded as we are by physical spaces and other bodies. We overlook the immense power of our imagination, which allows us to go places unreachable by any other means. Great novels, memorable plays, and groundbreaking scientific and artistic breakthroughs are all born from this rich space of the imagination. Characters and stories that impact our lives are first created in the private imagination of others.

The limitless human experience called "the imagination" is a non-rent space for each of us, transcending racial, religious, and gender boundaries. It offers freedom from life's hardships and can lead us to places of joy, sadness, excitement, and tears. Despite the rise of artificial intelligence, it lacks the genuine humanness unique to humans, a quality that comes from God. We should be careful not to arrogantly take the place and space that belongs to God alone, as He has given us more than enough to work with, just as in the garden.

For example, we can never stand or physically exist in a place beyond our reach, like the galaxies or many mountain tops. But there is something built-in part of our humanness of humans, called imagination, unlimited in its reach and above seemingly endless galaxies that our ancestors could not. It is pretty easy for me to believe what the Scriptures revealed: the far-reaching, thoughtful creation of spaces of existence that was done with the forethought and knowledge that someday His crown creation would develop the ability to see *"the heavens declare the glory of God and the firmament shows His handiwork* (Psalms 19:1). And this is not over. If our generation does not destroy what we have, future generations will yet see and observe what we cannot now see. It is the mystery of God's created spaces. This is the arena that we explore in this book. Think further: How did Einstein develop a theorem that so accurately locates mass existing in dynamic times and orbit so their locations years from now can be known? So, we hail to science. We give physical science the glory. And yet, no science can be established that was not birthed in the human scientist's imagination. Imagination creates science. It is folly to think any science could have existed without this space of imagination.

So, I contend that to understand spaces is to understand the mystery of all existence: In the beginning, God created spaces, and he made common sense in each of us—and even the choice to function without it. He created the ability to understand created things around us. If, as the Holy Scriptures teaches, the heavens declare His glory and the skies proclaim the works of His hands (Psalm 19:1), then we are left with no other conclusion that He created all a space with the ability to see Him there. Use your gift of imagination, and you will discover things about this universe that no science ever will.

Spaces of Evolution

Many people argue that it took billions of years for life to evolve, but I question how something as complex as life could arise from countless moments of nothingness. If life cannot spontaneously generate in a short span of time, how could it emerge after an eternity of nothingness? Can we truly attribute the creation of life to time when time itself would have had to come into existence before anything else? Another point to consider is the role of science in all of this. The scientific method relies on the repeatability of events to produce consistent results. However, we must be cautious in applying this principle to the concept of the "big bang".

Additionally, our perception of time is tied to our point of reference. Without a frame of reference, we may lose track of time altogether. This becomes evident when someone wakes from a coma and immediately seeks to establish their whereabouts and the current time. This phenomenon is mirrored in the story of "Rip Van Winkle", who experiences the disorienting effects of being separated from the flow of time. Time continues to progress regardless of our individual experiences.

From the beginning of time, the relationship between space and time has been governed by consistent principles, which are scientifically comprehensible within the context of the universe. Space and time are inseparable, each relying on the other for human experience. Referring to the creation story, the distinction between day and night and the corresponding measurement of time established by the sun and the moon are significant in establishing a point of reference for space and time. These principles remain relevant to this day.

Let's consider this: Why did God, who could have created the universe with a single breath, take six days? It was to create this delicate yet powerful gift of time and space for us. It's as if He and everything else wanted to offer us the steady rhythm of time and space. So, before creating us, He brought them into being. Think about what happens to humans in space without a point of reference for time. To survive, they must establish their own, lose their sanity, or develop a strong desire to die. We exist and thrive in spaces that contain an awareness of who we are, when we are, and how we exist. Evolution and the Big Bang have left us with existence without a fixed point of reference. There is no meaningful human existence without an absolute point of reference. "And the evening and the morning were the first day..." God created spaces with a point of reference both within and outside of ourselves. This is where we must begin to understand who and what we are.

"Don't Big Bang Me—I Am More Than That!"

I believe that the account of the beginning of everything as described by Moses makes more sense, whether one is religious or not. I think that alternative theories like the "Big Bang" require more faith to believe in than "the evening and the morning was the first day." According to this belief, time-space was created alongside other spaces. I also believe that understanding who we are, who we are becoming, and who we want to be must start from this point. Without God, "in the beginning" or in the present, nothing else matters. As the Preacher said, "all is vanity." This implies that we are insignificant in the vast cosmic universe, and the counterculture philosophy of the Sixties might be correct: we are just a tiny part of the universe, so we might as well disconnect from it. This conclusion is reached in a closed system where God is absent. It is the only option if no one else exists in this universe. This book begins where Genesis begins: In the beginning, God created spaces and the rhythm of time to exist in it. He is present and never silent.

Therefore, we must admit that while the Holy Scriptures is not a scientific work of origins, the Prophets of God did not hesitate to fulfill their task. They delivered the words of God to their people without apology for speaking for God. Just as with Adam and Eve, they allowed everyone to use their free will to decide whether they believe or not, holding them accountable for their choices. If someone is content with explanations that suggest they are a product of impersonal evolutionary spaces and have no room to consider the creation spaces of origin documented by the prophet Moses in Genesis, then they are free to make that choice, and this book will not be of assistance. Nevertheless, it is a journey worth exploring if one is even a little curious to understand more about what makes us who we are and who we can become. I claim that this book of spaces based on the Bible is a journey into the spaces of existence that can guide us there.

Who Gave Me Spaces?

I am drawn to this place like a hummingbird seeking nectar, as it represents the essence of understanding created spaces. It reflects the belief in how "us" came into being. Considering this space is akin to constructing a home without a secure foundation. For instance, the Apostle Paul stated, "For no one can lay a foundation other than the one already laid, which is Jesus Christ" (1 Corinthians 3:11). John also wrote about Jesus, "In the beginning was the Word, and the Word was with God, and the Word was God... Through Him all things were made; without Him nothing was made that has been made. He created all things [spaces], and without Him, nothing was made that was made" (John 1:1, 3).

It is important to note that light was the first creation, illuminating the dark spaces of our world. Subsequently, the heavenly spaces were formed. "Let there be a vault" (1:6); we now call the sky the beautiful expanse that could be seen even before anyone was there to witness it. God took the time to create spaces that were not only "good" for existence, but also good for enjoying life (Genesis 1:31). I have often pondered why the earth and heavens were filled with wonders that seem unnecessary for our survival. Why populate the heavens with stars that we do not need, except to marvel at? It is puzzling to think that our survival hinges on the vast celestial bodies. I argue that the concept of "survival of the fittest" does not apply to heavenly bodies.

Furthermore, if it does, what purpose does it serve? Thus, it seems that unlike the unique nature of Earth and its interrelated ecosystems, survival was not the sole purpose of creation. After all these years, we have not discovered other spaces beyond Earth that could sustain our delicate existence. This realization might make us feel isolated and alone. However, on the contrary, we know that Elohim, or the forces behind the "big bang," do not consider "us" as the most valuable aspect in making our space the only one capable of sustaining us – and even then, only in limited and obedient ways. The other spaces in the universe seem to exist solely for our enjoyment and for exploration. Achieving proximity to them takes an eternity without Divine transport.

Still Beautiful After All These Years

There is a flow to biblical history and nature, despite the tragic human choices that have marred it throughout history. The Potter has continuously demonstrated his loving interest in molding us into something of beauty, regardless of whether or not people believe in Him. His goodness, much like rain, falls upon both the just and the unjust.

Look at the Book:

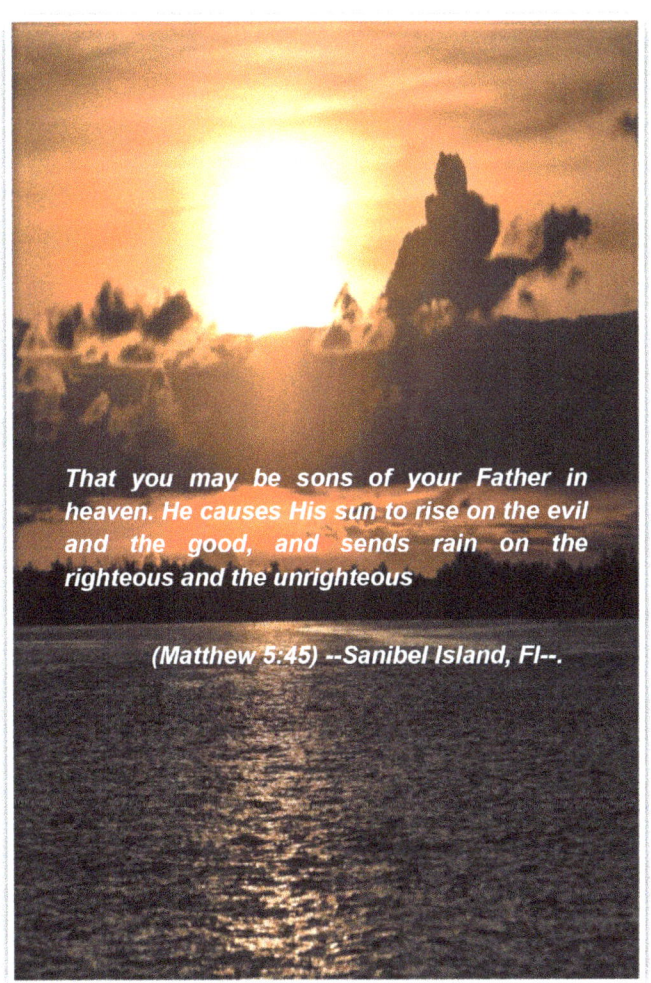

That you may be sons of your Father in heaven. He causes His sun to rise on the evil and the good, and sends rain on the righteous and the unrighteous

(Matthew 5:45) --Sanibel Island, Fl--.

When Jesus spoke these words, it's important to note that he referred to nature as "His" - meaning it belongs to his father. Jesus emphasized the connection between his rule over nature and his deep care for serving all of his creation. Despite humanity's rebellion, the world remains remarkably beautiful, a testament to God's continued interest in nurturing nature for all to appreciate. Everyone, whether they have the Bible or not, is welcome on this Earth, which is filled with indescribable beauty. By opening the eyes of our soul, we can go beyond science and see evidence of God's glory and splendor in the spaces around us as described in the Scriptures.

I want to share some thoughts with you on the importance of recognizing and caring for the world around us. When it comes to our relationship with the divine, many people seek tangible proof, but we are encouraged to look beyond the physical and instead look up towards the sky where we can see the wonder of creation. I recently had a conversation with my daughter about why I am passionate about conservation and believe in the need to address global warming. I explained that I feel a responsibility to care for our planet, as it is our inheritance. I believe that by taking care of the Earth, we are following the guidance given to us by Elohim to watch over and protect this beautiful place and all its inhabitants.

I believe that the instruction in Deuteronomy 25:4, "Do not muzzle an ox while it is treading out the grain," reflects a general stewardship and compassion for all living beings and the Earth they call home. After all these years, the Earth remains a beautiful and miraculous place. God has designed it to be not just a place of ecology, but also a place of awe and wonder, and this beauty continues to inspire us.

From the vastness of the sky to the smallest particles, every aspect of our world has been intricately designed and supplied to support life. The Earth is a finely tuned ecosystem, and it is our responsibility to care for it and ensure its continued existence. God's love flows towards us, and He wants us to appreciate the spaces He has created for our existence. Let's look up and understand the wonderful world around us.

Mysterious Shadow Spaces

"From the darkness came light, and formlessness gave way to beautiful, varied forms in the expanse (Genesis 1:1). The great lights were differentiated— one was named the sun to rule the day, and the other, the moon to rule the night. These expanse rulers each governed their domains (Genesis 1:16). Yet, between them, something enigmatic emerged: shadows. Unlike the explicit creation of light, shadows mysteriously followed suit and endured. Their ability to cloak both in darkness and light has captivated creative thoughts throughout history.

While light and darkness are distinct, shadows traverse the broadest spectrum between them. Each form illuminated by light casts its own shadow. Every individual cast a space of shadow, a concept too profound to delve into here. Mountains cast their own shadows, as do valleys. Every living and non-living entity, biotic or abiotic, contributes to the existence of these enigmatic shadow spaces. Thus, wherever humankind ventures, the space of existence casts the space of shadows. Silhouettes, whether of beauty or anguish, trail along the spectrum between life's dark and light spaces, accentuated by shadows.

How should we respond to this unexplained, elusive reality?

It should inspire humility before God, for He is the God of light and also the God of shadow."

Look at the Book—David said:

"Even though I walk through the valley of the shadows

of death

I will fear no evil

For you are with me"

The Genesis account describes vast spaces filling the void. Magnificent mountain terrains and low valleys fill the earth, reflecting energy and producing sustainable resources for nature: oxygen, water, fire, gravity, plants, infinite microbes, and quantum existence. These elements all occupy their own space and share it with everything else. We can learn from understanding the intersections of spaces we exist in. For example, one person can harm another while both breathe the same air. In other cases, we exist in shared spaces without the knowledge it takes to share, even though our joy and relationships depend on it.

Spaces of Value: Two Sparrows and a Strand of Hair

Matthew 10:29-31 spoken by Jesus, is most profound. The Genesis account describes vast spaces filling the void. Magnificent mountain terrains and low valleys fill the earth, reflecting energy and producing sustainable resources for nature: oxygen, water, fire, gravity, plants, infinite microbes, and quantum existence. These elements all occupy their own space and share it with everything else. We can learn from understanding the intersections of spaces in which we exist. For example, our joy and relationship depends on it. In other cases, we exist in shared spaces without the knowledge to share, even though our joy and relationships depend on it. When considering spaces of existence, It offers profound insights into a demonstration of Divine value by comparing nature to nurture in Christ. The contrast of value from nature's sparrows to the child of the Father cannot be missed. Moreover, should not be taken lightly. It applies directly to one of the purposes of this book, which is to discover who we are—to learn and appreciate the value of our space. Jesus makes this astonishing

Divine argument and conclusion about us: "You are more than many sparrows." A single sparrow cannot fall beyond my notice. So, much, much, more you are. You cannot slip through my gaze. You cannot go unnoticed beyond my love. My eyes are always on the sparrow. She cannot fly or fall hidden from my face. My care has no boundaries beyond which you can move. The space of my care is too fantastic for you to move beyond my caring eyes.

The Value of "us."

So, Elohim, the Almighty God of Creation (Genesis 1:1), sees not only the sparrow fall but also the space the sparrow and every other bird leave behind. This is not simply a poetic expression but a profound attempt to convey the immense value Elohim places on us within His created spaces. He who designed the eyes of an eagle, from where He soars, sees us in every conceivable detail.

The first six chapters describe what I refer to as the "Elohim Space." If the followers of Christ were to create a model of spaces, Elohim Space would be at the summit: "For as high as the heavens are above the earth, so great is his love for those who fear him" (Psalm 103:11). As we construct this descriptive model throughout this book, akin to biblical architects, we are developing a biblical blueprint of existence. True to the Book, we must commence where the Revelation did, with God—Elohim—in the unique space at the pinnacle. Therefore, we dedicate a bit more time to honor the One who occupies a distinct, unshared administrative space. Here, we provide only limited treatment. Who can truly describe God's space except within a human space filled with limitations? Nevertheless, all is not lost, for our aim is not perfection but rather adequacy, which I believe is attainable.

I will introduce the most challenging concept here, which is directly related to my biblical theology of spaces. It is referred to as God's "omnipresence." This means that the laws of physical spaces or spaces of matter and how we

Jesus...

"Are not two sparrows sold for a penny?

Yet, not one of them will fall to the ground outside your Father's care.

And even the hairs of your head are all numbered.

So don't be afraid: You are worth more than many sparrows."

-Matthew 10:29-31-

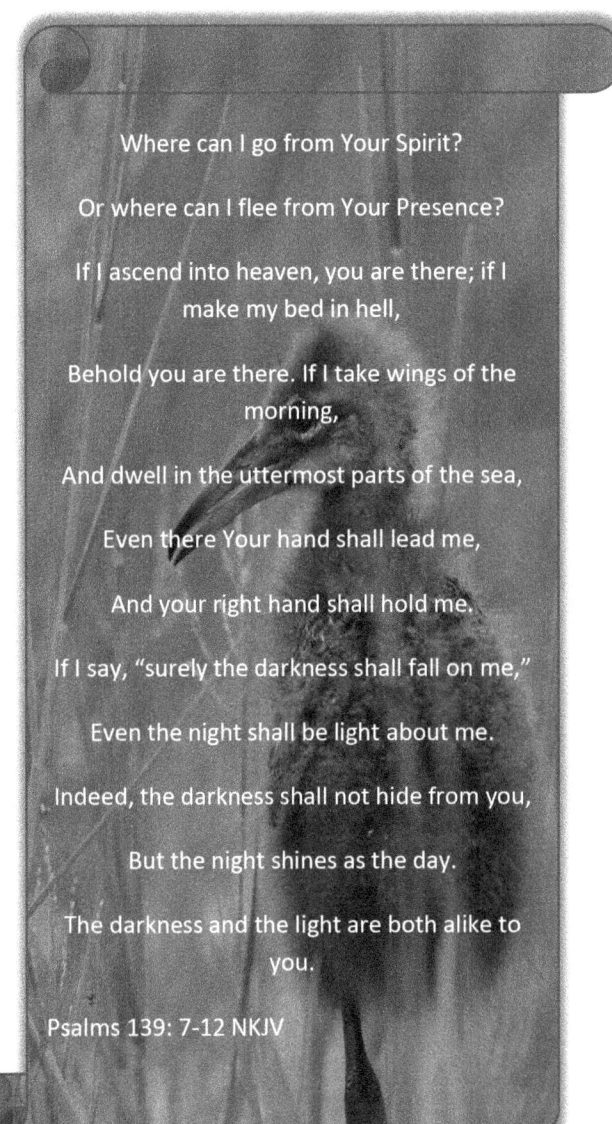

Where can I go from Your Spirit?

Or where can I flee from Your Presence?

If I ascend into heaven, you are there; if I make my bed in hell,

Behold you are there. If I take wings of the morning,

And dwell in the uttermost parts of the sea,

Even there Your hand shall lead me,

And your right hand shall hold me.

If I say, "surely the darkness shall fall on me,"

Even the night shall be light about me.

Indeed, the darkness shall not hide from you,

But the night shines as the day.

The darkness and the light are both alike to you.

Psalms 139: 7-12 NKJV

interact with them cannot apply to Him. This essence of God differs from the manipulation of cinematic spaces, as expertly depicted in Marvel's productions. In these productions, characters often possess superhuman abilities to defy the laws of physics without a built-in rocket or other energy source to move from one place to another, often in an instant. The significance of this description is that God is everywhere, a concept that is profoundly deep. The true depth of this indescribable description is worth grasping, for every word used to describe God inherently limits His unlimited nature—yet our pursuit is adequacy. God's omnipresence moves us into an unfathomable space for the human mind to comprehend. Why? Because we have no human point of reference to grasp that God is fully present in every space of His universe. Like we do, he cannot take our physical bodies from one place or space and just go to another. He cannot leave who He is behind or even a part of Who He is. There is no parking space for God in any space in the universe. If the heavens cannot contain Him, neither can the Earth. It was what startled Moses in His meeting with God on Mount Sinai. God asked him to build a temple so that He could be among His people. Moses wanted to know how God could dwell in a Temple when the heavens could not contain Him. God never explained it because he would not understand it. He is a God who asked Job who knows the eagle's path in the air. This is not so unusual. We live in a world of nature where so many things we accept but can never explain. We are not to approach this from a perspective of ignorance but from a perspective of humility. The vast world of unlimited knowledge would come our way if we were willing to see in humility why angels worship Him continuously. They know who He is, to the level of worshiping Him. That was the meaning of why God wanted to dwell among His people. It is so they could know Him enough to worship Him. To see the value of His interest in a sparrow that falls as much as in His throne room where angels sing in continuous chorus, "holy, holy, holy Lord God Almighty." Furthermore, I say this with the utmost reverence and worship and in the full authority of the Scriptures, that even hell cannot hide from Him (cf. Psalm 139:8 KJB). He does not zoom in like an app. He is imminent to each believer whose body is "a temple" space of the Holy Spirit (1 Corinthians 3:16). Not to be overlooked, He is ever present to hear the cry of saints and sinners alike to hear all those who call on his name (Psalms 145:18-19).

"Someday, he will judge even the thoughts and every idle word because he exists close enough in that space to do so. When I was a boy, I heard a song I remember well. It had a lasting refrain: 'You cannot hide from God no matter how you tried.' And I tried, even before I learned I could not. "No space is beyond Him. No space is hidden from him. Moreover, in his great love, it is not like a surveillance camera purposefully set up to catch people if they do wrong. The Apostle Paul in the Roman city said to the Athenians that God was not "unknown' as they thought. However, that he was near in case they wanted to call on him. He is near enough to hear them. He hears each person who calls on him. He hears the concern of their deepest longing (Acts 17). In the last book of the Bible, Revelation, there is a last written invitation to all. It says, "And the Spirit and the bride say come…." Moreover, of special interest, he said, "He that is thirsty" come…and drink of the water of life freely" (Revelation 22:17). That is

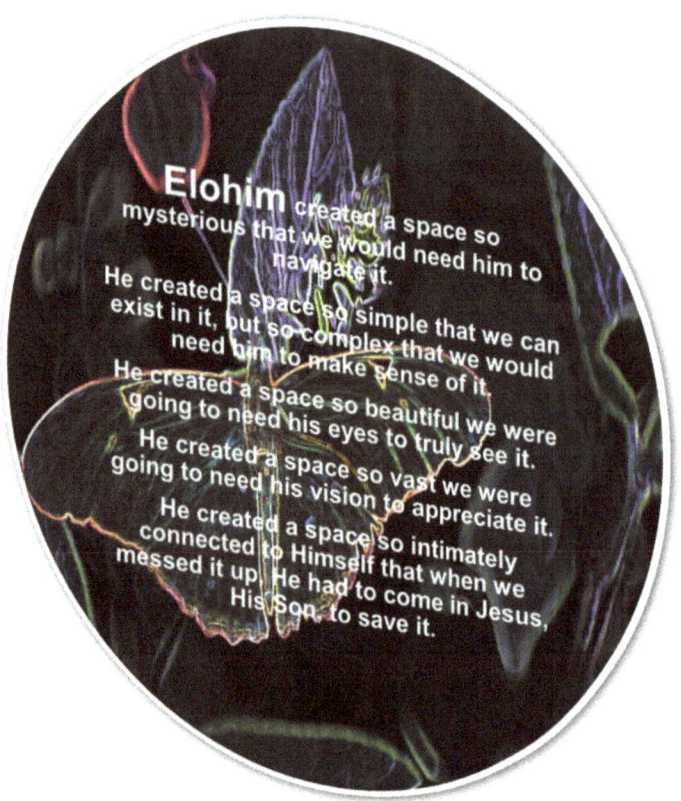

who He is. That is who he calls us to be. We need to be filled with who He is and reach our fullest potential in Him. It means no sounds of this world are unheard by him. From the frightening crack of lighting and the rumble of thunder all the way to the frail sounds of butterfly wings, his ears are attuned to his creation. He is near. He hears it all. He is as much present in church as he is in a club or a prison cell. Sometimes more so among the darkest of life—those who need him most. Indeed, David also said, "You know when I sit and when I rise; you know my thoughts from afar" (Psalm 139:2). It means when a sparrow falls—even a thousand sparrows at one time he sees each one even before their wings fail (Matthew 10:29). And he sees the one alone that fall among them all.

Shared Spaces

Another element of the nature of spaces is that there can be no existence without the sharing of spaces. There can be no adequate progress without a survival level of understanding of them. Today, there is a remarkable indifference to the spaces of our world on which we depend. We last only for a moment here. We depend on spaces that have been provided for us from antiquity. However, we are given the existing space within us for a moment. We are here to change these massive global spaces with the space we cultivate within ourselves. Here, we have the delicate spaces of existence not only for ourselves but also for our world. It is not

a choice only for some elite segment of our world. It is a choice space for all of us. We all live in this delicate shared space.

I once was traveling on a country road. I saw two eagles on a narrow electric pole that could track the open heavens with a flight of speed and freedom at any time. Standing on the edge, they shared space and made room for each other. I observed that it was the only way these mighty birds could exist there and make it work. I paused with my camera to learn the importance of shared spaces for survival.

A Universe Space by Space

Throughout this book, the core content is the structure of a model that represents the universe. Despite theories that the universe originated from randomness, it is clear that there is a designed structure and miraculous consistency to all aspects of existence. This book aims to present biblical evidence to demonstrate the consistency and design found in the spaces of our universe. Over the past forty years, this biblical research structure has aimed to understand the nature of our existence and how to function successfully in the universe. The excellent task of this book is to aid in this understanding.

To comprehensively understand the universe, it is crucial to consider it "space by space." The book will identify and consider eighteen significant universe categories spaces, each with potential sub-categories of influence. While this understanding cannot be complete, it aims to provide substantial insights into our existence and biblical wisdom. Please note that the information presented is not exhaustive, although additional spaces are included that are beyond what the model identifies.

Some chapters deal with "overlapping spaces" like Korah's song, as she indicated in Psalm 95:10: "Love and faithfulness meet together. Righteousness and peace kiss each other." Moreover, the Apostle Paul spoke of internal spaces that contrasted and collided when he shared his struggles: "When I try to do good, evil is present with me" (Romans 7). Then, some spaces flow within the private places of our lives, often unexpressed, yet significantly influence who we are and who we are becoming like stormwater running down until they settle in low spaces of the soul and can stay settled there for a lifetime.

Other spaces erupt gently or take more overt forms or aggressive behavior. We are not alone. We constantly influence our world, and our world constantly influences us. We need to identify these influences if we desire to manage them, influence them, and navigate a positive path through them. For I contend, there is no getting around them. It is why Jesus asked the Father, "I pray not that you take them out of this world but that you keep them…" (John 17:). So, another of my goals in this book is not to avoid spaces, good or bad, but to face the spaces of our lives to learn and lead our lives through them. So that the prayer of Jesus, to be kept even in evil spaces, can be accurate in us.

In the end, a model is weak and static on paper, as in this book. Words on paper can speak of rain, yet they are best read if the page is not wet. So, we deal here with influences of spaces that are constant "pressure" like silent gravity on us—like earth's gravity that we cannot see, yet it is constantly and relentlessly press down on us. Alternatively, like rain and strong wind, we cannot see, but they can blow us away if we do not run for the cover of protected spaces. I contend that the existence of every moment, even when we dream, seems to be a battle of the influence of spaces. We explore them here to know how to navigate them. The model structure or description is a static tool of a dynamic life situation.

Simplicity and Complexity

The descriptive models used here attempt to show simplicity for understanding, and at the same time, they can hide the vast complexity of our daily existence. Nevertheless, we need to function in both simplicity and complexity. We do not have a choice in the matter. Those who seek simplicity when life is so complex will not find it. For those who want to make the best of life, simplicity as a goal is not an option. The effort should be to seek each day to understand its complexity and not to run away from it. This book can help. It could be understood as breathing, which could be so simple to do, and yet each human breath has with it the complexity of what it takes to be alive and to live. A model or a book is like that. Like a snapshot of a breath. It is like snapshots of spaces of existence constantly moving in different ways and with different influences and reactions to these spaces of our universe. Each is being influenced in other ways by the *same* spaces of existence. Even if the spaces are the same and unified as the night sky, each responds in various ways.

Spaces are dynamic. Often, they are confirmed in site yet hidden inside. They are constantly moving and shaped like clay in the hands of the potter of existence. Here, I attempt with a model description to take a snapshot. "Slow" the process down to reflect, look, learn, and live like the Prophet Micah said to get to the space right: "He has shown you, O mortal, what is good. And what does the LORD require of you? To act justly and to love mercy and to walk humbly with your God" (Micah 6:8). So here is where we begin on this journey of the spaces of our lives. *Getting Back to the Beginning Spaces so we can navigate those we face today and tomorrow.*

GOD' SPACE – PART ONE

THE GOD OF THE BIBLE

SPACES

"In the beginning God created the heavens and the earth…" (Gen 1:1): He Created Spaces of Existence, and for Existence.

1

THE ELOHIM SPACE – ABOVE THE REST

Elohim Jehovah Yahweh

Alpha & Omega

His revelation-space is to each person, province, and peoples under Him.

(Psalm 46:4-10; Isaiah 40: 21,22)

LOOK AT THE BOOK:

"ONE GOD AND **FATHER OF ALL**,
WHO IS **OVER ALL**
AND **THROUGH ALL** AND **IN ALL**."
(Ephesians 4:6 emphasis mine).

We begin this journey of spaces in the space above all spaces—the Elohim Space. I contend the Bible passage above speaks of spaces. It begins with a statement of unimaginable relationship to all that exists. He exists in relationship to every other space: "*overall, through all, and in all.*" It means God the Father exists in a dynamic and unique space. It means He alone occupies that space.

It means He occupies everything. It means nothing can exist without Him. It means He occupies everything He has made, and nothing made can occupy Him. "He is over all, through all, and in all" is how the Apostle describes Elohim's exclusive position and existence. This passage, with its repeated declaration of inclusion in the word "all," leaves no room for misunderstanding or confusion as to the space of God in His universe. We begin here in the understanding of ourselves and our universe because there is no other place where the Bible begins. The one with the bible and the one without the bible have no other meaningful space to begin. Let me break this passage a little further:

1. First, Elohim is **"One God**." This declares His ultimate uniqueness, for there is none like Him. It is not as some religions teach that we are who He once was. That is utterly false. His ranking or position is unreachable.

2. Secondly, with all the good qualities of the human father, such as love, protection, and provisions, this One God" inhibits this unique space as the Divine **"Father of all**." The original language carries the force of what a good father does for his children. His positional space does not take away from what he provides for us in our space. He does not deal with us in the space of a ruler (although He indeed is). He deals with His creation as a loving Father does for His children. The takeaway is to teach us how God our Father thinks of us. We are to think of ourselves as no less valuable. He calls us children. It speaks to who we are. Whether we are saints or sinners, a God of the universe still cares for us like a good Father does his children. Although we do not all serve him as his child, we are all children of God.

3. Thirdly, this passage moves into mysterious and deeper waters with the Greek preposition (*dia*) translated as "through." It is a word of **agency**. It is a word of *action*. It is a word that opens the mysterious possibility that the God who can make sparrows sing and eagles fly, turn troubled waters still as a pond, and make His children into His agents of His purposes and His love in His world. It implies He is not a distant God but can work His will **"in" and "through"** us. It is why we can pray, "Oh Father who is in Heaven...thy will be done on earth as it is in heaven." This is no small space in which each human is welcome to occupy—the loving relationship of the father space of Elohim.

4. Forth, **"and in all**." The last description moves us to a revolutionary space. It speaks of *residence*. It speaks of *home*. It speaks of holiness, for he cannot dwell in unholy places. However, He can dwell in the holy place through the blood of Jesus Christ, whose cross sacrifice purifies the sinner and makes them a "temple of the Holy Spirit" (1 Corinthians 6:19). Yet I must admit, the simple point is without Him nothing made that was made without Him (John 1:1-3). It is difficult to understand, yet inconceivable, that no space can exist without Him.

The model created to illustrate the universal spaces of existence to discover who we are and who we are becoming and even to determine who we want to be is made up of eighteen interconnected circles—the heart and contribution of this book. Each one represents a distinctive influential space of human existence. At the center of circled spaces (as illustrated above) is the circled space symbolic of the space of "us" or the "me" space—inside and intersecting with all the other outside influential spaces. Spaces of our world near and far that function like gravity of dynamic influences all around us. But at the "overhead"—at the top bridge only by the cross- this unique space of Elohim—a circled space representing God's unique space in the universe. This is the unique space featured in this book's first six chapters. It was the only Circle I gave such treatment. But even then—even if the world were filled with the description of Elohim, it could never be enough.

In describing the Elohim space, it is like picking up a handful of sand on the seashore to study and feel humbled looking at the vast ocean covering grain of sand infinitum at unreachable depth. "For now, we see only a reflection in a mirror; then, we shall see face to face. Now I know in part, then I shall know fully, even as I am fully known" (1 Corinthians 13:12). We have yet to study to show ourselves approved, rightly dividing the Word of Truth—even if all we have is what we can carry in our hands. So, we continue this journey into this "Elohim Space—Above all the Rest."

Space of His Nature

The disciple John recorded an important prayer by Jesus in John 17:3 to further illustrate the value of what we know of Elohim. "***<u>Now this is eternal life: That they may know you</u>***, the only true God and Jesus Christ" (emphasis mine). In his gospel concerning God, John left no room for misunderstanding the connection between two critical spaces that merge into each other like one: There is a unique space of life called "eternal life" that is inextricably fused with the space of the ***knowledge of God***.

Some spaces collide like negatively charged clouds intersecting a positively charged one in nature, which can create such energy exhibited by the power of lighting. However, here, John is stating with unmistakable clarity the fusion of two spaces into one: The knowledge of God placed in the space of human life produces a unique space called "eternal life." Its emphasis on "eternal" is not meant to be its enduring length alone but its Divine quality. It is a quality that is also lasting. It is of such quality that it cannot end. The life we all have in our bodies will someday. This life of Elohim moves us into a redemptive space of "life" unending. In Elohim, we are drawn to a space of life that has no end.

It is why Elohim's space is placed at the top of the circle: His unique life-giving space is available to every person through the Cross. Here, in the "knowledge of God," they find their own space of who they are, who they are becoming, and who they can be for all eternity. It is a grain of truth we can carry for all eternity.

Space of His Name

In Old Testament times, names were not simply used for identification. They were also used for description. So, the names of God in the Bible are a rich source of the knowledge of God. An example of such connection: "She will give birth to a son, and you are to give him the name Jesus because he will save his people from their sins" (Matthew 1:21). And re-emphasized in verse twenty-three, "a virgin will conceive and give birth to a son, and they will call his name Immanuel (which means "God with us). When Matthew recorded this, he was attempting to be poetic but prophetic. He was telling his readers that they know who Jesus is by the name He was to be called. Such names had within them both the space of content and character.

There are at least twelve distinctive names for God used in the Bible, especially in the Old Testament, each highlighting the space of who God: (Elohim et al., Jehovah-rope, Jehovah-Jireh, Jehovah-Nissi, Jehovah-rope, Jehovah-M'Kaddesh, Jehovah-shalom, Jehovah-thickens, Jehovah-Rohi, Jehovah-Shammah). Since I have made this the subject of another book, I would not dwell on it here. It is essential as a guide to understanding the relationship between names and characters in the Hebrew historical culture. Names of God are invaluable in understanding and often especially in the context in which they were introduced in the biblical narrative. I contend that to **know the space of God is also to know the space of us**. To know God is to know who we are. It is the reason that with just Ten Commandments, among them is one not to take the Lord's name in vain. This act was associated with Divine judgment on the one who did so (Exodus 20:7). Why? Because God wanted His people to know and experience, His name represented a unique space. His name was more than a name. His name represented a space of holy power.

"Elohim" is the name of Moses in the Pentateuch, which God uses to describe the mighty and awesome God of creation. No one is God's equal. He occupies a space that only He alone can.

Saint Augustine, the great philosopher and theologian from the Fourth Century BC, captured in but a few words what I am attempting to describe in thousands of them. So, this book can be viewed as an extension of Augustine of Hippo's verbal model. God the Father, Son, and Holy Spirit—three Persons represented in the triangle's three points, yet One God, each acting in the creation of "us"—who we are first as created beings.

God the Son: The Redemptive *Bridge Space* of the Universe

If I were to develop a model of spaces of the universe and, in it, seek to find the most critical symbol on which all things redemptive hang, it would be the symbol of the cross. For it is a space—abridge space that is most critical to the understanding of who we are, who we are becoming, and who we want to be. It is the symbol of the cross, rooted in the Earth, its peak pointing to the heavens, with its extended arms outstretched to welcome anyone who would come to Christ who hung there in historical space and time. He created what I call a "bridge space." For of all the spaces of the universe, I contend there is no space so loving, redemptive, merciful, and gracious as the space the cross of Christ created. The very first message of the Christian Church created on the Day of Pentecost laid out clearly this unique space in the universe. The Apostle Peter, the former space disrupter in Acts 4:12, declared this to the powerful religious leaders of his day. These were leaders who were still fuming with zealous hate from presiding over the death of his Lord. Nevertheless, this former space disrupter boldly said to them, "There ***is no other name given among men whereby we must be saved***" (emphasis mine*)*.

The Apostle Paul, three centuries before Augustine, also captured the essence of this unique "bridge space" of the cross. Young Pastor Timothy wrote, **"For there is One God, and one Mediator [in the cross] between God and mankind, the man [incarnate] Christ Jesus"** (1 Timothy 2:5 emphasis mine). This is not hyperbole or some mystical philosophy. Peter, Paul, and Augustine pointed out a critical time and space—a "bridge" space, a "mediator" space, a redemptive connecting space—bridging humanity's space with God. A space that can only be accessed by the cross of Christ. It is a space accessed through blood and sacrificial death—the atoning death of Jesus Christ that occurred in historical space and time. Along with Peter and Paul, then John added his vision to this unique space of the cross that only Christ can occupy. In Revelation, Chapter 5 narrates a vision he saw.

Look at the Book:

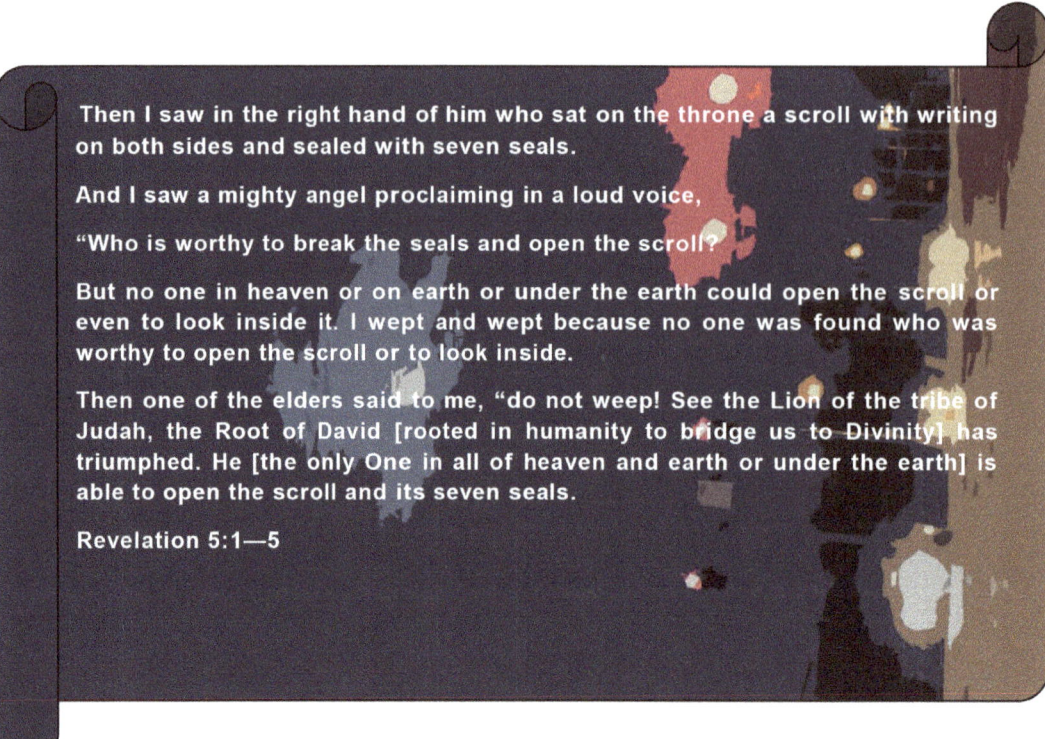

Then I saw in the right hand of him who sat on the throne a scroll with writing on both sides and sealed with seven seals.

And I saw a mighty angel proclaiming in a loud voice,

"Who is worthy to break the seals and open the scroll?

But no one in heaven or on earth or under the earth could open the scroll or even to look inside it. I wept and wept because no one was found who was worthy to open the scroll or to look inside.

Then one of the elders said to me, "do not weep! See the Lion of the tribe of Judah, the Root of David [rooted in humanity to bridge us to Divinity] has triumphed. He [the only One in all of heaven and earth or under the earth] is able to open the scroll and its seven seals.

Revelation 5:1—5

Again, look at the Book.

I contend, the most incredible lyrics ever written—the most excellent song yet to be sung:

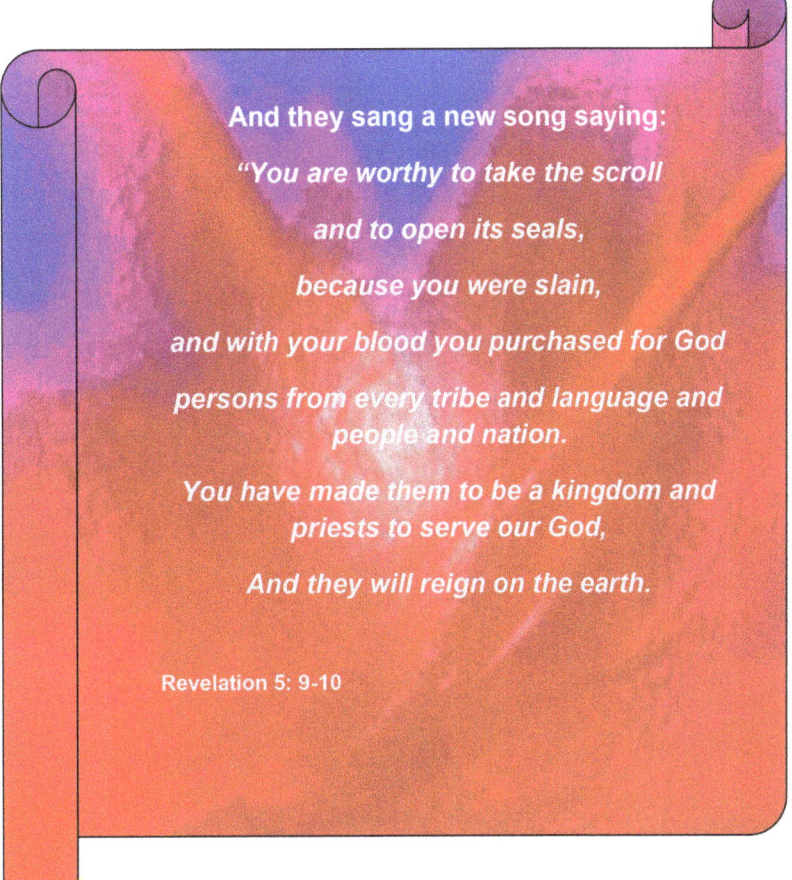

And they sang a new song saying:

"You are worthy to take the scroll

and to open its seals,

because you were slain,

and with your blood you purchased for God

persons from every tribe and language and people and nation.

You have made them to be a kingdom and priests to serve our God,

And they will reign on the earth.

Revelation 5: 9-10

Potter As Close as Clay

Look at the Book:

"Woe to him who quarrels with his Maker—one clay pot among many. Does the clay ask the potter, 'what are you making?' Does your work say, 'He has no hands'?" (Isaiah 45:9).

"But now, O Lord, you are our Father; we are the clay, and you are our potter; we are all the work of your hand" (Isaiah 64:80).

"Now in a great house there are not only vessels of gold and silver but also of wood and clay, some of honorable use, some for dishonorable. Therefore, if anyone cleanses himself from what is dishonorable, he will be a vessel for honorable use, set apart as holy, useful to the master of the house, ready for every good work"

(2 Timothy 2:21-22).

Does not the potter have the right to make from the same lump of clay one vessel for special occasions and another for common use? (Romans 9:21)

There are narratives in the holy Book that exalt God, like Isaiah 6, which says, "I saw the Lord high and lifted." He is exalted throughout the sacred Scriptures. Nevertheless, this same God inhabiting high spaces also occupies lowly, like a potter and his clay.

Such narratives speak to God's position and perception of us. They talk to God's intimate knowledge of us, as a potter knows the clay he works within his own hands. And like the potter, God knows our limitations and potential to be a vessel of high honor for His use. He knows us more than we do ourselves, for as a potter forms vessels, God forms us. It is why we need Him to understand "us:" Who we are, and our place in our world. It is the fundamental reason the top circle on my 18-circled model of spaces of existence begins with Him. There was no other biblical place to start.

Look at the book:

"You Know"

2

THE ELOHIM SPACE – DEEPER THAN ALL THE REST

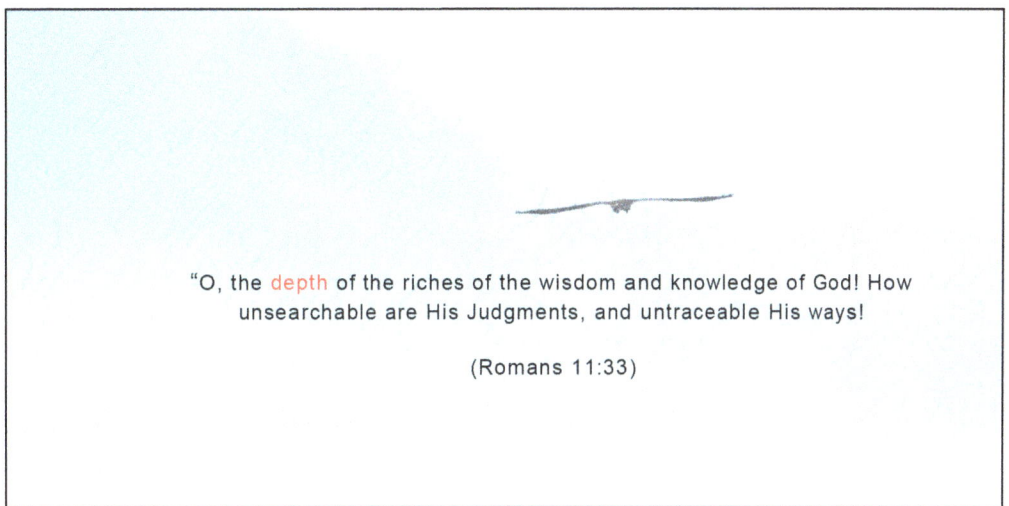

"O, the depth of the riches of the wisdom and knowledge of God! How unsearchable are His Judgments, and untraceable His ways!

(Romans 11:33)

"O the Depth…"

This leading passage of this chapter on Elohim Space confronts us with the overwhelming nature of looking "into these things," as the Apostle Peter revealed in First Peter 1:12. Such things made the Apostle Paul cry out as if to say this is too challenging for me to consider; too rich for my mind to research; too unsearchable for my limited faculties to fathom; too deep for me to dive.

I know those deep waters. I know that space is revealed in the Scriptures. Study the panorama of redemption from Genesis to Revelation each day for a year. Please do it again each year as you research each book topic, and there will be many moments like the one the Apostle Paul expressed. Even a casual reader of the Word in the Spirit can become overwhelmed and cry out from a spiritual space in the soul, *"O the depth of the riches of the wisdom and knowledge of God!"*

This is no ordinary space because it is the space of the depth of God's love and grace. We must learn to cherish that space where we are taken like an out-of-body experience to this unique space of the depth of God's revelation to us and in us. This space of devotion space and spiritual awareness of His presence—the "depth" is like a wilderness experience, but you are not alone because the depth of the presence of Elohim fills the space. It is a space where if your soul is silent, the stones in this wilderness will rise and cry out, "O the depth of the riches of the wisdom and knowledge of God!"

We must be careful to understand that this is not a space of God's presence; we must go to a physical building called "church" to experience. It can be experienced in the presence of a "burning" bush—a fire in the soul. Moses could experience the space of this depth of God's presence on a high mountain (Exodus 3). Jonah prayed in the Spirit from the belly of a big fish in the depths of the sea (Jonah). Queen Ester did while she walked towards her king between life and death.

We can experience this depth of Space of God at any level—low or high. This is the overwhelming beauty of this depth of Elohim space. It is there for everyone who would seek that space. The practical benefit of this experience is that it is a guide to understanding our own space. I contend that anyone who understands who they are or who they are becoming should never take lightly that space of who or what overwhelms them: "O the depth of the riches of the wisdom and knowledge of God!"

Depth of Content—Depth of Christ

I must also be careful to point out that one does not experience this "depth of the riches and wisdom and knowledge of God" by content alone. This knowledge space is introduced, intersected, and converged with " the depth of the riches" of first "the wisdom." There is this dept of the "riches of the **wisdom** and **knowledge** of God. This convergence or intersection of Elohim spaces is not by accident or just a play of words. It is critical. It can be broken down in this proverb: You need knowledge to understand God's world. You need wisdom to be under the God who made it. So, therefore wisdom is here first mentioned because it is wisdom that leads to His word, which then leads us into the overwhelming "depth of the riches of wisdom…." (To explore this further, this is more fully developed in my book on "The Death of Wisdom The Rise of Folly" (Christian Faith Publication, 2023). This depth is more than content; it is the space where the content carries you. It takes you to a deep space where Elohim richness is stored. In short, it is a space in wisdom that carries you to a love for one another that defies logic. It can take you to places where there is nothing but dry bones, where you see yourself as broken, lifeless spices scattered in the valley of your life. And He comes running after you with resurrection resolve, shouting, "Live!" And the brokenness of spaces of your life begins to mend— "bone to bone" (Ezekiel 37:12-14), and He infused it with His musical score that overwhelms you because the rattling is the sound of life—your life coming together because of the transformative power that Elohim space brings.

The Space of Sin Meets the Space Savior

She was a woman without a name but carried like a burden so many descriptions. They were not good ones. Yet, to all the labels that followed her, none was as damaging or harmful to her life as the space of the law and religious leaders. It was a space that could have her killed and killed by rocks pelting into her soft, delicate skin that before attracted many men looking for satisfaction from what she offered. Now, they wanted to take revenge on her unpleasant life or their religious hypocrisy. They did not want to do their dirty deed themselves, and of all the people, they dragged her to what they perceived as a space of the law. But in their ignorance and lack of wisdom, they did not know He was Elohim in the flesh to which they came.

So, there she was, already condemned even as her accusers asked for judgment. They brought in their self-righteous bag, only condemnation and death. She was kneeling alone in historical disgrace and shame. The long, vicious arm of the law had sought her out even in her private space. But she was not alone there because the depth of Elohim's space of love and care also reaches into those spaces. Her accusers say she was caught in an act forbidden by the law. And they wanted Him to know they brought her to Him—an Elohim space showered with life to take away hers. They came from the only space they knew—the space of the Law—a space of condemnation and never conversion. There is no space for rehabilitation in the space of the law. It comes from a different space beyond the law.

The sharp edge of the law meant two pointing to one—the woman and not the man or men involved. Alone in adultery. Alone in the judgment and conclusion of the Law. She saw no defense and expected none from the men surrounding her, including Jesus. Why should He be any different? He was a man like all the rest. No woman would dare show up at such a killing of another woman—he who taught that He came not to destroy the law but to fulfill it. There could have been no solution to this problem confronting Christ: Give life when the law that demands death is in session. Only wisdom of the highest order can resolve this deadly situation.

She stood alone in a space of condemnation. The Law was not on her side, as it is often the case of the vulnerable, weak, and needy among us. Adultery with its deadly blunt and deadly force of Hebrew Law and order laid bare before Him. Her accusers—judge and jury not of her piers faced her down with eyes of deadly expectations. It was a clear-cut case until Christ confronted the religious crowd.

He stood in defense of her—faced down the law with His love. He faced down the Low with His mercy. He faced down the law with his grace. Faced the accusers with the one thing that the Law could not overcome: "the depth of the riches of the wisdom and knowledge of God" required to meet both the requirement of His love and life and the very Law He gave that demanded death. Who on Earth can satisfy both? Who inhabits such a space of lighting where two opposing forces meet and stand in the middle yet satisfy both? And would vouch for a woman without a name but with a bad reputation? Who can stand in that volatile, guilty space? At this critical point in this guilty lady's life, only one person in the universe occupied that space. And you wonder how He could exist in the space of Law and grace that historically before the cross crashed into each other with lighting force? A space of peace in the middle of conflict. Only He alone could create. It was like finding a salvation space between opposite charge clouds. It was like finding a safe space where lighting inhabits. And He stood in the middle of it all between the charge of the law. And He saw it as only He alone could. "***He that is without sin, let him cast the first stone.**"*

Do not miss this. The depth of the richness of this story could not be understood if you miss this: He was the only one there that day who was qualified to cast both the first and the last stone, *__for He was without sin.__*

But He did not, for He had already committed to die for her. "Neither do I condemn you go and sin no more" (John 8:11). Do not miss the love in the "I" space.

He could say that because He would give her, like the woman at the well, a satisfaction she would never find in any other man. Israel never saw such love before grace and mercy but available in the Lord. Grace offered the woman a life that she did not have under the law. And mercy held back judgment and death, which she earned under the law. They both come together in this One who offered this unique space that only He alone could occupy and satisfy.

Like a good rain over her sinful soul, he offered her a new beginning. He provides this nameless lady a space where she can live where these religious leaders, with their heightened belief that they could judge her and others. In contrast, they live in their sinful spaces, condemned by the law they so publicly floundered. It is a space that Paul describes with a new description written across her life: "There is therefore now no condemnation to them that are in Christ Jesus" (Romans 8:1). All this is but a meager sampling like a grain of sand on the shore, lined by the ocean filled with the "depth and riches of the wisdom and knowledge of God."

The Extent of Elohim Space

Previously, we considered Elohim's space using the language of Paul, who, in looking at Elohim's salvation, used the language of biblical spaces when he used the word "depth" (Gr. "Bathos") to cry out from his soul "**O the depth** of the riches of the wisdom and knowledge of God" which is the lead Scripture of this essay. We now use another dimensional space emphasizing the physical in the word "extent." It is a concept of space that includes all physical spaces. We often do not think of God regarding physical spaces. But here is the extent of God we traverse the physical spaces of Elohim. It is like having the ability to dive into something to understand and experience. The extent is getting on the ocean, seeing how far the sea takes us, and learning along the way to this extent where the horizon seems always moving. The more you know, the more it expands. This, of course, challenges our understanding of God and expands our awareness of Him. It is not to make us afraid to travel beyond the shorelines. It is as Jesus told Peter, "Put out into the deep and let down your nets for a catch" (Luke 5:4).

Another important continuing lesson on spaces was exhibited in the language of geographical spaces Jesus used in Luke 5:4: "Put out into the deep and let down your nets for a catch." Again, both distinction and expansion of spaces are seen here. Peter was a fisherman by trade. If there is one thing the fishermen learn that is essential to success in fishing, it is where to go to catch them. One can see that Jesus, who was never a fisherman, knew the spaces of their existence. This Lake of Gennesaret, where Jesus taught in Peter's boat, was the largest in Israel. There was no hint in the Life of Jesus that He ever went to this famous Lake (also called the "Sea of Galilee") to fish. Yet Jesus knew where the fish was in this immense sea to instruct this experienced fisherman, Peter, where to take his boat. This is as much Theology (the study of God and His works) as anything else. Why? In its effects, this act transcends the divine knowledge of where fish are located in the Sea of Galilee and where everything else occupies a space in the universe.

Elohim's knowledge cannot be limited to the geography of Galilee. The "extent" of His knowledge, both biotic (living things like fishes) and abiotic (non-living like the sea), extends to the entire Universe. He could have never made it if He did not know it in every single detail. It is why one looks at this simple statement with just a little imagination and pauses in awe of the extent and practical implications of His simple instruction to a Galilean fisherman. And no less important in Matthew 12:13 to a man with a withered hand to "Stretch out your hand!" And as the man did, his hand was restored to full use. I contend no spaces of all existence are ever beyond His reach. And I argue that the person who "connected the dots" of a little of it in the "advanced" machine or biological discoveries (however crucial to human life on this planet). As Mary (Sylvia Tilly S4E2) observed in an episode of Star Trek Discovery: "Life is but one heartbeat in the entire lifespan of the universe." In the end, one can never know who they are, who they are becoming, or who they can be if they do not know the Potter who made them and every other in existence in this universe.

THE FOOL SAYS IN HIS HEART

"THERE IS NO GOD."

-PSALM 14:1-

Why Did God Called Some Among Us Fools?

I contend that each time civilization understands just a little more of this universe, instead of seeing how vast God is, it attempts to make Him more minor and nonexistent. The period of the Enlightenment declared He was dead because they were discovering more. Some modern secular cultures studied the world. They learned a little more about it and thought they owned it all. They thought they had made it all. Elohim, if He existed, was a crutch they did not need. It was but an opium for the people. With such advancement and enlightenment, Elohim was no longer needed. As their leader said, "All this will I give you if you would bow down and worship me" (Matthew 4:9). And like fools at a cynical parade, they bowed down. And some never recovered from their disbelief to this day. They first began to teach it in their university. There could be no room for Elohim in a thinking space. A vege was driven between faith and thought. A closed ideological system with only humanity inside that terminated at every level of our institutions. Alone in the universe, even as we seek answers as to why our children are shooting each other. Why civility is hard to find? Why do racism structures yet remain? Why is poverty still pervasive in a land and world of plenty—even as we all bleed the same? Why do plagues of biblical proportions still pop up in an enlightened age?

As we need Elohim to pray to Him more to "deliver us from evil," foolish hearts abound. "Where there is no vision, the people perish" (Proverbs 29:18). It is the height of folly to live as if we are the only ones in the universe when, in historical space and time, One called Immanuel—the Son of God—paid us a visit from His throne room someplace outside and apart from our Universe. His name is Jesus, for He shall save His people from their sins" (Matthew 1:21).

It is a twist of folly that humankind can grow so elite as to eliminate God from their calculation, consciousness, and consideration. Yet if they do the same with the Universe, that is, entertain the thought of removing it as they do God, they will cease to exist. This is not some vague philosophy. This is reality 101. Just because you increase your knowledge of an apple, or the moon does not make you either. The fact that one would study, research, and contemplate a thing makes them a learner, not a leader—a servant, not a savior: More of clay and not the Potter. It is the twist of folly to think or believe otherwise. It is the reason the song of the Psalter is so emphatic. Only fools say in their hearts, "There is no God." It is the height of folly and irrationality to look at a simple 🦋 and conclude we are alone—much less this vase extent of our ecological space.

If we want to know who we are and who we are becoming seriously consider our conclusions on the evidence around us. Elohim in never silent. It is that only the wise listen to Elohim spaces.

Let's Go A Little Deeper

Albert Einstein postulated that time, space, and matter cannot be considered apart from one another. And in his most famous equation …$E=MC^2$. He pointed out that "C" represents the velocity or speed of light, estimated at 186,000 miles per second. "E" is the energy contained in a stationary body. And "m" is its mass. But here is the rub: For this to work together, there must exist this all-important mysterious element called "time"—an indispensable element of any equation. And even with time, a second agreed to be 9,192,631,770 vibrations between two levels of cesium-133 (atoms); even with this preciseness of vibrations, the mystery of space between the vibrations still exists. We still do not know the basic questions from mathematics, physics, science, and abiotic or biotic sources concerning how, why, or what their existence is. All of which this book answers is based unabashedly on the propositional revelation of Elohim in the original revelation of His Holy Scriptures through His Prophets.

Geography is spaces of light, energy, mass, velocity, time, and space; I contend that it does not matter how brilliant the minds that study them are. It does not matter how practical the results are born from them. If we rise each day out of sleep to a world we would fall asleep again and again without any answers to these basic questions: You do not know why, how, or Who put these existing vibration spaces together in harmonies like the waves and the fishes, and combustibility like volcanoes and titanic shifts below the Earth, and in the most combustible elements call the sun that Elohim said literally rules the day (Genesis 1:16), we are as the Apostle Paul argued in 1 Corinthians 15:19 "If our hope is in Christ is for this life alone, we are to be pitied more than all men." Each time we go to bed or wake up without answers to these fundamental questions: Who are we, who are we becoming, and who do we want to be? From Elohim's space of absolute answers, we are getting older but not wiser.

Without an answer to who created and established these spaces of existence and why they were made, we remain just creatures of the darkness of folly—even as the Son rains down His light upon us. It is why the Holy Scriptures conclude we are fools who worship equations and miss their real revelation. Solomon—a king who asked God for wisdom and got it even from the secular world's testimony, wrote: "The wise heart will know the proper time and procedure" (Ecclesiastes 8:5).

The Heavens and the Earth were given to declare Elohim's glory (Psalms 19:1). As they learn more about anything on the earth, the foolish glorify only themselves. It is like anyone placing empty hands in their line of sight and pronouncing to themselves, "Look what I have made for me."

I offer my discourse of these passages: *They speak of the entrance of categorically restrictive space of our existence here. First, we all enter a restrictive space: how we came and how we see others go. It is an experience common to all that the Book describes. We come into the world with nothing but our bodies and even leave with less, for we leave it behind. This is true for the one with the Bible and the one without it, for it is devastatingly brutal in its facts and conclusion.*

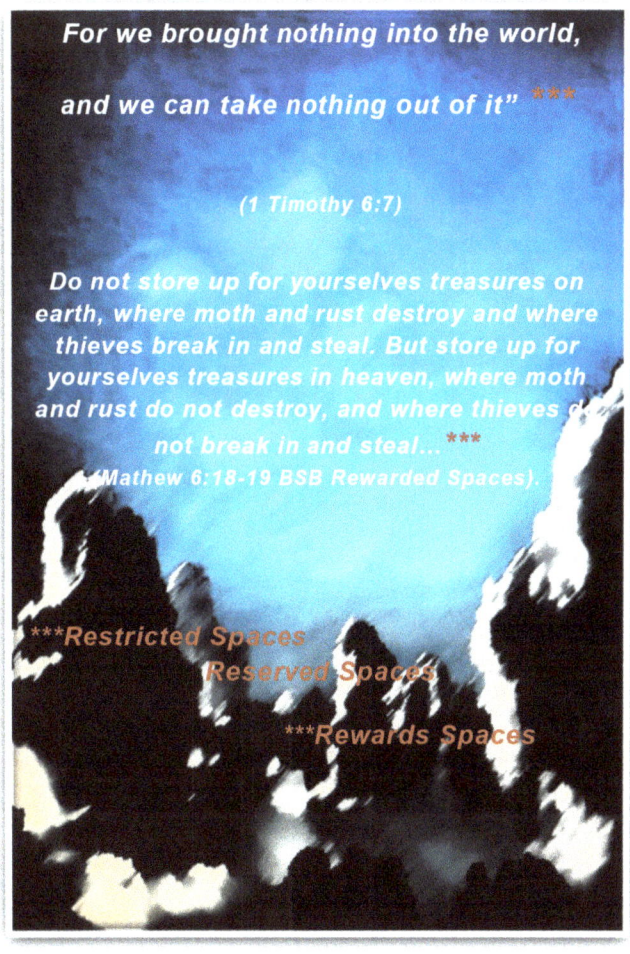

It is God who brought us into this world. And it is God who takes us out of this world when our time is up. (As one of my members as a Pastor told me, "You never see a U-Hall connected to a hearse). But here is the blessed hope. We can purchase heavenly spaces through redemption in Christ, and as we serve Him while we are here, we will have stored up treasures in Heaven that we will meet us on the other side: Luggage claim carousel Matthew 6:18-19 (graphic quote above—from restricted spaces to **reserve** *spaces, to* **reward** *spaces.* That is what Elohim Space offers us. It is the purpose of this book on spaces is for each person to know they have the power to purchase or claim space in heaven, like a heavenly safety deposit box space where one can make deposits of a lifetime of doing good—serving the bank manager of the Universe—Elohim.

There was a man in my hometown village on a small Caribbean Island. We called him Brother Conner. He was a big man—like the tallest tree in the village forest. He noticed how many of the kids each year got nothing for Christmas. Their Island was too hot for the North Pole reindeer. So, he started a little banking system. He asked each kid to bring even a penny during the entire year. He had their names on an accounting ledger, and pennies after pennies all year began to add up. Just before Christmas, they would line up to receive their deposit. For many, it became their life's biggest and most consequential lesson. They were amazed as to how much was stored for them. Christmas was never the same for those who stored up little by little treasures all year long. It was always there at the end of the year, just before Christmas.

Elohim created a deposit space for each person to come to His Son in confession of Faith. And He guards this space and ensures all deposit of good in this world is assured in His unto that great day. It is not the amount of success one has in this world that makes good deposits, or education, or fame. It is simply based on the good done to others in your life. "As off as you have done it to the lease of these, you do it for me." That is how the account gets built. And the devil's stock market cannot affect it. "Lay up for yourself treasures in heaven." It is a space where "robbers cannot break in and steal (Matthew 6:18-19). This is the "extent" of Elohim's space to include an extensive banking system that reaches into heaven's secure vault.

Elohim Practical Extent Spaces

There was a man with a restricted hand. Jesus told him to "stretch it out." In obedience to this simple ask by Jesus, the man's hand ventured into extended physical space. We now move to a more practical expression or outline of the extent of Elohim's space. When He told Peter to launch out into the deep for a catch, it revealed His knowledge of the inhabitants of all physical spaces of the Universe. It could not be limited to the workings of the biotics of a man's hand or just the fishes in the ocean, but it speaks of the extent of the physical universe. "He counted the stars and knew them by name." This was not hyperbole. This was an expression of the "wisdom and knowledge" of God. He knew not just where the fish were located but all of the fish of the sea and the birds in the sky. And He knows the location of you and me. So, when He who never owned a boat and was said to be a carpenter spoke to someone like Peter, "put out into the deep…" it demonstrates Divine knowledge of physical spaces and who and what occupies them. It is even amazing that Peter did not argue with Jesus as he often would, like letting Jesus know the Peter was the fisherman. In this instance, Peter just went out into the deep as Jesus ordered him, and he saw the catch come in. He who never cast a line instructed where to cast his, and he has good cash. Jesus, in His instructions to His disciple Peter, spoke of distinctions of spaces and knowledge of their varied conditions. He can, in wisdom, direct all His followers where it is best for us to be in His will because He is the Lord of Spaces. The spaces within us and those without. So, when He says to us, "launch out into the deep," He knows the spaces of the deep in which He is instructing us. One day, He astonishingly condemned a fig tree because He saw it using the space given but not producing fruits (Mark 11:12-25).

First, I want to establish the parameters. That is what I mean by the word "*Extent*." I would identify the "extent" of Elohim's presence in the spiritual realm and what we would more readily understand when thinking of physical spaces. In its most concise understanding, it is the question: What do we mean when we speak of the "presence" of God? It is a language often spoken in Christian communities around the world. We say, "the lord is here." Even in more complex forms, we used the past tense. We say the lord was "here" or He was "there." But was Elohim truly "here" or "there" more or in any greater way than He is in any other place? Or even at any other time? What do we mean in our attempts to localize God? What do we mean in our efforts to use limiting language to refer to Elohim, who cannot be limited?

For example, we can refer to Elohim, which is eternal, and speak of Him in periods and times. We can speak of Elohim in His throne room beyond the third heavens as if He is any more there than the throne of our hearts. As we speak of Him in this world when we say "our Father" in a powerful relationship space. And in the same breath, acknowledge "Who is in heaven." So, we are moved into a vast Elohim space that is "reachable" beyond reach. It is an awesome space that is far beyond fathom and near beyond belief. Elohim is extreme beyond measure yet immediate as the breath we breathe. No language exists that can express this extent. There is no song to fully capture this "extent," which I am attempting to explain here. I am a beggar at the Temple of Elohim, telling another beggar where I have found a little bread of understanding. So, they can find it as well. This book of spaces is about this.

Judy inspired me in the following Illustration of the "extent" of spaces. She was a financial adviser at a bank I do business. In one of our meetings, my being an author came up. The typical question authors face—one which I rhetorically try to dodge- was asked of me: "What are you writing about? Judy asked me. She leaned forward in such anticipation for an answer my usual rhetorical answer was not going to work. So just a little, I thought, not realizing I was going fully in I am writing a book about spaces of the Universe. How they exist, and how we interact with them. Judy, instead of saying "ok" or "Thank you for that…" To my surprise, Judy leaned further over her desk and became more inquisitive. I abandoned all pretense of secrecy and decided to lay out a more developed writing story. At least I told myself what harm I could do to explain to someone a little bit of what I was doing. However, it turned out to be more. Because the matter of spaces in the universe is so vast, you do not know where it will end once you begin. The extent of space is so vast and unlimited that it has no end. So, the following is how I attempt to explain to Judy the extent of practical physical spaces and how we can understand and interact with them.

I must add, although I am often so hesitant to discuss anything I am writing about, I am so amazed when I have ventured to do so; how someone so detached from this can be so inspiring that it could enhance the writing and the years of research. So, the following is a more extended version of what a financial advisor's questioning inspired the following illustration on the "extent" of human spaces. It was like I gave her an experiment to get a conceptual understanding that moves from the immediate to the extreme. In doing so, in about ten minutes of conversation, I laid out the physical landscape of a way to understand the Universe, our place in it, and it in us.

1. **A PRIORISM SPACE STEP ONE**: It is the belief that some knowledge of the physical spaces of existence can be derived from general principles. I contend that anything that exists—human or non-human, living or dead, seen or unseen must occupy a physical space to exist. Nothing can exist without occupying space, from quantum spaces to the vast universe. So, think of yourself as occupying your space. Whether at your home, in an office, or any other place. You exist in the body that is uniquely of your space. That is the primary space of you. It is your personal space within your skin. If you are a person with or without the Bible, it is still beneficial to know this is a space that God created before it became "us." It was lying there separated from life, much like our loved ones or others would see us after we die. When my wife died after two years shy of forty years of marriage, I did not want to see her body space without her occupying it. However, you go with the flow in a large family to keep things low. They insisted, so I did. Now, despite all the wonderful memories, seeing her lifeless body remained vividly in my mind with a strong awareness as a man with the Bible that she was no longer there. It was just the space she occupied on her journey on this Earth. I contend that to know who we are, who we are becoming, and who we want to be, we must first confront that the space we occupy here is that—the unique space given to us for our temporary journey here. This knowledge of God and knowledge of ourselves directly affects what we value here. Someday we all are going to leave this space for another. This is so for the one with the Bible and the one without. But this is just the beginning of the immediate space of "us."

2. **A PRIORISM STEP TWO**: Nothing exists in isolation—nothing. Nothing can exist alone without shared spaces, whether immediate or extended. As long as you are "home in the body" (1 Corinthians 15), you occupy a personal space but never without a public dimension. Depending on where you are, the space outside your skin is filled with various objects you can see and those you cannot see, like the various chemicals and particles that freely flow inside and outside of us. Some sustain life, but other nasty stuff in the age of viruses and variants can even kill us. The idea is that we exist in space within that is within and in shared immediate space occupied by other objects and elements all in our immediate space. We are never alone. No such space exists. We can never exist alone. It is important to understand that as we consider spaces of existence. Consider the space of the air that we breathe. It occupies a unique dynamic space because it bridges these two dynamic spaces. I am always mystified by the thought that the air we breathe on the earth from the beginning of "God breath into man…. and mankind." that this air is recycled but is never replaced. ***So, we breathe inside of us the same breath of Adam and the very physical breath of God*** (Genesis 2:7). It is more than we all bleed the same. We all breathe the very same breath. It is how we live; in a pandemic, it is how we die. Let us face it: we cannot exist without occupying space, and we cannot exist without sharing spaces. We can never exist alone. You can always see and feel the space around you. It is a reality of existence, and it all comes with its strong influence, like gravity, on who we are. Think of yourself then as occupying *personal* space. Then notice that you are never alone in a very profound way. You are in touch in a very real way with every other human being who walks the same earth and breathes the very air as we do.

In your space, look around you, and you will see or even feel the many other people, things, and matter that also occupy space. It is the fundamental nature of existence. The one who thinks he or she is better than you yet is so dependent on the same necessity for existence. It is folly (the subject of my book, The Death of Wisdom: The Rise of Folly) not to be aware of this when considering who we are—the one with the Bible and the one without. We must confront this to understand ourselves—who we are.

3. **A PRIORISM STEP THREE**: So that my lists of existing spaces do not get too long, let's take some big leaps or transitions to get at the "extent" of physical spaces. Not only are we not alone, but we also exist in shared spaces with both living and non-living (biotic and abiotic) spaces. We can (and also fully supported by the Holy Scriptures) move from the *immediate* spaces shared around us into the continuum of *extreme* spaces all the way to Heaven. Now, of course, we can travel by various means to the far extent of this earth compared to generations before us. But we also know from common experience and logic that just because we cannot reach a space with our physical presence could never mean that that space does not exist. It is the age-old question of the great historical philosophers: *Does a tree fall in the forest if no one sees it or hears it?* If we visit the forest often enough, we will see evidence that it does. Because there are spaces we know exist even if we never see the spaces. We know the deepest ocean has a bottom, even though it will never physically go there. We know it is a common experience that spaces exist all around in a continuum that we cannot see. We cannot follow the journey of the wind. It goes to places we cannot. Yet we know from wherever it goes; it brings each of us the breath of life.

4. **A PRIORISM STEP FOUR**: Extreme Spaces. So, we move in spaces from inside our skin to the immediate spaces around us, to spaces we can see as far as our eyes can behold, and spaces we know exist but cannot see with our eyes. We also know we can move from such immediacy to spaces too far to fathom, too extreme to experience, too beyond to behold. So, you can get the progression of spaces all a critical part of existence in this universe. It is critical to understand where our physical bodies hold us back from going and where our yes though able to see so far yet cannot behold, then even there, this extraordinary gift part of the distinctive image of God—Elohim in us called the imagination can take us any place anytime we would like to go. You are sitting in a place reading this book that occupies its own space. To get even a little far fetch consider: If you are in your home, the home is on a street, the street is in a town, or a village, or city. If you are in America, the City is in a County, and the County is in a State, the State is in a Country, the country is in a hemisphere or a continent, the continent is in this world, this world is in a solar system, that is in another infinite of connected spaces all the way to where God and His angels occupy their unique heavenly space. If this is not so, it would make no sense that Jesus taught us to pray, "O Father who is in Heaven…thy Kingdom come thy will be done on earth as it is in Heaven…" it is a prayer where spaces are distinct yet merged carried by the breath of prayer. A space where the Christian can sit in their living room or shack on earth and touch God in His throne room. Such is the possibility of the existence of connected spaces and learning how to ride like the wings of birds on connected spaces from earth to heaven and heaven to earth. So that

there be no confusion, these spaces exist, or the Scriptures are false, and Christianity based on the Holy Scriptures is nothing more than a fantasy. All would be vanity, said the Preacher Solomon. But his more certain conclusion is "Fear God and keep His commandments, for this is the whole duty of mankind" (Ecclesiastes 12:13).

5. A PRIORISM STEP FIVE: So, we have moved to the far reaches of space where all prayers are heard by one with the Bible and even those without who cry out to Him. "Now I know God does not hear sinners, but if anyone is a worshiper, he hears" (John9:31). This extreme or ultimate space is not fiction. It is reported in the Scripture as real as any other physical place like mountains, hills, rivers, and oceans. All spaces that exist. And the extent is that from the person sitting in their living room or out in the perry grass fields to the far-flung throne of God, all are connected in spaces, as I have tried to illustrate above, from this universe and beyond. One constant exists in the continuum of the immediate to the extreme. On some level, one can then imagine a unique, singular space that connects all existence. Yet without destroying the beauty of distinctions of unique spaces. This is how from the immediate to the extreme where God is spaces are all connected. It is what is meant when the Psalmist said even "if I make my bed in hell you are there" (Psalms 139:7-10).

This I have just described above is the heart and mystery of spaces—all different, immediate, and vast, but all connected. This is no small thing. It is the mystery of the universe divided yet connected by spaces. Although you cannot see the country like astronauts, you know it is there. And the space of this Divine gift of imagination takes you far beyond any astronauts will ever see. It is like Bruce Hornsby's song "Dreamland:" 'Hey you can slip away slide away into dreamland" (LyricFind). The space of your imagination is a gift from the image of God that can take us places where nothing else we possess can go. It is forceful, fast, and not limited by space or time. It is part of who we are. Many of our accomplishments as to who we want to become begin in this personal and powerful space. But I am not done yet. There is more.

6. A PRIORISM STEP SIX: Now, let me take one deeper dive before we return to *immediate* space. For here is the depth of the mystery of who God is. For example, although you are in your immediate space—the space between you and everything else and to the extreme can be connected through the imagination, which is like space travel that can take us where we might want to go; that is how we move in lighting speed faster than any spaceship by God's gift of our imagination: From the immediate to the extreme. Christians are invited to that real space that Isaiah saw (Chapter 6), John saw in a vision in Revelation (1), and others. They saw beyond the edge of our galaxies into a unique space called the "throne room" where the God of the Universe holds Court. So, this is not some flight of fancy for the person with the Bible. I call in my works the reader to "look at the Book!" For the one with the Book, it is as real as any other in the universe.

Here is a critical depth of the knowledge of God and the uniqueness of who God is. We are created in His image. But what he did Was limit us by "presence." So that although we cannot be present among the stars, we can walk out, and through His image of imagination he gave us, we can, by this gift of imagination, be among the stars. (Now, I must admit not all imaginations are created equal. Like everything else, the Potter decided the depth of each person's imaginative perception in how He forms the clay). It is what makes great artists. They can fill a canvas with what resides in their imaginative space. It is a gift afforded to all but extremely special in some. We are all created equal in essence and human value. But not equal in abilities. And this is across the board. There are supreme individuals but no supreme race. But, to the critical and amazing point I am making here about our topic—the depth or extent of Elohim's space. *He gave us the ability through His image to be present in any place through our imagination, which He does in Person. That is, the distinction of God, who is above all, is that we can travel to any place we want by imagination. However, God does not "travel." His space of existence is not limited to the immediate, like sitting in a living room. He can sit or stand in real-time and through eternity, past, present, and future, <u>everyplace in full personhood</u>. That is how Big God is. And this is only a starting view of His **Presence**. Do we dare attempt to illustrate His **Power**? Look at a butterfly or the ocean; you will find clues everywhere. Open your palms and look at those mysterious, unique lines you take everywhere. There are clues of His revelation all around. He is just as present in butterfly's wings as in His throne room in Heaven.* **His presence cannot be divided because he is One God in person, in presence, in purpose, in place, and in space everywhere.** Again, I must point out that this is not a presence like the everywhere presence, like the wind or atmospheric presence. However, it is difficult to grasp as we have no earthly example to draw on, only His revelation and our innate imagination. In brief, where we go with our imagination, He does not have to because he is already there. It is expressed in that he said, "I am alpha the beginning of and the end." And guess what? There is no traveling in between. We shall now dig just a little deeper into this. To the one with the Bible this is an awesome description. It could be for the one without as well. Certainly, Elohim wants each person to know who He is so that all can come to the knowledge of God (1 Timothy 2:4).

"I am Alpha and Omega"—Unlimited Space

There is no higher calling of human language than when called upon to describe one's God. I contend this is so for any religion or religious group. It was so for ancient Jewish scribes who considered the name of God so holy that they would not attempt to put it in writing. It is like describing the eagle's way in the air, which was one of the questions God, speaking of himself, asked Job if he knew (Proverbs 30: 19). So, we approach describing God with a certain awe and humility wrapped in humans' limitations. But what gives me comfort is that God purposefully did not present himself as a vacuum space. He filled the prophets with knowledge of Himself. Indeed, He filled the Cosmos space with the display of His knowledge and splendor in the space of his entire Universe. He filled it with the little ant with energy to work about all summer to be ready for winter.

He filled this space with mysterious things that walk the Earth and beautiful birds that fly above it. He filled this space with all the creatures of the land and see, and most of all, He filled this space with how He designed, created, and loved you and me. Despite how difficult to describe, He did not leave us without ample descriptions of Who He is and what He is like (Hebrews 1:1-3).

The language we use to describe ourselves is of the utmost importance. It is so with God in the language or concepts He described himself. One of his descriptions employs what I call the "Language of Spaces" in Scripture. At the top of the descriptions yet, it is found in the last book, Revelation 22:13: **I am Alpha and the Omega, the First and the Last, the beginning and the End.** Here are but some notes on what this simple description says of the vastness of Elohim's space:

1. In *Alpha,* He is the beginning of everything.

2. In *Alpha,* he is not saying he is the beginning of himself. It means he is the Space from whom all other spaces flow. So, in Alpha we find a name of action. A name of Space. A space without which there would be no other spaces. So, it is the reason David in Psalm saw him as the space maker:

The following is based on the same biblical divisional process, "Spaces of Revelation," in the Father's gifts for Christ. To think of spaces in these divisions is to apply them towards understanding. They are meant again not as the end of content but to aid the pursuit of it:

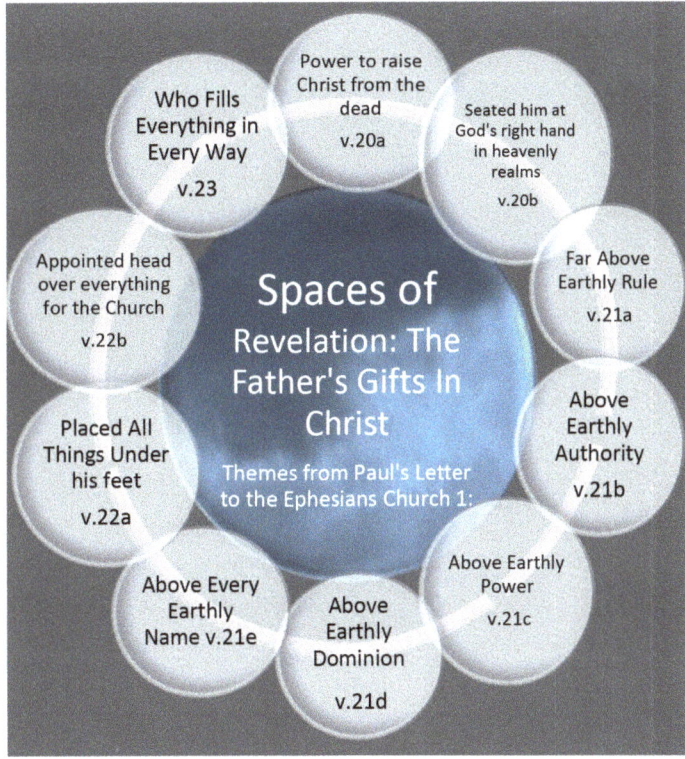

3. **In Omega,** God is the end of all things. It is a way of saying God has the last word in everything. Solomon said, "Now all has been heard; here is the conclusion of the matter: Fear God keep his commandments, for this is the duty of all mankind. For God will bring every deed into judgment, including every hidden thing, whether good or evil" (Ecclesiastes 12:13). This is the practical import of this description of God. It was not meant to be a poetic description. It is not hyperbole. It is a description of God's space that shows he encompasses the space of all things. Even that which is often thought of as hidden.

4. **Omega,** as part of the full description, is like a musical title that is meant to include all the awesome lyrical spaces of the song. It is one sung by all creation. And its lyrics fill the full spectrum of time to eternity. In His name "Alpha, and his name Omega the music of His existence fills the entire scale. He is the God of time and, at the same time, the Elohim of eternity and then some.

5. **In Alpha and Omega, the beginning, and the end.** *Here Elohim is the beginning without a beginning and the end without an ending.* There is, of course, design on Earth that represents such a space. The circle is one of them. It has no beginning. And it has no end. But even that simple geomatic item still falls short. The scriptures clearly say he is alpha and Omega more than a circle, which has neither.

6. **The best description of this God's space is "Alpha and Omega,"** I learned in one of the choruses I sang as a boy in Sunday School singing about God:

3

THE ELOHIM SPACE – CREATOR AND CHANGER OF TIME

(Photo by Kady Garcia 13 yr..)

Her Name is Time

Like a mother with her newborn baby, Elohim holds the space of time in His hands. He alone births time. He alone can change it someday into eternity: a space of time or existence without emerging death and its troubles—a metronome of life that will never end. In the meantime, although her days are numbered, she provides the days of our lives—the cadencies of our existence from memories to possibilities.

Time moves to the beat of Elohim's drums, who started it all with a creation song and a chorus of all nature joining in. It is difficult to understand time without Elohim. Otherwise, where do we begin? No other in history has been reported to have created her. No other set her in motion. Not even the mighty evolution is ever said to give her the necessary interconnected ecological birth or the "big bang" for that matter." Who started the first bang? Who continued the tune? Who carried its reverberations to the time of now? Where did the big bang go? Where will it end? Einstein said that for anything to exist, time must be in the equation. Like a dark hole, they seem to gobble up time more than anyone or anything, even for the most minute lifeforms. But through all this time, she, like "Old Man River," just keeps moving along. Why? Because she was created along with humankind. She may not have needed us, but we needed her. We could not exist one moment without her: "And the evening and the morning was the first day" (Genesis 1:5). And so began the rhythm of the dance of time. To this day, we are still dancing to her tune. We still exist in her metronome space. We still function in her stable staccato. Elohim started creating songs on the rhythm of time, and the universe of nature is still singing and dancing to her tune.

Look at the Book:

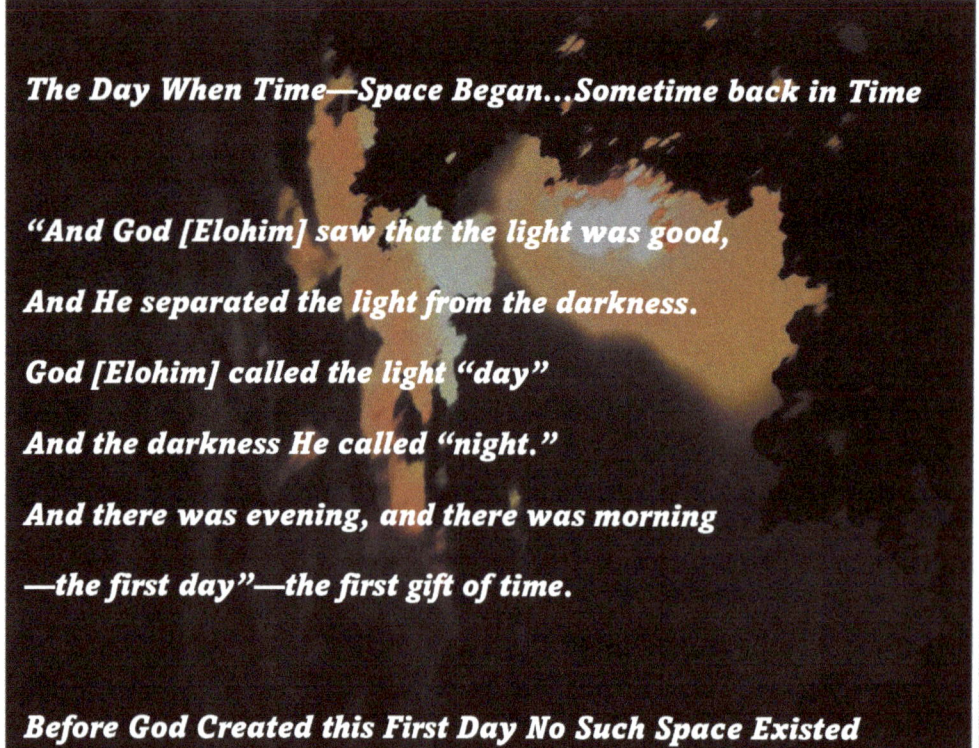

The Day When Time—Space Began…Sometime back in Time

"And God [Elohim] saw that the light was good,

And He separated the light from the darkness.

God [Elohim] called the light "day"

And the darkness He called "night."

And there was evening, and there was morning

—the first day"—the first gift of time.

Before God Created this First Day No Such Space Existed

Like every other creature born of its kind, we came into this world in a ready-made time capsule called the Universe. And as we grow into this prior ready rhythm of space and time, they must learn to exist in it. Sometimes they must run for cover from its blistering sun and learn to exist in its shade. Each must learn to live within this rhythm of space—the shifting changes of the seasons. "For everything, there is a season, A time for every activity under heaven…." (Ecclesiastes 3:1-8). The season rolls in on its own time. She waits for no one. She has no limits but her own. We cannot stop her. However, she can and will someday stop us. She lives only by her own rules. So, to exist, we learn from them and live by them if we want to survive. We can learn how to understand her, learn her parameters, and the value she affords us. However, we cannot change her. We can only allow her to change us in the time she allotted us to learn who we are, who we are becoming, and who we want to be. That is the value and power of time. She is a gift from Elohim that is so valuable to us that we cannot transcend what it affords. We live at her disposal and discretion of this mysterious creative gift call time. She can, like an eagle, take wings and fly away beyond the reach of each of us as a cloud hangs over us. And like the earth stays beneath us. Alternatively, the gentle ocean breeze envelopes us. In the end, she wants only for us to accept her as the welcome friend she is and learn to respect her timely value, this precious gift she is to all humankind. It is the nature of this space called time, both its directness as well as illusiveness, that Paul admonished the Christian followers of his time: "Pay careful attention, then, how you walk, not as unwise, but as wise, redeeming the time, because the days are evil" (Ephesians 5:15-16 BSB).

Time Mysteries

It is a mystery that we humans exist in a time-space continuum, helpless to do anything to time. Yet, she can do so much for us and to us. Let us face it: when we are hurt, she can be a healer, and at the same time, she can order more pain. Rehabilitation is a valued reliance on her. Without her, there is no rehabilitation. When we have time to heal, then she is our friend. But in other circumstances, like deadly force against the tubes we need to breathe, she, however precious, can extinguish our existence. It is because of this understanding that the prophets of old, like Hosea, declared, "It is time to seek the Lord" (Hosea 10:12).

We speak of time like her fate is in our hands or subject to our will. So, we say we are going to use her to our advantage. We say we are going to measure time. We will make the best of her, buy, sell, tweak, and see how much we have of her. Yet all the while, we are helpless to change her in any way. When it comes to time, it is all talk if we do not change ourselves. She may give us the space in which to change. But she cannot change us. We are at liberty by our choices; sharing will only change us for better or worse. She remains in her own rhythm and dance even as her perceptions of our own space change. As the great singer-poet Bob Dillion, in his Album Time out of Mind (1997 Song: "Standing in the Doorway"), lamented, *"Yesterday everything was going too fast.*

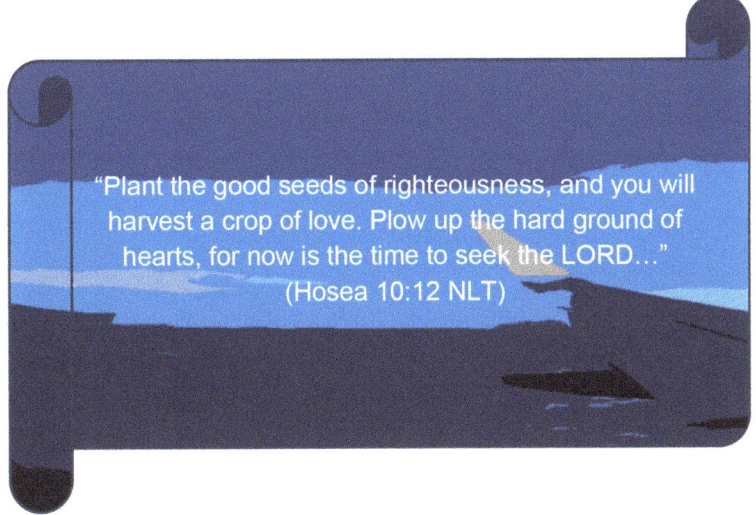

"Plant the good seeds of righteousness, and you will harvest a crop of love. Plow up the hard ground of hearts, for now is the time to seek the LORD…"
(Hosea 10:12 NLT)

Today it is moving too slow." And Sheer told us everything she would not say if she could just *"Turn Back Time"* (2009). We can all share that sentiment, wishing we could go back in time and change things. Nevertheless, sadly, it is but a pipe dream.

She is like a marathon runner for one of the mysteries of time. She never runs backward. Sometimes, we wished we could, but only for a little while. We would change a thing or two. But she does not listen to us. She bothers us to listen to her, although she can never listen to us. She does not flow backward. How we wished she did—this mysterious lady called time. She can come like a cool breeze on a hot Summer afternoon giving us a desirable respite. And in a moment of time can change into a raging storm. It can push us to sleep in a wink while at the same time leading us into a space of constant events, deadlines, demands, urgencies, and anxiousness—even as Elohim reminds us, "Be anxious for nothing, but in everything, by prayer and petition, with thanksgiving, present your requests to God" (Philippians 4:6). It is but one of the ways how we are instructed to use this space of time wisely.

Time's and Eternity

Elohim, who is eternal and created time as a necessary space for us to exist, entered time so that we can transcend her to the next level of eternal existence. Elohim exists in eternal space and makes us in His image to also exist in that space. This will happen at the end of "the evening, and the morning was the first day." As there was a "first day," so there will be—and now is a period of "the last days" so frequently mentioned in the Holy Scriptures (2 Timothy 3:1-5; 2 Peter 3:3-4).

One cannot read prophetic books without the clear statements that there is a time coming when time and days, as we know them, will end. And something called "eternity" will commence. So, a specific period is expressed in the rhythm of days when the dance with time will end. The Prophetic Daniel heard it from Elohim this way: "But you, Daniel, shut off the words and seal the book, until the time of the end. Many shall run to and from, and knowledge shall increase" (Daniel 12:4 ESV, emphasis mine). So, Eternal Elohim comes crashing into time in the Person of Jesus. The Apostle Paul wrote in Galatians 4:4-5 "But when the fullness of time had come, God sent forth his Son, born of a woman, born under the law, to redeem those who were under the law, so that we might receive adoption as sons. He crashed into time, so He transformed us to exist in eternity.

Time and the Christian

Elohim, who created time, declared to his servants how we are to live in this space. Here are some general principles:

1. **BE STILL - PSALM 46:10**: *"Be still and know that I am God."* You cannot win against time, so do not fight her. There is a calm space of God that each of His followers must know and appreciate. But it can only be known in the stillness of spaces. There is a time for everything under heaven. And it is always

time to be with Elohim. As you enter this space, you will find Elohim Space. You will first learn Who He is. And you will then learn more about who you are, and who you are becoming.

2. **BE SEEKER - ISAIAH 55:6**: *"It is time to seek the Lord."* When life's circumstances come crashing in on you, and you want to give up—do not! Treat circumstances as a call space to come to Elohim. Treat trials like a Divine alarm. Treat it like a stopwatch, like a call from Elohim's space to yours. Like a time to turn your gaze upward to the space of the hills from that space that is the source of your strength (Psalm 121:1,2). Elohim who created you to take the time to seek Elohim. It's time to turn your eyes upward away from your space to seek Elohim's space. It is a large space. There is always room I that space.

3. **BE SENSITIVE TO THE TIMES - EPHESIANS 5:16**: *"Redeeming the time, because the days are evil"* (Ephesians 5:16). Time is like a speeding train that makes no stop until the end of the tracks. Only Elohim can put the brakes on time. In the meantime, we keep our eyes open to what is happening in our world. We make full use of what we see as we care to make a difference. The only way to "redeem the time" is to live redemptively in it.

4. **BE A SERVANT IN TIME – JOHN 9:4** *"While it is daytime, we must do the works of Him who sent Me. [The] night is coming when no one can work."* In the broad sweep of things, God's people are left here to produce fruits for Elohim's kingdom. It is like living since Genesis in an endless Summer. Now Fall is here. Winter is soon upon us when the flowers fade. And the ground can no longer produce. The Sun is hidden by the clouds of Winter. And the long night when no one can work is fast approaching. So, Jesus said to his followers in a sweep of time's conclusive pressures, Keep working now that the sun is shining upon you. The long night is about to begin. And there would be no more opportunity to work in the space of time. Work before time retires.

5. **BE SAVVY WITH TIME – ECCLESIASTES 3:1** *"There is a time for everything, and a season for every activity under heavens."* It is a mystery of time that we have no control over her. But we do have a significant control over what is called "timing." The great ones up at bat long cultivate the master of timing. Times come like a fastball, but you have to know when to make the swing. The same applies when the ball comes at you slowly or with an unexpected curve. You still must cultivate the art of knowing when the moment comes to swing at bat. I planted an avocado tree in my backyard. It took some seven years to bear fruit. Yet when it did, I did not know when to pluck them. It is too late; they become brown inside and are not good for eating. Too early, and it is hard inside with the same result. I learned that sometimes they are ripe to pluck but not ripe to eat. The avocado tree in my backyard taught me to let my space for avocados get ahead. I had to learn to develop patience if I wanted to enjoy the fruits from my avocado tree. Sure, one can last without eating avocado. But one can hardly succeed without learning the value of timing. It is the wisdom learned to be savvy with time.

6. **BE SANCTIFIED –LEVITICUS 20:7** *"Sanctify yourselves therefore and be ye holy for I am the Lord your God."* God told Moses when He appeared to him in a burning bush. He wanted Moses to respect holy spaces and function in the space of his holy space—the space of obedience. so, Elohim said to him,

"Do not come any closer, take off your sandals, for the place where you are standing is holy ground" (Exodus 3:5). Peter expounded on this space in the New Testament when he wrote of the believer's separateness for the world (1 Peter 2:9-12).

I have often wondered why I never saw a school curriculum with a lesson on time, especially in the field of the humanities other than the pure sciences. I know in certain scientific research, it must be considered, as there can be no adequate science in any field, as Einstein demonstrated, without its consideration. But serious thought in the ongoing existence of humanity time is often left behind. It is always there for what we want or should not do. Its space can be an ever-present friend until it becomes our enemy. That is when time itself forces us to consider its value in our existence. Whatever humans decide to do, they will need time to do it. And once time is passed, it can never be reclaimed. It is one of those special spaces that demands respect and attention.

Time a Blank Check From Elohim

Let's face it. What if we were given a bank account at birth with no cosigners? It is in your name only. Only you and you alone can draw from it anytime at your own choosing. All you know is that you have this account, but you do not know when the dollars will run out. Knowing this, how would you spend that money? How would you use that singular special account?

At your birth, you were given this space call time. It is in your name only. No one can use it for you. It is the only source of time you have for you to live and exist. But here is the catch. You have no knowledge of when this valuable source of existence called time will run out. How will you then live with time, not knowing when it will run out? But you know for sure it will run out no matter what is in the news or not. No matter who is president or not. No matter who or what is trending in social media or not. No matter what religion, race, class, gender or not or any other identity you deem yourself in this world or not. No matter your health status. You do not know when and no one can lie to you about that reality. You know your time account is going to a zero-balance sheet. How would you spend your existence? Who or what would you choose to be while you have a choice when you do not know which one will be your last? Let me deliberately billable the point of time—give you a further summary of my assessment of time-space that can inform us on how we live in this precious Elohim space:

- Time is like a song. Each life determines its title, lyrics, tune, and rhythm. And no one knows when her lyrics will end, or her last song will fade to silence on this side of space.
- There are many who do not believe in absolutes. But one of the absolute certainties of time is its uncertainty. It is folly to deny there are no absolute spaces. Who we are and who we are becoming depends on what we believe about her.
- Time is not a gift that keeps on giving. So, you must make the best of it while you have her.
- Time is the rhythm of our spaces. We can keep up or lag. It's our choice.

- Time is the rhythm of space. It has its own rhythm in its innate independence. We must learn its rhythm in all its varied themes. Sometimes, we must dance to the beat of its drums to get ahead. Other times, you must know when to refrain from dancing to its sounds.

- Time and space are immersive with each other. They are the inseparable components of existence on this Earth. It takes time for each person to inhabit spaces.

- Time is often experienced as the flow of life. It is an experience like a stream. Yet, for us to make sense of it like spaces, we have to break it up into manageable bits. Like music, life on one note or score is boring, and it can be to the point of not wanting to listen anymore.

- The essence of time and space is their varied and constant challenge to us to make sense of them all. We make sense by being sensible about time and space. No one can understand all there is about the spaces inside or outside of us. But time requires we like eating we take a bite at a time. The simple act of eating can teach us how to understand time. That is why The Apostle says, "rightly dividing" the Word. Because it is an effective way to deal with anything that is too big. Even a small meal requires it. So, we break it down into manageable bits to digest. For example, so many people came to me as a Pastor for some time. They would begin by talking about their problem, often in global terms. Using language like "my life this or that." My task was always to try to get at the pieces. "Why do you feel that way about your life? Is there something that happened to make you feel that way? When I help the person to see, it is not so much "life," but it comes in specific spaces of that life, light shines on the problem, and possible solutions come. The spaces seem more manageable and even controllable. If it is because you lost your job or someone close just left you. Then we focus on that.

- Sometimes, good stuff comes out of a bad situation. Hope rises and is a solution to life that is one step at a time in bits and pieces. When the journey seems long, you must focus on the little steps you can take just ahead of you. Time affords a slower pace than we often take.

- It is good that time offers itself to us already broken down in bits and pieces. Time allows us to break it up into manageable bits or periods. It is a good thing time offers us. It gives us a period, a break, a time to figure out who we are, who we are becoming, and who we want to be.

- Sometimes, I come at the truth from a different perspective, like I am doing now with the space of time. It is because time is worth the time for us to understand its mysteries. So, I contend, time is too big and overwhelming to take it on whole. Indeed, it is the nature of time. It does not mind us breaking it up so we can manage it. It tells us here I am, take me, and use me well. I am not your master. I am a gift from God sent here to serve you. I am yours. Respect and cherish the space I give you to be the best you can be.

- Time is one of the most natural things in the world. It does not cry when we misuse it. We are the ones who cry. Time is like the old Mississippi river that just keeps rolling along.

- So, what can I add to this mystery space-time? I contend that time is important but also important for everyone. Time is valuable. And it is so for everyone. What makes the difference of who we are and who we are becoming, and who we want to be all comes down to the choices we make in the moments of time allotted for each of us.

- Time is not dependent on the nature of our circumstances. It is dependent, no matter our circumstances or station, on the quality of our soul. "For what shall it profit a man to gain the whole world and lose his own soul? Or for what shall a man give in exchange for his soul (Mark 8:36). So, time value is in the value we give it in who we are.

- Although time is a gift to everyone, what is important is what do we give back to time in the fleeting moments it gives us. Jesus gave his truth about time and his role in it. Speaking of space and time to all his followers: "While it is daytime, we must do the works of him who sent Me. *Night is coming, when no one can work*" (John 9:4 emphasis mine).

- I must also point out that Elohim, who created time, has also created blocks or periods in which he deals with His creation in certain ways. A period of time he set aside for specific action. For example, the term of period of grace as opposed to the period of the law from Moses to Christ. The period or times of the Gentile is when God is given a time for His true Church to be born and spread throughout the earth, to Gentiles. That time-space will end when God takes his true Church—called out ones out of this world and once again turns his attention back to His geographic space and his people.

A Coming Time and Space of Judgment – A Graphic

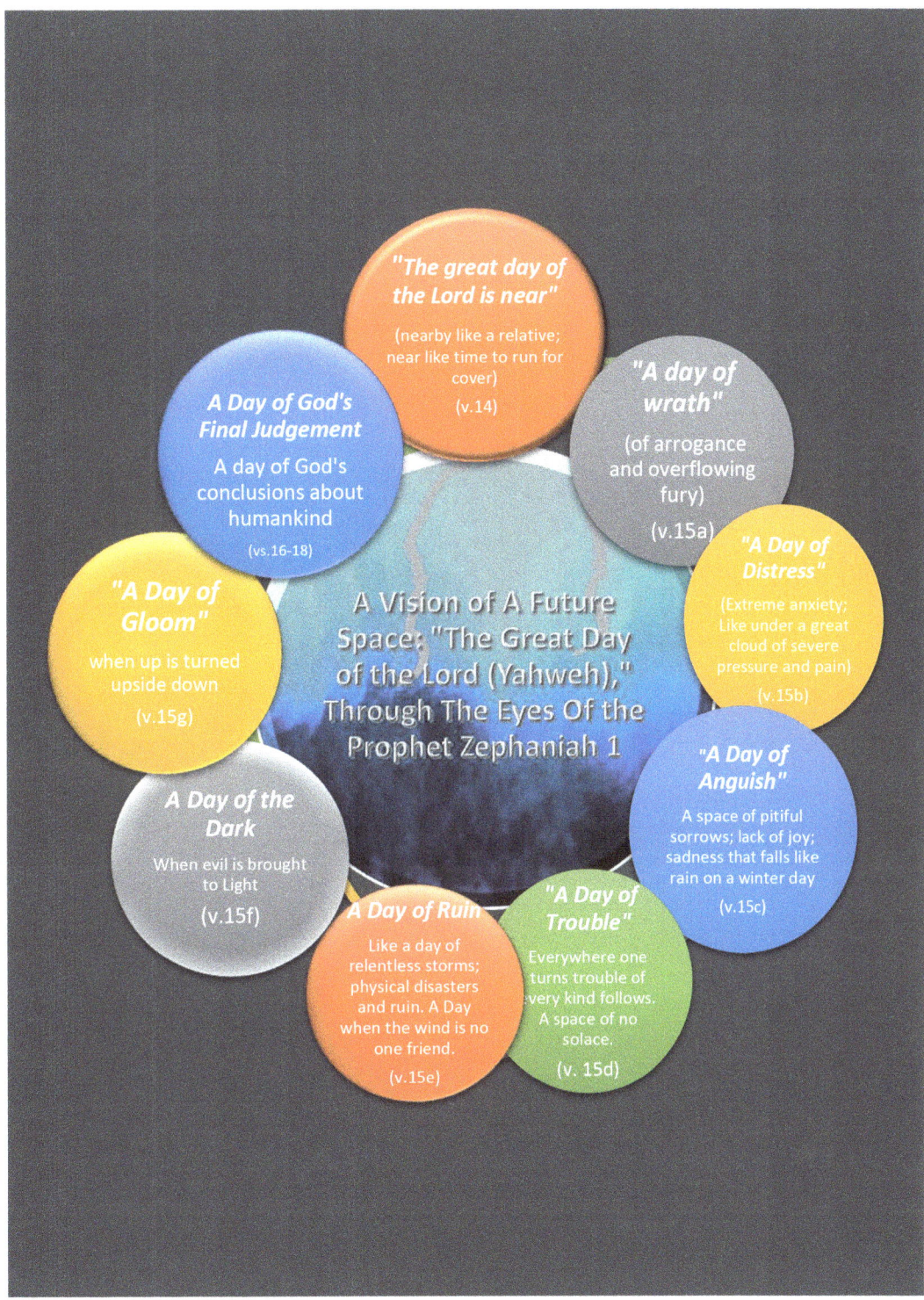

4

ELOHIM SPACE – THE GOD OF US

The Narrative of "Us"

"But God, because of *his great love for us*, who is rich in mercy, made *us* alive in Christ even when *we* were dead in transgressions— it is by grace *you* have been saved"

(Ephesians 2:4-5)

The most wonderful space in the panoramic flow of the Bible is its narrative showing Elohim who could have maintain an aloft distance after creating us but did not. From the beginning of Moses narratives suggested in Genesis 3:8 in Hebrew language of Divine intimacy that Elohim would walk among them on a regular basis. After creating Adam and Eve, he would *"come down in the cool of the evening"* to interact with them. And more astonishing, after mankind rebelled against Him by listening and following their Creator's arch enemy, Elohim found a way of redemption and forgiveness of this worst of sin—revolt against Elohim.

Throughout the entire journey of humankind on this Earth to this day He still in various ways seeks to be near us (James 4:8). To say that Elohim is a God of "us" is not hyperbolic. Indeed, it could not be. I wished with all my heart; I could find the words to express and describe this massive river flowing from the heart of God like a river with all the force of Divine love to every single person. And that is whether they believe in Him or not. This river flows and meanders to every corner of the human stream from Genesis to Revelation to everyone in this panoramic space. This space of the *Elohim of us* is the heart of everything in the Holy Scriptures.

Exhibit Cain

When Cain murdered his brother Abel because of the quality of his sacrifice to Elohim, he cried out to Him for protection from those who wanted to exact revenge on his life. And Elohim placed a "mark" of protection on Cain. He gave him a survival space to exist from his Avengers. What kind of God is this that would let a cold murderer go free? When things got desperately evil in Genesis 6, humankind's thoughts and actions became so evil that Elohim wanted to crush them all. He raised up a holy man named Noah, who found grace. Gave them 40 years of showing mercy—created a space of grace; built an ark to save them from a coming flood. All the while Noah was building an ark for their protection, they engaged in four decades of partying while Elohim was planning their deliverance. Forty days. Enough time to repent. How do you explain forty years? And this while they engaged in four decades of partying: "Eating and drinking, marrying, and giving in marriage, up to the day Noah entered the ark (Matthew 24:38).

Exhibit Abraham

Of great historical and yet future significance of this Elohim concern for us—a space that was going to change both the historical and future order began in Genesis with the call of Abraham. This Elohim space of concern for us was going to change civilization for all time. Elohim gave Abraham a three-part space of promise in Genesis and He was going to Keep each of them to the end. All three earthly dimensions of this promised space have already been fulfilled, but their completion is yet future. and the third is yet to come to complete this promise space: (1) He promised Abraham PLACE. This is why Jerusalem is called "the promised land." The geographical space has already been fulfilled, but more is coming in the spiritual dimension of the space. Abraham understood this to be so when it was said of him as a man of faith in Hebrews 11, "he looked for a city whose maker and builder was God. 2) Elohim promised Abraham a PEOPLE. He was going to make his seed into a great nation. But again, this space was going to be larger than just Israel, for it was said through Abraham's seed that all nations of people would be blessed. (3) And most significant, He promised a PERSON—Jesus Christ, who would come not only a Savior of his people but the whole world, said declared in John 3:16. This is again a concise summary of the panoramic redemption's space entirely laid out in the narrative of the Holy Scriptures. It fully demonstrated Elohim as a God of us. Promises are given concerning all of us for us. And Elohim is a promise keeper.

Exhibit Moses And Others...

He raised Moses as a deliverer of His people; to show His redemption and love. He raised Joshua to show he would fight their battles and give them victories against their enemies. He raised up prophets, priests, and kings to lead them and reveal His word and ways. He raised up ordinary people, men, and women like Ester, to be a queen and show his love for his people—to save them from extinction. At every turn, at every crossroad, when mankind acted horribly, like at the foot of Mount Sinai in Idolatry and shame, His mercy abounds. The law was broken in species but never His love, grace, or mercy. And to cap it off, one of His great servants in his great treatise on the Gospel rejoiced, "But God proved his love for us in this: "While we were still sinners,

Christ died for us" (Romans 5:8). What do you do with such a space of love? Like the writer of Hebrews cried out, "How shall we escape if we neglect such great salvation?

The God of us is the central theme of the entire Scriptures: "Emanuel" expressed this central truth in one word— "Behold the virgin will be with child and will give birth to a son, and they will call Him Immanuel" (which means "God with us" (Matthew 1:23).

Humanity will stand without excuse before a Holy God because of this redemptive space provided and their rejection of that provision. The actual *evangel* body of Christ lives in that uncontaminated and global redemptive space—a space in Christ and absolutely nothing else. Any criterion based on social or political litmus tests is spiritual contaminants. Only the blood of Christ matters. We sing it over Robert Lowry's 19 Century testimony in song, but we do not often reflect that space to the world: *"What can wash away my sin nothing but the blood of Jesus. What can make me whole again nothing but the blood of Jesus"* (1876). We need to enlarge the space of the Blood and not the space of the battles. Jesus commissioned His followers to widen that space. It is the most critical "space task" Hum gave us directly. He said the harvest space is excellent. He said the labor space is small, and we must pray for it to be enlarged significantly since the space of the evil forces in the world is rapidly increasing. The thief comes but to rob and steal, but He came that we might have life and have it abundantly. The Bible, in its entire narrative, describes a God of us. And the "us" includes those often despised among the "us" (Luke 4:8).

Exhibit Elohim's House—Will God Really Dwell among Us?

In chapter 8 of 1 Kings, a grand celebration is at a very important event. The ark of the covenant of God to Israel, which was like a symbol of the continued promise of Elohim's presence, was heading home to the promised land Jerusalem for the dedication of the great Temple King Solomon had built. This was no ordinary event. It represented the prelude and celebration of Elohim's meeting among His people. Everyone was present, from priests to peasants, from the prosperous to the poor, from the mighty to the masses—all invited to this unique space built to meet with Elohim. Animals for sacrifice to Him were so many the narrative said they could not be numbered (v. 5). Each thought destined to be slaughtered was not alone, for in that act of their spilled blood was the symbol that He would someday shed His Blood for all humankind like a sheep to the slaughter; silent in His act of sacrifice (Isaiah 53).

This would be a space for a keynote address from the King who spearheaded this big and significant project. But King Solomon, the most powerful and wisest person who ever lived, did not feel it was a space for a speech. He felt the occasion was a space for prayer. That alone would be significant enough that he wanted to take this occasion to pray rather than to praise. But such was Solomon's choice to get to the significant part: Like the time God gave him a choice of what he wanted on his anointing King. Instead of asking for riches and power, he asked for wisdom to lead His people. Here again, at such a grand occasion, he chooses to take the less aggrandized path and turn to prayer. But this space of prayer was not important to my lesson here. It was again what Solomon chose to pray about, the important lesson for all God's followers. I contend the prayer as an act would be significant enough. But the deep narrative of his prayer must not be unnoticed. He was not just prying to Elohim but trying to understand Him more. After spending years building the temple, pause in prayer to understand why Elohim would build it. So, he revealed the questioning, apprehension, and doubt and laid it out like a soil blanket to Elohim, all enfolded in a provocative question like standing next to a wailing wall and not next to a well-built and beautiful Temple. He asked at the celebration of this monumental achievement if this temple was really going to serve its purpose: "Will God really dwell on earth?" (1 Kings 8:27).

This is not hyperbole. This is not philosophical speculation. This is a wise man questioning all the planning from Moses, given the detailed plans handed down through his father David and to him building the most majestic building with the finest of materials from all over the then-known world. He is discovering an empty space in his soul with one big question mark: The great, unique, vast space of God's dwelling fit into a temple among His people. However, one thing was clear to him. God must think it possible to have spent so much time, leadership, details, contribution, and talent from woodworkers to those block makers, and layers to iron fabrication and design, to the finest of gems of the highest quality by those with the highest quality of skills in each area. And now it was done. Nevertheless, he still had an unsettled space in his heart. However, he had the wisdom to seek God when the spaces around him did not make much sense. He prayed. God was asking for a space too small for him to inhabit. If God could not dwell in that small temple, he could not dwell in each of us. To launch out into the deep things of God is to understand this Reality of the ability of God to inhabit any space in which He is invited. I contend, here, that the Scriptures fully support Elohim as a God of us. It is one of the most essential spaces in the panorama of redemption. It is the space where the love of a holy God meets the abject sinfulness of His creatures.

"HERE I AM! I STAND AT THE DOOR AND KNOCK. IF ANYONE HEARS MY VOICE AND OPENS THE DOOR, I WILL COME IN AND EAT WITH HIM, AND HE WITH ME. TO HIM WHO OVERCOMES, I WILL GIVE THE RIGHT TO SIT WITH ME ON MY THRONE, JUST AS I OVERCAME AND SAT DOWN WITH MY FATHER ON HIS THRONE"

(REVELATION 3:20).

In this prayer from Solomon, his view of God and how God can do or not do changes his perspective of his task. He sunk deep into suggesting that with whom he perceived God, his greatness could be too great to dwell among you and me. Or our work on earth is too small for Him. He learned that our space is not to understand all God is doing but to focus on what He asks us to do. Some spaces collide. When they do, we must get in sync with God's space. The conflict of spaces hits us each day if we associate with others, even when we live with them. Love, mercy, forgiveness, longsuffering, humility, and many other spirits fruits function like oil to ease conflict and smooth those spaces when they come together.

The collision of spaces is a significant part of existence. However, it must be avoided when our space is against Elohim's. This is the "collision of Spaces." Sometimes, spaces are in harmony with each other, and at times, they crash into each other. This was a time when Elohim's Space came crashing into the perception of the King of His people Israel. His view of God did not include a space for God as a Temple.

5

YAHWEH – SPACE OF THE WARRIOR GOD

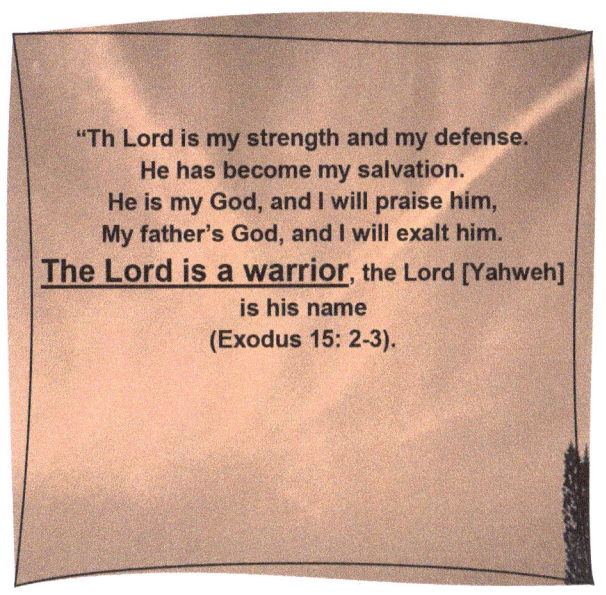

"Th Lord is my strength and my defense.
He has become my salvation.
He is my God, and I will praise him,
My father's God, and I will exalt him.
The Lord is a warrior, the Lord [Yahweh]
is his name
(Exodus 15: 2-3).

In nature the battle for survival is fierce. What in Darwinian theory is termed gently "natural selection," like a disinterested scientist just looking at the data, is on some level of nature considerable brutal. It is true in nature as it is in humanity there are some who maintain their spaces of existence by taking others out of theirs.

The "survival of the fittest" (Darwin theory given a more fitting title) is not a sport. It is true in nature. It is true in the human condition. It forms the basis for justification of all kinds of evil in this world. It is no longer enough for one to show their strength by just being strong. They show it by constantly taking advantage of the weak to demonstrate they are strong. But not just in nature, and the human condition, but in the unseen world of spiritual forces as well. My book "Deliver Us from Evil: A Prayer for Our Times" (Christian Faith Publishers, 2021) is an exposition of this space. Here, the considerable power of evil, like prey, seeks out the spiritual and marks them for destruction (1 Peter 5:8).

We are not called upon to take vengeance on those who act against us. We are admonished, on the one hand, to defer to God. "Vengeance is mine, and I will repay sayeth the Lord (Romans 12:19 ESV). On the other hand, towards our brothers and sisters in the Christian community, we are encouraged against any "survival of the fittest" ideology. There is no room for ambiguity "We who are strong ought to bear the failings of the weak and not to please ourselves" (Romans 15:1).

The tradition of thinking about God, even in any given culture, is that of benevolence—kindness, compassion, love, and understanding. But in a world where evil is constantly in battle mode and high alert, the Christian God cannot be just a God of love and mercy. Although these spaces of Elohim are critically important, in the selected text, "Yahweh" is the existing One, strong and mighty, who cannot be defeated in any battle. Here, Elohim, the God of Creation power, is expressed as Yahweh, the Warrior God to His Children. To know God in that space is also to know who we are, who we are becoming and who we want to be. Do we want to be in the winner's circle? Or do we want to be on the losing side? We each have a choice of the spaces of existence we want to occupy.

Look at the Book:

Exhibit - Moses and Miriam Sang of a Warrior God

It is the story of a solemn song. Pharaoh, after the plagues Elohim inflicted on him and his people, ordered Moses and the Israelites to get out of Egypt. Even to the point of telling them to take their belongings, their possessions, even their silver, gold, and leave! But it lasted but for a moment. Pharaoh soon changed his mind. He called up his best commanders, chariots, and forces and set out after Israel. Israel at this space and time had no armies. They were slaves in Egypt. They were vulnerable to the overwhelming military power of Pharaoh's army. They had no attack weapons like swords and no defense like shields. And no training in any battle. Egypt had developed their own with trained worriers to use them. Even if they had a supply of ammunition like the Egyptians, they would not know how to use them. Long years of slavery had drained any birth of a collective spirit to fight. They could run but not hide. Their progress took them to a space like lambs in an open field surrounded by lions. From this perspective, the war seems to have been over before it began. Israel had no chariots to flee the coming mass of Egyptian warriors. They could not make a run for it, for they were confronted with a deep river ahead of them. They were journeying along a path hemmed in by mountains on either side of them. And the worst was that the Pharaoh's efficient and well-equipped army was in hot pursuit behind them. The sounds of their rapidly moving chariots were getting closer. There was no physical place to escape in any direction. They were cornered in a death trap. The

Who is the King of glory?

The LORD [Yahweh- the existing One] strong and mighty,

The Lord invincible

in battle.

deliverance from the Egypt Plan seems to have all but disappeared. Death seemed imminent. No words of an author can tell of the terror that must have filled the souls of the people. Slavery at least kept them alive. It was like the old saying "out of the frying pan, and into the fire" as the Israelites clustered at the raging river's edge with no pathway out in any direction. Moses carried "the rod of a Warrior God," who told him to use it to fight the battle. He told him to stretch it out towards the waters. And the waters parted. On the other side of the deep waters, with all of Pharaoh's mighty army at the bottom of the sea, they gathered to sing about it.

Upon reflection of this historical event, Moses, Miriam, and the people sang a song. It was a warrior song whose lyrics traverse the landscape of war and having prevailed over their oppressors, their enemies, being hurled into the sea. And all of Israel learned that day that their God was also a mighty Warrior among all his mighty attributes He showed Himself to be. So, they sang and gave Him a new name "The Lord [Yahweh] is my Warrior"—a battle cry of victory (Exodus 15:3).

So, this is the initial space of the Exodus story. The story can be defined as a space when God Elohim showed himself as Yahweh, a warrior God. However, this is not a conjecture. It is what the Israelites who experienced it in historical space and time described Him to be. They experience a God who was to them a Warrior. But to what does this historical space apply today. When we look at a biblical story—even one such as Jesus Himself told- it would often be followed by a question: What is the story's meaning? How does this story apply to my situation? How does it apply to the state of my life? The narrative is not given as content to study but as conduct to be lived.

Sometimes the student of the Bible might get the story. The narrative is straightforward, and the event of the story is laid out. But its application is not so straightforward. Sometimes, the application of Old Testament stories is made clear in the New Testament. Often, they are given in the Old Testament by other servants of God separated from the events themselves. For example, what were Moses, Miriam, and the congregation of the Israelites singing about? What was the Israelites to learn about the "rod of God" in the hand of Moses? More specifically, what were the people to think of their God as a Warrior God moving forward? I contend the answer, and the application of the warrior song can be found in the words of the Prophet Isaiah 54:17:

"No weapon forged against you shall prevail…"

Miriam sang the Warrior song after the Warrior's event. Every child of God now lives in that Warrior space. They can sing her songs before their challenging events, for it does not matter that the road up ahead seems impassable. You turn to the left and the right and mountains are in your way. You look behind, and your enemies are tracking your every move with GPS precision, coming after you. What do you do?

You can imagine the impossible: No weapon forged against you shall prevail. You can imagine that you are not helpless. For what the "rod of God" represented in historical space and time in the hands of Moses is still available to you. Your Warrior God is present to do battle on your behalf. Stretch out your rod of faith and see mountains move. Stretch out your rod of faith and see rough waters parted and rough places smooth. This is what it means to live in the Warrior space of God.

This is not hyperbole. It is a spiritual reality for those who consciously and daily practice living in this Warrior space of Yah-Weh: "No weapon forged against you shall prevail." It is a special unique space of God to sing and dance about—a Warrior God.

Exhibit - Ben-Haddad Faced a Warrior God

The Bible narrative, especially in the Old Testament, is filled with other examples of a warrior God. A God who stands ready to defend His people stands ready to battle on His people's behalf. In 1 Kings 20 Ben-Haddad King Aram mustered his entire army to come against Israel in Samaria. He believed his own army could do the job, but he wanted to have overwhelming force and leave nothing to chance. In those days, a king could get other kings to join to ensure victory with the promise or prospect of sharing in the spoils of land and other valuables. So, King Ben-Haddad got an additional thirty-two kings with horses and chariots to join him. However, when the day of battle came, King Ahab of Israel defeated all of Ben-Haddad's armies. They fought Israel on the hill and lost. Ben-Haddad, to save face, said the reason for the loss was that the space of geography favored Israel. So, he altered the strategic location of his attack. But again, no matter the location of his attack, he lost every time, although he came with more forces and weapons. The application came from the Warrior God, who told His people He was not just the God of the mountains, but **also the God of the valleys.** Their God defeated the large armies of the Arameans that covered the countryside and every other front they came at God's people. It did not matter where the enemies of God's people came from; the Warrior God of battle in the mountains was the same in the valleys and the plains. God here took an interest in winning the battles and pointing out to His people that he would be a warrior God no matter the vantage points of their enemy. Long before Sir Winston Churchill gave his great speech outlining the various locations, "We shall fight them on the beaches…" Elohim already demonstrated to His people that He would fight His people on any battlefield (1 Kings 20) and never surrender fighting for His people. He is a Warrior God.

Exhibit - Judges of Israel Represented a Warrior God

During the period of the Judges in Israel, despite the rebelliousness and waywardness, God still raises up warriors among Israel to deliver them time and time again from their enemies. He did so because he was a warrior God who looked over His children. He was the same one who represented Himself as a cloud by day and a fire by night as a warrior of His people. God inhabits the space as a mighty worrier of His people. Even at a time when they deserved to fail, He fought for them. He is a Mighty Warrior who loves His people and will fight for them.

As we examine the spaces of our lives and try to determine who we are, who we are becoming, or who we want to be, it is indispensable that we consider our God, who will be who He is to us: our Mighty Warrior.

Language of the Warrior

The narrative of the Scriptures, like massive oak trees scattered across the biblical plains, is filled with the language of One who sees His relationship to his people as a Warrior. The thousands of words present a vast space for understanding a Warrior God. Here are but a few:

"Mighty Army."

The most powerful and dramatic illustration of God as a Mighty Warrior—Yahweh, is found in Ezekiel 37—his vision of the valley of dry bones. This is the biblical space from which this warrior description of a "Mighty Army" is drawn. It is like a play with God as the producer and the director. The Producer opened the scene with a strong physical and emotional impact. The lead actor is placed by the Spirit and laid down smack in the middle of a valley filled with dry bones. What is riveting and striking about this is that God sent him carried by His Spirit in this dramatic valley all alone. He has no supporting cast for what he will see unfold before his eyes. He had only the Spirit of God in this opening scene being taken back and forth among them. The opening scene, or the story world, is that of death in the valley. It is what the dead, dry bones represent: death. In the second scene, there is a striking dialogue between the leading actor and God, who places him in the valley. He is challenged with a question: "Son of man, can these bones live? The leading man among the dead dodged the question by saying, "O Sovereign LORD, you alone know." The script continued with God speaking to the leading man among the dead: "Prophesy to these bones and say to them, 'Dry bones, hear the word of the LORD! As the words of the Prophet spoke the word of the LORD to the bones, the score of this drama began. It first came as just a noise that turned into a rattling sound. Then one can see, along with the rattle, a resurrection of bones connecting and coming together all over the valley. Sounds connecting to sound. Dead bones connected to other dead bones, and this while they were still dead and lifeless, for there was no breath in them. But the score was getting louder. And the bones were not just connecting but seemed to be multiplying in the valley so that they were numerous. This scene was like a horror movie.

But then the Director quickly spoke again to the leading man, Ezekiel, a Priest, and Prophet, and called out to him to speak to the dead bones again and tell them to "live!" As the Prophet cried out, "Live!" The breath of God, like coming from the four corners of the world, crashed into the valley of dry bones, and they did the impossible. They live. What is striking is what they became after they were given life. They became a reflection of who they serve. The script read, "They stood up on their feet—a vast army. Indeed, the implication is not hidden. They became an army under the command of One who would lead them into victorious battle—A Warrior!

Jericho's Walls - A Warrior Won

The walls of Jericho were not made to keep its inhabitants in. They were fortified to keep outsiders out. There was a historical space and time when many outsiders wanted to get in. It blocked their path on their way to the promised land. And it so happened that their God was a warrior God, and the walls came tumbling down, down, and down. That was the kind of God He was. No walls built could block his power and purpose. No walls can stand in our way when we are following Him.

"Armageddon"

Armageddon, the last war, the final battle, the war of all wars is coming. It is the war where good and evil spaces collide. There is no space for a draw. One side must win. One side must prevail. Only the greatest warriors of all time will show up. The greatest battle ever fought in that space, and the greatest warriors assembled will be there. It is yet to come. This will be the one that genuinely determines world domination. The battle will truly determine who will rule the universe. It is a battle that has been raging in the dark side of existence since time began. There it will finally come to fruition in full display before a watching world—Armageddon.

All of Hell will come to battle. The Beast and all that accompany him will be there. The warrior and Overcomer Jesus Christ will lead Heaven there. There, the ultimate question of the ages will finally be determined: Who or what will finally win out—God or Satan, good or evil—in a historical battle yet to be called "Armageddon?" There, on the greatest battlefield of history and of the future, not only the fate of the world but Heaven will be determined as well.

However, unlike all battles that have ever been fought, the uniqueness of this battle is that the strategy for this one has already been tested in the future. Although it is yet future, it has already been battle-tested. Before the world began, the fate of evil had already been determined (Revelation 13:8). It was determined in Pharoah's armies at the bottom of the sea. In a wilderness and high on a mountain, it was determined with "it is written…" (Matthew 4:7). On an old rugged cross just outside Jerusalem called Golgotha, the outcome of Armageddon was already guaranteed. And when, on the third day, he broke the sting of death and came out of the grave, Easter had already won over Armageddon. The script of victory had already been determined in language, which cannot be denied: "Upon this rock, I will build my church and all the power of s of hell will not conquer it" (Matthew 16:18 NLT). And John on the Ilse of Patmos, in the Spirit on the Lord's day, saw this final battle victory by the greatest warrior for humankind's redemption in which the outcome is already determined in the predictive language of absolute certainty –the greatest words of hope and inevitability ever written. The Director has seen fit to release the end of the story summarized in these warrior words: "…*The Lion of the tribe of Judah has prevailed*" (Revelation 5:5). There will be victory. The victory space is assured for every believer.

6

ELOHIM SPACE – GOD THE SPACE MAKER

He made Learning *Space* even in the whom for David.
v.6

"Clean Spaces of confession and Forgivness"
vs.2, 7, 10

"Loving & Forgiving Spaces"
v. 1

God is a Space Maker Outside:

"In the beginning Elohim Created the heaven and the earth...(Gen.1:1)

Inside:

"Create in me a pure heart, and renew a steadfast spirit within me"

(Psalm 51):

"Praise Spaces on my Tongue"
vs. 14, 15

"Teachable Spaces"
v. 13

"Spaces of Obedience"
v. 12b.

"Joyful Spaces"
vs. 8, 12

I contend that this series concerning Elohim Spaces, as illustrated in the main graphic model of this book, is indeed above all the rest; this final part six is not yet exhaustive. However, it is central to understanding the model on which this book is based. It is also central to applying the model based on the spaces of existence. In all our consideration of spaces of existence, we can never lose sight of this constant reality that God is indeed a "Space Maker." I contend if we are to find answers as to who we are, whom we are becoming, and indeed whom we want to be; we must gather our thoughts, ideas, and especially spiritual focus and understanding that God is a space maker. In the graphic above, I attempted to show that He made the space inside our skin. And He made the space outside of us as well. It means we do not have to "reinvent the wheel." The task is to understand how we can live within the wheel.

We do not have to seek to establish new spaces of existence relentlessly. But to live an effective, successful life, we must learn to live in and through the spaces afforded us through existence. This sentiment is popularly found in the various versions of Theologian Reinhold Niebuhr's popularized prayer (1932 -1933):

"Father, give us the courage to change what must be altered. Serenity to accept what cannot be helped, and the insight to know the one from the other" (Shapiro, Fred R. (April 28, 2014). *"Who wrote the Serenity Prayer?" The Chronicle of Higher Education.*

In the center circle of the model, which we will consider next, is what I call the "me" space. I do not mean this in some "looking out for just oneself" way. In the model, it means that for purposes of understanding existence, the individual—although God is above us all, is at the center of his or her universe. It is to acknowledge that we who are the center of our universe yet need God, who is above us, to understand who we are. In this chapter, I contend that one of the chief reasons we need God to understand the "me" space—you" of existence is to understand one of the chief natures and is that He Elohim is a Space Maker.

We cannot understand or comprehend the spaces of the universe without Him, for He is the One who made it all. Let us again launch into the deep to consider what I am considering in the proposition that our God is a Space Maker. It is that each person recognizes that God is the creator of the spaces around us—many we cannot change, and the Creator of the spaces within that we can change or alter, as Theologian Reinhold describes it in his prayer. Long before this popular sentiment in this prayer, King David in his prayer expressed the same sentiment:

Look at the Book:

"Create in me a pure heart, O God, and renew a steadfast spirit within me" (Psalm 51:10).

The entire 51 Psalm of King David is a striking representation of David reaching out from his inmost being, crying out to Jehovah to fashion, as a potter would the clay new spaces within him. This was serious business he had with God. He had used his power and prestige at a most vulnerable time in a lady's life. He saw her taking a bath and lusted after her. Although she was married, David used his power as a ruler of the people to have her, then had her husband, who was serving in his army, killed. God had some serious work to do in the heart of the King. Fortunately, with the help of the Prophet Samuel, he could look inside his "me" space. He did not like what he saw. Despite his power, position, and place, he did not like what he had become. He turned to God for a "do-over" of his "me" space. David made it seem easy, but most people, including those with the bible, never go there. David did. His comprehensive list of the renewal of the "me" space is worth incorporating into any believer's life.

- *"Blot out my transgressions:"* (v. 1 - Get rid of that which is contrary to your will in my life).
- *"You teach me wisdom in the inmost place"* (v.6 -Let me learn your wisdom from my folly).
- *"Cleanse me with hyssop…wash me….* (v.7 – I created a mess that only you can clean).
- *"Let me hear joy and gladness…"* (v.8 – Let me hear pleasant sounds from my life again"
- *"Create in me a pure heart…renew a steadfast spirit within me"* (v.10 – God the space maker, let your spaces be in me and sustain me).

Elohim is a warrior and defender of battles that come from without and a Space Maker for battles that come from within.

In PSALM 118:5, the Psalmist speaks of the concept of spaces: ***"When hard pressed, He brought me into a spacious place."*** He said he was in a space where he was "hard pressed." It is a translation of the Hebrew word "may-tsar" that speaks of internal distress or troubles. The restricted space makes one cry, like a jail cell. And his answered prayer was to break out of these restricted spaces. Like a rabbit out of a trap and a bird escaping from a cage, he experiences the spaces of freedom. Like freedom to run, fly, and experience joy in the space of your skin. The space where the body space is set free—hard pressed.

Another concept of the Psalmist is a space of "callousness." In Psalm 119:70, he said that there were arrogant people who cultivated spaces of callousness or what can be described as a space of unfeeling indifference to others in need. This is a destructive space in any relationship. It is a space that prohibits one from feeling another's pain. It is a space where empathy calls and knocks at the door, but no one is home. Or if she is home, she answers only to those she selects worthy of her concern. A space where the cries from certain "others" are not heard or acknowledged. It is a cold space. It is an indifferent space. It is a space of existence within that remains unless the love and mercy of Jehovah can fill it. And He can because, as illustrated above, He is a Space Maker. It is who He is. It is Who he wants to be to us.

I can think of no other space in the Old Testament narrative as Jonah in his disobedience in the belly of a "great fish"—a sperm whale known to have a throat large enough to swallow a man whole. Regardless the narrative did not leave it to natural design alone. It says, "God provided a great fish to swallow Jonah. And Jonah was inside the fish three days and three nights" (Jonah 1:17). Elohim can do that because He is a Space Maker. Like the Psalmist, the narrative said, "From inside the fish [this most restrictive physical and spiritual space], Jonah prayed to the Lord his God [for no space is restricted to Him]. He said, "In my distress, I called to the Lord, and he answered me (Jonah 2:1-2). After Jonah prayed from that restricted space as he described it in detail, this ended with "And the Lord commanded the fish, and it vomited Jonah onto dry land" (Jonah 2:10).

The New Testament writers also described this restrictive space in various ways. The Apostle Paul writing to the Church at Ephesus, said, "Stand fast therefore in the liberty wherewith Christ has made us free" (Galatians 5:1). This is an admonition towards real freedom space not only of the body to stand, but spacious freedom of the soul to live unrestrictive in the love of God. That is what the Psalmist was experiencing in answering prayers from his God. PSALM 118:5 The Psalmist spoke of the concept of spaces when he said the following illustrated in the graphic: "He brought me into a spacious place." He said he was in a space where he was "hard pressed." He was like in a jail cell. And it was like his prayer to God was like a jailbreak. It freed him from a space described as 'hard pressed" to a spacious place like an escape to freedom.

We can only skim the biblical narrative to reveal the value and availability of the Christian journey into this space. If one studies the life of Jesus of Nazareth, one sees that His journey as He walked among us was one of empathy. But concerning Him, it comes to us with a word with more divine force than human empathy. It comes to us with the force of such description from the gospel writer Matthew 9: 36: "But when he saw the multitudes, he was moved with compassion on them, because they fainted, and were scattered abroad, as sheep having no shepherd." Christ's life on Earth was a continuum of life in this space.

The Space Between

This is a review of Elohim's fundamentals as a pacemaker. In the beginning, He paused to look in our direction and saw a vast, formless, dark void. Then, He began his mightiest, majestic, and major act of human existence when He formed, designed, created, and established spaces—and spaces between spaces.

And then God created a life of all magnificent forms, including ours, to experience and inhabit those delicately connected spaces. From simple life forms to the complex, He created separate yet inextricable and interconnected. Like the invaluable air we breathe, or the food we eat, or the magnitude of important human and non-human relationships we have. Elohim made spaces that can influence and even inhabit us. And like a keen balancing act, God gave us the power of choice, creativity, imagination, of spiritual consciousness spaces of his Divine image within us. They came with the awesome human power and ability to change those spaces within and without us significantly.

With great love and empathy towards us, all is not lost despite the emergence of original sin and evil to corrupt these spaces, create fragmentation, dislocations, and destress. The power to change spaces—our own and that of the world—for the good of all is possible. I contend that the historical Jesus Christ came into our space to make that possible.

That is what this book is about. It is an exploration of spaces within and without that constitute our existence. It is a consideration of the human condition in which we exist and the Elohim gift of the ability to transform ourselves and our world. It attempts to understand the complex spaces of existence: Who we are, who we are becoming, and getting to the space of who we want to be. Life at its best is a constant quest toward understanding physical and spiritual (external and internal) spaces and how to navigate effectively and exist between them.

Reality vs Reality

I must again emphasize that the creation story is not meant to be hyperbole. When the Scriptures spoke of such *beginnings*, it was not meant to be a romantic idiom. It has not come to us in a genre based on fictional characters and circumstances. This Divine "stuff" occurred in historical space and time. The Apostle Peter, one of the most practical and non-ideologues of the disciples of Jesus, said, "For prophecy never had its origin in the human will, but prophets *though human, spoke from God* as they were **carried along by the Holy Spirit"** (2 Peter 1:21). If the Genesis story is but figurative (as some believe) and not meant to be a historical record of the Judeo-Christian acts of Elohim in historical time and space, then all of Scripture and indeed all books base on these reported acts of Elohim are futile.

It would be like living in a place where no one is home. Living in the finite, without any infinite reference point for morality, conscience, social order, indeed life itself. If there is no Creator, then no one is home in the universe, and there is no reference point for life and its meaning—no meaningful interaction with anything. As was proposed during the volatile Sixties, we would be just an insignificant cog in a meaningless universe. But the humanness of our existence inside and out from within, with a reference point called the "image of God" in which we are made, tells us in silent consciousness that we could not be alone in our Universe. I contend it could not be so. It would deny what we know in our internal space: We may often feel alone inside but never alone outside. If we do not know God, we will inevitably create one. This is humankind's anthropological and religious history in every place they are found.

This book, and indeed all my theological works, are based on the belief in the truthfulness of the historical and original writings of the Holy Scriptures. I contend that there can be no adequate understanding of the human condition and its salvation without this special revelational space that Peter and all the Prophets, including Jesus Christ himself, declared (Psalm 40:7; Hebrews 10: 7).

Spaces of Choices and Conclusions

Looking at the Christian Church today and her frequent representation of the secular world, it is difficult to conclude that from the record of the beginnings in the Holy Scriptures, one of the most powerful spaces God created in us was the power of choice. It is foundational to the Christian cause. It is critical to the Gospel that we proclaim that it is decidedly based on human's choice to accept Christ or reject Him. It is unmistakable that what was given to Adam was not given by Elohim ignorant of the outcome. Elohim knew what a disastrous outcome awaited given the choice to Adam and his wife Eve. But Elohim valued human choice as so important. He laid it all on the line. A large segment of the established churches today seems unwilling to value this space of choice that Elohim, we claim to follow, gave willingly to each of us. We often then occupy that critical space of choice Elohim created in every human soul and fill it not with the wisdom of Elohim but with our folly.

This book is a deep dive into those spaces that influence us and how we can influence the spaces of our world for the good of all. It is like looking at the building of a home: the foundation, the walls, the roof, the laying out of the rooms, their design function, and furnishing room by room, space by space. This is not a "shack" building. This is the most important multi-room mansion ever built, from foundation to roof, interior to exterior. It is our own. Built with our own life and experiences and the choices we make. Human choice is one of the most valued gifts of God. For it is to that same space in every heart to which the Gospel must appeal. The same space of choice Adam and Eve applied to select sin is the same space every person must apply to accept the Savior. This was a singular space of choice for mankind's destiny in the Garden of Eden. It is yet a single space in the heart of everyone today regarding their destiny. My point is to be clear: I contend if the Church, in its self-righteousness, seeks to destroy human choice, it also destroys the vehicle of salvation. "Choose you this day whom you will serve" (Joshua 24:14), would have no meaning if we represent a lost world we take lightly their space of choice. And that is so even when the result is not what we desire. It is this point of choice that Christ gave His people that caused Him so much pain. He saw them as sheep without a Shepherd and lamented how they chose not to come to Him. This was no small thing to the Historical Jesus Christ. It should never be small—this *choice space* for His followers today.

7

GRAPHIC ILLUSTRATIONS OF ELOHIM SPACE

The following are some illustrations of different passages using the language of space to apply to the nature and work of Elohim. They are topical in nature in the flow of the passage. They are not exhaustive but are a biblical tool for further development and application. Each graphic has a central theme in the inner circle, which is then outlined in the surrounding circles. The first graphic has an important emphasis on the "allness" of Elohim's love and concern as expressed by the Palmister in the seven distinctive ways expressed:

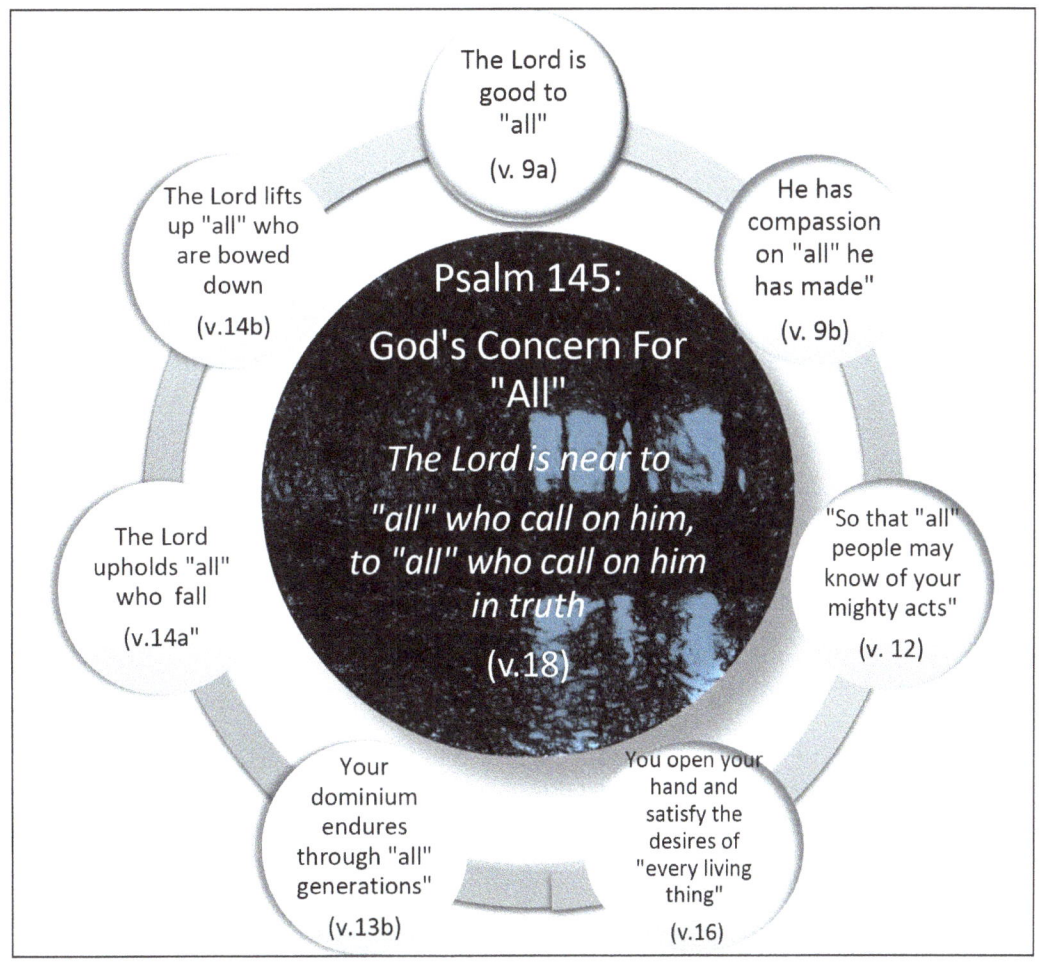

Ezekiel was a Prophet when his people were taken captive by the Babylonians. He was called to inspire his people to keep their faith, to still trust in Elohim, and to give them real hope for restoration to their homeland and deliverance from the hardships of exile. But God had to first reveal to His Prophet that He was a God of restoration and deliverance. He often revealed Himself to Ezekiel through visions. The following graphic chronicles the vision Elohim revealed to Ezekiel of His power of restoration and redemption:

Early in the history of Israel, they had come to know Elohim by His historical acts, all recorded in the Plentitude and historical books. With other Prophets, Elohim reveals what they did not know or even imagine. Through Isaiah, in one of the most moving redemptive passages in the Old Testament, Elohim reveals His love. It is a love letter from Elohim to His People. The following graphic chronicled that lonely, hard, and sacrificial road His Son would take to redeem His people and the world:

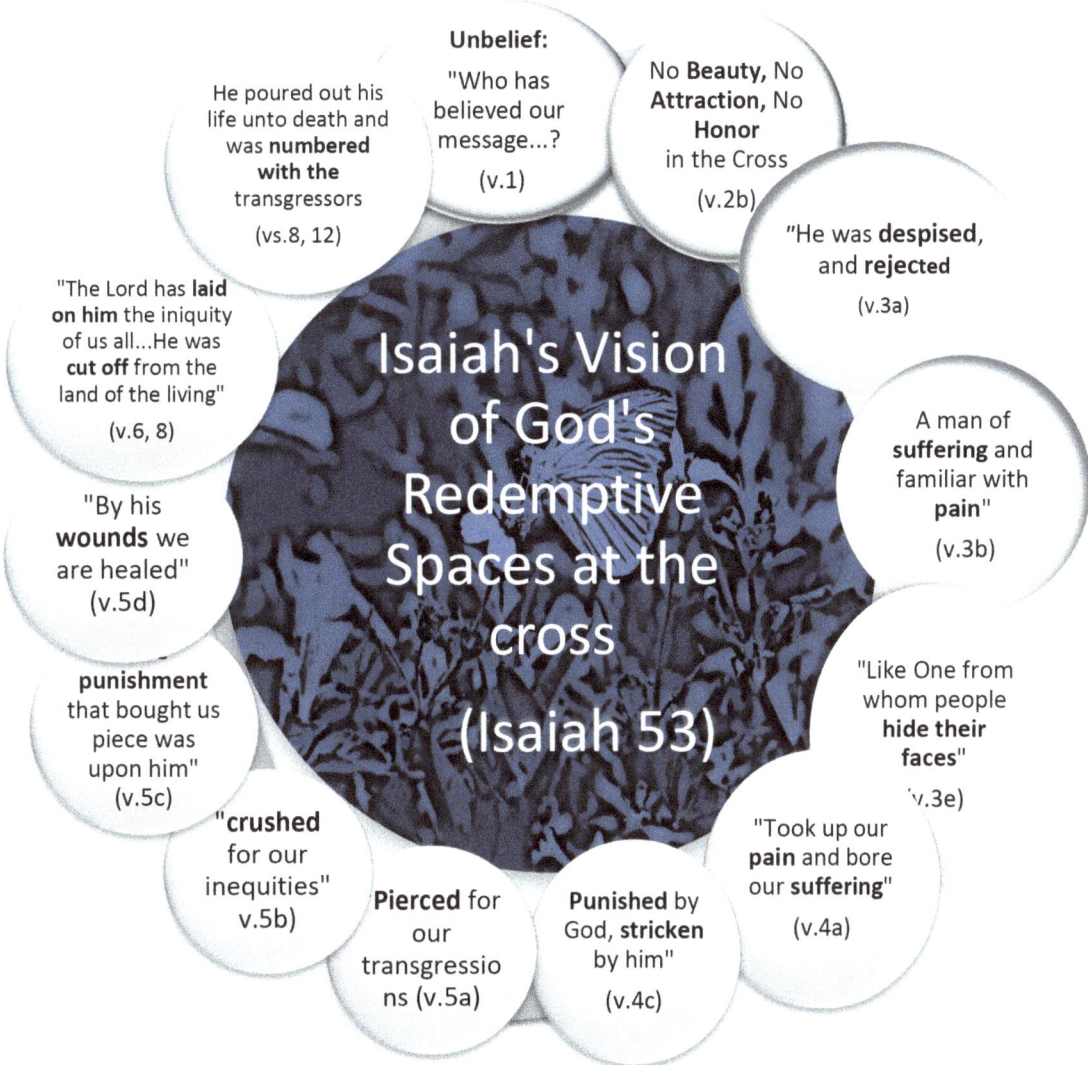

Isaiah, one of the Prophets, had a rare experience. In a vision, Elohim-Jehovah opened the windows of Heaven and gave the prophet exclusive access to His throne room. The following is but a chronicle of some of what He saw and heard.

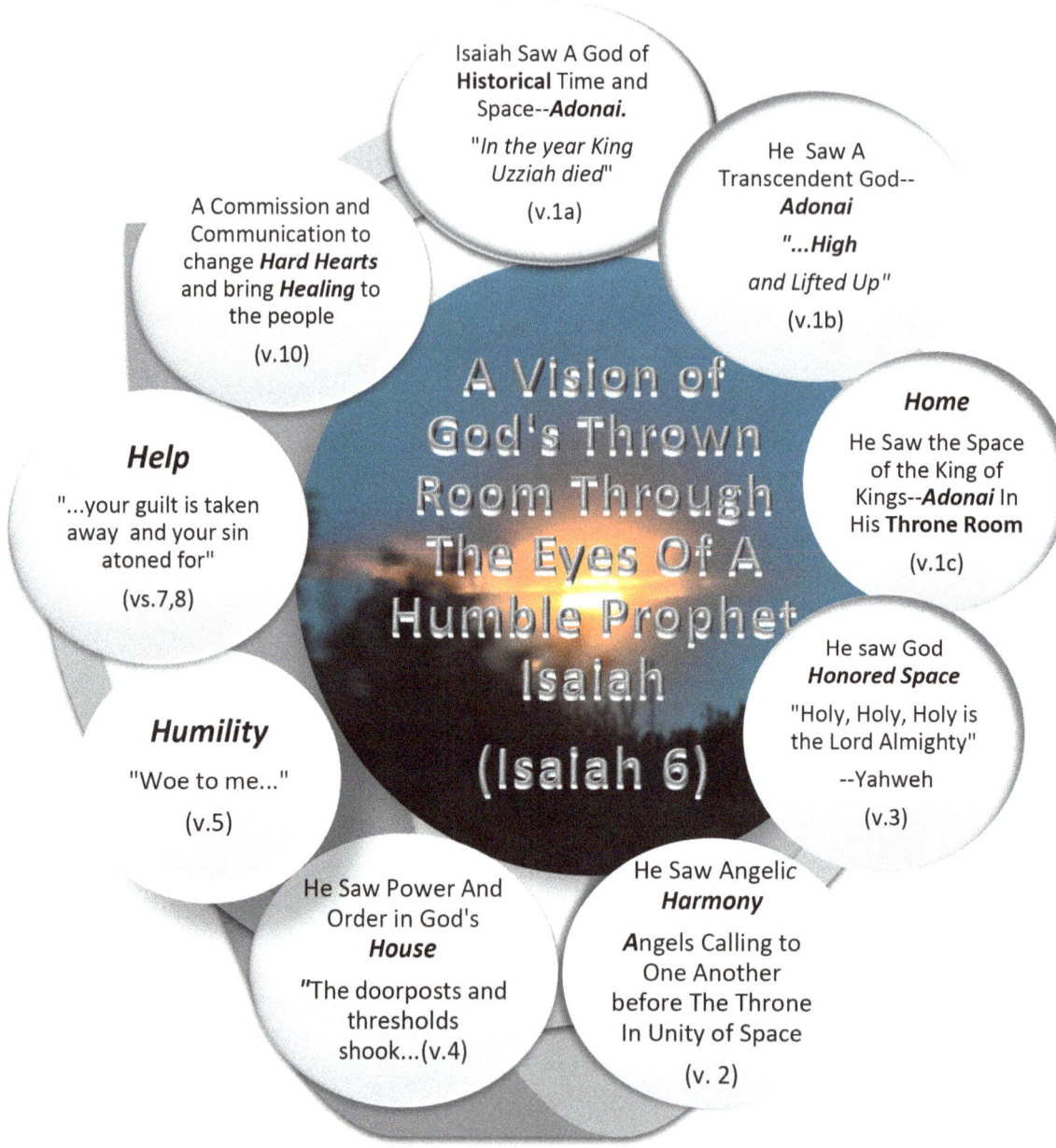

The book of Psalms is a rich source of for understanding Elohim Space. We are made in His image; I contend that part of his image is that of this inner sanctuary or "inside space." This Psalm at the center of the graphic shows that God Himself is represented as having this "inner space" of His existence. It is the Elohim inner space that we are called to notice. We see the demonstration of His power all around us in His works. But we can only glimpse His inner space of His love, compassion, grace, mercy—and so on, as He reveals them through His Word. He tells us what pleases him inside, contrasted with those that do not. Again, the following graphic, or as I think of it as an attempt of "rightly dividing the word of God," is intended to guide understanding God's inner Space of what truly pleases Him.

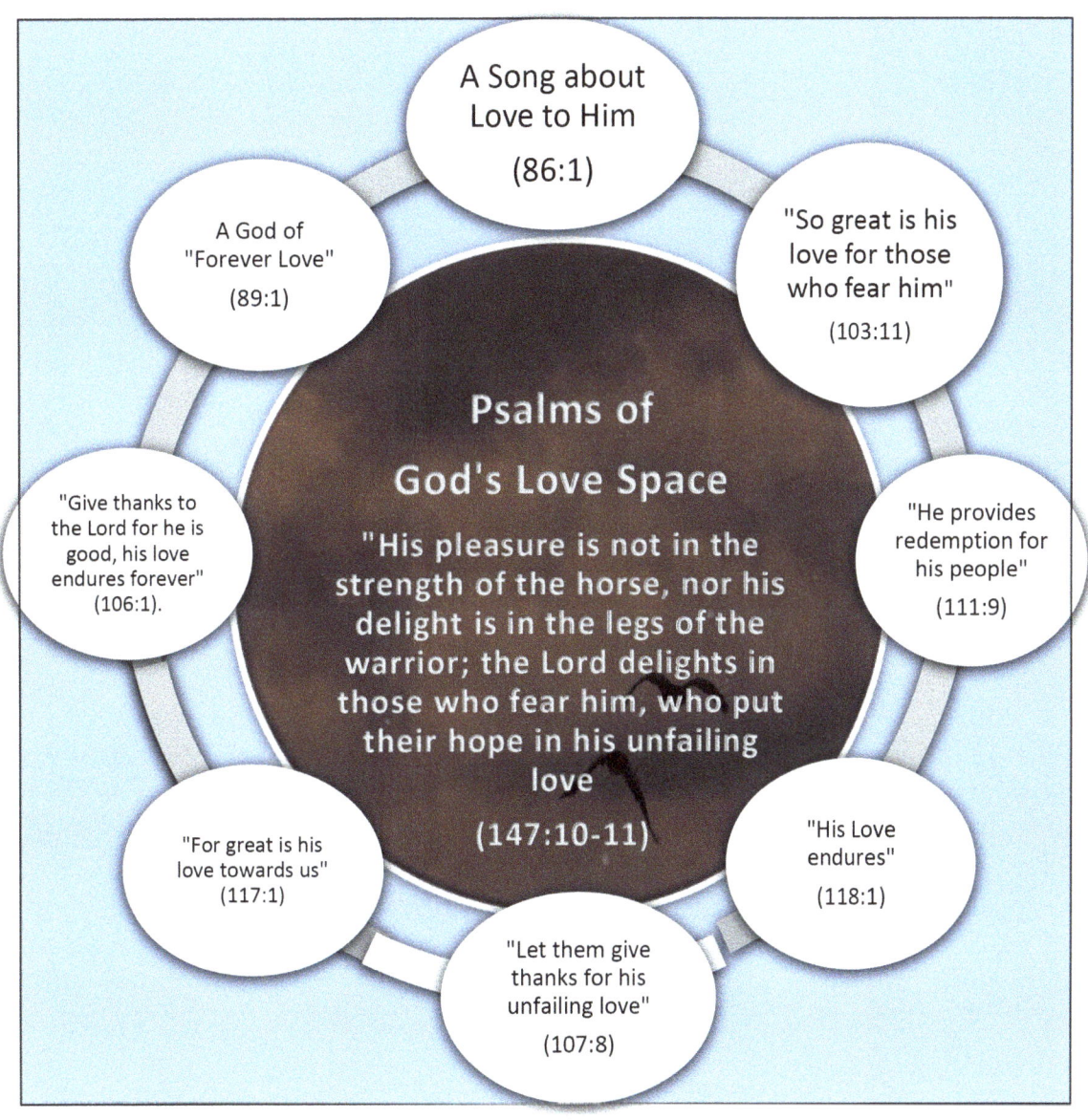

In the following graphic the Psalmist once again pulls at us to pause and consider the mighty works of Elohim. He does so, like with the chorus of a song repeated repeatedly, not for poetic effect but for much more. He wanted us to focus on a "Who done it?" series to make a point of the song moving us toward a God who did so many wonderful things for us. It is an acknowledgment and testimony to Elohim-Jehovah, who does mighty acts on our behalf. He is here revealed as Jehovah Elohim of provisions not just for us but for himself "purchased long ago the people of his inheritance:"

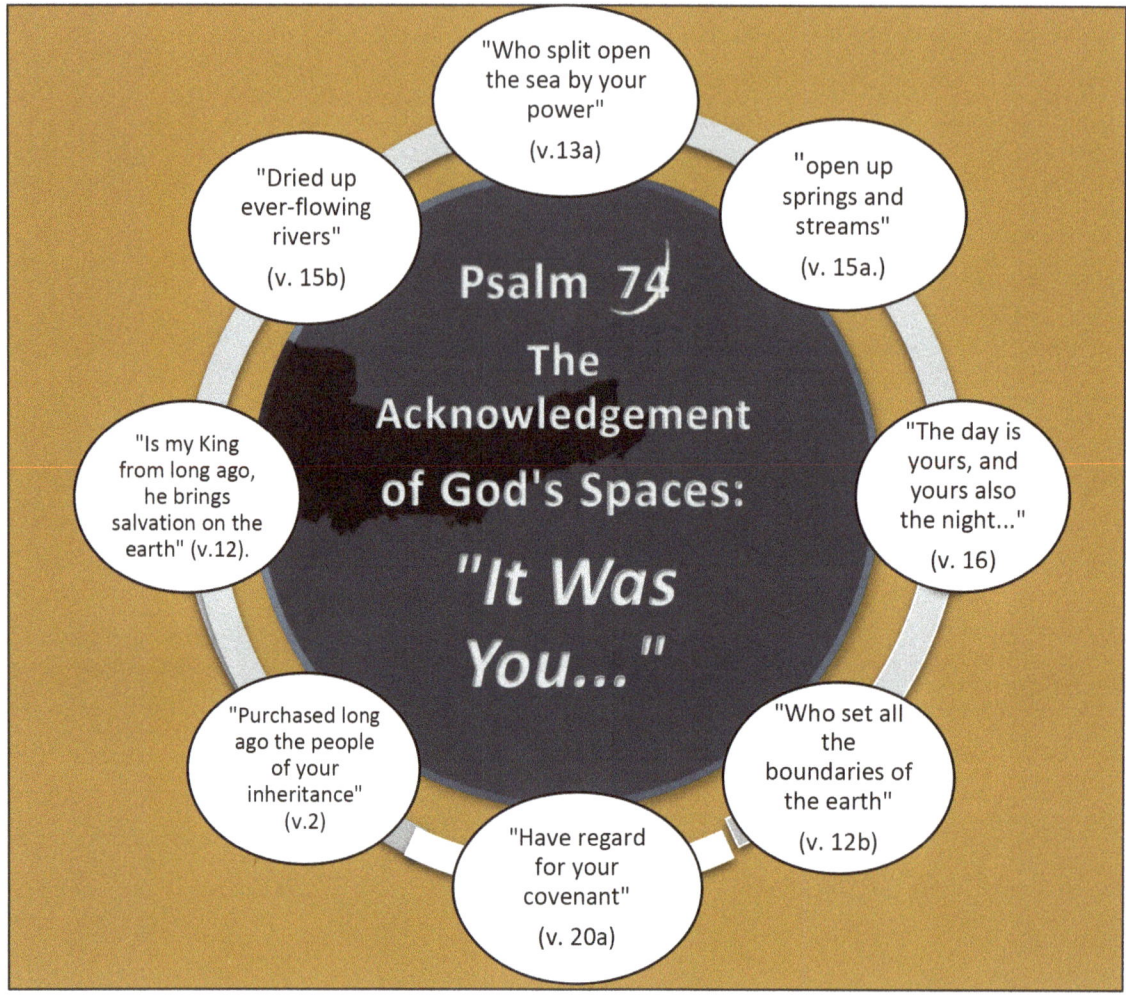

In Psalm 24, the language of Elohim Space is employed to illustrate who among us can qualify to go to 'the mountain of the Lord." It is like a shortened version of the Ten Commandments. That is who can ascend to His holy presence? It is a question that was not left unanswered. The graphic division of the passage is centered on both descriptions of the necessity of approaching Elohim's presence. And in so doing describe the holy presence of God as well. Again, the graphics are simple, but its content can be exhaustive, for it is a revelation into the Divine holiness of God and what He requires of mankind. In this final graphic, I return to Ezekiel's first vision the Lord gave him, as He did in the Prophet Isaiah's call. Here, this is an extended version of Isaiah's special invitation to the throne room and what it was like in this unique God's Space.

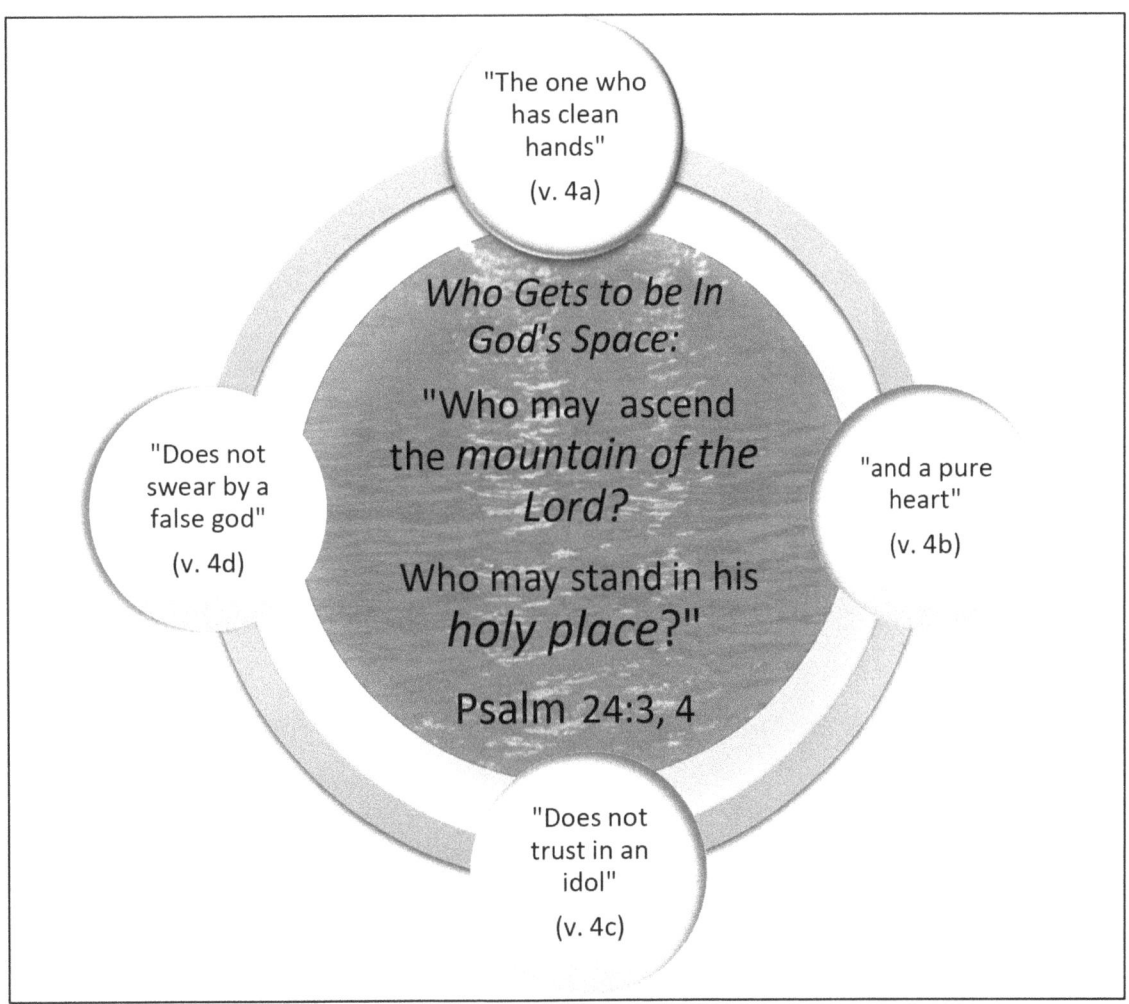

"The one who has clean hands" (v. 4a)

Who Gets to be In God's Space:

"Who may ascend the *mountain of the Lord?*

Who may stand in his *holy place*?"

Psalm 24:3, 4

"and a pure heart" (v. 4b)

"Does not trust in an idol" (v. 4c)

"Does not swear by a false god" (v. 4d)

God's Ultimate Space Through The Eyes Of His Prophet And Priest

Ezekiel Chapter 1:

Visions of an "Awesome" Vault of Separated Spaces:

Between Living Creatures and The Living God; The Created and The Creator; Those who give Praise and Him Who is Praised. Those below the Vault introduced He who was high above the vault.

(v.25)

God's Voice Thundered Above the Vault

"Then there came a voice from above the vault...what look like a throne...high above on the throne was a figure like that of a man...This was the appearance of the likeness of the Glory of God.

(vs.25-28)

Visions in Historical Space and Time:

"i was among the exiles by the Kear River, the heavens opened and I saw visions of God"

(v.1)

Fire and Motion In the Throne Room

"The appearance of the living creatures was like burning coals of fire or like torches. Fire moved back and forth among the creatures; it was bright, and lightning flashed out of it. The creatures sped back and forth like flashes of lightning.

(v.12-14)

The Introduction:

A Sky Vision of Light and lighting glowing in a Powerful Northern Windstorm

(v.4)

Order in the Court

"Each one went straight ahead. Wherever the spirit would go, they would go, without Turing as they went.

(v.12)

Attending Court

Specular Living Creatures With Human Forms, and non-human Quad Faces With Court in Session

(v.5)

Wings For Worship

"They each had two wings spreading out upward.

Each wing touching that of the creature on either side; and each had two other wings covering its body.

(v.11)

Faces to be Feared

A Lion's Face: Ruler of its Domain. An Eagles Face: Queen of all Heights.
An Ox's face: Mighty, Stable and Strong.

A vision interconnecting with the Human Face and Form:-the many spaces of God's Realm.

(v.10)

Devine Dress

Creatures with wings, Legs like a calf, gleamed like burnished Bronze. Under their wings were human hands. And when they Move they do it together in their spaces.

(v.6-9)

8

ELOHIM: THE GOD OF *"THINGS TO COME."*

"The revelation from Jesus Christ which God gave him to show his servants what must soon take place. He made it known by sending his angels to his servant John, who testifies to everything he saw—that is, the word of God and the testimony of Jesus Christ.

Blessed is the one who reads aloud the words of this prophecy and blesses are those who hear it and take to heart what is written in it, because the time is near"

(Revelation 1:1-3 emphasis mine).

Is there a future for life on this Earth?

It does not seem there has even been a time filled with so many possibilities and pessimism on so many levels for the future. Many are asking what would become of our children. What kind of world are we leaving them? Is the American dream still valid? Will democracy survive? Will we be able to contain future predators like pandemics that are sure to attack us? Will global warming be or undoing or some other natural or unnatural disaster? And what of wars—with enemies now on both sides with weapons of mass destruction: Conventional, nuclear, chemical, cyber –will we ever find a way to avoid using them? Can we all ever get along? And what of our political leaders? Could we survive the ones and their followers who want to lead us to hell in a divisive handbasket? Does the Bible have anything to say about these and other critical questions of the future?

This is the challenge of our world. Thcsc arc but a fcw of thc daunting questions of this chapter. We want to ask Elohim these questions. We want to learn what Elohim's future space is. Who is He in the future? Can we rely on Him? Is the Christian God big and powerful enough to handle this world and the universe's future spaces? Does He even care about our future space?

I contend that history is indeed going someplace in the consistent story world of the Holy Scriptures. I further contend this is even consistent with our rational minds. We hardly believe there is no rhyme to the reason of our lives. Just live, and let's die. Is that all there is? We can hardly believe that the actors and actresses on the world's stage are simply making their Shakspearian entrances and exits, and that is all. We can hardly believe the show has no significant end—no grand finale? No final recognition of the performers? No final recognitions of the great ones from time memorial who, on their entrances, contributed so much good to all humanity. And is there even no poetic justice for all the bad actors? What of the haters, murderers, and the slave and sex traffickers, even of our children? And what of those among us who felt they were more supreme than all other members of this world and created political and social systems to maintain their discriminatory evil ideologies—those who entered the stage and trafficked in human misery with impunity?

What of those who became powerful among us and used their power to kill and plunder humanity, others who polluted the world with their greed? They all exist on the world stage, leaving with a free pass and no Divine accountability. No one to answer in the future? Image no Heaven and no Hell—imagine that! There are no rewards for the prudent and wise and no punishment for the perverters of truth and justice. I contend there is something in all of us that says this cannot be: No justice and no judgment, all pain and no gain, all suffering and no salvation, all wars, and no peace, all sacrifice, and no rewards—life fizzles out in the end with no balance sheet? I contend, the Bible agrees there is an accounting coming. It draws a line in the sand for all civilizations, all nations, all peoples, and all individuals to stand before Elohim's future court session. We will not be judged by a jury of our pairs but by the Elohim of all the heavens and earth- a space of accountability that only He alone occupies.

In the End

In the end, no one gets a free pass to the heavenly space if they never knew Jesus. In the end, Jesus asked, "What good is it for someone to gain the whole world and **forfeit his own soul?** (Mark 8:36 [emphasis mine). In the end, Jesus challenged us to His Divine logic: "My Father's house has many mansions. If it were not so, would I have told you I am going there to prepare a place for you? And if I go and prepare a place for you, **I will come back and take you to be with me**, that you also may be where I am" (John 13:2-3 [emphasis mine). In the end, the Apostle explained to the Christian Church: "For we MUST all appear before the **judgment seat of Christ** so that **each of us** may give what is due us for the things done **while in the body** (2 Corinthians 5:10 [emphasis mine). Psalmist declared: "The wicked go down to the realm of the dead, all the nations that forget God" (Psalm 9:17). In the end, "weeping may endure for a night, but j rejoicing comes in the morning" (Psalm 30:5). In the end, "We will not all sleep, but we will all be changed in a flash, in the twinkling of an eye, at the last trumpet. For the trumpet will sound, the dead will be raised imperishable, and we will be changed (1 Corinthians 15:51). In the end "And if I go and prepare a place for you, I will come back and welcome into my presence so that you also may be where I am" (John 14:3). In the end "And this Gospel of the Kingdom will be preached in all the world as a testimony to all nations and then the end will come" (Matthew 24:14). In the end only one life will soon be past, only what done for Christ will last. In the end, you and I must all stand before the throne of God." In the end, "Blessed is the one who reads aloud this prophecy, and blessed are those who hear and obey what is written in it because the time is near (Revelation 1:3).

The Bible Prophets Saw the Future Coming

Ultimately, no one gets a free pass if they never knew Jesus (one mediator…). In the end, Jesus asked, "What good is it for someone to gain the whole world and **forfeit his own soul?** (Mark 8:36 [emphasis mine). In the end, Jesus challenged us to His Divine logic: "My Father's house has many mansions; if it were not so, would I have told you I am going there to prepare a place for you? And if I go and prepare a place for you, **I will come back and take you to be with me**, that you also may be where I am" (John 13:2-3 [emphasis mine). In the end, the Apostle explained to the Christian Church: "For we MUST all appear before the **judgment seat of Christ** so that **each of us** may give what is due us for the things done **while in the body** (2 Corinthians 5:10 [emphasis mine). Psalmist declared: "The wicked go down to the realm of the dead, all the nations that forget God" (Psalm 9:17). In the end: "**We shall all stand before the judgment seat of Christ,** and everyone will give an account for all the deeds done in our bodies whether good or bad" (2 Corinthians 5:10). In the end, "weeping may endure for the night, but joy comes in the morning" (Psalms30:5). In the end, "We shall not all sleep, but we shall be changed for the trumpet shall sound and the dead in Christ shall rise first" (1 Corinthians 15:52). "I go to prepare a place for you, and I will come again and receive you to myself" (John 14:1). In the end, "and this Gospel of the Kingdom shall be preached in all the world and then shall the end come" (Matthew 24:14). In the end, only one life will soon be past; only what is done for Christ will last. In the end, you and I must all stand before the throne of God (2 Corinthians 5:10)." In the end, "Blessed are those who read this prophecy aloud, and blessed are those who hear it and take to heart what is written in it because the time is near (Revelation 1:3).

Let us face it. It is true that the Bible's prophets all saw disaster coming. But they also saw great deliverance by Elohim as well. But I cannot make clear enough that the distinguishable mark of the biblically planned future is that this future space of disaster or deliverance will be on Elohim's terms. Yes! Much disaster is coming. So will be deliverance. But both will be on Elohim's terms—period! For He who made the world and now holds it together by the word of His power is also the God not just of the past and the present, but Elohim God of the future. He has demonstrated this in various ways through the narrative of the Holy Scriptures and the historical Person of Christ (Hebrews 1:1-3).

In the model graphic below (opening of chapter 10), I have created an alliterated what I called "Timothy Trail" (my approach to the scriptures based on 2 Timothy 5:17 used throughout this book). This graphic is limited, but it is meant to outline the unlimited ways in which Elohim God has demonstrated to his Creation the ways in which He has shown to be the Elohim—the Mighty God not only of the past and present but also of the future. Each graphic model used in this work is centered around an important theme. The theme here is

Revelation 1:1-3 "The revelation from Jesus Christ which God gave him to show his servants **what must soon take place…because the time is near"** (emphasis mine).

In the case of Elohim as a future God, it must be remembered that when the Bible was completed (the selected sixty-six books, the canon of the Bible), no less than one-quarter of its content was prophetic. (This is unique and astonishing for any non-fiction literary work of antiquity to its own merit). For it means it can be objectively reviewed in the flow of human civilization and history. And even now, despite the many verifiable historical fulfillments like the destruction of the Jewish temple, the scattering of its people, and her return of Israel as a nation in the recent century, coming back as predicted to their homeland from all parts of the world, the marshaling or the outline of the ten-nation confederacy that would someday rise up against Israel; the setting up of the outline of political and banking digital infrastructure for one man control of the various economic, social, and political system called "the man of sin" or the "anti-Christ."

These are all coming together for the "man of sin"—a powerful dictator, a charismatic leader, and Lier all coming together for one of the worst evil leaders this world has ever known. He is called the Antichrist because he would represent all that is evil in this world against Christ, who represents all that is good. He will deceive many because of the lies, as his persuasive momentum would be based on lies, deception, and violence. This is directed to individuals groups and nations, who will be deceived. So, controlling would be his power in the world against God's people, and the only one capable of defeating him in a coming battle called Armageddon is the visible return of Jesus Christ himself to put him down. Those who study from the grammatical, historical, and literal interpretation of the Holy Scriptures can see in our own times the continued development of the evil landscape or "story world" stage in which the characters, economic, social even religious structural space of what the Bible repeatedly called "in the last days" as well as the coming "day of the Lord" as being near.

9

ELOHIM SPACE OF PROPHETIC REVELATION—*PRAYER*

The following graphic models I create are an outline or biblical structure of approach to grapple with a particular theme. Here, the theme is taken from what John was told about the Isle of Patmos. He would be shown things that would soon take place. Here in this graphic, I wanted to show in some limited ways the narrative of Scriptures has revealed The Elohim spaces of the future. The Bible presents us with a blueprint of the future and in some events, a measure of significant details to show us what will soon occur.

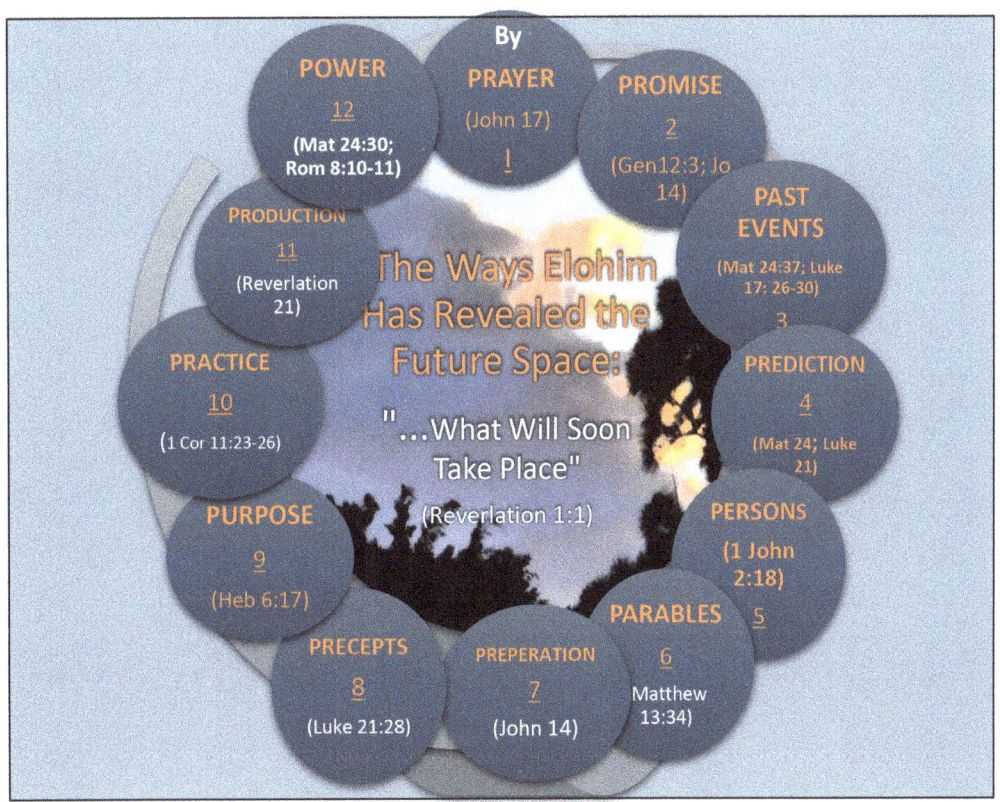

The "Timothy Trail" of Things Soon to Come

The Future Revealed by Prayer

Prayer reveals the deepest perception of a person's mind, heart, and soul. Even as a ritual, it is solemn and serious. However, it is more at its heart, for it is a space directly directed from the human's heart to their God. As a form of communication, it is not a space of slack. It is not a space for a joke or careless chatter. It is as serious a communication that exists among humans. So, when in moments of great joy or deepest sorrows, we are given privileged entrance into this prayer space of another, we must realize we are given access to enter into a most spiritual and holy personal space. We enter a space where truth is demanded, and discovery is pure. There is no space at all given to falsehood, fear, or failures.

As an activity, it can be trusted to reveal the deepest seriousness of intentions. It can be trusted to reveal the deepest longing possible of the human soul. Pain comes here for reprieve. Loneliness soon leaves her behind once she enters this space, for she knows a listener is always here. Poverty comes here to find riches. Despair comes here to find hope for a better future. The lost come to be found and are found here. The sick, the dying, the poor are never blocked from this space. No dividing walls exist here. This space is relentlessly open to all who call on their God. No voices of hate, condemnation, or shame fill the air of this space, for love is its gatekeeper. So, when one seeks prayers as a means of the future, or understanding of the future, I contend, we are dealing with the most honest desire and representation of that person's personal space. Here are but a few biblical examples that gives us a window into how God open up this space for us to see His future space:

David - 2 Samuel 12:23

By

PRAYER

(John 17)

!

David, the second King of Israel, rose from being a shepherd boy to becoming one of Israel's most famous and successful kings. As a boy with but a slingshot and his faith in Elohim, he defeated one of Israel's worst enemies, the Philistines. He was less than half the size of their 10-foot giant warrior. He ran one of the most successful military campaigns, taking Israel to the pinnacle of military and social success. He brought Israel out of the disarray of the previous years into the most successful and glorious days Israel has ever known. He often personally led many of Israel's battles and successful campaigns. Sometimes, however, his able commander Joab would lead the battle. Was such a time during a battle, he stayed home, and as he took a walk on the roof of his palace, he looked down and saw a young woman bathing named Bathsheba. He was overcome by her beauty and inquired of her. He learned she was the wife of a Hittite soldier, Uriah, out fighting the Ammonites under his command.

However, this important intel did not stop him from lying to her. Bathsheba later told the King, "I am with child." He began a plan of coverup. He recalled her husband Uriah so he would sleep with his wife to provide the cover of his adultery. But Uriah, as a dedicated man of battle, refused to sleep with his wife. David moved to plan b. He sent him back to war with a sealed letter to seal his fate. There, on the front, he was going to be legally killed, but the cover was not enough to cover his sin. For Nathan, the prophet knew and told David a story of his sin that he would never forget. Bathsheba went into mourning. After mourning, David married Bathsheba and thought this third coverup phase was completed.

But the biblical narrative reported: "But the thing that David had done displeased the Lord, the God of Israel [the Elohim of the past now confront David in His servant present circumstances. David is going to meet Elohim through His Prophet Nathan. First, David is here, meeting the God of the past in the deeds he had done. Then, David also confronts Elohim in his present circumstances. He knows the past; He sees the present as He sent His Prophet Nathan to let David know He sees it all. He was also aware of what the future held for him because of the sinful deeds he thought were covered by Him. He is aware of his past sinful deeds. He is aware of his present guilt. And moreover, He was aware of the future consequences. This awareness was not simple for David, but it was the space in which everyone functions. Being exposed to his past deeds, David is then aware of the coming consequences.

Again, this is true of every person, and what the future holds for each of us is known to God. David confronted this God who knows the end from the beginning. Perhaps if he were aware of this on the rooftop, he would have looked down and up to the hills where his strength comes from, as he later would recall. David admitted his sin. The kind of sin that calls for death. But his life was spared, but the son born of this evil union was going to face death. All the prophesies concerning his seed must have crossed David's mind. The prophets had declared that the Messiah of Israel would come through his seed.

There is much in David's prophetic words which I cannot fully develop here. For in this prophetic word of Nathan, Elohim is revealed to the King that he was a God of the past, fully engaged in the present and knowing what was to come in the future. This is no small thing for a man of victorious battles to face. This is no small thing for a successful leader of Israel who was given a prophetic promise that it was through his seed—the seed of Davin that the Messiah, a Deliverer of Israel, would come. Moreover, now he is facing a sentence that is going to take away his seed borne through an act of sin. A prophecy of not just life through his seed but in his time, the child born of his seed and his sin will die. For although there was an eternal prophetic covenant through his seed, the world would be blessed. Now, however, death was assigned to his seed as well.

He was driven to fasting. He was driven to prayer. But the space of God's future judgment was already there in that space. As a worrier in battle fighting with the soldier's panoply of weapons, his sin led him to that private prayer space. He learned the prophetic answer to his plight in that space through prayer. David learned a prophetic lesson that should inform all the inhabitants of this earth for generations to come: "**You will go to him. He will not come to you**" (2 Samuel 12:23).

The announcement of this prophecy, which David gave through prayer, applies to every person. Here and now, he was a king who took thousands of men to successful battles but became beside himself when his son in the relationship became seriously ill. From this tragic story, one can read David's prayers that have encouraged many of God's servants down through the ages who have fallen into sin because of their lusts, especially Psalm 51 of this specific event.

Now what is the point of all this extended context or *story world* for just a line in the script:

1. We must learn in this Old Testament narrative, which is also extended in the New Testament in the Teaching of One called the Son of David, who laid out this future for everyone to know. "For there is nothing hidden that will not be disclosed, and nothing concealed that will not be made known and brought to light (Luke 8:17). One can live their entire life in a *space of secrecy*, but nothing would remain secret in the future before a Holy God. (*Suggestion for life application*: There is no "right to privacy" in the biblical prophecy. In practical terms and application, even though Elohim knows everything, the believer should pour out all their secrets to Elohim. Acknowledging the secrets of your life before Elohim prevents the enemy of your soul from using them to bring you down).

2. Another lesson of the prophetic narrative in the life of David is that in the future, one can go to a place to meet their mother, father, brother, sister, or any other earthly relative, but they cannot—contrary to many beliefs, none can come back here to meet with us. This is also the teaching of the New Testament. When one prayed and requested that Abraham get to talk to his brother. This could not be done because, as stated in the answer to his prayers, "there is a great gulf fixed between …." (Luke 16). One has to be prepared here to be ready there. No one leaving here in Heaven can then reach back to warn anyone here. The gulf is too wide, and the bridge is too far to reach any loved ones that left us. One is eternal destiny, which is sealed when they leave here. Elohim is the God of the future. But He has determined that choices must be made in this life to be prepared for the future. (*Suggestion for Life application*: Embrace the thought of this separation space of death when our loved ones die. Do not spend any effort trying to bridge this gulf. It is far better to focus on getting ready to meet that divide by living life now, pleasing God)

3. There is the answer to David's prayer that revealed prophetically that there will be continued development to extend the lives of many, but in the end, as Bruce Springfield sang in Atlantic City, "everything dies… that is a fact" (LyricFind). There will be no development of any pills, therapies, or frozen schemes to give anyone the ability to escape death. The best scheme is not to attempt to avoid it but to embrace it as a natural part of the gift of life. It is but for a season. What is important is to prepare for it. David concluded the lesson learned: "Though I walk through the valley of the shadows of death, I will fear no evil, for you are with me." This is the best and wisest lesson to learn when facing the future. It is to be prepared because "the time is near." (*SLA-Suggestion for Life application: Do not focus on the longevity of life facing the future. Focus on your quality of life today, and the future will take care of itself. We cannot change the future, but we have the ability to change today*).

When tragedy hits you, like David, someone you love leaves. Let it drift away over time in the past. Get yourself up in the present as David did. He wrote some of his best poetry in his psalms from this space (Psalm 51). He continued to play music that he loved. And he continued to serve his people long after his loss. In other words, in the middle of his loss, he continued to live. He learned that his God was a God of the future. Moreover, like the Apostle Paul, "his grace is sufficient for me." For he is Elohim of the present and the future as well. *(SLA: Do what King David did. Even in the face of tragedy and disappointments, make every effort to move on and live).*

In conclusion, I must also point out that David, who had received great promises as a leader of Israel, also received no less a promise to answer his pain. God promised David he would see his son again. As a servant of Elohim, he would see that he got to his son. "You will go to him" was a promise" (2 Samuel 12:23). If not now, then, in the resurrection, David will meet his son. (SLA [Suggestion for Life Application]. Moreover, to all those who have lost a child of any age, even before birth. The way to prepare to meet them is like David, who repented and discovered that Elohim has a designated place and space for sinners. He has one for each of us: "Against the O Lord I have sinned," as he asked the Lord to "blot out his transgressions" (Psalm 51)." And through grace for both you and your child, the prophecy is that you will meet them again in the future.

A Criminal Prayer

"Jesus Remember Me When you Come into Your Kingdom" (Mark 23:42-43)

After some three years of earthly ministry reaching out to the poor, the lame, the destitute, and the suffering—doing good to everyone in need, the time of his sacrificial death arrived. Many prophets, especially Isaiah, had said this was his mission. The point of our reference here is that Isaiah had foretold as he hung on the cross between two criminals. "He was numbered with the transgressors" (Isaiah 53).

One of the criminals began to hurl insults at Jesus: "Aren't you the Messiah? Save yourself and us." It sounded like a prayer for salvation, but it came from a place devoid of reverence for Elohim. The other criminal said as much to him: "Don't you fear God?" he asked, "since you are under the same sentence? We are punished justly, for we are getting what our deeds deserve. Nevertheless, this man has done nothing wrong." He defended Jesus, who asked for no defense. And then this prayer that seems to come like a string out of tune, not of this world. The disciples did not hear it, for they had scattered in fear. But this criminal on the cross next to Jesus found a space in his heart of belief. He found a space of penitent and prayer and directed his attention to Jesus. He gave an extraordinary prophetic prayer: "Jesus, remember me when you come into your kingdom."

1. This was a prayer focused on Christ's future.
2. This was a prayer that was focused as well on his future. A future that saw past the pain to a place without any pain. He saw past in the sun's heat in this world to a more comfortable place with Christ. A prayer that saw past his own suffering to a future where there would be none.

3. It was a prophetic prayer because, in but a few words, it captured the cry of his soul for fellowship with Christ beyond the Cross. In the depth of his prayer, he did not see a Christ on a Cross but a King in his Kingdom. He saw past the kingdom of this world that had placed Him there. And so, he prayed to be remembered because somehow he saw the Kingdom coming.

4. If a common criminal could see Christ beyond the cross and envision a future Kingdom and King, then this is the prophetic message of this prayer: All the world can listen to it, a prayer that can become anyone's prayer two thousand years later and closer to that which will soon take place: "Jesus, remember me when you come into your Kingdom." This is a prophetic prayer for our times.

Jesus Prophetic Payer: "Deliver us from Evil"

I have written an entire book on this important prophetic prayer, so it is not my intention to dwell on it. I would like to highlight just a few prophetic points from this prayer.

1. Jesus' prayer envisions what many of the Old Testament prophets declared: that evil days are coming. To pray from a place to seek deliverance from something is because that something exists and poses a threat to every Christian.

2. The prayer can be taken to be extended not only to the present order of things when evil is present. But His prayer is an extension beyond the general period to refer to his Upper Room prayer when he said, "I pray not that you take them out of the world but that you keep them from the "evil one." This prayer extends not simply to be delivered from the general evil times in the last days but to be delivered from the personality or the person behind the evil of the times. So, Jesus, in His prayer, envisioned a future when His people would be "delivered from the evil" and later "from the evil one."

> ### (SLA: Suggestion for Life Application):
>
> Jesus prayer for us is an example to follow. I suggest praying the Lord's prayer found in Matthew…each day. It is to find that space of prayer to understand the evil times, and to understand the evil one, so we learn to pray always "deliver us from evil." Because we were going to face a prophetic future that was going to require us to understand and pray such a prayer.

10

ELOHIM SPACE OF PROPHETIC REVELATION—*PROMISE*

Prophetic Promises

Take a journey with an imaginary thermal instrument across the landscape of the Bible, and you will come across numerous *hot spots* of prophetic promises. I have walked along this journey each time I have researched a subject and related topics for a book. I vet the subjects and themes throughout the bible narrative. It takes time, like a year for each subject and related topic. But it is like a truth fire that burns away the trash of one's folly space of personal opinions they might bring to the subject.

For example, on the theme of this chapter, I have come to understand two major, large smothering fires of Promises. One is the Old Testament, which can be interpreted as an Old Testament promise," covenant," or even Divine agreement. The other, the New Testament, is correspondingly the same as a Divine Promise. So, both the Old and the New Testaments are predicated on a prophetic promise made in them.

From the Garden promise made in Genesis and culminated in Revelation, the writer of Hebrews said of Jesus, "Then said I, lo, I come in the volume of the book it is

Side Bar- "Vet It!"

"Vei it!'—take it through the entire Scriptures." In my college classroom hallway, my professor said, when I had stopped him to get his critique on a model project I was researching in 1975. I thought he was joking about that assignment. It would take at least a year to do what he was asking. However, he was a Harvard graduate with impeccable scholarship and decorum, not given to jokes. I was in serious trouble, so Why did I ask?

I often crammed for classes, but this was beyond any class assignment. This was a life assignment. I love creating communication models for biblical understanding and thought to share them with him for his valued counsel. I was encouraged and delighted with his critique. He even recommended publishing until he got to the part I must do next: Vet everything through the Scriptures---Genesis to Revelation before anything else.

It had taken me a whole year to get through a devotional reading of the Bible. In college, we studied book by book or section by section on any given topic. To research the entire Bible on one subject or theme well was the job of the great scholars in the ivory towers. I was not one of them. I had gotten a degree in Communication and just love creating models as tools to communicate biblical teaching. It was an unreasonable difficult ask to have to go through the entire bible with each element.

I remembered feeling like the rich young ruler in the Gospels. When Jesus told him what to do to enter the kingdom, to sell all he had and give to the poor, he walked away sorrowful. The narrative said this because he was very rich. But this poor student's heart was in the same place. I walked away sorrowful, and my only solace was thinking my teacher could not be serious about this extracurricular challenge.

I do not know what the young ruler did with his sorrow confronting Jesus' personal challenge to him. The Gospel writers did not say. I hope that he did what Jesus told him to do out of his sorrows and found joy in obedience. What I did with mine changed my life and enriched my soul. My only regret I am not able to thank my professor Dr. Smith, Moody Theological Seminary, for the challenge. Each time I have written a book I have research its subjects through the entire Scriptures.

Now I could not venture to write a book without having spent this year long research journey vetting it in the Scriptures before I even begin to write an introduction. I vet it! Like through a spiritual washing machine to make everything clean.

written of me, to do thy will, O God" (Hebrews 10:7 KJV). Thus, it is. Throughout the Old Testament, the Prophets looked ahead to the Messiah. Then the Messiah came in historical space and time, and His message was that "the Kingdom of heaven is at hand." This prophetic fulfillment of His first coming that dominated the Old Testament shifted in a continued progressive revelation now focused on the prophetic promise of His Second Coming of Jesus, which is yet to come. One of the outworkings of the prophecies in future events is revealed through Elohim's establishment of His Covenants, Agreements, that we call here His Promises. As we have noted, these prophetic promises are extensive. We consider here only a few highlights.

Again, what can easily be missed is that the major divisions of the Scriptures are divided according to two prophetic promises. Old Testament or promise and New. This is corroborated by the numeric distinction of BC (before Christ) AD (Latin: *Anno Domini* translated "in the year of the Lord."

There is the Old Testament—meaning the Old "Covenant" or promise. And the New Testament carried the same meaning. A new covenant based on a new prophetic promise. We can conclude then that the Bible as a whole is a document of promises of things pass, things present and of "things to come." I will then just give a broad overview of how promises have been specifically developed in the narrative of the Scriptures to show us what will soon take place.

The Garden Promise

The very first prophetic promise hot spot was found in the sin-contaminated soil of the Garden of Eden. Other promises throughout the Bible were given with expressive drama. This crucial promise opening scene was like those old British movies I enjoyed watching but often lamented how slow they often took to develop. Here in the opening scene at the garden, even the script was written in a poetic style and description that can easily be missed how these lines set the progressive prophetic development of the entire Universe:

"And I will put enmity between you and the woman, and between your seed and her seed. He will crush your head, and you will strike his heel." Genesis 3:15

Genesis 3:15 sounds simple enough but let us use scripture to interpret scripture. Let us use the "Timothy Trail" in 2 Timothy 3:15 for this opening prophetic salvo and see if we can decipher the plot of the entire Scriptures. For this is what it is.

1. In any episode, script development, or opening scene, you want to present to the audience what is called the "story world." The obvious story world is the garden. But once the script begins, the story world becomes a prophecy. It would be a story that spans the entire space of existence of everything and

everyone on this planet and everything in this universe. In other words, this script presented a story world that included the entire universe.

2. In every story, you have a voice. Who is telling the story? For example, Moses wrote these opening lines of the script. However, he is not the voice. His will come later in the establishment of this drama. However, like every good writer, Moses gives the voice up front, and it is clear that it is the prophetic voice of God. It is the most powerful voice in the drama of this world. Moses gives voice to God. And here, although we can develop much as in in the voice of **Authority**: "I <u>will</u>...;" the voice of **Action** í will <u>put</u>; the voice of **Association** and **Alteration**: "I will put <u>enmity between</u>" and so on. But here, like the cinematographer, I want to take the liberty to focus the lens on the nature of the entire open script and show that the view is not on the present but entirely on "things to come." It would take thousands of years to predict and develop. The Elohim voice was laying down the opening prophetic script of the serious drama of the universe.

3. In any good opening drama, it is critical to introduce the importance of the characters who will interact in this prophetic outworking of this plot of the ages. First, Elohim will be personally involved throughout. This cannot be missed. He was the voice of things to come, speaking to all the characters, even those yet unborn. He was going to be present, so his "I will put..." be done on earth as it is in Heaven.

4. The scriptwriter, Moses, did not leave out the main characters. They were going to be the development of conflict between God and Satan, the Man and his offspring, and the woman and her offspring. In other words, every single person born of a woman is a part of this drama, for "we shall all stand before the judgment seat of God...." No one is omitted from this drama. Each person is written in the Script. Each person was going to have the opportunity to have salvation as a result of what Elohim would do with the central character in the drama of this world order—Jesus. "And she [Mary] will give birth to a Son, and you are to give Him the name Jesus because He will save His people from their sins" (Matthew 1:21). And in the end, Jesus will put the enemy of all God's creation in his place—Hell. "And the devil, who deceived them, was thrown into the lake of burning sulfur... (Revelation 20:10).

The Abrahamic Promise Space

One of the Bible's most far-reaching and detailed prophetic promises is the one given to Abraham. In theology, it is called by his name—the "Abrahamic Covenant" or promise as it was given to Abraham; again, Moses recorded this prophetic space of revelation. This is so far-reaching that this special prophetic promise dominates the outworking of civilizations past, present, and future. Here, the Elohim of the future is taking one of His humble servants, Abraham, and launching him by prophetic promise space into the future. It is important to note that this is not just for intellectual investigation. We learn of God's prophetic promise space so that we learn and experience today that He is the Elohim of prophetic promise. What He says comes to pass. His promises can be trusted today because countless of His children from the dawn of time have found Him so.

God Gave Abraham in Genesis 12:1-3 a significant promise. He gave him a promise divided into three parts, all of which are stamped in human history, like a seal from the threefold promise that would be central to the future of everyone on this Earth. And that is so whether they believe in Him or not. God just laid it out; what he promised to do then and now cannot be disputed as the truth. Here is the tree-fold promise to Abraham that not much is left to be fulfilled. It was prophetic when it was given. We today are living in its fulfillment. It is another way that God demonstrates to us that He is a God of the future. Here again, the narrator is Moses. As he introduced what I termed "the Garden Promise," he does here by stepping out of the script to let the most important voice to mankind get through:

First, The Promise of A Place

"The Lord had said to Abram, "Go from your country, your people, and your father's household to the land I will show you" (Genesis 12:1). Then came a series of "I will" from the voice of God: "I WILL make you a great nation, and I WILL bless you (Genesis 12:2a). Here the first part or section of the prophetic promise space is that of a land. Abraham had land already, but God called him to give up his land. That was not easy. He was called to leave his home, people, and land for another. However, the requirement was simple compared to what God wanted to do. He was asked only to obey, and the land would be his. And Abraham did, and the better part of that story and history from that point is dominated by travels and circumstances getting to that land and sometimes losing it to their enemies, which was also predicted by the prophets, even for a long period of time and generations being scattered to all ends of the earth and God in his covenant and in many living, people today seen prophecy of the land fulfilled in the reestablishing of Israel as a nation in our times.

Secondly, the Promise of a People

"I will make your name great, and you will be a blessing. I will bless those who bless you, and whoever curses you I will curse" (Genesis 12:2,3a). We would have never heard of Abram's name if this promises first of the place, and then as a people, if the promise were not continuously being fulfilled to this day. Again, what is important is not to discard this reality as a matter of chance but as a distinct continuum of Elohim's prophetic space, which all of us must reckon with. Moreover, this is the one with the Bible and the one without the Bible for the Abrahamic Promise to fill all the spaces of us permanently.

Third, the Promise of a Person

From the prophetic promise of the Place came the promise of a People inseparable from this land. However, the most significant dimension of this prophetic space as it was for the Garden Promise was the central theme of messianic redemption in the main character of "Born of a Woman." Even his tribe was prophetically given to the place where he would be born. Moreover, here in the third dimension of the promise of a Person through whom the entire world would be blessed is found in the shadows of the Abrahamic Promise and throughout the continuum historically revealed in the Person and work of Jesus Christ. And astonishingly, He, as the seed of the woman, through the line from Abraham, fulfilled the promise that through him *"all the peoples of the earth will be blessed through you"* (Genesis 12:3b emphasis mine). This is the section of the promise that dominates the theme of the New Testament. Moreover, this is the dimension of the promise that is now filled in present space and time as the Gospel of Christ—the good news of redemption in Him has been proclaimed since He came born of a woman and began His ministry of blessing the people. Among them were the lame, the blind, the poor, and anyone who would come to Him. The blessing of eternal life is afforded freely to them as He was to Israel.

As one can see, these prophetic promises created hot spots of revelation throughout the landscape of the Bible. Much can be said of the continued development with progressive revelation in which the Old Promises were continually developed throughout history. For example, the next extensive promise or covenant is further established, called the "Davidic Covenant" found in 2 Samuel 7:12-16. Elohim described this prophetic space that would be developed after David (emphasis mine):

When your days are over, and you rest with your ancestors, I will raise your offspring to succeed you, your flesh and blood, and establish his kingdom. He is the one who will build a house or my name. **And I will establish the throne of his kingdom forever.** *I will be his father, and he will be my son. When he does wrong, I will punish him with a rod wielded by men, with floggings inflicted by humans' hands. But my love will never be taken away from him, as I took it away from Saul, whom I removed from before you.* **Your house and your kingdom will endure forever before me; your throne will be established forever**

In John 3: 16, the disciple John also extended this prophetic promise.

For God so loved the world that he gave his one and only Son, that whoever believes in him shall not perish but have **everlasting life.**

The everlasting life yet to come is based on an eternal prophetic promise. It is but one of the ways in which God demonstrates the nature of his prophetic space that spans the length of existence in time and beyond—a space reported by the prophets to be of endless duration—eternal.

(SLA: Suggestion for Life Application):

Elohim is a God of Promise. The child of God must practice living in this radical space of home. The is what Elohim promise can give each one of us. It says there is always hope for there is always Elohim. He calls us to hope in Him. Hope though, is not living in the future. It is living today knowing Elohim got your future covered.

11

ELOHIM SPACE OF PROPHETIC REVELATION—*PAST*

Revelation through the past could easily seem like that of the previous chapter—revelation through "promise" because the promises we selected as made in the past look to the prophetic future. However, now we look at past events like a porthole in which one can look back to learn what the future would be like. This is considered because it was one of the many ways Jesus answered his disciple's questions about the future. He took them to the past to teach them to a future space. A past space intersecting with the future. Here are two examples from Jesus.

"As it Was in the Days of Noah" (Matthew 24:37)

Jesus was sitting one day on the Mount of Olives. This is the reason His whole prophetic discourse is called the "Olivet Discourse." His disciples had followed him there because they were filled with questions about the future. Often Jesus would speak publicly, and his disciples would listen and learn along with the others. However, they felt the questions they had were better asked privately. They had just passed by the temple, and Jesus had made a prophetic comment about the temple that must have astonished them. The temple, which was the center of their lives and that of their people, had just commented that every single stone of it was going to be "thrown down." It did not rest well with them. It just raised deeper questions among them. So, when they got to the eastern edge of Jerusalem, where Mount Olive is situated, they came to Him privately. *"Tell us, when will this happen [the destruction of the temple], and what will be the sign of your coming and the end of the age?* Jesus did not mention the time. However, we now know it was in AD 70. It was only a few decades beyond their historical time and space. Their follow-up question, however, stretched to our time. Since they were asking about the "end of the age."

Now Jesus laid out a litany of details that would characterize the season of the future end of the age for His disciples. For our purpose in this chapter on two historical periods in the "past," Jesus identified as a prophetic event of the past that significantly points to the future. I think this to be informative of Jesus to include this approach to understanding the future by looking at the past. It was a question of time. Jesus told them first, *"But about the day or hour, no one knows, not even the angels in heaven, not the Son, but only the Father"* (Matthew

24:36). Here is His first critical historical event he drew upon to illustrate the time of the end of the age without giving a day or hour. He appealed to a period that each of His disciples would be familiar. He told them: *"As it was in the days of Noah so that it will be at the coming of the Son of Man* (v.37). Jesus then began to describe what the people were focused on before the flood of Noah's times. *"For in the days before the flood, people were eating and drinking, marrying, and giving in marriage, up to the day Noah entered the ark; they knew nothing about what would happen until the flood came and took them all away. That is how it would be at the coming of the Son of Man…Therefore, keep watch because you do not know on what day your Lord will come.*

Again, let us apply the "Timothy Trail" to this passage to understand what this historical event tells us about our world's future.

- If you want to understand the space of the future, look no further than the past. God has written revelations about the events of the past to teach us what to look for at the time of the end.

- Indifference to the message of redemption was a dominant feature of Noah's time. This is suggested in Jesus identifying several normal human activities like "eating and drinking, and marrying and given in marriage up to the day…" What is critical about this is the climate of lack of urgency for Christ's second coming that would prevail. There will be a space of a lack of urgency. I must be careful in saying this because I do so from a spiritual sense and only the implication of Jesus' warning to his disciples: I prophesy that this characteristic of indifference concerning the urgency of the end times would be evident among the church community. I contend if this historical event is directed to those outside the community of faith alone, then why would Jesus give such a stern warning to his disciples to "therefore keep watch…"

- To restate this critical prophesy, the people in Noah's day were clearly indifferent to the practical problem of a flood. However, they were also spiritually indifferent. It is that spiritual indifference I contend Jesus was speaking when He said to his disciples that they should *"understand this: If the owner of the house had known at what time of night the thief was coming, he would have kept watch and would not have let the house be broken into. So, you also must be ready because the Son of Man will come at an hour when you do not expect him.*

- Jesus reveals that the Father already sets the future space for the Son of Man's return. And this unique space is coming on a Day that no one in heaven knows but the Father. What is the most unique and critical space of that day? Nobody knows what day it is. Yes, of course, if one knows what time a thief is coming to their house, they would indeed be prepared. However, that is the point, since you disciples—servants of God, since you do not know it would be foolish not to treat every day as the day He is Coming. The sad failure of the past of the people of Noah's day is that they never allowed for their prophetic ignorance of future events. They did not believe it as well because there was a message from God to all the people, and except for Noah's family, they did not care.

"It was the same in the days of Lot" (Luke 17:26-30).

The Gospel writer Luke combines these stories because of their historical and prophetic similarities. They both speak to the typical involvement of people obsessed with pleasing themselves and unconcerned with the dangers around the bend. In the case of the times of Lot, the social climate was doing anything that satisfied them, but Jesus mentioned more of an economic focus of "buying and selling, planting and building" until Lot left town and the fires of God's judgment fell on the city. Again, what can be said of Noah's time also applies here. The point to make is Jesus' example of looking back to past events to get directions on what to look for in the future. As we look into the future, the most important of these stories is the theme that ran through both events. It was the suddenness of future change. At a time when you least expect it, radical events change, impacting the present order as we know it.

Jesus implied this much when He told his disciples in answer to the question of what would be the sign of the end of the age. He said it would be like "two men will be in the field: one taken and the other left. Two women will be grinding with a hand mill; one taken and the other left," but although these events are difficult to decide as to what period of time such events would happen, such as is these kinds of events more the time of the rapture of the church in the air rather than the Second Coming of Christ upon the earth. One thing is clear: both call for us to "Therefore keep watch because you do not know what day your Lord will come. That is clearly the focus of Jesus appealing to these past historical events to prepare his listeners for a future that faces us with a tragic space of prophetic indifference and a call to all his followers to stay alert as we face the future, for the Lord is sure to come at a time when we are not going to expect Him. We see that in the future space, looking at these two past events.

SLA (Suggestion for Life Application):

Embrace the past if only that there is nothing you can change in that space. Its baked in. But its effects on you is what you can work on. So, get to work with what you can do preparing for a better future.

12

ELOHIM SPACE OF PROPHETIC REVELATION—*PREDICTIONS*

One of the fundamental ways in which Elohim has revealed the future is by predictions. That is the nature of prophecy. Except is not the general understanding of "predicting" something based on the odds it will happen. God is not informed by taking poles. Elohim does not work on future odds attempting to predict what will happen. He does not run the world like the stock market. When the prophets of Elohim predicted something, it came with the force of Elohim's character. It came from a space in which Elohim cannot lie.

God is not a man, that He should lie
Nor a son of man, that He should repent.
Has He said, and will He not do it?
Or has He spoken, and will He not make it good? (Numbers 23:19).

Even then, for the sake of the people, there were prophetic procedures so the people would have confidence that the prophet spoke for Elohim. They would be given short-term predictions of what would happen in their lifetime. Then, the people were assured of God speaking through them as they could verify that their words correspondingly would occur beyond their lifetime. Jesus himself often did the same many times as he got closer to the end of His ministry. He wanted to assure them that what he had predicted for the future would come true. So, He gave them short-term predictions, like when he told disciples they would find a colt tied ready for him to ride into Jerusalem. He told Peter that a cock would crow three times as a reminder of his denial. He told them that he would be handed over to death, and in three days, even as the prophets of old had said, he would rise again. So, He fulfilled a short-term prediction hundreds of years ago from the prophet Isaiah (Isaiah 53).

So, the godly prophets were serious about their predictions. They were men and women of truth and were not about hiding their credentials, whether interpreting powerful dreams or predicting the people's future.

Their product was always true even when it cost them their lives. If they were true prophets, the people would be assured that their words would come true. Jesus came as a fulfillment of many predictions. However, like a true Prophet, Jesus never relied on the fact that he was fulfilling so many long-term predictions of the ancient prophets as Messiah. Like a true Prophet and Master Teacher in His times established His own credentials in making predictions that would be realized in the lifetime of his disciples. He predicted Peter's denial down to the precise number that a cock would crow. He predicted a donkey would be waiting to be available for his triumphant entry to Jerusalem. He predicted his eventual death for three days and that He would rise again on the third day. He predicted the Holy Spirit's coming and His Church's birth.

With these and other events in historical time and place, He was establishing His prophetic credentials so that they would have a firm assurance that the far-reaching predictions of things to come beyond their lifetimes and to us as well will not simply think of "blind faith" that the Christian movement is often said to have. However, a faith rooted in fulfilled predictions in historical space and time by a Jesus who is the Way and the Truth. He predicted the falling of the temple in a precise way that when it did, it would be stone by stone. That there would not be one stone remaining upon another. He would be gone at this time, but many, especially the early followers, would be scattered in various parts of Asia Minor by then. However, this tragic event of the destruction of the center of Israel's life by an enemy was going to signal the truthfulness of his other claims, especially his prediction that he was coming back for them. So, when the disciples saw the Temple fall, although it was heartbreaking, it would also lift their spirits. As they partake of the communion and remember why he told them to remember Him, it was more than a remembrance of historical significance. They would also do it in remembrance of Him until He comes. The Temple would be in rubble, but a better day of redemption and restoration would come.

I must here give the word about what is illustrated in the model at the start of this section of "P's." They are presented in graphic overlapping circles. This is because Elohim in prophetic space cannot be separated from the other. The graphics are but an aid to help us consider the subtle differences to understand the whole better. In our effort to understand His space, He asked us to divide the word correctly. Done on the basis of Scripture, it can enhance our understanding of the same. For example, here is a prophetic revelation through prayer—the first circle (#1) on the top.

It is easy to overlook that Jesus' prayer that he taught His disciples revealed a prophetic element of "prayer." He taught His disciples to pray, "Our Father who is in heaven hallowed be thy name." However, along with this acknowledgment comes the request "thy Kingdom Come" and towards the end, the further exaltation "for thine is the Kingdom the power and the glory." All of these sentiments are a prayer that moves from the present needs of daily bread to future glorious blessings. This prophetic space of Elohim must dominate all of our lives. We are asked to pray for the future and work for His Kingdom. I would think that since the Kingdom is assured from the Divine perspective, praying for the prophetic Kingdom is in every way for our benefit.

The Apostle Paul, in the flow of biblical servants of Elohim, was not of the official stream of historical prophets. He repeatedly opens his letters, "Paul an Apostle of Jesus Christ." However, he did not shy away from prophetic descriptions of things to come, especially focusing on the continued personification of the human condition in the last days. His most extensive description was given to his son in the Faith, young pastor Timothy. Whereas many of the ancient prophets focused on political and national relationships, the apostles took the spiritual to scapple to the inner space of the population inside and outside the church. Here is a simple graphic that first appeared in my book "Deliver Us from Evil" A prayer for Our Times" (Christian Faith Publication, 2023 p.34): This Pauline description is framed in the context or space of "the last days" (2 Timothy 3:1). This period began with the first coming of Jesus Christ. We live in that prophetic space until He returns the Second time. This is our world—the spiritual shape of the present order: Here is the list:

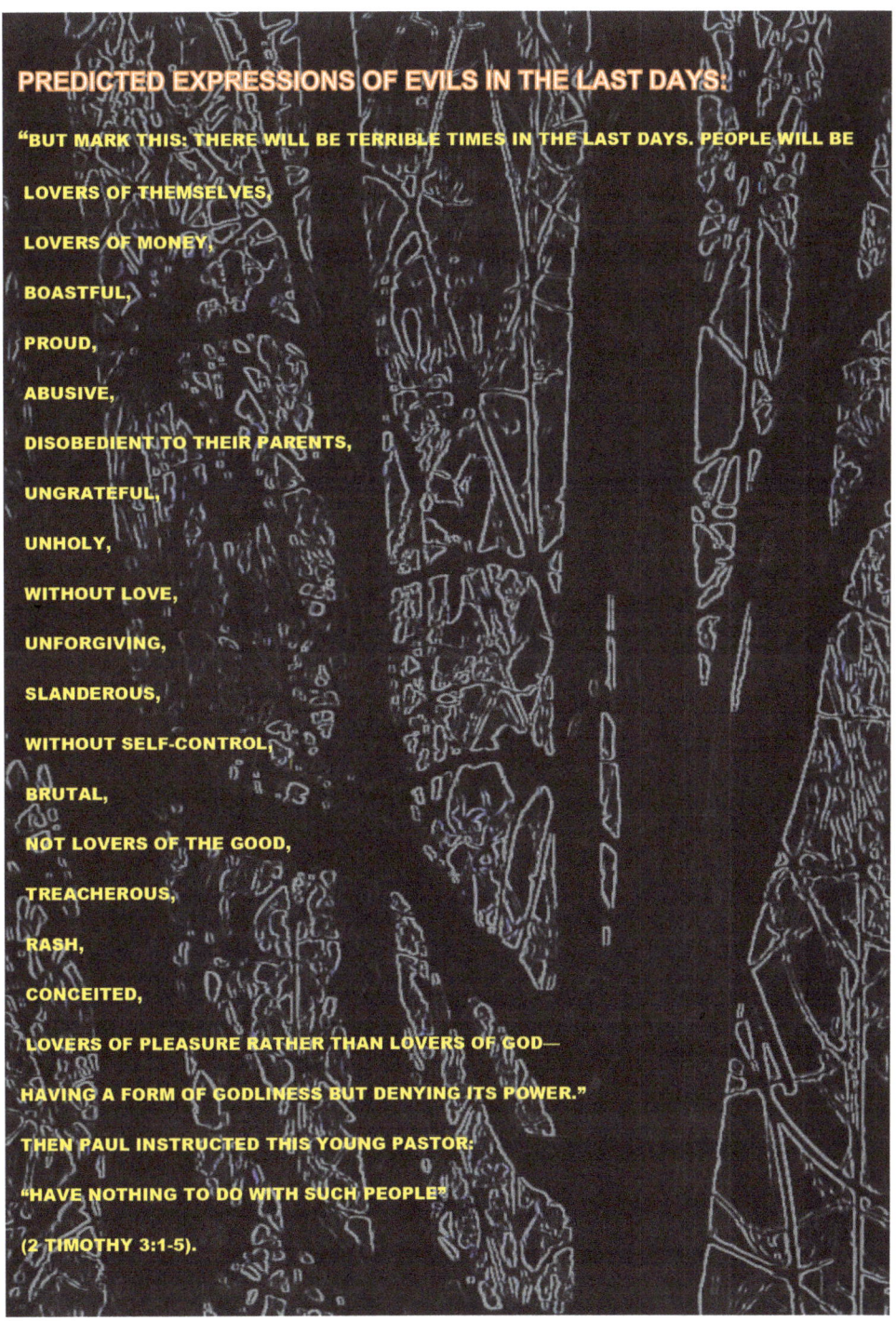

PREDICTED EXPRESSIONS OF EVILS IN THE LAST DAYS:

"BUT MARK THIS: THERE WILL BE TERRIBLE TIMES IN THE LAST DAYS. PEOPLE WILL BE

LOVERS OF THEMSELVES,

LOVERS OF MONEY,

BOASTFUL,

PROUD,

ABUSIVE,

DISOBEDIENT TO THEIR PARENTS,

UNGRATEFUL,

UNHOLY,

WITHOUT LOVE,

UNFORGIVING,

SLANDEROUS,

WITHOUT SELF-CONTROL,

BRUTAL,

NOT LOVERS OF THE GOOD,

TREACHEROUS,

RASH,

CONCEITED,

LOVERS OF PLEASURE RATHER THAN LOVERS OF GOD—

HAVING A FORM OF GODLINESS BUT DENYING ITS POWER."

THEN PAUL INSTRUCTED THIS YOUNG PASTOR:

"HAVE NOTHING TO DO WITH SUCH PEOPLE"

(2 TIMOTHY 3:1-5).

Let us face it: one can look at this list and say nothing new under the sun has been going on for a long time. That is the point. They describe the period that began with the first coming of Christ, which began the messianic dispensation. But considering the Apostle Paul was not given to hyperbolic descriptions must be getting at something else. In the last days, evil will increase in the world. As we have now come to experience, the unthinkable will become *thinkable*. Take this notion as a guide in each of the items the Apostle mentioned, and you will get a picture of how we would characterize our age. For in so many ways the unthinkable is fast becoming thinkable and normalized. Today, we are witnessing the "normalization of evil."

However, the Apostle list is not the whole story. He also, in less predictive and more propositional, declared, "Where sin abounds, Grace did much more abounds" (Romans 5:20). And there is the prophet that the Apostle Peter quotes on the day of Pentecost, also referencing this same period of the last days. "This is that," he said, "which was spoken of by the prophet Hosea that in the last days I will pour out my Spirit on all flesh… (Acts 2:17).

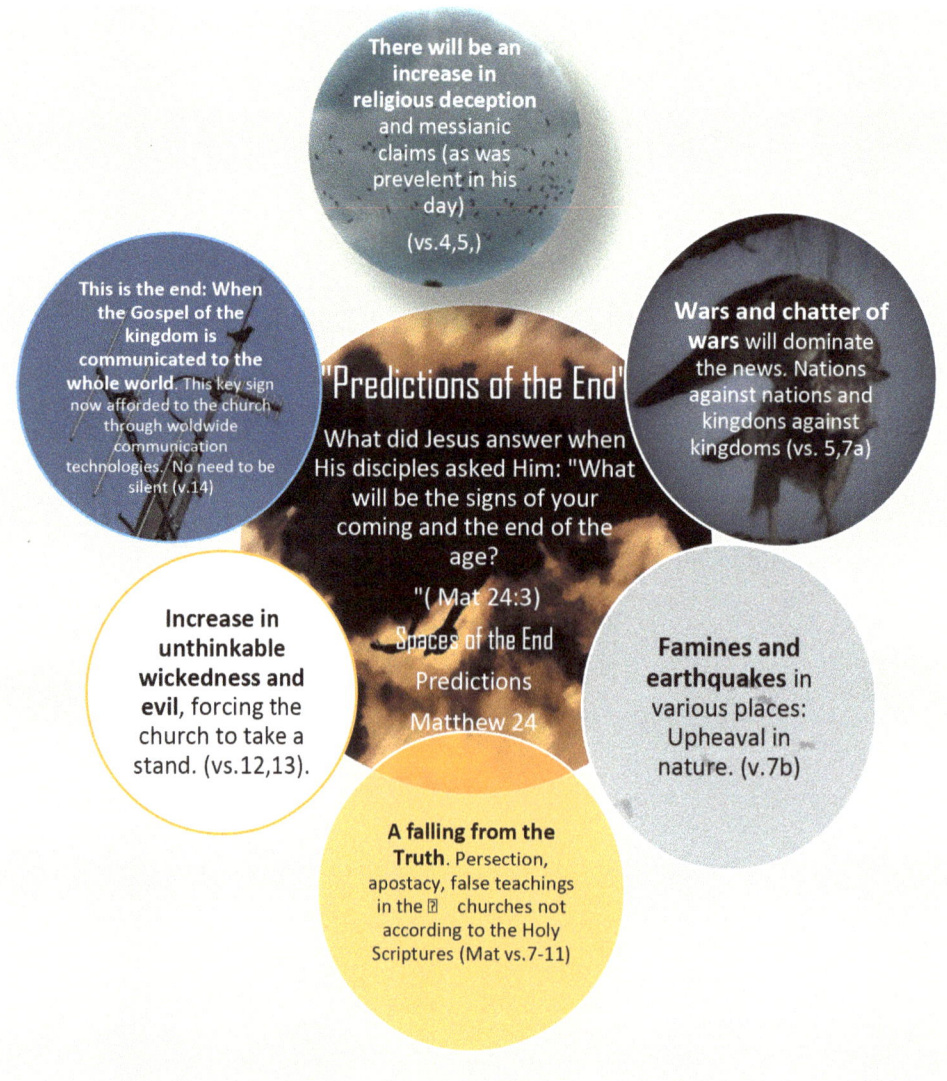

SLA (Suggestion for Life Application)

We are not called to make predictions. But we are called to make plans. So, plan your life and what you want to accomplish short-term or long-term. Plans presented to the Lord are like presenting the "desire of your heart." He said if you ask for bread, he will not give you a stone." Elohim encourages us to Commit our way to the Lord, and He shall bring it to pass. So, Plan, Pray, and purpose to believe he will bring it to pass for you.

13

ELOHIM SPACE OF PROPHETIC REVELATION—*PERSONS*

"But Thou, O Daniel...."

As a boy, I remember holding a little of what we called a transistor radio in my hand. We were able to carry the radio man outside the home now. It did not matter that it only picked up one or two stations, which we feverously adjusted to avoid the ever-present static. It was a fulfillment that made me, and many other youths believe that what men like Daniel prophesied would happen in the last few days. The Sunday School teacher on our little island school would tell us, "See what the prophet Daniel told us in Daniel 12:4 is now coming to pass. That was decades ago, before the cassette tape recorder, before color television, and like in a complete universe before the computer, the internet, GPS, and social media. Moreover, that is not even half the story. For that was even before man visited the moon. Moreover, here is the prophet, and his story got our serious attention each time there was some phenomenal, unbelievable technological development that we could see, feel, and touch. Moreover, here is the passage from Daniel that startled little boys and girls taught in Sunday School about the prophetic times in which we then lived.

Look at the book (Daniel 12:4 KJV):

But thou, O Daniel, shut up these words and seal the book until the time of the end. Many shall run to and fro, and knowledge shall be increased.

The rapid increase in humankind's ability to move "to and from" and the exponential "increase in knowledge"—these two phenomenal events of our lifetime unmatched by any other period of civilization on so many travel abilities and knowledge levels could it be just a luck of the prophetic draw? However, here is where it gets personal. The same Daniel who received this unique prophecy of future physical changes of our time also received the following prophecy in the social and spiritual realm Daniel 12:1-4:

Michael, the great prince who protects your people will arise at that time. There will be a time of distress such has not happened from the beginning of nations until then. But at that time your people—everyone whose name is found written in the book will be delivered.

Multitudes who sleep in the dust of the earth will awaken some to everlasting life, others to shame and everlasting contempt. Those who are wise will shine like the brightness of the heavens, and those who lead many to righteousness, like the stars forever and ever.

[But you, Daniel, roll up and seal the words of the scroll until the time of the end. Many will go here and there to increase knowledge]

"The Lion of the Tribe of Judea"

The Lion of the tribe of Judea—Jesus was given this title that proclaims future conquest over all His enemies at the end of days yet to come. However, before then, He lamented in historical place and time:

"O Jerusalem, Jerusalem, the city that kills the prophets and stones God's messengers! How often I have longed to gather your children together, as a hen gathers her chicks under her wings, and you were not willing" (Matthew 23:37 NLT).

Here Jesus singled out those persons He said, "prophets and messengers" who were killed. He did not tell us their prophecies were of Him, and the message was all about Him. Then, with the full knowledge, the city—this holy space He knew would be the scene of His own death not too long after he made this lament.

Jesus, the Person of Interest of the Prophets

From the time of creation, Jesus, the Son of God, was a Person of interest. It was revealed later that He was the driving force of creation. John, one of His closest disciples, said, "All things were made by him and without Him there was nothing made that was made" (John 1:1). However, this man of history, this central Person of prophecy, still humbled himself to the death of the cross. He alone reveal this unique personal Elohim space. He is a Man of History at the same time, the One who is yet to come at the end of days to open the seal of the book that the Prophet closed. Consider the following in Revelation 5:3-5 when the call went out for someone worthy to open the scroll to be unsealed. "But no one in heaven or on earth or under the earth could open the scroll or even look inside. John was heartbroken and "wept and wept because no one was found who was worthy to open the scroll or look inside." Then an Elder went to John, who was in tears, and told him:

Do not weep! See, the Lion of the tribe of Judah, the root of David, has triumphed. He is able to open the scroll and its seals.

The prophet Daniel closed and sealed the book until the end. Moreover, in the end, the only One of all the ages—the focal Person of "things to come" is worthy—the Lion of the tribe of Judah. One would think that the Roman Rule would take center stage and not a loan Galilean named Jesus. He came at a time when imperial Rome held an iron clad on everyone, including Jesus. His very birthplace and growing up years, even to his departure under the Roman government. There was "peace," but it was an uneasy one. Roman garrisons were fully in control of every place. Moreover, to prove it, even the Temple of Israel bore an emblem of Caesar. This messianic Person gave initial hope that it all was dashed when He was crucified by Roman soldiers and mocked and treated like a common criminal. While all the time through the prophetic space, even at this time, He was the Lion of the tribe of Judah who, on the wings of the eternal prophetic continuum, would, in the end, "triumph."

"Until the Man of Sin is Revealed"

This person of the prophetic future space is not included here, even for honorable mention. Indeed, he would be the most dishonoring person who ever existed. He will emerge on the prophetic scene to dishonor the authority of Christ. He would rise in opposition to him. When it was said that the Lion of the tribe of Judah prevailed or triumphed, it was more than He could open the scroll before the Elohim's thrown. It was because He came and fought this beast of a man, called names such as "the man of sin" 1 Thessalonians 2:3-4), "Blasphemer (Revelation 13:6). "lawless" (2 Thessalonians 2:8), A liar and deceiver (John 4:1-3); and there are many other expressions of his evil character in the Scriptures. His main purpose will be to lift himself up above Elohim's space. Throughout the Scriptures, Elohim is revealed as existing in a space that only He alone can and does occupy. But even before the beginning of time, Lucifer attempted a coup to overthrow Elohim and failed. At the end of time, he will attempt to do it again, alluring many with his big lie and even performing what would be considered miracles. This would be his big attempt at deception, and many will fall prey if the true Christ does not return to stop him.

He will be one of the most mysterious Persons in Bible prophecy. He would have extraordinary powers of influence and charm. Those who resist his mark 666 as a sign of ownership and allegiance will die. There are many other mysteries of his character and person, not the least of which is that he would be one of the most physically handsome men in the world. His looks alone will take him viral. This would enable him to deceive many as the social order is primed for such outward superficial folly. Volumes can be written of this prophetic person. However, in keeping with the New Testament writers who spoke of him, he did so in the context of a warning. I do the same here. It is simple to warn and be on guard when a deceiver is coming. His spirit of deception is already growing among us. We have constantly been primed to believe lies and to be deceived by the rise of folly. The antichrist is coming. He is not the real one. However, many will believe he is. All the evil in the world would be personified in this prophetic person.

"I, John…was on the Island of Patmos…On the Lord's Day"

John was a prophetic person. A casual reader of the Scriptures could easily miss what he was. Indeed, his calling and service could easily be missed by those serious in the study of Revelation. He did not do his introduction by saying like Paul explained, that he was an Apostle. He did not have any ranking to identify. He simply described himself by what he was about to do. He was the only person in the Bible who described himself as being called to write. He said Jesus called him to write to the churches:

> *On the Lord's Day, I was in the Spirit, and I heard a loud voice like a trumpet behind me: "Write on a scroll what you see and send it to the seven churches…. (Revelation 1:10-11)"*

John turned around as the voice was coming like a trumpet behind him. John said he was someone dressed and looked like the "son of man." Although he was seeing a vision, the voice that appeared came through the vision as real. It was and remained throughout his writings the voice of God. Later in revelation, he would narrate what he saw in his voice as a narrator and writer. However, in his letters to the churches, he wrote all these letters in the voice he heard. Here he further explained his calling to be a writer of this unique style of ancient writing called the apocalyptic. This was an unusual style of literature then, as it would be in ours. This made the task he was called to do even more critical and important, dealing with symbols, visions, voices, and characters of the future. However, it makes their meaning no less true than any other writings of the Scriptures.

> *"Do not be afraid. I am the First and the Last. I am the Living One; I was dead, and now look, I am alive forever! And I hold the keys of death and Hades. Write therefore, what you have seen what is now and what will take place later (Revelation 1: 17-19).*

(SLA -Suggestion for Life Application)

John was tapped by Elohim who knew he had the skill and vision of a writer. But he did not know it—not until God told him to "write." Then he discovered he could. The Church is still being blessed by his obedience and faithfulness in the task.

We often define ourselves by what we want to do—by what we see in ourselves. It is far better to know who we are and what we are capable off by what Elohim calls us to do—the space Elohim calls us to occupy. From Abram to John to Paul obedience to his call is our vacation. In John, the revelator we see we can be banished by others yet call by God to fill a space in His will we never thought we could. God calls different ones with different skills and styles and each of us has something He can use. All that is required to full our vocation is obedience (Revelation 1:1-5).

14

ELOHIM SPACE OF PROPHETIC REVELATION—*PARABLES*

Parables are commonly defined as *earthly stories with a heavenly meaning.* For this chapter essay on parables in the Elohim prophetic space, I would define the ones selected as *historical stories with prophetic or future meaning.* All parables are applicable for teaching. However, Jesus selected some parables to focus our attention on future events.

His parables often speak of urgency or readiness. His followers should cultivate as we live in this period, known to the prophets as the end of the age. They were illustrative of the theme of both John the Baptist and Jesus himself when they burst on the New Testament scene declaring: *"Repent for the Kingdom of Heaven is at hand* (Mark 1:15; 3:24). It must be understood this was the story world in which they ministered in historical space and time: That the messianic Kingdom dispensation has begun. And this is why Jesus so often began His parables by stating that he was describing the Kingdom with His parables.

All of Jesus's parables were then given to reveal something about the future. They were like prophecies of the future in the form of stories. For example, over and over, He said, "The kingdom of heaven is like a mustard seed (Matthew 13:31-43) is like a treasure (Matthew 13:44-46) is like a pearl (Mt.13:45). This should not be taken lightly that the great Master teacher Jesus appealed to everyday stories of His times to reveal days to come.

The context of our discourse here is to illustrate How parables were used in ancient biblical times to forecast the future. Although we did not identify the "dreams" category, they were often used to " see" the future. For example, Joseph was called the dreamer and was hated by his brothers for this gift. It was because what he dreamt was not interpreted too kindly towards them. He saw that as the youngest, he would rule over them. And they would have none of it. However, since Jesus used parables so often, we would want to check this source to illustrate what is coming in the future.

Ten Virgins

Although this parable is a tragic story by Jesus, it became one of the most popular, influencing various art and sculpture in churches during the Middle Ages. However, at the heart of the story, it is about the prophetic future. The beauty or tragedy of this story is in its simplicity of context (a wedding), a choice (to prepare or not to prepare), and a conclusion by Christ (those who were ready for Christ and those who were not).

The Setting

Jesus is outdoors at a mountain telling various stories of the Kingdom. It is a place where the consequential elements of His Kingdom story could be missed. He was not the setting point to any tragic consequences He was about to reveal. Indeed, the setting is a wedding. Who would expect any bad outcome at a wedding? It was a beautiful setting of hope, love, and nothing but joy. But Jesus, like a skilled tragic storyteller, did not hold back on its tragic story because of its beautiful setting.

The Telling of the Story – (Jesus recorded by Matthew [25:1-12)

"At that time of the kingdom of heaven will be like ten virgins [or bridesmaids] who took their lamps and went out to meet the bridegroom [to lead the way in the wedding processions]. Five of them were foolish, and five were wise. The foolish ones took their lamps but did not take any oil with them. The wise ones, however, took oil in jars along with their lamps. The bridegroom was a long time in coming, and they all became drowsy and fell asleep. At midnight, the cry rang out: Here is the bridegroom! Come out to meet Him! Then, all the virgins woke up and trimmed their lamps. The foolish ones said to the wise, 'Give us some of your oil; our lamps are going out. No! they replied, 'There may not be enough for both of us…go to those who sell and buy some for yourself." While they were gone, the bridegroom came. The bridesmaids who were ready went into the wedding banquet. And the door was shut.

The Meaning of It

- The Kingdom of Christ is coming.
- It will seem among many of Elohim's servants that He is delayed in His coming for His bride, the Church, and His Kingdom people.
- Some will give in to this delay and become weary even in well-doing. However, some, even in their weariness, made sure they were ready for when the call came that the Bridegroom—Christ had come.
- Those who are ready will go into this glorious gala of celebration with all God's children from all ages.
- Those who were not ready were left out. As Bob Dylon sang, the lyrics from his song, "Trying to get to Heaven before They Close the Door" (Time Out of Mind, Album 1975).

SLA: Suggestion for Life Application

- No matter the circumstances of your life live in the wisdom of knowing you have the Oil of the Spirit in you. He said He keeps us "sealed [even when we sleep at times] till the day of redemption yet to come.

  Jesus did not tell this story to be dramatic but to be true. True to what is living wise is being ready to meet Him. And fools when we are not ready for His coming. For "what shall it profit one to gain the whole world and lose his own soul" (Matthew 16:26).

  If you have never done so here are the simple steps to be ready. (1) Pray to God and admit that you are a sinner (as we all are) as stated in Romans 3:23. (2) Ask Elohim to forgive you of all your sin. Here is a simple prayer "Lord I admit I am a sinner before you. Forgive me of all my sins. Make me one of your Kingdom children." You pray it. You believe it. He does it. It is that simple.

- That is called the "sinners prayer." You may not often here these simple steps spelled out like this in the church you attend. But this is a prayer that one can pray any place. Chances are a lot of people in churches never prayed this prayer and assure their salvation. They are like the foolish bridesmaids and would not be ready Because this simple prayer or versions of it spoken in any language, even the silent ones of the heart. It must be made to enter Elohim Kingdom. There is no shortcut to this (John 1:12; 3:16).

Two Builders

We turn from a parable of ten virgins to two male builders. This goes to show that Jesus has more to say about His Kingdom than just the numbers or gender in these varied parables. It is the choice of the participants, not a numeric feature or gender, which determines the relationship to the prophetic Kingdom space. For this story, we follow the same three-part outline to consider this Parable.

The Setting of the Story

Matthew said that Jesus looked out and saw the crowds; he went up to a mountainside and sat down. His disciples followed him there, and He began to teach them. This began one of Jesus' most extended teachings, which was called the Sermon on the Mount. It covers some of the great themes of the Gospels. He began with those who are "blessed" and typified the character of those who would inherit the coming Kingdom. Like the "poor in spirit for theirs is the Kingdom of Heaven. He moved on to how his followers are to be salt and light and take a stand against crimes such as murder, adultery, divorce, and love for enemies, and giving to the needy as He had quite a zeal for helping the poor. So, this was a time of far-reaching subjects on the whole condition of the community and the kingdom's demands.

Towards the end of this sermon, He closed out with a similar theme of the five wise and five foolish bridesmaids to a wise builder and a foolish one. So, the story comes at the end of one of the great extended discourses in Jesus' ministry, which began with the blessed and ended with a story of two different builders.

The Telling of the Story (Matthew 7:24-27)

Two builders set out to build what could be termed their dream home. One of them constructed his home on a rock. Jesus described him as someone wise because he heard Jesus' words and followed them. When he got the double force of rain coming down and streams coming up, with the lateral force of the wind. Jesus said his house "did not fall because it has its foundation on the rock." There was another builder in the story called a "foolish man" who built his house on sand. A similar weather pattern came upon his house, and it fell. Jesus said, "with a great crash."

The Meaning of the Story

- Usually, Jesus would explain a parable after the telling of it. In this case, Jesus gave the meaning before the story. So, it was of primary concern how he gave the meaning at the start at the outset.
- The meaning of the wise builder referred to anyone who first hears His words. That is, to listen and then practice them. That man represents all my followers. They are my wise followers of me.
- The other builder who built his house on sand and lost it in the storm of life is symbolic of all those who hear His words but do not practice them. It means their lives will end in a crash. Nothing they constructed for their lives will last when the storm of God's judgment comes against them.

SLA: Suggestion for Life Application)

- In building your life check out whether or not the teachings of Jesus forms the foundation of how your life is lived.
- Since Jesus used the analogy of a home would you check with Jesus what kind of curve appeal you would employ? Would you let Him have free range of your home with access to every room and its use? Or would you shut Him out of certain areas? Would you let him take a look at your closest?
- Would you let Jesus build your foundation? Consider making Jesus the foundation of your life. Will you let Him have full access to every part of your life, or shut Him out of certain areas? Build your life on His teachings, secure a stable future, and find strength in His words (Matthew 7:24-27)., are you looking to your job, money, earthly relationships, pleasures the sand of life on which you build?
- To secure a good solid foundation for the future Jesus said in this simple story: Learn my words and follow them and you will have nothing to fear when the rain fall, and the streams rise up, and the life's circumstances blow on you from every direction. Elohim says you would exist in His stable space. You will not fall for I will be your Rock (Matthew 7:24-27).

15

ELOHIM SPACE OF PROPHETIC REVELATION—*PREPARATION*

PREPERATION

7

(John 14)

Foxes prepare holes spaces in the ground. Large and small birds work tirelessly to prepare nests in trees and crests of rocks. Land and sea turtles prepare places on earth for their eggs to be safe and their young to thrive. Individuals and nations are all relentlessly preparing for a future yet cultivating the folly of the past.

There are trips back to the moon. There are planned changes in the energy supply from fossils in the ground to energy harvest from the wind and sun. The old faithful combustible auto engines giving way to electrical force—

EVs they are called. We are now warming up to global warming from decades of uncertain debates about whether to be prepared. I contend that it would be folly not to do so. We are preparing to fight cancer and diabetes, and many other illnesses that have eluded us for years. We are sending rockets targeting asteroids to test how we can blow them up before one blow us up on a collision course with Earth. The first try targeting a "moonlet" without the threat of collision with us was successful on September 26, 2020. So, what is my point? What it my concern about all these global preparation efforts for the future? *I contend we relentlessly preparing for our own future space, often without much thought or regard that God-Elohim is also preparing His.*

History is Never Historical Space Alone

One of the major tasks of Elohim is His revealed preparation to bring civilization—including all the created Universe to closure. He is preparing for a day of reckoning when all of history, from the material to the spiritual, from biotic to abiotic, will crash into their determined future. From Elohim's perspective and revelation, history had never been about only the past. This must never be missed. I cannot make this point of history enough. I contend that to understand history at its fundamental level is to understand today and the future as well.

The concept of "*let bygone be bygone*" and "*what is done is done*" or the casual disclaimer "*what is past is past*" I contend is not true. If that soliloquy was true, then what of forgiveness? Is not forgiveness for what was done in the past? How could God forgive or even reward those forgiven without dealing directly with their past? It is not folly to think of the past as only in the past when Elohim is bringing all the past to meet Him in the future judgment for which he is preparing. Indeed, what of us? Are we not the living expression of our past heading to the future? Is not our very body we carry the embodiment of our past? If not, where did our education go from birth? And what of all our experiences are really past?

We cannot ignore the past either in this vast universe or in us. He is preparing a future, considering, and dealing with how we got here, and the journey of our history is ever before Him. Indeed, He is fully preparing for it. will face the future when a big change will happen. That includes separating the sheep from the goats, the wheat from the weeds, and sinners from the saints. He has to get multitudes of his followers from ancient of times into his abode, and he has to get all those who reject Him—Satan and his followers to a place prepared for them called "the lake of fire." getting the saints into heaven, and Satan and his followers into a prepared lake of fire. Elohim has a lot yet to do to bring civilization to closure. According to his prophetic plan, this world order cannot survive his justice. He plans to institute a new order of things.

"I go to Prepare a Place For You" (John 14:1)

In the meantime, before the end, Jesus said He would prepare a place for His followers. I am interested in giving attention to Jesus' words in a prophetic sense. For then, the prophecy is that of a period of time, which is, as we already noted, the period of the last days. Many things will occur in our space of existence or space (many of which we have already considered). Here, these words of Jesus open up an expansive space from the time He left Earth to heaven and, upon His return, includes this period space of *preparation*. This is one of my Sunday School teacher's favorite topics growing up. It is like teaching slave kids about freedom; people in prisons about liberty is coming. It's like telling kids who came to her class from one-room homes about essential things we take for granted now, like indoor bathrooms, kitchen, and water, when all of these things her students never knew. One room, and here a teacher is standing before her students at the bottom of the economic ladder from an already bottom space, declaring with unwavering certainty that there is One who lived among us. He did many miracles here, then said He was preparing a big one "over there," then He chose to describe it as having "many rooms." For an audience like that, everyone was like pack my bags with whatever little I have and *let us go*.

Our modern convenience spaces can tend to make Jesus' "many rooms" prophecy seem less distinct from what we can gain in this world with a little luck. This is why these words are part of the narrative for those who have trouble envisioning heaven.

Look at the Book:

Here are some general observations of this space

- A space devoid of troubles. Dump all the trash of this world in a basket and leave it here. It is a place where there is no room for any trouble. "Let not your heart be troubled."
- My purpose for coming was to provide salvation. My purpose for leaving is to provide a space for you.
- This space is described as "in my Father's House. It is a big house containing "many rooms." It is so that all the people of my Kingdom from all generations will be accommodated.
- If it sounds unbelievable, I understand. However, if it were not so I would have told you. Moreover, I am coming again to receive you and take you there so you can be with me forever.

Jesus was more of a Teacher than a Theologian. I could even consider Him an "anti-theologian." However, I mean it in a more strategic sense. For example, I looked to theologians with their vast knowledge in seminary, struggling painfully to explain those "deep truths" in the Scriptures. All of the word of God was seen more like a "deep truth" that needed to be analyzed and explained, and one had to learn even the rules of explanation. Over the years, after theological studies and degrees, I have learned to stand back and see the Word of God the way ordinary disciples heard it. They read a narrative in the Old Testament about their lives. They heard Jesus telling them stories that they were familiar with from everyday life.

We, scholars, and researchers of the Word of God, are not called to give people "deep" truth. We are called to give people the truth. This truth is wrapped up in a relationship with a Person of the Bible –Jesus Christ. Jesus looked at this great scholar Nicodemus and told him, "You must be born again." Even then, he struggled because he came at it as a scholar. Jesus had to bring him down to real, every day, practical knowledge of how one is born. He had to see this common space before this Theologian could understand the import of being born again. Nevertheless, it must be acknowledged it was this "deed" conversation that gave rise to the most profound yet the most popular in its simplicity that a boy could learn and grasp: *For God so loved the world that He gave his one and only Son that whosoever believes in Him would have everlasting life.* It is easy to overlook the narrative that this central passage of all of Scripture was first given to a great scholar well versed in Law and Prophets (John 3:16).

Nevertheless, when I look at Jesus, I see no such unreachable intellectual space. I see a Man describing heaven in the most humble and deeply personal of ways as "my Father's house." Quite astonishingly, he added personally in coming back to get us there, "So where I am, you can also be." I see not a space that in any way whose joy or excitement, or glory of being there can be described as a space without the relationship of that space with him. So, His theology is this. If you know me, you know that place. It is a space of my indescribable presence. It is a Jesus Theology that says this place cannot be described to us while we are here. Its description can only be experienced when you are "in my Father's house." That is what I mean when I say Jesus was more of a teacher. He used the simplest illustrations from the most common elements or concepts to express the most far-reaching and deep truth. His selections are impeccable, and his applications are always personal and relational. He alone can speak with such personal and relationship force: I go to prepare a place for you where I am, you may be.

"Prepared as a bride adorned for her husband"

In historical times and places, Jesus told His disciples that He would prepare a place for them. Toward the end of His Revelation to John in Revelation 21:21, we read a remarkable narrative

---

"I saw the holy city, the new Jerusalem, coming down out of heaven from God, prepared ["hetoimasmenen" GRK. "to make ready" or, "having been made ready"? as a bride adorned for her husband."

There is a direct connection between the action of preparation and the nature of the act. Here again, there is no action without the intersection of relationship spaces. This action comes with the force of love. She comes dressed in holiness, mercy, and grace. She comes clothed in a designer's original for a special time and space. At the end of the day, a new space is called a new Jerusalem. One not made with human hands. Abraham saw it. He left his home for a new place because "he looks for a city not made with human's hands but whose maker and builder is God.

Piece by piece, the parts come together. These parts, once again, cannot be understood or interpreted clearly without taking note of the symbolic relationship in the act. One has somehow to put oneself in the heart of a bride as she is in her dressing room preparing to make a grand entrance to the Kingdom scene that awaits her. All the eyes of the saints are there. Abraham and Sarah, parents of the promise, will be there. Noah and his family, who hung with him for forty years preaching, will be there. Moses and his brother Aaron and Rahab, Ruth, and Naomie are going to be there. Jerimiah and John, Peter, and Paul, and hopefully, you and me and every last child of God will all be in the audience of this big new final space called "the new Jerusalem."

In a world where nothing is exciting anymore, a population and people difficult to be thrilled with, a people who are constantly being poled to show we are heading in the "wrong direction." Take heart, for if you have a relationship with Jesus, He already said, "I am the way." his GPS cannot lead you in the wrong direction. If your destiny relies on social order, the country's direction, or even the world, I cannot vouch for them because the Bible does not. Why would Elohim prepare a new space if the old space is do good? There is a wedding day coming, and it is not far away. There is still an open invitation prepared for anyone who would accept it.

"Prepared for the devil and his angels"

Despite the beauty of heavenly weddings and attendants, sadly, the Bible always presents us with the dark side. Not everyone is going to go to heaven. Not everyone is going to choose Christ. As it was in the days of Noah, there were eating, drinking, and the like until Noah entered the ark, and the door was shut. Jesus reminded His disciples of that tragic reality. Throughout the scriptural narrative, the final separation is given. We hear much in the traditions and songs of Heaven. It is because that is what lifts the soul. However, if I am writing about the prophetic space of Elohim expressed in future preparations, the true balance must include alternative preparation. My point is simple to say here, the expression of preparation for a place prepared to followers of God, it must also be acknowledged that hell is not an idea. It is not an imaginary space. It is not hyperbolic language.

The discourse that brings us here is from Jesus himself responding to a question from His disciples about the "end of the age." In his response, he gave a story about separating those on the left and those on the right. And in so doing, He made clear where one side was going in contrast to the other. He did not just point out the location. However, he added that it was a place that was not prepared for humans. It was a place that He had "prepared for the Devil and his angels [the Devil who before creation started a revolt and was cast out with the angels that followed him] "(Matthew 25:41). So, all those who in their time on Earth did not trust in the living God but follow the one who revolted against Him, they are going to go to that place prepared for him. God prepared a space for his followers. Those who did not follow God will end up in a place that was never prepared for them.

"If He did not spare the ancient world" (2 Peter 2: 5).

"In Those Days" (1 Samuel 3:1)

To survive, individuals must be conscious of "times" or the "days" they live. They determine who we are and who we are becoming. We are neither alone nor isolated from our times. We are shaped by our times. We are all shaped by what determined the "*in those days*" biblical reference to life." So, 1 Samuel introduced us to the gravity influence of our times. "In those days the word of the Lord was rare; there were not many visions" (1 Sam3:1). In this, the prophet Samuel looked back as did the Apostle Peter looked back to the ancient world to show how Elohim is preparing for their deliverance from the great suffering in which they were enduring (2 Peter 2).

"*My times are in your hands*" (Psalms 31:11).

The Psalmist understood this perspective: God is One who prepares. With knowledge, his life was shaped. He said, "*You, God, are my God. Earnestly I seek you, my whole being longs for you, in a dry and parched land where there is no water*" (Psalm 63: 1-4). "*I will praise you as long as I live.*" It is a way of saying I will praise you all eternity. "*Your word, Lord, is eternal. It stands firm in the heavens. Your faithfulness continues through all generations. You established the earth, and it endures* (Psalm 119:89,90). It is no small thing that God is not caught off guard. He knows the times in every generation, is prepared, and provides accordingly.

"*Do not boast about tomorrow*" (Proverbs 27:1).

Do not boast about tomorrow, for you do not know what a day may bring.

Solomon considered the time from a practical perspective. He concluded that in existence, the space of time includes everything. From planting to uprooting, to weep and to laugh; to mourn and to dance for birth and death, for living and dying, "*there is time for everything and a season for every activity under heaven* (3:1-8). He describes a space like a large boulder moving down a steep mountain, unstoppable until it does. Moreover, no one knows when or where. It is still a mystery how much we do not know of our existence. However, Elohim, who knows, provided what we needed to be prepared. One of the important preparations of our times is to be prepared when we no longer have it. When we no longer have this precious *space*, we constantly move through varied spaces of our existence, called *time*.

Preparation For What? Isaiah, Daniel, Hosea, Miriam, Joel, …

Like watchmen and women on the walls all day and night, these were ordinary men and women called to an extraordinary task—Prophets and Prophetess of Elohim. They stood in historical space and time with eyes that saw beyond themselves and their time. They stood with ears open to hear from God and tell a message not of their own minds but that of their God. Like weather reporters, they stood in the storms of their day and told the people about the severe storms of things yet to come. Like hurricane and tornado warnings, with coming force, no one can withstand them without His unique space of protection in the Messiah.

Despite their varied periods and times of ministry, there was one recurring theme, one recurring message, and one recurring warning: Prepare for the coming day of the Lord. Prepare for the Day of the Lord. Justice and judgment are coming for the wayward ways of His people and all those who turn their ways away from His truth. The great "day of the Lord is near," as they told the people to prepare.

Isaiah: At a time when Israel was losing their way, the spoke of a future where *"All the stars in the sky will be dissolved, and the heavens rolled up like a scroll; all the starry host will fall like withered leaves from the cine, like shoveled figs from the fig tree"* (Isaiah 34:8). They thought of him as a troubler of Israel for the warnings he gave. *"For the Lord has a day of vengeance, a year of retribution, to uphold Zion cause."* Some things endure even time: *"The grass withers and the flowers fall, but the word of our God endures forever."* A Change of Space: "A new heaven and a new earth." Isaiah saw this change of *space*. He saw a *space* change: "Former *things will not be remembered, nor will they come to mind"* (Isaiah 65:17-25). He sought to tell the people the truth to be prepared and free from future disasters. Furthermore, He told them with uncommon eloquence that a Deliverer was coming, although His people would ignore Him (Isaiah 53).

Daniel: He spoke much of preparation for the broad sweeping landscape of nations. He laid out the historical successions of the present and future. He saw far and long into the future. He gave us information about our world to prepare us for it. His declarations of the end of time are today's news. Daniel, who began as an interpreter of dreams and visions, had many dreams and visions and dreams of his own.

He saw four beasts revealed to be four nations, all represented by different beasts. Later, this development of future world history was seen through the image of a man with different types of earthly materials representing Nations and rulers in the flow of future history. His contribution to revelation for our preparation is like giving us where to find water in the desert landscape of our time and what is yet to come.

The point to remember from Daniel's revelation of preparation is that there is a continuum of space of nations, civilizations, or times, of periods of significance of future/historical spaces coming upon the earth. Spaces that, if understood and appreciated, can determine who we are who we are becoming, and who we want to be

Hosea 9:7: "The days of punishment are coming. The days of reckoning are at hand. Let *Israel know this. "In such a time yet future "they would say to the mountains cover us and to the hill fall on us." such is the times that we will face. (10:8; 12) "Sow righteousness for yourself, reap the fruits of unfailing love, and break up your unplowed ground, **for it is time to seek the Lord until he comes and shower his righteousness on you.**

Joel 1:15 *"The Day of the Lord is near"* 3:14 *"Multitude, multitude, in the valley of decision, for the day of the Lord is near in the valley of decision"* (Joel 3:14). There are many "valleys" recorded in scriptures. The popular ones include Ezekiel's *Valley of Dry Bones and David's reference to one of the most popular Psalms, "Valley of the Shadows of Death."* Joel's Valley of a Future Period of Time is less popular but nevertheless most informative of our world today. He spoke of a figurative valley of indecisiveness. He spoke of a valley in which time it would be most necessary to decide because the 'Day of the Lord" would be eminent. However, a time when great numbers of people of the earth will gather in this valley of indecisiveness. A valley where the people were not prepared because they simply could not decide who they wanted to serve Heaven or hell—Hope or despair—God or money—The broad way or the narrow way that leads to Life.

Obadiah 1:15: "The day of the Lord is near for all nations." They were men and women steeped in the exclusive traditions of Israel from the time of Abraham. They considered themselves large or small a voice to their people. However, we will foretell relationship space unthinkable—that God's day is coming for Israel and all nations. Little people spoke of a time when God's message would be freely spoken to all "nations." This is no small thing.

Micah 4: *"In the Last Days"* Prophets after prophets tell of this time call *"In the last days."*

(SLA -Suggestion for Life Application)

- Since Elohim demonstrated His Space of preparation for the end of days, I contend, it is wise to do the same. As the ancient Prophet Amos said, "Prepare to meet thy God" (Amos 4:12 KJV).
- It is a coming appointment each of us must keep. Let's be ready and help others to be ready!
- If you know what time the "Day of the Lord" would be what would you start doing to prepare for that specific time?
- Think about what special talent or skills you have that you can use to prepare yourself or others for the "Day of the Lord."
- Live as if the "Day of the Lord" is going to be today.

16

Elohim Space of Prophetic Revelation—*Precepts*

PRECEPTS

<u>8</u>

(Luke 21:28)

There are overlaps in the flow of these spaces, as shown graphically above at the start of this section. The distinctions highlight the unique forms of expressions that the Bible writers historically gave them. As stated, this is an effort to take the *Timothy Trail* approach of "rightly dividing the word of truth" (2 Timothy 2:15).

Some of the uniqueness of these divisions can be subtle yet very applicable when discovered to personal understanding and development. They are like wisdom teachings, often hidden just beneath the surface of what we think we know. Teaching may be subtle, but hopefully, they will be informative and applicable to personal development. The idea of prophetic revelation through precepts is to seek out those sayings or teachable expressions that look to the future in the Holy Scriptures. Sometimes, they are less obvious than a promise, parable, prayer, or prediction. However, hidden in the narrative, if one looks with a focused eye, such as through the eyes of precepts like gems, they are discovered and can change our perceptions and lives. The following are but a few of them. There is much more than what can be considered here.

- ✓ Check One: "Be sure your sins shall find you out"
- ✓ Do not wait until you meet God to meet Him. Meet Him now. Live with Him now. Serve Him now. Death bed confession is not guaranteed.
- ✓ *Life is a continual gift each day. It is death that comes but once. It is death that needs the* bulk of preparation.
- ✓ History is heading someplace.
- ✓ Your happiest days are ahead of you if you know Jesus as your Savior. It may sound old and outdated. But sometimes, the best of truth and values seem that way.
- ✓ PROVERBS 27: Do not boast about tomorrow, for you do not know what a day may bring.

Choice and Consequence

Even a casual reading of the Bible reveals it is a Book of precepts. It reveals principles and rules that guide the reader down the right path. Here are a few receipts that deal with the future outcome of present behavior.

Look at the Book:

You plant wickedness you reap evil (Proverbs 1:31).

Do not be deceived: God cannot be mocked. A man reaps what he sows. Whoever sows to please their flesh, from the flesh will reap destruction; whoever sows to please the Spirit, from the Spirit will reap eternal life (Galatians 6:7-8).

"God is Not Mocked"

One does not have to have a law degree to conclude that the courts can sometimes make a mockery of its citizens. In principle, one would think that justice would be justice in practice. However, it is often revealed throughout history to this day do not treat everyone the same under the law. It is not too hard to say. In some cases, it is deadly wrong. In many cases, justice is raised up like a flag in full mask and used as mockery by some groups.

Even Jesus suffered mockery from both religious and human court justice. He carried a cross in mockery. A crown of thorns was placed on his head in pain and mockery. The same was true with nails pierced in His hands and feet, and He was raised on a cross in Mockery. Soldiers participated in gambling at His feet. They did it in mockery. The entire system of Jesus' trial was an exercise in religious hypocrisy and civil mockery. They tried and convicted One who did no wrong. The crucifixion stands for many things, but let it not be missed that it stands for the flagrant failure of human justice, religious and civil—especially volatile when they intersect as it did with Jesus—an innocent Man crucified.

However, what is my point here? In the end, Jesus will have the last word for all who did Him wrong. He will come again not as a Savior of humankind but as a Judge of all the earth. I believe the force of God's coming justice is the force of the context of the treatment of the human's court system with His Son: I contend, in the times of the end of time in His court when all shall stand before Him, there will be no such miscarriage of Justice: "Those who sow to the flesh shall of the flesh reap corruption. Those who sow to the Spirit shall of the Spirit reap eternal life (Galatians 6:8 KJV).

Judgment begins in the beginning by dealing with sin and ends in the future by dealing with its outcome. The precept is that the condition or sin will not go unpunished. From the beginning, God told humankind that they had choices but would have consequences. There would be consequences when spaces crashed into each other when spaces were held accountable for the ones they made.

The idea that humankind can do whatever they want, whenever they want, is not a biblical teaching or concept. Among men, the idea is to express or do something to break the law, whether moral or civil, as long as one does not get caught or can get away with it. However, this contradicts the biblical prophetic precept: "Be sure your sins will find you out" (Numbers 32:23).

"What you reap you so" cf. 2 Co 9:6 and Galatians 6:7 God is not mocked you reap what you sow.

"Be sure your sin will find you out"

Many people find solace in secrecy. It is the idea that some things are private and should remain that way. As a fashion and celebrity photographer, I remember that many years ago, there were rules of the game. One of them I remember is never to take a photo of a celebrity in the act of eating; among other things, I follow the rules. Even celebrities have private moments they want to keep private. You may have been given an "all access" pass, but it comes with the knowledge if you want to be invited back, you do not reveal everything you "think" you see. Again, the context of my point is that Elohim is all access. He sees and knows everything. Everything you ever did is going to be on His Facebook of life. Everything with be exposed. The right to privacy does not apply to sin. In the judgment, you are either covered by the blood of Christ, or you are exposed.

IN PRECEPTS OR PRONOUNCEMENTS Teachings of His coming"

LUKE 21: Signs of the time

Before long, the world would not see me anymore, but you would see me. Because I live, you also will live. This is a space in the ultimate perspective - which is a space of the Spirit and of Jesus Christ and a place in us that they choose to occupy. They pull me in, and I am on a space of unworthiness. The more I see His glory in me, the more I see it is but the value that he himself placed on me to live here. I have no furnishing that would make him desire me other than what he himself put there. Spaces of the heart, body, and soul. There are many things in Scripture that I believe without having the ability to understand it all. My understanding is adequate but incomplete. ACTS 1:7 "It is not for you to know the times or the date the Father has set by his on authority." The next verse, 8, gave us spaces in geography and time. ACTS: 2 As the Spirit began to move among the assemble, there were strange behavior patterns, much more for a drunken party than a religious one. So, the apostle Peter felt the need first to 1) Give a defense of the behavior that was not of a drunken stupor, as it was "only nine in the morning." but in a more positive defense, it was a 2) Development of what the prophet Joel predicted would occur "In the last days, God said I will pour out my Spirit on all people...."(Acts 2:). The Deliverance that was promised v. 21: "And everyone who calls on the name of the Lord will be saved." Then 4) He went on to DECLEAR the Gospel through Christ Jesus. ACTS 13:36 "Now when David had served God's purpose in his own generation, he fell asleep; he was buried with his ancestors

Romans 13 11-14 "The day of the Lord is near." Each will give an account to God (v.14).

1 TH 3: 5b). "I was afraid that in some way the tempter had tempted you and that our labors might have been in vain." Here, the Apostle was not above being afraid that bad stuff could happen. He was human, and it comes with its own challenges. Good for us, he did not fear admitting his fears in the ministry. 1 Thessalonians

4:13, the Apostle Paul wrote, "Brothers and sisters, we do not want you to be uninformed about those who sleep [the space of death for the believer is described as "those who sleep] in death so that you do not grieve like the rest of mankind, who have no hope. (v.4). For we believe that Jesus died and rose again, and so we believe that God will bring with Jesus those who have fallen asleep in him (v.15).

According to the Lord's word, we tell you that we who are still alive, who are left until the coming of the Lord, will certainly not precede those who have fallen asleep 16 For the Lord himself will come down from heaven, with a loud command, with the voice of the archangel and with the trumpet call of God. And the dead in Christ will rise first. After that, we who are still alive and left will be caught up with them in the clouds to meet the Lord in the air. And so, we will be with the Lord forever. Therefore encourage one another with these words. 1 Thessalonians 5:1--3 "Now, brothers and sisters, about the times and dates we do not need to write to you, for you know very well that the day of the Lord will come like a thief at night. While people are saying "Peace and safety," destruction will come on them suddenly, as labor pains on a pregnant woman, and they will not escape.

11 Peter 3: 8, The Day of the Lord to come And the elements will melt with a fervent heat. Fire is coming…. v12 cf. 2 Peter 1: "when we told you about the coming of our Lord Jesus Christ in power." Here we also see a description of eternal space where past, present, and future collide in the present. With God, both past and future extremes exist in His present aspect. The human mind or logic cannot fathom it. However, it was not meant to be a logical analysis, just to be a glimpse of God's full awareness of everything past, present, and future. It is not an issue or problem with Him.

17

Elohim Space of Prophetic Revelation—*Purpose*

A Purpose Behind the Promises

These elements were considered in these essays, and I did not impose them on the Scriptures. The alliterations came from the Scriptures, as indeed they should be. Each one has a biblical and prophetic meaning and application. That is what I am considering here. So, as we come to this matter of *prophetic purpose, What is it that is being considered*? Or, to be more specific, what do the Scriptures have to say about the prophetic purpose? Here is a passage by the writer of Hebrews 6: 17-20 with my highlighted emphasis on the point of this essay:

*Because God wanted to make the **unchanging nature of his purpose** very clear to the heirs of what was promised, He confirmed it with an oath. God did this so that, by two unchangeable things in which it is impossible for God to lie, we who have fled to take hold of the hope set before us may be encouraged. We have **this hope as an anchor for the soul**, firm and secure. It enters the inner sanctuary behind the curtain, where our forerunner, Jesus, has entered on our behalf.*

Let us once again look at the Bible study method of the "Timothy Trail"—rightly dividing this passage to see what treasures the anchor of our souls are depositing for us.

First, we get at the theme, the framing, or the story world, of this passage. It is concerning what Elohim did to expressed the secure nature of what He promised. It is about Elohim wanting to describe the nature of this *purpose space*. Elohim is describing this space, so we have no doubt of its nature. Now let us break it down further. In brief: it is about What God wanted us to know about this unique prophetic *purpose space*:

o A ***Perfect*** **purpose:** "*to make his purpose clear purpose.* A purpose that is explicit, and without ambiguity. It is to give His Kingdom people clarity of His revelation purpose, and its establishment in truth.

o A ***Perpetual*** purpose. It is perpetual because a God who can change all things is Himself unchangeable. He does not change by changing circumstances. Therefore, His established purpose is expressed as "*the unchanging nature of His purpose*"

o A ***Provisional*** purpose. The revelation of His purpose is not arbitrary. It was and is established as an inheritance of His people: "to the heirs of what was promised." He wanted to make sure His promised inheritance goes to the right people. Here Elohim is again emphasizing how important relationship is to Him. His gifts and provisions are established on the relationship between Him and His children.

o A ***Pronounced*** or declared purpose. This is so that His people and the whole world can hear it. So, He "*confirmed it with an oath.*" It is a binding pronouncement of His purpose. An "oath" connects this communication with His Holy Character. It connects the purpose based on His Personal character. There is no God if there is no future as predicted and promised. His purpose is true and true. "*unchangeable things in which it was impossible for God to lie.*" This is the standard in which there can be no alternative truth.

o A ***Practica***l Purpose. God's revelation of future space could not be like leaves shaken in the wind— follow wherever the wind blows. It could not be like the waves flowing and returning and constantly moving, for the waves, which is what they do. They move, but not so with the revelational purposes of God. We can "take hold" of Elohim's purpose space. For like the anchor of a ship that sinks deep to the floor of the ocean, anchored in a rock. We can hold on like a ship at sea, holding steady because of the surety of its anchor" for the soul, *firm* and *secure.*

o A ***Penetrating and Powerful*** purpose "*It enters the inner sanctuary behind the curtain….*"

Elohim Secret Purpose

It was and is a penetrating and powerful purpose of Elohim that had the capacity to disrupt generations of religious thought traditions and even teachings. It would rip across religious lines, tribal ways, and laws. His purpose was to shatter all racial lines and social status, and some were going to be angry enough to kill to maintain the established social order. People, some of His choice servants, were going to shed blood trying to fulfill this purpose. Elohim had held His own purpose. Held it close to His heart. He kept it a secret from Genesis to Jesus. No one knew his secret mission.

Even when angels sang at the birth of Jesus, they did not include this hidden purpose in their chorus. They sang about Jesus but not about Elohim's ultimate determination because he kept it a secret even from His angels. Even when Jesus openly declared His mission in the Temple, no one even got a hint. Up to Pentecost and the coming of the Holy Spirit in spectacular fashion, even then, Elohim held a council. Even then, He kept this radical world-changing purpose a secret. Hidden in the mystery of the ages, it was made known in secret to the Apostle Paul before it was made known to the Church. This wonderful mystery almost split this young ragtag group of disciples when it was revealed. What was this mystery hidden from prophets, priests, kings, and the people as well?

Elohim had a long purpose that in His Church, Jews, and Gentiles (all non-Jews) would be "heirs of what was promised," members of one body, and in His church through Jesus and in His Kingdome, there would be "distinction in Christ." All from every tribe, every language, every nation, all who would come to Jesus would fully participate as **heirs of what was promised:** Jews and Gentiles bond and free for will be all one in Jesus" Here is how the Apostle explained the world. Best kept secret (*and, still is today when looking at the typical composition of local churches*):

It was not until Jesus confronted a Pharisee named Saul (before Jesus changed his name to Paul), a man bent on crashing the young church community, that Jesus revealed His secret purpose held from Abraham through all the Fathers and prophets they prophesied and did not know the ultimate perspective of their mission. It was and often still is the world's best-kept Greek word, "Evangelion," from which we get the word to evangelize – to share the good news of the Gospel. ("Behold I bring you "good tidings of great joy" is what the angels sang at the birth of Jesus. (a word first associated with Jesus, never in association with any political or national movement). It is the reason the first four books of the New Testament are called the "gospels." — meaning "good news" of the Gospel). It was particularly "good news" for the Gentile world, which was never thought of as being included in its purpose. It was considered the mystery of the ages revealed through the Apostle Paul, a dual citizen Jewish and Gentile. He was imprisoned because, as a Jew, he ministered the "good news" (Evangelion)" to the Gentiles.

Look at the Book to see how Paul revealed it. (Ephesians 3: 1-9):

For this reason, I, Paul, the prisoner of Christ Jesus for the sake of you Gentiles—Surely you have heard about the administration of God's grace that was given to me for you, that is, mystery made known to me by revelation… This mystery is that through the gospel, the Gentiles are heirs together of one body, and sharers together in the promise of Jesus Christ…. this grace was given me to preach to the Gentiles the boundless riches of Christ….

Elohim's Purpose Here

- HIS CHURCH – Elohim's immediate purpose was to leave His followers here for each to be the world's light and salt of the Earth.
- His followers were to be as one, and He and the Father are one. It is for what He prayed. So that a watching world when they look at the church would see Him.

  His purpose was to leave us here to show to the world how to love. "By this shall all men know you are my disciples if you love one another (John 13:35).

His purpose is for us to take the good news to the ends of the earth. It was His final command to the young movement: "Wait in Jerusalem...you shall receive power (Luke 24:49).

- His purpose was to "keep us to the end so that we may be blameless on the Day of Our Lord (1 Corinthians 1:8)

Elohim Ultimate Purpose

- His ultimate purpose is not to leave us here. And that is dead or alive when He returns. This is no longer our home.
- He is preparing us here for something better there. The Apostle said (1 Corinthians 9:24) Earthly crown does not last. There is a heavenly crown (symbolic of participating in his reign), one waiting for each believer.
- All God has for each of His followers is in a world used for that purpose. "Salvation" means everything God has for us. 1 Corinthians 13:11-12)
- His purpose is to demonstrate the "incomparable riches of His grace" (Ephesians 1:21; 2:7)
  His purpose is to see that the work that He has begun in us is completed Philippians 1:6).
- 1 Co 13: 11 "The hour had already come for you to wake up from your slumber because our salvation is nearer now than when we first believed" c.12 "The night is nearly over; the day is almost here. So let us put aside the deeds of darkness and put on the armor of life." The language of space is used for understanding.../ this language also continues in the following verses. 12,3,
- TWO AGES" Present age and the one to come" (Ephesians 1:21); 2:7 "in order that in the coming age, he might show the incomparable riches of his grace...

(SLA -Suggestion for Life Application)

The Believer must understand and live in this space that Elohim ultimate purpose is not to leave us here.
In many regards we must learn to live here as strangers. Examples of how:
Give some of what you earn to others, thereby laying up treasures in heaven.
Learn to practice forgiveness. We want God to forgive us our depts we must forgive others starting with our families, friends, co-workers and even enemies.

18

Elohim Space of Prophetic Revelation—*Practice*

What are we to do with prophecy? How will we respond as prophetic wave after wave comes ashore in our time? How are we to weather the storms of *things to come*? Indeed, how can we weather the storm of things already here?

In our effort to understand Elohim's revelations of Himself, we come to a unique space—the space of *practice*. As we have an "overlap" of spaces, as is noted in the graphics above, each dimension of Elohim spaces, although overlapped, is to understand relationships and distinction. So, what is distinctive of "practice" in revealing Elohim? It is that someone practices something with a focus on themselves. You do not practice a given sport to gain an understanding of the coach. However, that is the revelational uniqueness of this biblical form of "practice." The object of this practice is to understand the "Coach better." It is to deepen the understanding and relationship in the past, present, and future by practice, practice, and practice. Let me illustrate this with two prophetic practices commanded by Jesus in historical space and time for all believers of all time.

The Practice Of *Prophetic Posture*

"Look up!" (Luke21:28)

Let me continue with this sports analogy. It is like Coach Jesus giving us a prophetic posture, one for our times. In any sport, posture is one of the first things learned. If you come to play with a bad posture—no matter your stats, you must unlearn it and get the right posture to get to the next level. Bad "posture" and body alignment relative to the task will only get you so far. The coach will first teach you how to align your body for action. Whether to throw a ball, or to hit it, if you do not first get the posture, it becomes difficult to get the play.

So, Jesus is telling his disciples that at the end of days, there are going to be many events that will arise. These events could range from spiritually distracting to dangerous. They can make you "miss the ball." If you are not careful, they can make you lose heart. So, He gave them a posture to practice that can guide them to see Him in the various events coming at us, whether good or bad. A prophetic posture is needed. Elohim knows what is coming. He wants us to exist in the right prophetic space for our own survival—yes! But for His glory.

So, we can be necessary to survive. till maintain the practice of Posture., receipt, an act, a teaching that can guide them through these events that come at the end of the age.

Look at the Book:

When these things begin to happen, [signs of the time] **stand up and lift up your heads, because your redemption is drawing near"** (Luke 21:28, emphasis mine)

The "posture" given by Jesus to His followers is clear. When they end times events including "wars and rumors of wars" and "pestilence" [like on a global scale as Covid] and other signs of troubled times, the posture in dealing with the various perilous times is to "Stand up and lift up your heads." What does that mean? We can let Scripture interpret Scripture:

I lift up my eyes to the hills. From where does my help come? My help comes from the LORD the Maker of heaven and earth (Psalm121:1-2 Cf. vv. 3-8, BSB emphasis mine).

Jesus is giving an important guide. He taught the posture for the end of time is to look up. It is not a looking up to ignore what is going on around. It is not a "look up" of indifference to social needs around us. It is a *looking up to get strength* to help others and carry out our mission. It is a looking up to gain the hope and strength to endure what is going on. It is a looking up as an old song refrain said, *"Turn your eyes upon Jesus. Look full in His wonderful face, and the things of this earth will grow strangely dim in the light of His glory and grace"*

This looking up can be physical. It is the kind of verse that a Shepperd boy or one working among the rouged terrains of valleys, the fields, and mountain and waterfalls of the monument of grandeur can produce such verses. However, this is not a song on the level of *happy talk.* No! This is from a space where the Psalmist sees vicious lions roaming. Ultimately, this is a spiritual "look up" for a "hook-up" to where our strength comes from. "My strength comes from the LORD, the Maker of heaven and earth."

Practice of the Prophetic Supper

"Do This!" (1 Corinthians 11:23-26 emphasis mine)

"For I received from the Lord what I pass on to you: The Lord Jesus, on the night he was betrayed, took bread, and when he had given thanks, he broke it and said, Take, eat; This is My body which is for you; **do this in remembrance of me.** *In the same way, after supper, He took the cup, saying, "This cup is the new covenant in My blood.* **Do this whenever you drink it, in remembrance of me.**

For whenever you eat this bread and drink this cup, you proclaim the Lord's death until he comes."

These instructions invite us to engage in an important Jesus-established ritual that seems outside our present turbulent, busy space. We are invited to pause as one would for breakfast, lunch, or supper. It is difficult to engage in such while on the fly. In some homes, selected ones are important for family time. In the large family in which I grew up, there were no tables large enough to seat everyone, so we were scattered wherever we could find a place to pause, and even so, we ate together. It was like Jesus gathered His spiritual family and appeared in the "upper room" where Jesus participated in the Passover meal—Reflect Remember to Report This ritual of the Lord's Supper and its precepts could easily not be seen in a prophetic light. For one thing, its prophetic teaching is intrinsic to the past. Jesus, in His private time with the Apostle Paul, established this unique ceremony for the church, and they were to do this "in remembrance of Me." On its surface, it seems like a ritual of remembrance. However, the precept from the ceremony is not limited to remembrance. Paul gave the precept: You do two things whenever you eat this bread and drink this cup. One, you proclaim the Lord's death and the key to this precept "until He comes." The beauty of this special ceremony is the overlapping spaces that it brings together as one: Remembering Christ's death in historical space, proclaiming this death in the present, and thinking at the same time of His eventual return. In these times, this ritual should be participated in often. (During COVID, we were all closed off from our usual fellowship. As I was alone, I practiced the Lord's Supper several times a week. It became such a personal and precious time to remember the Lord in this special ceremony; to stop now would be like moving away from a close relationship I have come to cherish. So, I never stop. Covid may be gone, but Christ is closer).

Despite the fact that one of His own betrayed Him, he still wanted to have family time with them.

SLA: Suggestion for Life Application

- I recommend making the communion ceremony personal. It commemorates the death of our Savior, symbolically proclaiming it in the present while looking towards His coming.

- I use fat-free water crackers as symbolic of the unleavened bread of ancient times. I also selected the wine (or bread) our Jewish brothers and sisters used for their Passover Celebration. I am mindful that it was during the Jewish Passover that Jesus participated with His disciples in this special ceremony we now call the Lord's Supper or Communion. I have often sought the council of a Rabi friend for what precepts I can learn from such overlapping spaces.

19

ELOHIM SPACE OF PROPHETIC REVELATION—*PROVISION*

I contend to understand the ultimate provision for God's creation, beyond any human's intellect to grasp. If we cannot now understand all the provisions of our Earth—not to mention the uncharted Cosmic Universe, how could we even venture to understand much of anything about Heaven? How could we grasp beyond what the Black Spirituals envisioned in their songs, rich with hope and aspirations about a place provided "*when We get over*" to this place and *space* "*beyond Jordon's stormy banks?*" How can we form an adequate image of a *space* where no one travels on dusty slave trails of blood and death, but the inhabitants are transformed into a place with "*streets of Gold?*" A place where all God's children can *take off their shoes* and walk all over His "*Habon?*" How could we fathom such a provision in our modern conveniences? How can we radically change our modern perspective to envision such a provision of Heaven? Do we even dare to try?

Keep Heaven Real

I heard a preacher of my youth describe heaven in a way that got my attention. And I was never able to shake off his description, as I had done so many other religious things in my youth. His words were real, raw, and down to earth with sincerity and concern. He said *if you were to go there, you would not have to call for a doctor because no one ever gets sick. You would not have to call for emergency attention because no accidents of any kind ever happen. You would not have to call the police officers on anyone, for no such thing happens that you would ever need them. There are no lawless people there, and no crimes of any kind are there. There is no need for repairs of any kind everything works.* And he ended with the unforgettable statement: *No one ever calls for an undertaker there, for no one ever dies.* I listened and thought I did not know much about heaven, but if what this preacher said was true, it was enough for me. I want to go there.

I am now a man up in age. I have read and studied what God has provided for His children. I have learned much since my youth and have seen many days of trouble. I have experienced much in this world. Some that often drives me to tears just thinking about this journey. As David described it like in the valley of the shadows of death. These have only enhanced to appreciation of this old preacher's insights to describe to me in my youth this unforgettable place etched in a sacred place in my soul. Even before I knew what to do to get there, God was already preparing the way for that meeting. He had already provided for me and for all who desire Him. Through all the ways I have researched and studied the way and the provisions of Heaven. With all my extended research and studies, there is nothing; no Theology has improved on that preacher's description of heaven as a place and space where all the multitudes of ills and troubled circumstances we live with daily in this world are gone. As one gospel songwriter Curtis Stewart (First recorded by Johnson Family Singers, 1948) humbly requested, *"Lord, build me a cabin in the corner of Glory land."* He was keeping it real.

I do not need to know all the magnificent details of this cosmic universe to believe in God and the unimaginable provision for those who love Him. It is beyond human's capacity to comprehend Elohim's ultimate provision for the future. He taught us to pray in this world: "Give us this day our daily bread." However, He does not ask us to pray for that which is to come of future provision. That is beyond what we are asking or envision what He has prepared. Notwithstanding, let me yet offer some additional revelation and description of what this chapter bravely announced in its opening title. That is a limited essay on Elohim's future revelation of His provision.

What is Elohim Building for the Future?

Let me take a less emotive approach and a more reasoned review. As a builder, I know that you need a great architect to build something great. You also need a good engineer on your team because the structure must achieve the intended occupancy. Of course, if the building is in Heaven, there are no structural concerns to contend with like down here. No earthquakes, no tornadoes, tropical storms, and wind loads or uplift to contend with. However, you most certainly need a designer with artistic flair and abilities. And looking at the world in all its glory, who can suggest anyone greater than Elohim, the Almighty Creator? Truly, who is most capable of designing Heaven? In our world, we see beauty as even a gift to us of form and function. I contend that Heaven is going to be immensely spectacular from this reasoned perspective.

Taken from a different view. I do not know what kind of ark Noah built. However, Elohim will have to up His production and design plan. For one thing, imagine a place beautiful and vast enough to house all the saints of all time from different cultures and styles. And if Heaven in anything it would be a pleasure to be. However, when I look up at an endless sky when I hear and see the vast galaxies seemingly uninhabited, I know He has the space he needs to make this vast project happen. He can do it. Just look up. There will be no sign warning "oversized Load." Since John saw the New Jerusalem coming down from heaven, the production team has cleared the way for eternity to begin. And there is only one name for the credits: King of Kings and Lord of Lords.

We know from biblical hints that the production team is already at work now. This place would not be made of any earthly materials. We know this Earth was contaminated with sin. It is like wood left out in the rain or iron left out in the sun. No material of this world can be used on Heaven's construction site. The prophets said there would be a new heaven and a new earth. No used items will be employed there. Even God's children cannot get there without a material body change. It will be a change from the body material from the earth to a new body material not of this space (Corinthians 15). If it is one thing made clear as to what Elohim is providing, everything shall be made new. There will be no new wine in old bottles and no new creation in the old flesh. Elohim is not going to recycle us. He will make all things new. That which is born of the flesh is the flesh. That which is born of the Spirit is Spirit. This spiritual process is called a "new birth" because it is new. What is provided in Heaven will be consistent with what is now new in us. It is what makes us strangers in this world. Therefore, our new creation is not of this world and does not belong here anymore (2 Corinthians 5:17).

A Look at the Body Now

He said we will all have a "new creation" (2 Corinthians 5:17"). Then He said He is going to provide a Body to go with our new creation. The corruptible must put on incorruptible and the mortal immortal" for we shall be changed (1 Corinthians 15). There are no used parts here on this heavenly production line. There are no replacement parts either. There are no hearts to beat that can stop. No brains that can deuterate. There will be no exercise needed to stay fit. No garbage to take out, for no waste is ever produced.

At a loss to write this essay, I took my lead from the old preacher who had already gone to this place he described. I find it a lost effort to try, with any increased skills, to describe heaven in any way that would be different from the space this man described. In the end, I learned from this preacher's approach to describing heaven: If you try to say heaven is this or that with all the positive things in Paradise, I did not get it. In our world, at any moment when we think of paradise, something will soon come to bring us back to reality. Although I am positive, I must confess that I best envision heaven and how great and blissful heaven would be when I think of all the negative stuff left behind here. It is a way of saying Elohim will make everything new. Then I get it. So, think of everything that gave you pause in this world. Things that you wished would go away. Then envision a space without them all. In that space exists some solace and sanctification of what heaven is like. This is what is expressed in the Book: There remains a rest for the people of God. No wonder Elohim, after Creation, is said to have rested.

For example, I did this exercise by thinking about my mom. In her later years, I left the Island of St. Kitts to a nearby island as a teenager to find greater opportunities that were flourishing on other Islands—the American Virgin Island (Just 4 hours by car here, a lifetime by sailboat then). No matter how opportune the place is, it cannot dampen the pain of missing home. So, heaven is like that. It is like never having to feel the loss of those you love. Then, over the years, I would visit once a year at Christmas time. I remember that one year when I had to introduce myself to my mom. My look and my voice were not enough for her to know it was her youngest son who had come to visit. O, the hidden pain of the intermitted question, "Who are you? Words were soft-spoken but hit me like a bolder—pulling me to a devasting reality space and robbing us of any overlapping spaces of who we were to each other. Mom does not know you are. And I remember the old preacher's approach to understanding what heaven must be like. Heaven is a place where I do not have to say, "Mom, it's me, Arnold...you know, your son." And you look in your mother's eyes, searching gently for clues of who you are; at the end of this silent search, finding none. In that space, I feel the depth of what Haven must be like beyond any words to describe it.....

Elohim, in His wisdom, has so designed our body that although it brings us pleasures. It is best known for introducing us to all the things we loathe. Shakespeare spent his skills as a playwright exploring this tragic situation of the human condition. In the third soliloquy, his most famous line in Macbeth, "to be or not to be," brings into dramatic focus the life tensions that can cause questions as to whether Macbeth should live or die. In the famous American poem "Life," Paul Lawrence Dunbar spoke about the troubles in life and the often out-of-proportion sadness that comes with it. "A minute to smile and an hour to weep in," along with "a pint of joy and a peck of trouble" and the thought that never a laugh that the morns come tumbling down. Of course, all of life is not sad. It is both joy and sadness. However, it is the nature of life that the sadness has long and lasting memories, while the joys of life seem so momentary. My point, however, is this. Elohim has provided a life to come when all this sad side of life will be no more. To understand God is to understand this significant, lasting, and eternal provision of joy, unspeakable and full of glory.

A New Body is Coming

This is not out of some science fiction movie. All of Elohim's children will be provided with a new and vastly improved body. It will be like one description says, "the glorious body of the Lord Jesus Christ" (Philippians 3:21). The one that traveled to the third Heaven to greet His Father after the resurrection, a lightyear journey of unfathomable distance. They say the light of some stars is just getting here since the so-called "big bang." Billions and Billions of lightyears that Jesus in his new Body did like a weekend trip to see His Father. Within three days. Moreover, that also included a trip in the other direction. Just this body's "physical" quality and what it will be made of is unthinkable. However, Jesus and the other disciples and Apostles who wrote about it reported it like everyday news. On the first day of the week, the ladies who went to look at His body thought they were seeing a ghost. That is, until He spoke, they understood that voice to be that of the Jesus he knew. However, in a new body without any connection to Mary but to the cross, for he maintained in this new body the nail prints in His hands from the cross. All Elohim's children will see those prints in His hand as a reminder of His great love.

There will be no production of pain or loneliness there. Pause and think about all the things you see and hate in this world and imagine Heaven as a place and space without it all—every *darn* last bit of it!

"Fear Him…" (Luke 12:1-12)

Jesus gave one of the most definitive declarations on the final end of His follower's body found in the Scriptures.

The Setting of the Teaching:

The framing of Jesus' teaching on the physical body of believers began with an act of deliverance of a man whose body was not working for him to speak. It was a body without a voice. Jesus declared that the reason the man was mute was because a mute demonic spirit took up residence in the man's body. Luke did not see it as important to mention without request, or if the man did. He just told us how Jesus reached out to the man and cast the mute spirit out.

The man began to speak to the amazement of hundreds of people gathered to hear Jesus. However, not everyone was amazed by this miracle. Luke noted, "But some of them said, 'By Beelzebul, the prince of demons, he is casting out demons" (Luke 11:14, 15). After this encounter, the crowds, which were already large, began to increase in numbers. Jesus continue to teach in this hostile context (Luke 11:53). Jesus began to focus the attention of His teaching on the vulnerability of the Christian bodies in a hostile world. He warned His followers against unbelief. In this context, he also had the strongest words against the religious leaders of His day. However, in the middle of all this, he focused on his disciples and with lessons about the body and its future. Here is a summary of what Jesus taught about the body as a context for his prophetic statement on the body:

- **The Body needs Light to be Healthy**. "no one lights a lamp and puts it in a place where it will be hidden or under a bowl. Instead, they put it on a stand so that those who come in may see the light. Your eye is the lamp of your body. When your eyes are healthy, your whole body also is full of light. However, when they are unhealthy, your body also is full of darkness (Luke 11:33-35).
- **The Light Within:** "See to it, then, that the light within you is not darkness. Therefore, if your whole body is full of light, and no part of it is dark, it would be just as full of light as when a lamp shines its light on you (v.36).
- **Examples of Darkness (Luke 11:**39-52) Jesus brought to the attention of his followers how "the Pharisees and the teachers of the law began to oppose him [Jesus] fiercely." They who were most familiar (or should be) with the Law and the Prophets set themselves up against Israel's greatest Prophet, Jesus Christ. In so doing became the symbol of a physical body dressed up on the outside with horrible darkness on the inside. A darkness that exists in opposition to the Light of the world. Moreover, Jesus warned His disciples of this dangerous space on that basis.

The Stating of the Teaching (Luke 12: 4)

I have selected the above narratives of Jesus as the "setting" to show how the physical body formed the "framing" of what I believe is Jesus' definitive statement concerning the end of the human body as we know it. So, the setting is a discourse on the body, and now we come to the statement. What was Jesus' definitive statement of the body that no believer should take lightly? Jesus illustrated or framed His statement on the question of who we are to fear.

Look at the Book:

"I tell you my friends, do not be afraid of those who kill the body and after that can do no more. But I will show you whom you should fear: Fear him who, after your body has been killed, has authority to throw you into hell. Yes, I tell you fear him"

(Luke 12:4, emphasis mine)

The Meaning

There is much to unpack here in these words of Jesus. I must then rely on my "Timothy Trail" as a guide. That is attempting to, as the Apostle Paul advised, "rightly divide the word of truth" (2 Timothy 2:15):

- **Division Space One *Relationship*.** Hash and direct words of warning were going to follow. Nevertheless, Jesus wanted His followers to know that ***relationship matters***. He spoke to them from the perspective of personal friendship: "*I tell you **my friends**…* ". It means all Jesus' sayings and warnings and even judgments. When dealing with his followers, He always wanted them to see His space of love and friendship. Immediately after this, he launched into an illustration to show how much he cared more about them than sparrows.

- **Division Space Two – *Fear:*** The disciples were a small group in the middle of thousands of people that day. The religious leaders, from the time he healed a man from demonic possession, considered it an affront to their authority and claimed His authority was from the Devil. They grew hostile even more, and Jesus did not back down but called their hypocrisy out with a series of "woes." I contend Jesus called out "fear" as a follow-up to His relationship in the form of a command so that they gather that they were to pay special attention to not slip into fear. Because if they opposed Him, they would certainly oppose His disciples. So, it would mean that in any circumstance, do not let fear rule you. It is as if Jesus is saying do not fear. We all go through fearful situations but are not to be ruled by them. I was on a country road traveling home when I blew a tire on my truck. I tried to change it, but the lug were stripped. I called AAA for help, but no one in a radius of fifty miles reported trying but no one came. Here I was on an isolated section of the long road home. Hurricane IAN was heading to that area. From 10 AM to the darkness of night in an area where carcasses of alligators littered the road. No water, no food, everything primitive to survive all night. I went to bed in my truck reading a book by St. Augustine's "Confessions" from the fourth. Century. The worshipful spirit of Saint Augustine visits me there in the darkness of the night with a little light to read his works. Moreover, I had no fear of waiting for delivery to come 32 hours after I got stuck on the road.

- **Division Space Three - Fearless:** No fear, particularly "*of those who kill the body.*" There will be those who will come against you, and your body will be their target. They are going to want to destroy your body. Do not fear them. In fear, I have separate "fear" in general as a hindrance to Christian service. However, a different perspective beyond just fear itself, but the specific fear of those who come against your body to destroy you. Do not back down. Furthermore, the reason is the heart of this discourse.

- **Division Space Four - Limitations:** The limitation of your enemy who wants to destroy you. Do not fear them. However, even if they succeed, do not fear them because all they can do is kill your body. Then Jesus makes this astonishing claim to his disciples of what comes after: Jesus is saying do not fear anyone who wants to kill you because when they do, they cannot do any more than that. They are stopped at a "dead end" road when they kill you. However, remember there in that space, do not even then fear, because they top your body yet cannot stop me. I am still here for you even then. Still, fear me, for I have the power of life, death, and judgment even after this point.

- **Division Five – *Your Death is not the end of you or Me.*** It was Jesus, before a Roman secular ruler, who thought he had that kind of authority over life and death. He told Jesus do you not know that I have authority to save you? Jesus replied, "You would have no authority at all except it was given to you" In this teaching, Jesus is encouraging his disciples to realize He is the one to be feared because of the authority He has to control what happens after this world kills their bodies which we shall all face. This world, some slower or faster, kills us. Jesus knows that. Moreover, He means to tell us He, not those who want to kill us, has the last word: "But I show you whom you should fear. Fear Him who, after your body [not you, your body] has been killed, has authority [the same word used by Pilot] to throw you into hell" [very strong words]. Moreover, for emphasis, he repeated, "*Yes, I tell you fear him.*"

- **Final Division – Jesus Cares; Back to Fear (Luke 12: 4-6).**

These, it must be agreed, were some of the strongest words Jesus gave to His disciples. I sometimes wonder what Jesus' thoughts were. Could you not say after they kill you [and that was bad enough], that I have the power to raise you? However, for a reason, I do not think I would ever know, He said, "*I have the power to throw you into hell.*" But I must quickly add I find solace in the words that followed:

Are not five sparrows sold for two pennies? Yet, God has not forgotten one of them. Indeed, the very hairs of your head [your body] are all numbered. Don't be afraid; you [including your body that grows hair] are worth more than many sparrows."

I contend, Elohim is the one who gives value do your body. And that value cannot be destroyed by anyone. So, fear Elohim. His eyes are always on you. And every part of your body, soul, and spirit leave not his attention and care.

SLA: Suggestion for Life Application

- When the world cares come at you hard, see Paradise through them.
- Recall and Reset: When life's troubles come your way, remember they are not the only things coming. Heaven where all your troubles will be over is coming. Jesus said: "In this world you will have tribulation but be of good cheer I have overcome the world.
- He actually said that. Put it to work. Be happy!
- This is how I fight my battles. I pause and think about all the things I see and hate in this world and imagine Heaven as a place and space without it all—every *darn* last bit of it! That is how I fight my battles. I know they will not last.

Elohim will provide a new body.

Do not be afraid being in the one you have.

It will not last, but you and I will; you never beyond my concern and my care.

Luke 12: 1-6

20

ELOHIM SPACE OF PROPHETIC REVELATION—*POWER*

Look at the Book:

*Then the sign of the Son of Man will appear in heaven, and then all the tribes of the earth will mourn, and they will see the Son of Man coming on the clouds of heaven with **power** and great glory (Matthew 24:30).*

Power Predictions

*I saw heaven standing open, and there before me was a white horse whose rider was called Faithful and True. With justice he judges and wages war. **His eyes are like blazing fire [symbols of power], and on his head are many crowns [power and** authority]. He has a name written on him that no one knows but he himself. He is dressed in a **robe dipped in blood** [Jesus' sacrifice], and his name is the **Word of God** [sword of power].*

*The armies of heaven were following him [military power], riding on white horses and dressed in fine linen, white and clean. Coming out of his mouth was a **sharp sword** [power] with which to **strike down the nations. He will rule** power] then with an iron scepter. He threads the winepress of the fury of the wrath of God Almighty [all power]. On his robe and on his thigh he has the name written: **KING OF KINGS AND LORD OF LORDS** [POWER Revelation 19:11-16; 20:1-6 emphasis mine).*

Elohim knows how to make an entrance. We missed the first big one when He hung the world and the entire Universe in space by the word of His power (Hebrews 1:3). But in His Second Coming, He has determined in His sovereign will that the whole of creation will see it. And the specular nature will be a combined space of *power and glory.*

"Vengeance is Mine and I will Repay"

It is one of those power statements that is easy to gloss over while reading. We have so conditioned ourselves to think of Elohim as purely benevolent that we can hardly associate Elohim as possessing "vengeance." So let me do a limited "Timothy Trail" to explain it so that it becomes feasible or necessary to see His *space of vengeance.* Our lead-off passages above make it clear that Elohim—the God Almighty of Creation, has prophetic armies for battle called "*the armies* [plural] *of heaven.*" He is coming with overwhelming force.

In Sodom and Gomorra, in historical space and time, we see the kind of massive destruction that a significant number of angels can do. In future space and time, He comes with "armies of Heaven." This is no small army and no small battle. This is not a little prophetic squabble. From the time of Eden Satan made his first move to corrupt the entire human race. He made the first power move in this battle often described as "*the battle of good and evil.*" So, it has been going on for a long time. Elohim is going to bring it to an end at the *end of the day.* So, consider who or what Elohim is talking about when He said, "Vengeance is mine, *and I will repay*"? Who is the object of God's repayment and retribution?

Look at the Book:

> Then I saw the beast [Satan] and the kings of the earth [Gentile's nations], and their armies gathered together to wage war against the rider of the horse [Jesus Christ] and his army [armies from heaven come together as one army]. **But the beast was captured** [by the power of Christ] and with it the false prophet who had performed the signs on its behalf…. the two of them were thrown alive into the fiery lake of burning sulfur…. (Revelation 19:19-20)

This is what ultimately "*vengeance is mine*" looks like in a power prophetic showdown yet to come. This is the ultimate target of Elohim's vengeance –Satan, not us. This is what Jesus asked us to pray "*deliver us from evil.*" He is going to do it. And the earth will truly be free at last when He does.

Look at the Book:

> The Lord is not slow in keeping his promise, as some understand slowness. He is patient with you **not wanting anyone to perish, but everyone to come to repentance.**

But the day of the Lord will come like a thief. The heavens will disappear with a roar; the elements will be destroyed by fire, and the earth and everything in it will be laid bare (2 Peter 3:9-10).

Two important distinctions is to be made here.

First, it must be understood that God's vengeance is *not a description of His character*. For example, when a Judge listens to both sides of a case and makes a judgment according to the law, we do not say the judge is vengeful. We may say he or she is tough, decisive, hard, but not vengeful. This is understood in civil rule, for a Judge is expected to do that. In the same way, the *"Judge of all the earth"* (Colossians 3:6) executes his judgment in authority and power. He is doing what the law of justice demands. He is doing what we expect a just judge to do; and what is rightly expected of Him. Indeed, it is because He is holy that his holiness demands it.

Of course, this is never arbitrary. For like a good civil judge he weighs the evidence direct and circumstantial. And with Elohim and his judgment, clemency is always available. His grace offers clemency for the guilty, and His mercy withheld judgment for "everyone who come to repentance (2 Peter 3:9)." But there is sure to be recompense for those who do not accept repentance.

Second, this passage can seem "vengeful" if it is considered to deal only with humans. The force of this passage is its ultimate perspective or the ultimate object of His vengeance. Take Elohim's "vengeance" to its prophetic space, and everything changes. For there, the ultimate perspective is Satan, who, because of his evil reign upon the earth, will be the object of Elohim's mighty and powerful vengeance.

Satan in the Garden of Eden used soft power against Elohim. He produced a plan to tempt both the woman and the man to get them to sin. He succeeded to the point of plunging Elohim's creation into sin to this day. Now, in the future battle, Satan will not use the *soft power* of evil's diplomacy. It would not be as in the Gospel; he took Jesus up to a high mountain to tempt the Lord through his evil persuasion for forty days. This is going to be physical. This future war would come with a direct clash with physical weapons. There will be blood. Swords would be raised and used. The Lord and His army from Heaven against Satan who is future represented in *the beast and his followers*. Satan will try and bring all the power and evil against the Lord Jesus—the Son of Man. But he will be defeated by the forces of Heaven's army led by the One who testified *"All authority in heaven and on earth has been given to me"* (Matthew 28:18). This will be demonstrated for the whole world to see in time to come against evil and the evil one (2 Peter 2:4-6).

PERSON OF JESUS: How to Use Power Graphics

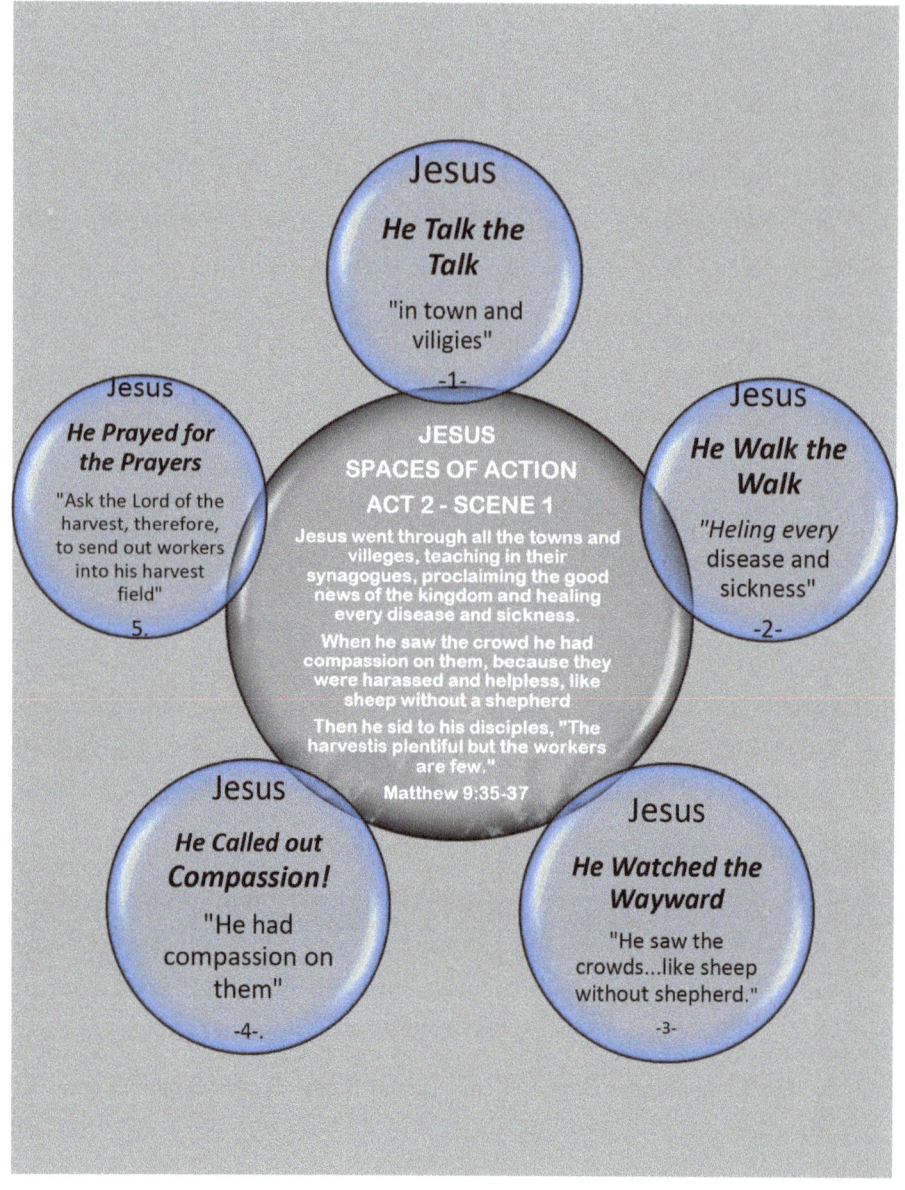

SLA: Suggestion for Life Application)

- Do not fight your weaknesses. You will just get weaker doing so. Life would wear you out. Embrace your weakness and embrace God along with them and you will have power over them all. *"I [you] can do everything through Him [Christ] who gives [you] me strength"* (Philippians 4:13).
- The Apostle Paul said, *"when I am weak, then I am strong"* (2 Corinthians 12:7). A great gospel singer and writer said it this way: *"If I never had a problem, I never know God could solve them"* (Album "Soulfully" Song, *Through it All"* by Andrae Crouch).
- Samson was the world strongest man but lost his strength when he relied on his physical strength alone.

21

Human Desire To Hear From God

"The days are coming,' declares the Sovereign Lord,
When I will send a famine through the land—
<u>*Not a famine of food or a thirst for water,*</u>
<u>*But a famine of hearing the words of the Lord"*</u>

-

(The Prophet Amos [8:11]—some 760-750 AD to his people)

In the flow of biblical history, there were times when the people of God turned away from Him to serve other gods in the secular nations around them. He added difficulties to their days when they persisted in their wayward ways and sent plagues in their path. In the middle of their distress, they would cry out to God, Jehovah. He heard them and forgave them time and time again. He chastised them with national crises of various kinds, even including several extended captivities over historical space and time. He did this to garner their attention and to mold them into His will and ways. However, it would be like a passing breeze on a hot Summer day that soon dissipated. Furthermore, the heat of dissatisfaction descended from God and His people.

These historical cycles of crisis and considerations, failures and forgiveness, disasters and deliverance were never because God changed from His great love and compassion for His people. It must be understood that it was because they changed their love and obedience to Him. Indeed, I must also point out that His heavy hand of discipline came crashing down on them because of His great love. It was a historical example of what the writer of Hebrews offered as a necessary path to holiness: "For the Lord disciplines those he loves, and He punishes each one He accepts as His child" (Hebrews 12:6; cf. 7-14NLT). I contend it is as if Israel took the limitless love of God and tested it to the limits. They took this knowledge of God's relentless love for them yet repeatedly disregarded His decrees, ignored His instructions, and tested His teachings.

The most extreme example of this occurred when Moses, upon God Jehovah's invitation to come to the mountain to receive the laws for the people. While Moses was at the top of the mounting meeting with God, the people were at the bottom of the mountain, making their own. They began to worship the work of their own hands. Moses came down from the mounting to see the people indulging in idolatry that must have angered his soul. He took the tablets of the law and cast them down. They were shattered and scattered like the people did as the hand of God's discipline was severely directed against them. Even then, the mercies of God never failed as Moses was given the opportunity to return to the mountain, and God yet again gave His law and love to the people.

It is important to understand what this incident teaches us about God:

- The crashing of the tablets with the laws written in God's own hands was more than a historical incident. It was a symbolic solemn reminder for all time that we understand who God is in His relation to mankind. We pause at the bottom of the mountain to learn God is the ultimate Lawgiver. As such, it has real-life ramifications for how we think and act in relation to His rules for life.

- We have in this incident the revelation of God of Love and concern for His people but also a God who demands accountability. He is then more than a *lawgiver*. He is a *law arbiter*. It is an incident that illustrates in the flow of human history that He alone is the ultimate Judge of "all the earth" (Psalm 7:6-8; 94:1-2).

- If there was doubt of this in Moses casting the Law to the ground in pieces, then seeing the aftermath of this in the Hebrew community at the bottom of the mountain as death like a plague ravaged the community so that hardly any families were speared.

- The judgment of death came calling in the camp of Israel. The same hand of God that delivered them judged them that day. They turned to Him in great sorrow and wept for their deeds. But regrettably, this was not the end of it. As they soon forgot the great deliverance from Egypt's bondage, so did the experience at the Mount soon fade as they journeyed away from it.

- God has a divine interest in continued loyalty to His will.

- God is not a God who relishes in punishment but One who requires righteousness before Him.

God of Forbearance

As a student of the Bible, I have often felt that Israel in the Old Testament narrative, took the love and mercy of God to an extreme, requiring so many forms of disciplines. They seems to have been in a class by themselves constantly putting God to the test.

Until, one day I reflected on my own wayward ways growing up. So many times, I did not listen to my parents, teachers, other guardians, and followed my own ways.

Now I know it was a pathway to understand His mercy, His grace, his forbearance with me and all His children. It was to take my eyes off Israel and see Him in His abundance of love, grace, and forgiveness to all of us can come to that space:

"But God demonstrates his own love for us in this: While we were still sinners, Christ died for us" (Romans 5:8)

I must also be quick to point out here another striking cycle in the flow of the biblical history of God's people. I contend it is a historical period more relevant to the Church today and one that underlines my prophetic purpose of this book on God. We have considered in our introduction the often-tragic cycles of repentance and restoration. What if there was a period when there was no resolution of the down cycle? What if the people simply decided to ignore God's call for repentance and reformation? What if, like the disciple Matthew recalled, "We played the flute for you, and you did not dance; we sang a dirge, and you did not morn? (11:17). Is there anything worse for a musician? Or a dancer in a musical on stage but all ignored by their audience? No one is listening. No one is cheering for no one there. Imagine with me for a moment if the player of the flute was God. And He was a dancer as well. But no one for whom he plaid the flute listened, or no one for whom He danced looked on and cheered. He performed, but they walked away in indifference as God danced for them.

He sang from the heavens, but they never looked up. He played the harp upon the moving waves and the scales of fish unnoticed. The birds sang His tunes, and the elephants stride by His majestic beat. He orchestrated the rhythms of the mountains and whistled on the wind, but no one saw Him or felt His Divine moves in all of this.

I am drawn in the writing of this book to a time in Israel's history when God stopped this distinct dance with His people, to this dispensation when God hung up his flute on heaven's walls. It was a time when the frequent periods of the people's reproach and regard, decline and devotion, crisis and care did not follow each other. Something emerged among the people so lost when this historical cycle ceased. It was a period when the people's hearts were so hardened; their spiritual eyes so blind they could not reflect on Jehovah God. They no longer had eyes to see him. It was a time when they could not listen anymore because they had lost their spiritual ears altogether. Again, I must make clear there was never a period in human history when God stopped attempting to reach His people. It was that they came to a point where they no longer wanted to reach out to Him. It was like a one-sided marriage. Their minds became so dull to God that all the memories that would at least move them to consider their God, to reflect on their knowledge and memories of His greatness and how in love He had guided them. They now seem to have been afflicted by a mind-invasive virus infection that rob them of any ability to think of God—their God.

It is in these dark days of chronic despair and depression that their God, the real Explainer in Chief, who yet loves them and who never slumbers or sleeps, called a man of fields—a shepherd called to be a spokesperson to deliver God's judgment against their continued indifference. I contend in this book that God's words to the prophet Amos more than ever before apply to the moral and spiritual condition of our times: ***"The days are coming,' declares the Sovereign Lord When I will send <u>a famine through the land—Not a famine of food or a thirst for water, But a famine of hearing the words of the Lord"</u>*** **(Amos 8:11).**

I contend these days of spiritual drought and silence are here. And the need for revival has never been more urgent, as no crisis, plague, or unusual disaster no longer leads to God's knowledge. We no longer consider Him the "Councilor and Mighty God" in Chief. For every disaster, we look to baseless stories for the base of our lives. We look to hear from our pre-selected pundits and not God's prophets in His word. Others want to hear only from science and ignore the Savior. Masses seek cures through only medications—a cure for all that ails them and not for the Master—not to the Messiah. Others turn to politics as their God as they conveniently ignore His precepts. So, God is speaking through unusual disasters, events, mysterious plagues, and pestilences in our time. We will find answers, but none will last. We would run out of answers that neither politics, medication, science, and even human pundits cannot solve. Only "Christ is the way, the Truth and the Life…" Now, I know it is easy to ignore such statements of Jesus as if they were given for romantic consumption. However, these are words from the Greatest Prophetic ever lived. His followers predicted the kinds of pestilences we now face. That is Who He is. To know Him is to know the future. That is who He is. It is what this book is about.

22

THE GOD WHO IS NOT SILENT

"For prophecy never had its origin in the human will,

but Prophets, though human, spoke from God

as they were carried along by the Holy Spirit."

2 Peter 1:21

"Carried Along"

If there ever was a time we needed to hear from God, it is now. He has never been silent since our first parents, Adam, and Eve. God, it must be understood, is not a silent God. He is a God who "spoke to our ancestors through the prophets at many times and in various ways… (cf. Hebrews 1:1-3). This brief introductory statement by the Hebrew writer demonstrates God's distinctive nature as a constant communicator in various ways to His creatures. Any adequate understanding of God must begin here. He created the world through His communication. He sustains the world in the same word of His power. Moreover, He communicates His will and ways to us in various ways. The writer of Hebrews added in the introduction of the letter that the fullest revelation of God was the incarnation of His Son, who was fully God among humans in historical space and time (Hebrews 1:3). When He spoke, He was not speaking as a human prophet. He was the voice of God directly speaking to the people. However, the prophets who spoke their words were of no lesser value, for the value, across the board, was God's truth. Notwithstanding, since Jesus is not now here in his human body, it must be understood that we are not at a loss for His communication to the people, His teachings, His history, and His involvement with humankind through the ages is what the Scriptures are all about. They are the revelations of God to man written down. They are not the only revelations of Him. But they are the fullest we have because they are the ones that explain all the others. For example:

The heavens declare the glory of God (Psalm 19:1 – 6).

We would not have known how the heavenly role in the understanding of God except the Prophets and Psalmist told us to look up and see Him in splendor. We would not have known that we are constantly in the thick of His handy world. Moreover, we would not have known who made us. We would not have known how He did it and what was His thoughts about what He did. That we are "fearfully and wonderfully made" (139:14). We would not have known that every person, however tarnished by sin, yet have a part of God within them—made in the image of God. The possibility of knowing God and who we are, are all made possible by the availability of the Scriptures that have come to us through, among other things, the blood of the saints. We can now take it lightly. But it has not come to us without severe persecution and bloodshed. The prophets spoke for God as His spirit moved them. But they all did so at the risk of their lives. Being a prophet was one of the riskiest tasks in Old Testament times. And they did so without any pay. It is what makes the Scriptures sacred. They spoke for God and not for themselves. And they suffered for doing so.

So, the point is that one's knowledge of God is determined by their knowledge of the Scriptures. The prophets did not know about God from "private interpretation." They were holy because they received the holy word of God. I contend that the average Christian today knows more about what is happening in the world than what is happening in the Scriptures. Yet, to understand what is happening in the world, the Christian Church cannot do that without knowing what is happening in the scriptures. There is a statement in the Scriptures concerning the priority of the Scriptures in the mind of God, which is beyond my ability to explain. It is a simple statement, but it points to an incomprehensible space that the mind of His followers is not able to understand its depth: "I will worship towards Your holy temple And praise Your name For Your lovingkindness and Your truth; Fr you have magnified <u>Your word above all Your name</u>" (Psalm 138:2). I have underlined the distinctive comparison. Even as this is also rendered not that the word is not "magnified above His name, but in some translation as equal to His name still leaves us with a priority of the Scriptures unequal to anything else which can be considered. In other Scriptures, other dimensions of importance are given, for example. When the large crowds who followed Jesus left Him, He turned to His disciples and asked, "Will you also go away? In their brief response again is this statement, "To whom must we go, you alone have the <u>word of eternal life</u>" (John 6:68). Yet another comparison of the Scriptures description of the Scriptures by Isaiah "The grass withers and the flowers fall, but <u>the word of our God endures forever</u>" (Isaiah 40: 8). I contend the conclusion of the Scriptures concerning the Scriptures is clear: There is nothing on earth that is equal to the Word of God. Why? Simple stated: The story of God the Father, Son, and Holy Spirit is the story of the Scriptures. The real story of mankind is the story of the Scriptures as well.

It must be understood then that mankind, with all the varied forms of communication and information on and around our planet, has no other place to go. Left with no other place to go to make sense of the often-senseless world we now live in. We have grown exponentially in every aspect of human knowledge and the world except in the knowledge of God. For ages, His Prophets have called us to search the Scriptures, for in them, you find out Who God is. Jesus made this clear: "These are the very Scriptures that testify about me" John 5:39). I must quickly point out that I am not saying we seek no information of our time in any other source but the Scriptures. I contend we must, however, balance all sources of information about our world with the Holy Scriptures. The late Evangelist Billy Graham, whom I heard preaching on the radio as a boy growing up in the Caribbean, explained that the believer must hold the newspaper (the prevalent news source at the time) and the Holy Scriptures in the next. We must do this if we want to understand God in the context of our times. Of course, we have come a long way beyond the newspapers and research journalism. However, we have searched for everything else but the Holy Scriptures for ages. It is like times gone by when the Prophets spoke of a vast drought in the land, not of food and water but of hearing of the Word of God. Time was when at least God's people sought to hear of His Prophets. Now, the national prophets who spoke divine truth to power and the people seem to have all gone into hiding under the cloak of political pandering. There is no other place to go to find Holy Words revealed as a "lamp to our feet and a light to our path" (Psalm 119:110). There is no other place to find the truth that sustains. "The grass withers and the flower fades, but the Word of God lasts forever" (Isaiah 40:8). No other place to go to find the means for the cleansing of the soul. "Where can a young man cleanse his ways by giving head to the Word" (Psalm 119:9).

Prophets give each of us the green light to know God. Astonishingly, these men and women called by God to reveal themselves to us did not come from prestigious stock. The very people among whom they emerged had slavery as a part of their resume. And when they were not slave under foreign governments and evil tyrants, they wandered the earth as nomads looking for a place to settle and call their own. And when they found that place, they could hardly keep it before some other power would take them into exile again and again. Yet these Prophets who would tell us of God came from such a lowly people existing often vulnerable among some of the great kingdoms and civilizations that traverse this Earth.

Let us face it. If we were giving our choices to God as to who would speak for Him, would we have even suggested a beauty queen such as Ester, whose ticket to fame and prestige was solely based on her good looks? Yet she now has a book in the Bible named after her because God did. I contend that this beauty queen in historical time and space demonstrated she had more than her beauty but her belief. She had more than external features but strong inner faith that revealed a God of power to her people.

When Israel was drenched in idolatry, and the God they once knew became an afterthought to their self-indulgence and decadence, would we suggest to God to turn to a young country boy who grew up outside the city and called him to speak to the city dwellers who would hardly give this country boy Jerimiah a hearing? But He did, and two books in the Bible are named after Him. One with his name and the other with his passion for his people: Lamentations.

Given a choice of personnel for God's Prophets, would you include a farmer who spends his days in the fields tilling the soil, plowing, and pruning? Such was the task of Elisha when he was called from among the fields to proclaim to the people God's prospective and precepts. I contend that working as a farmer Elisha would not make the cut speaking for God. Fast forward to the New Testament to Mary, the mother of Jesus, the greatest Prophet and King. She understood this when she gave a song of praise. "My soul magnifies the Lord. And my spirit rejoices in God my Savior, for He has looked with favor on the lowliness of His servant; surely, from now on, all generations will call me blessed, for the Mighty One has done a great thing for me, and holy is His name (Luke 1:46-49). None but God would have thought of such a woman from a poor family on the poor side of town with an even poorer reputation. "Can any good thing come out of Nazareth yet express the sum? Yet in that space, God called her to bear the greatest Prophet and Teacher who ever lived in historical time and space.

No one would rush to tap the like of Peter, a rash-mouthed fisherman, among so many others who were called from that common folk's trade to learn and tell their people the un-common truth of who God is. This band of misfits he led on the Day of Pentecost changed the world and initiated a movement with us today. Through God, they are revealed by message and mission to the world, revealing God to mankind. "This was spoken of by the Prophet Joel, who declared it to all. He boasted of no earthly privileges or prestige or even cash. One day, when a paralyzed man at the Temple gate asked for a few pennies, he told the man he had none. He spent his days for some years now with Jesus, and He did not pay them, for He himself had no earthly cash. So, except for rare occasions, such as the Apostle Paul, who was highly educated and worked as a tent maker. The majority of the Prophets of God were common people with truly little, if any, earthly goods, like John the Baptiste, who hung out in the wilderness. Some were referred to as "unschooled, ordinary men," which were then considered as a sign that "they had been with Jesus" (Acts 4:13). I contend that the glory of who God is does not rest with the teacher, the author, or even the prophet but for whom the Prophet speaks: God. This is the foundation of this book. It is to look at the revelations of the Prophets, the holy men, and women of God, in an effort to grasp some semblance of Who God is and what difference this knowledge can make in the life of anyone who seeks such knowledge.

The theme of my graduating class of 1973 at Moody Bible Institute was taken from the personal testimony of the Apostle Paul, writing to the Church at Philippi, "That I may know Him, and the power of His resurrection, and the fellowship of His suffering being conformed [becoming like Him] to His death" (Philippians 3:10 KJV). To this end, this book of God is written that in all our lives, we must talk about Him, for He cares for us (1 Peter 5:7).

Permit me to establish some general perspectives or guidelines for understanding this book, written on the most profound subject in the universe: God.

1. **God is not presented as a Definition but a Declaration**. It is not my attempt to define God. I am not capable of that. Even if I had the skill to write a thousand books on Him. I will come up short. He would remain undefinable. My attitude and approach, even my academic research, is more like a hungry beggar who, along life's path, found a little bread here and there and wants to share it with others.

2. **There is no mystery here. There is no magic. And quite frankly, there are no miracles.** If one needs miracles to know who God is, this book will not add to their knowledge. This book cannot add any mystery or magic if one fails to see such in the eyes of a newborn baby or needs additional miracles if one fails to see it in the oceans below or the sky and unreachable galaxies above. If one cannot see magic in the way of an eagle through a pathless air, riding the wind it never made or observed the landscape of earth and sky through eyes it never created eyes more defined or far-reaching in clarity and focus than those found in the sockets of its human co-earth dwellers, then there will be no magic or miracles found here. But if there is one who is a seeker or a beggar of divine truth who wants to know a little more about who makes plants grow and eagles fly, it can be found in the pages of this book. It is to understand the character and Person who is behind the already abundance of mysteries, magic, and miracles all around us, in the purpose of this book

3. **God is not, in essence, a gender God, a culture God of any political persuasion, or any of our common human distinctions.** He may have made us "male and female," but He is not. One can refer to God as "she." And although it will sound strange to our culturally conditioned ears it would be theologically correct. For God is gender-free. Moreover, each person who comes to be "in Christ" has no greater value over another regardless of social status, ethnicity, gender, nationality, or any other earthly distinctions. So, to come to God to understand Him, I contend we must leave all these distinctions, including liberal or conservative, Black, or White, and every color and ideological shade of difference at the door. That is of course, if we want to grasp who God is. We must leave all our human distinctions behind in our search to understand His. Paul spoke to the Church at Galatia, who were creating dangerous distinctions in the church, like different categories of Christians. He made clear they must be careful not to cast such distinction between God's Church and the character of Christ where no such distinctions exist. "There is neither Jew nor Gentile," he said, "there is neither slave nor free, there is no male and female, for you are all one in Christ Jesus" (Galatians 3:28**). It is the oneness

"in Christ" that best represents the nature of Who God is, and not the modern popular distinctions we so jealously guard. The distinctiveness of this book is more about Who God is and not who we are or what we call ourselves. Yet I must admit it is in the journey to find more of who God is that I learn much of who I am. I contend it would be the same for anyone who seeks after God. They will find this to be one of the great mysteries of life. One cannot learn more about God without understanding more of themselves. But the opposite is also true. As one seeks only to know themselves devoid of God, they become more ignorant of themselves and their world. The point being highlighted here has nothing to do with discarding one's culture, heritage, individual likeness, or common identity. God would not have made us distinct in many ways if He did not want us to embrace it. But such distinctions are not to be a value judgement over one another or to be used as a spiritual hierarchy in the body of Christ. It was at the heart of the Apostle Paul's conclusive testimony as he listed an impressive resume of his life and ministry: "But whatever were gains to me," he concluded, "**I now consider loss for the sake of Christ. Moreover, I consider everything a loss because of the surpassing worth of knowing Christ Jesus my Lord, for whose sake I have lost all things. I consider them garbage, that I may gain Christ** (Philippians 3: 7-8). I contend that to truly know God is to learn the priority of His distinctiveness and not ours. It is to know His identity and not settle for ours. It is to know and be careful not to bring anything we may have attained by nature, nurture, or any other venture, however successful by worldly standards, to occupy that space "in Christ" that He reserves for Himself alone.

4. **God is not a force in the universe like the wind that blows, like the energy flowing from our sun or like the rain that waters the earth, but He is a Person who can see, feel, think, and reason, and make it all possible.** So, especially for people of faith, as we gather to praise and worship God, we must be careful not to "reduce" Him to an atmosphere or a feeling flowing in the ever-increasing materials and often highly electronic produced effects in a given space. Like the story I heard of a parishioner on leaving service expressed how much the preacher preached that morning. When asked by someone what he preached about, they replied I do not know, but he really preached this morning. We must be careful not to let our zeal for God fly beyond our knowledge of him as the Apostle Paul warned, "I can testify about them that they are zealous for God, but their zeal is not based on knowledge. Since they do not know the righteousness of God and sought to establish their own..." (Romans 10:2, 3). Recall the experience of Elijah the Prophet of who was told by God to "go out and stand on the mountain in the presence of the Lord, for the Lord is about to pass by" (1Kings 19:11). There on the mountain the narrative continued: "Then a great and powerful wind tore the mountains apart and shattered the rocks before the Lord, **but the Lord was not in the wind.** Then, after the wind, there was an earthquake, **but the Lord was not in the earthquake.** Then after the earthquake came a fire, **but the Lord was not in the fire.** And after the fire, there was a gentle whisper" (1 Kings 19:11-12). There in that gentle, silent space devoid of the crashing sounds of the material world, the powerful life-changing voice of God was found in a whispering space. In a "still small voice" (KJV)." I contend each believer must learn to discover God in the still, small voice of their personal space that no one else or any other

sounds on this earth can occupy. To know Him is to cultivate that unique space in our lives where everything thing else is silent, and He can speak to us in a whisper and yet be heard in that personal space reserved for Him and Him alone. "You shall have no other gods before me" (Exodus 20:3; Joel 2:27). To know Him is to know and cultivate daily through the Word of God. It is a space where even we ourselves, despite all our concerns and travails, get out of the way to the lonely place reserved for God. It is so we hear only Him in the stillness of our souls. I contend modern modes of worship, with their ultra-digitally filled material presence and production, can perceptively preclude any pretense of a prophetic space in our souls where God can whisper and yet be heard beyond the winds, earthquakes, fires—the noise of our world.

("Eclipse" Photo by Freddericka Thompson - April 8, 2024, North Texas)

"DRAW NEAR TO GOD

AND HE

WILL DRAW

NEAR TO YOU"

JAMES 4:8

5. **God is not human.** It is to say He is not bound by the limitations of humanity. We have often used the expression "I am only human" as a general justification for our shortcomings. God has no such out. He cannot say "I am only God." For Him, it cannot apply. He can find no justification for weakness for in Him there is none. We are limited in time. He is not. He sees the end from the beginning. He declared at the end of time in Revelation 22:13 "I am the Alpha and the Omega, the First and the Last, the Beginning and the End." A human being comes into this world massively flowing with events before they came. And it will continue to flow unabated after their brief time on this Earth in their human's limited body. God made us human, but He is not. However, we can look at it this way. He said He made us in His image. So, imagine all that we can do. He can do it more. And the "more" is for Him or Her without limits, which brings me to my final perspective here on unlimitedness. He was before each of us. If there was a "big bang" He was there before. And He will be after if there is another. The astonishing thing is that although He made us human, he said He also made us like Him with a human spirit with a godlike essence in that we are also born with an eternal spirit. A spirit with a newly created body with the possibility to choose while we are here in this body to choose His Son who took on one of our body types and lived among us in historical space and time. I contend this is the perspective or goal of "knowing God." It is the essence of why we chose … as our class theme so many years ago: **That I may know Him and the power of His resurrection.**

This is why we seek such knowledge, not for intellectual curiosity or emotional comfort. We seek such knowledge not for its limited use in just living in this world. We seek this experiential knowledge of God for the radical unmasking of this world and all its troubles and limitations in the flesh so that we can be made anew in another body, much like the glorious, resurrected body of our Lord and Savior Jesus Christ.

The Apostle Paul appealed to the early Christians that they are not "uninformed about those who sleep in death. So, you do not grieve like the rest of mankind who have no hope" (1 Thessalonians 4:13 cf.1 Corinthians 15). This Divine information and knowledge is causally linked to a prophetic event in future space and time, based on the resurrection of Christ in historical space and time. And become the overriding present pursuit, priority, and purpose for every follower of Christ: "**That I may know Him and the power of His resurrection....**" That is the possibility, power, perspective, and plan of this knowledge of God. It is the ultimate prophetic reason for such resurrection for all God's followers why God called these simple Prophets to tell of Him. They filled many of them at the risk of their own lives to fearlessly tell His truth. They filled the overflow to our times the prophetic narrative of the Holy Scriptures. For them, He was not a God only of their times. He was the God for all ages of time. That all mankind may know Him. It is the fundamental reason we must care. To that end, is the purpose of this book.

23

"His Name Shall Be Called"

Spaces of God's Personal Names

Names in the Hebrew tradition were never arbitrary. They were given as are all names for identification. However, it must not be missed that in the biblical and Hebrew cultures, they moved beyond the identification of a person to the revelation of character. So, the elder son of Jacob was called Esau, which means "hairy" in Hebrew. He was in real life a hairy man (Genesis 25:25). Peter, "Petra" in the New Testament whose name meant rock, despite his wandering and denial of Christ, also lived up to his name as he became the "rock" of the New Testament Church. The most descriptive was the angel's message to Mary, giving her the name of her child and the personal connection to His name: "You are to give him the name Jesus because he will save his people from their sins" (Matthew 1:21).

Knowing the biblical names of God is a pathway to His Person—his unique Space in the universe. This essay is dedicated to this perspective. It is not meant to be exhaustive but descriptive, so we gain some additional insight as to why God was called or described in the different ways that He was.

I must also be careful to point out that language, especially English, cannot fully describe the essence of Who God is. We do so as Paul noted, speaking of God's love. *"For now, we see only a reflection as in a mirror, then we shall see face to face. Now I know part; then I shall know fully, even as I am fully known"* (Corinthians 13:12. What we have here in this informative description of the Apostle Paul is the limited and humbled landscape from which we understand the greatness of God's space. Imagine then the further obscurity that must exist in that space we attempt to occupy to reflect upon God's love and Himself.

To illustrate: I was a professional photographer at the height of the transition some twenty years ago from film photography to the new digital. Although many of us bemoaned the new technology, thinking it was robbing us of the creative dimensions of our craft, we learned how forgiving this new digital process can be in real time. I have taken what I would consider critical shots, say, like an eagle on a limb about to fly because it sees me coming. In a rush, with just a few seconds, you take the photo without the time to check the camera settings or even to try different ones. The time is short. Looking at the frames in my viewfinder on my digital SLR camera, all was lost. The outline of the eagle is there, but the details are not. So, I often see through a glass darkly on the field and must wait until I get home to see what I got. Although I have been doing this for some years now, I am still uncertain of the outcome until I get home. I place the disk in my computer in what amounts to an instant digital "dark room," and a few contrast and saturation slides and filters, and then details appear.

When we study God, we are not home yet. We saw the outlines; when we got home, He said He would show us the details. Here we see through a "glass darkly." Now, it must be noted that this does not suggest we cannot understand God. It means, as Paul said, "We do not have all knowledge. Why? It is not because the knowledge is not there. It is because "we have this treasure in jars of clay to show this all-surpassing power is from God and not from us" (2 Corinthians 4:7). **But God has seen fit to create in us the capability to know what we need to know to get us where we need to Go.**

The basic premise of this book rests on two declarations from the narrative of the Scriptures. As we have covered above, one is that God exists and has revealed and continues *to reveal Himself in many ways.* And second, that *He has created in humankind the capability of apprehending His revelation that is adequate enough for us to know him to the extent to love and serve Him.* These two biblical realities are the foundation of this and other essays about God. It is not to prove He exists but only to set forth the case that he does and what He demands of us. He exists, and He is not silent about it.

In this chapter, I will do something different from what is typical in Theology. For example, many of the studies of the names of God are riddled with historical speculations as to the specific meaning of various names for God. There is no certainty that one would trace genealogy to an original household. The etymology of the various names or words for God and any direct meaning only takes us so far, but not far enough to be fully certain of direct meaning or association based on the various names used in antiquity. We are left with cautious truth. What we say a particular name means is undoubtedly true from what the Scriptures described about God. The problem is then an etymological one and not a biblically descriptive one. The point is that we are etymologically limited by God's names used in antiquity. In such early stages, the word God was used to denote all kinds and concepts of deities. This must be recognized. As Dr. Henry C. Thiessen so described:

> We may know a thing correctly as far as we know it, even though we do not know all about it. We certainly set forth the attributes of God as revealed to man [kind], and these are to be regarded as true. We can also state the genus to which God belongs and note the differentia that distinguishes Him from others of the genus. A chair is a seat; that is stating the genus. It is a movable single seat with a back; that is stating the difference. A stool is also a single seat, but it is without a back; a bench is a long seat, usually accommodating two or more people. Thus, we can say that God is a Being and then indicate the ways in which He is different from other beings. (Henry C. Thiessen, *Lectures in Systematic Theology*, WM. Eerdmans Publishing Company, Grand Rapids, Michigan, 1971, p.54).

I will not take that approach of listing names and what they were purported to mean like a word study. Whereas one can say that there are twelve names of God as an estimate in the Bible, I find a rich volume of unfathomable descriptions of the God of the Bible that constituted what Thiessen called the "differential."

And what others of less theological bent would call the "meat on the bone." I find this to be the best and most fruitful approach to revealing the knowledge of the Christian God from the Holy Scriptures' own description of Him. I would call this the biblical-theological approach to understanding God and Who He is. It is not based on various names used alone. These are more like a doorway to the vast distinctive description of God's space in the Bible.

Here is the primary example, which I will deal with in further detail later: In Genesis 1:1, the Scriptures began, *"In the beginning God."* One can stop there and study with all due diligence the Hebrew name used and still not get its substance. Not until they expand beyond that etymological space into the revelation space that opens up all of the vast unlimited heavens, and all the earth and its vast depth, and all the vast creatures yet being discovered today, to fathom this space; this "differentia" in the Bible own description and revelation. If one steps into the space beyond the name, it is where the Scriptures, like making words and their meaning, come alive. Who did what, when, where, how, and why? The answer is found in the brief opening salvo beyond time, beyond comprehension, beyond speculation; this One referred to as "God" –the God of the Bible Who **"created the heavens and the earth."**

I contend all that flows from that space "in the beginning GOD" and what He did reverberates the space down through the ages in all of nature and the existence of humankind. How do you then attempt to define "in the beginning God"? Here, we are introduced to consider this space in which this God of the Bible moves, then and now, for all time. It is one of the fundamental revelations of Who God is. It is like a vast Scriptural garden filled with God's descriptive fruits of Who He is. There, in that space, there are various colors, tastes, and textures, some too small to notice and others too large to comprehend, yet more is yet to be discovered in the continuum of who God was then and now in His creative space.

I contend one can pause here for a lifetime and yet not discover the full implications of the knowledge of that space so simple, so vast, so incomprehensible yet adequate, even though we see through often distorted human lens Who He is. We can still know this God of the Bible: "In the beginning, He CREATED EVERYTHING. I contend that names are but places to start on the creative journey of discovering God's Space.

The God of Genesis

"In the beginning, God"—continued

I would like to consider this space Moses described with the Hebrew word "***Bereshith,***" *translated in English as* "***in the beginning.***" This word, Bereshith, initiated an account representing the world's most ancient oral and written history. It is like a survivor of the most ancient of times who comes to us to tell us a story about One, the Creator of the world and everything in it. The Scriptures tell a singular story in its antiquity, for there is no rival in its time. And there is none with such simple and profound details of how everything began. This survivor's story stands alone in its details of origin and its singular value to humanity. Whether one believes it or not, they do so without any alternative in antiquity. The Scripture's space stands alone in its details of origin.

It details the arrival of light from the words God spoke. Light is separated from darkness. Their mysteries are still with us today. They both exist but never together, for God "separated them." When one shows up, the other leaves without any battle or argument. Turn a light on, and darkness disappears without a fuss in that space. Why? It is because from the beginning, This God of the Scriptures "separated them." I contend that no physicist will ever exist to put light and darkness together in the same place. This was not a statement of poetry or even meant to be a scientific statement. It is just a simple truth that man can consider to this day to gain knowledge of Him.

Bereshith—the ancient history of the world—details abound on how the world was created. There are details on how this God of the Scriptures made the first inhabitants. Bereshith accounts for their original sinlessness. It accounts for the hell in our world from the original fall when mankind sinned against his Creator.

I contend that no one can doubt that something had invaded mankind from antiquity that reveals something is desperately wrong. Humankind, in all the greatness exhibited, yet evil always seems to follow. Bereshith—*In the beginning,* did not fail to tell the whole story with no rival. It spells out the works of art. It accounted for a global flood. Then, the repopulation of the world outlined the divisions of its people. There is an account of the rise of nations and nationalism. The development of Kingdoms and their contribution to good and bad civilizations is all laid out.

The unique history of the Hebrew patriarchs, their peoples, and journeys all the way to Joseph's death in Egypt, which took almost two thousand four hundred years BC (2369 calculated), is accounted for. It laid out the making of religion as mankind sought to worship. When this Book of Antiquity said that God separated the light from the darkness, it was not a poetic statement. It was not intended to be any scientific declaration either, however, since it is the God who created both light and darkness. Science He separated them; scientists are welcome to test whether light can show up without dispelling darkness in the simplicity of space.

How Did the story of the *Bereshith* transmit to us?

There is only three ways the record of Bereshith—the ancient history of the world recorded by Moses in the book of Genesis could have been transmitted to him:

- The Written Word so Moses and the people could read it.
- The Spoken Word so the people could hear it
- The Inspired Word from God through Divine revelation so the people could know, believe, and live by it.

24

PERSONAL NAMES OF GOD

"And this is eternal life: that they know you,

the only true God, and Jesus Christ, whom you have sent"

(John 17:3).

As stated before, we must be careful not to be too dogmatic about assigning certain specific meanings to the names used for "God." I believe that in the contextual biblical narrative in which they were used, we can yet gather the beauty and power of Godlike petals on a rose.

In this chapter, we dedicate ourselves to the biblical petals of the names used in the Bible for God in the hope of sharing light on the character and power of God expressed in his names. The following then are twelve names, their general pronunciations, and their meaning as employed in the narrative of the holy Scriptures. I must again be careful to point out that this is but a humble attempt to express some sense of uniqueness (if that is at all possible) to answer the question "What is in a name?" which is a unique challenge when such names are used for One in which the very concept of a name is limiting if we avoid limiting our knowledge of God to the study of names not look at the varied descriptions of his nature, power, righteousness, truth all his character lavished like uncountable stars in the Scriptures.

Elohim (El-lo-him)

I have considered this name above in the context of Genesis 1 verse 1: What is said before the name Elohim "In the beginning" and what is said after the name "…created the heavens and the earth. Elohim is like a sandwich made in heaven's kitchen cooked up by One who alone can mix all the ingredients that filled heaven and earth, including all creatures great and small, and said it was Elohim. *It was good*. Mankind can now feast on a meal from God's heavenly kitchen made from the visible act of his creative power—all of heaven spread out on the earth's plates. He called the fire and the power of this heavenly Chef in Chief *"Elohim."* He serves this in abundance "day after day" (Psalm 19:2). The "heavens declare the glory of God and the skies proclaim the work of his hands" (Psalm 19:1). So, mankind can come to his table and feast with him and get to know him whose name is *Elohim*.

It is a name of power and might. It denotes a power yet approachable by all who see His glory and acknowledge His handy work (it is used 2,570 times in the Bible).

I got up one morning while writing about these names of God. In some strange way, I was led to go outside on my patio, where I kept a Bible to sit and read. I do not keep the Bible open outside, but this morning, it was. And it was open to a passage that spoke of Daniel praying and giving a powerful description of God that began with "praise to the name of God." This was just before I sat down to write about His name.

In this context, Daniel heard of an edict from the king to kill all the wise men in Babylon who were called upon to interpret the dream of King Nebuchadnezzar. It was a unique situation. It was untypical because the king had forgotten the dream, and none of the wise men and astrologers could give the King the interpretation of a dream that they did not know. They could interpret the dream and begged the King to tell them, so they could serve him by giving him the interpretation. They told the king: "No man on earth can do what the king asks! No king, however great and mighty, has ever asked such a thing of any magician, enchanter, or astrologer, for it was unheard of in all the land that anyone could give an interpretation without the dream. The king ordered all of them killed, including Daniel and his friends.

Daniel and his friends…..prayed, and God gave him the interpretation that protected them all. This situation of God demonstrating who he was to Babylon is why Daniel said, "Praise to the name of God," which describes all His names.

"Praise the name of God forever and ever…"

Praise to the name of God for ever and ever; wisdom and power are His.

He changes times and seasons; he sets up kings and deposes them.

He gives wisdom to the wise and to the discerning.

He reveals deep and hidden things; he knows what lies in darkness and light dwells with him.

I Thank and praise you, O God of my fathers: You have given me wisdom and power, you have made known to me what we asked of you

You have made known to us the dream of the king.

Daniel 2:20-23

Jehovah (Je-ho'-vah)

"Jehovah" is the most prolific name for God in the Bible. It is used some 6,823 times in the Old Testament alone. However, the meaning of this name and the God space it describes may be the most difficult to grasp. This is even more astonishing when the God to whom it is ascribed states it in the simplest of terms: Jehovah the great "I AM."

The name first appeared in Genesis 3:14. God appeared to Moses with his voice speaking from a burning bush. In a lengthy back-and-forth dialog between God and Moses, a reluctant Moses gave God all the reasons or arguments as to why he was the wrong person for the job. He did so to the point that God was getting angry at his defensiveness to his will and purpose. This was no small thing. God laid the foundation for the call to go to Egypt to deliver his people. Moses must have known to some measure with whom he was talking. However, God was also willing to reveal more to Moses. For it yet appeared Moses needed to know more of who God was to accomplish the mission. So, he said to God, in one of the boldest of questions posed to God.

In Exodus 3, 13, Moses said to God (Elohim), "Suppose I go to the Israelites and say to them, 'the God of your fathers has sent me to you,' and they ask me, 'What *is his name? Then what shall I tell them?* Up to that point, Moses had failed to grasp the lesson from the burning bush that he was going back to Egypt, representing a God (Elohim) who had the power to speak through a bush on fire without it being consumed. Moses could have concluded some semblance of God's powerful space: If God can speak through a burning bush without the bush being consumed, God could also speak through him and protect him as he did the bush. However, a stubborn Moses, who had settled down in his comfortable space, resisted the call of God. He needed more revelation. And Elohim in his love and mercy gave it to him: *"God [Elohim] said to Moses, "I AM WHO I AM"* [*Jehovah*] *this is what you are to say to the Israelites:* **'I AM [*Jehovah*] has sent me to you"** (Exodus 3:14). God in this historical place and time on the mounting of a burning bush revealed a new name to Moses—Jehovah.

God revealing this new name wanted Moses to know that the God of creation power *Elohim* is also God *Jehovah* **WHO IS AND ALWAYS WILL BE.** Elohim wanted Moses to know he was not a God who in his great power created all things and then went away. Yes, he was Mighty, high, and lifted up in power above all things, but he was also going to be immediate. He was also going to be an **imminent** God existing always in real time and space for his children—no space even evil Egypt that enslaved His people was going to be hidden from His presence. The "Existing One"—the I AM was going to be there among His people as well.

As suggested in the English translation of Exodus 3: 14, "I AM" God revealed himself from the Hebrew name Jehovah: That meant "**being**" or "**existing**"—a name of "life." A name for *God's Life—the self-existing unique space of God*. He derives his permanent eternal existence or *being* from no other but himself. The "*I am that I am*" that we have come to know as the name "*Jehovah*" means he is "*all and in all.*" Each of us owe our existence to someone else. Even in the natural world ecological systems beyond us must exist in our world for us to exist in our lives.

It is critical. We could not exist without say, our parents. They could not exist without theirs. We could not exist without them going back all the way to Adam. But there is even more. Neither we nor they could have existed on any other planet that we know of.

The Earth does not need us to exist, but we cannot exist without it. We need its soil and habitat for food, its air for breathing, its water to drink, its ecology to endure. Yet all of it is not ours. We cannot live like a fish in its oceans and a fish cannot live like us on land. If the sun comes a fraction to close or the elements that temper its heat were to collapse global warming would burn us out of existence. If it moves a fraction too far life would be frozen in its tracks. We live on an ecologically dependent planet. That is the space in which we live.

Jehovah is his name—the great I AM that reveals to us his existence is unlimited for he always is and will be eternally. He can abode in the heart of the sun and the heat could not destroy him. That is why he could show up as the fourth man in the fire to save Shadrach, Meshach, and Abednego the flames could not destroy him or them (Daniel 3:14). It is the reason "no weapon forged against you will prevail…declares the Lord" *Jehovah* (Isaiah 54:17). Because no one or anything can put him out of existence, not even the forces of hell (Matthew 16: 18). What more can be said of that name? Except in all humility to acknowledge before him as his Son taught us to pray "*hallowed be thy name.*" *Moses! This is Who you say send you!*

This is the unique *space* that this name of God used some 6,823 times in the Old Testament, often translated as "Lord," occupies. It is a name expressing the basis of his covenant with Abraham, Isaac, and Jacob and even extended to us today in Christ. A name that expresses the basis of his covenant on his *eternal existence* and *Person*. His abode is in a self-existing space, depending on no one or anything. He is the self-existing God of life, existing in righteousness, holiness, love, glory, truth, and so much more, like a rose expressing its beauty and glory in its divine petals. *Jehovah*, the GREAT I AM, eternally exists yet can exist in each of us through the salvation of his Son Jesus Christ, simply by putting our trust in him (John 12:12).

El-Shaddai (**El-shad-di**)

God's Names are finite ways to express an infinite God.

What's in the Space of a Name?

- *God exists in a space that is and always will be infinite. It is a space that no one description or name can describe. But it is a space where all can come. It is a space where all of God's space collides. An unfathomable mental or spiritual circle can represent it. Like a rainbow so vast, its edges cannot be seen or defined because such edges do not exist. And if they exist, they could not "contain" him.*

- *He is a God who can and always "burst" the edges of names. Everything. He exists in an unlimited, undefined infinite space represented by a circle without edges, without beginning and end. A circle without height or depth with unfathomable, unlimited dimensions of Divine Space.*

- *God's names are all unique because they represent a space in which God is revealing himself to finite humans. God attempts to "break down" who he is to us on our level. Each of his names represents a Circle, which also means a space within the unfathomable larger circle of space.*

- *None of the circles representing God's name stand alone in two essential ways. (1) The space of understanding they exist is in the larger circle of infinite space. And (2) they do not stand alone because each of the circles/spaces of his names overlap. Which means we cannot fully understand one name without the others. We cannot fully grasp them without understanding the more significant, unfathomable space of God in which they all exist.*

In Genesis 17:1,2 a new name for God is introduced—*El-Shaddai – "I am God Almighty."* In the circle of this name, we see there is an obvious overlap with the names of God because one informs the other.

God made a promise to Abraham about his seed and called him to go to a place he knew not. A long and difficult journey to get to where God wanted him to be. That was the space through which Abraham was to understand God. He was a God who made promises. And a God who could and will keep them. However, if we draw our own human circle or space around that name, our understanding of God would begin to crumble. Why? Because the circled space of this name was given in the context and circumstances that defied human limitations in relationships. This promise was made when it was still humanly possible for Abraham and his wife Sara to have children. That time had come and gone for both Abraham and Sara.

So, when Sarah overheard the updated promise, which was so long and outdated, she was so amused that she laughed. Sara thought it was a joke by then. She had followed her husband on a long, dangerous journey of a promise that seemed to have fizzled out. So, in her long-established barrenness, it was like both she and her husband would have to be resurrected from their dead bodies. For as far as bearing children, they had long died. And in their lives, there were no such miracles among mankind. There was no such demonstration of power or blessings to be bestowed on anyone. There were no stories of such of which they were familiar.

However, in the circle—in the *space* of this new name- El-Shaddai had no place for laughter, doubts, lies, or impossibilities. For with God, all things are possible. This New Testament declaration was captured in the space of this new name revealed to Abraham and Sarah. This name expresses God Almighty, who revealed his sacred covenant to fulfill a promise of blessings that, from a human perspective, was impossible. However, not so with a *God Almighty—El-Shaddai,* who makes covenants not only based on his eternal existence as the great I AM but also based on his circle or space filled with all his promises and with his might not simple power to create, or to be in existence but the power to provide for all his promises against all human odds. It is a unique circle, a unique space, which focuses our attention on God Almighty introduced to Abraham and Sarah in a space to demonstrate God Almighty—El-Shaddai is a God who keeps his promises and is mighty to do so against all human odds. A God who can focus all his power not only to create all his creatures but to care abundantly for them as well. El-Shaddai occupies the circle and space of the name in the unlimited circle and *space* of who God is.

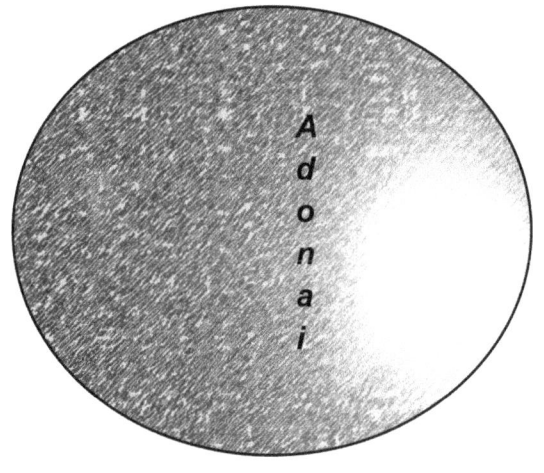

Adonai (a-do-ni)

Adonai occurs about three hundred times in the Old Testament. Elohim translated "God" in the Scriptures. Jehovah translated "LORD," and El-Shaddai translated **God Almighty**. Each of these personal names for God overlaps in their meaning, yet they have a focused space that helps us understand some unique dimensions of who God is. It is like one can study David as a man from the space of being a shepherd and a hunter as indeed they were roles he occupied. He can be studied as a fierce worrier who, from a lad, killed giants and, as an adult, led men into victorious battles. He could also be studied as a person of the Arts, a poet, a musician, a player of the harp, a songwriter, as we see in the book of Psalms, and as well be viewed as he was a great King of Israel. All are personified in the Bible in one called David. It is not so unusual then that God would have different names. He is called to personify who he is—Adonai – God Almighty.

Adonai is another name within the circles of God's other names, and all in the nameless unlimited circle of who God is. *Adonai* is translated in our Bibles by the word "Lord." It occupies a unique circle space, always rendered in the plural. So, it brings to our attention that God represents Himself to us as One yet in three Persons: God the Father, Son, and Holy Spirit. From its root and usage both in the plural for God and in the singular (lord) for man conveying *ownership, master, ruler, possession. It is a name that expresses in its circle God as ruler of his world, possessor of his people, master of the universe, and the lives of his children.* It is a space that identifies God's accountable relationship with his creation and his people. It is a name uniquely expressing the "right" God possesses as ruler and master of our lives. Although we do not often recognize this unique space, this demanding relationship with God, it does not change what this name represents him to be. The master and ruler overall. And that means as is made clear in its many uses in subsequent narratives concerning God and Jesus Christ, he holds all his creatures accountable. It is a name that brings the justice of God into that circle, who will someday make his enemies a footstool. "And Jehovah said into my Adonai sit [Lord]" (Psalms 110).

Adonai, whose name is so great worldwide (Psalms 97:5), will put everything under his feet (Psalms 8). He is a savior God but also a warrior God who will fight for his cause of righteousness and do so on our behalf against all the enemies that come against his children. The warrior God, the ruler God, the master God who demands servitude from all his children and the world. These and much more cannot be considered in the Old Testament (Psalms 114:7, 89:50; 113:5; 141:8; 109:21-28) and the New (Matthew 25: 14-30; Luke 19:11-27; 1 Corinthians 6:19, 20; Romans 6:22; 12:1; Acts 9:6) in the application and illustration of this unique name, expressed in this *circle/space* in the model of who God is especially in understanding the nature of the relationship each of his creatures have with him. to whom we are. another significant avenue and *circled space* of who God is. Adonai was not meant to be a poetic expression of God. It is meant to communicate and reveal a *space* where Adonai is occupied as ruler, warrior, master, and lord. Each time one of God's prophets was commissioned, this name filled that space because it is a name applied to commission and demanding action from all God's servants. The Adonai demands that "we present ourselves to Adonai as a living sacrifice holy and acceptable which is our reasonable service" (Romans 12:1). What more can we say of this unique circle? What more can we say of this unique space?

The response was summed up by the Apostle Paul as Saul, on the road to Damascus, confronted with the judgment and demands of this space expressed in God's name Adonai. "Lord, what will thou have me to do?" (Acts 9:6).

It is one of those names that must exist in a practical way. The force of this name is not the force of meditation but of action. It does not come with the force of blessings such as El-Shaddai from God but with the clarity of demand on our behavior towards him. Although we must understand God, the space this occupies comes to us not with the force of just *understanding* but *doing*. It comes with the force of not just appreciation or adoration as revealed in other names but with the force of action. "All power is given to me. Go into the whole world and make disciples of every nation (Mark 15:16). It is a circle that pulls us into a space of not simply being but acting and expressing the glory of all the other names to a watching world—Adonai, our commander, and ruler—the warrior of our faith.

Jahovah-jireh (je-ho'-vah yeer'-eh)

Jehovah-Jireh- the God who provides. In Jehovah, he is the Great IAM, and in Jireh, is the Great Provider. So, He is the one who exists to provide for all of us.

God, as we have pointed out in his essential being as the great IAM (Jehovah), cannot be divided even in understanding his name. So, each overlap with others, and even then, all is to be understood in the larger circle of unlimited, nameless space that exists without limit as a name—a circle and space without borders but very real as it is in that space where the Throne of God and all his attendant's host exist. Each name, then, is to be understood in connection with each other to understand that unlimited space of God without limits, without borders. A Divine space of existence, power, and glory in a circle and space without borders—without edges. The combinatory nature of the names we now consider falls within that proposition of the circles that, in the very verbal connections of these names, brings to focus this dimension of understanding who God is. In other words, this combination of names and meanings shows that no single name for God can be "complete" without this connection or reliance on the other. I contend that the complete human understanding of God exists is a recognition of all the Divine Spaces in which he occupies, functions, and expresses who he is.

In these names, we now consider two descriptions or additions to the name Jehovah, which are beautifully brought together to express something unique about God in such combinations of overlapping spaces.

Jehovah-rope is the first of these combined names represented in overlapping spaces as a symbol of the combined name. At the outset, their very structure of connected spaces or names shows they owe their meaningful value to the name to which they are connected Jehovah. As we have learned, Jehovah is a name existing in the space of God as the everlasting, self-existent in holiness, righteousness, truth, and redemption, among other moral attributes.

Another important dimension of these compound names of God is that their circle or space is infused with a historical event. Each name is revealed from a historical event that is unique to the name and informs its unique meaning.

Here is the circle of Divine *space* from which the name *Jehovah-rophe* fills. I love stories, for as a boy, one of the popular means of learning was listening to stories to gain moral and spiritual training. For example, I recorded a story in which every school child learned to teach us the hazard of greed. It was about a dog with a bone that one day, walking home, looked into a pond and saw another dog with a bone. At last, in his effort to get the other dog's bone, he dropped his in the pond and lost them both. They were simple, straightforward stories that helped us as children in moral training. However, as a child, I heard the story of Abraham, who gave rise to this name for God, Jehovah's rope, and that left me puzzled while growing up. It represented a space of who God is that I could not understand. I could not understand a God who would take so long to give this family a son, then turn around and tell his dad to offer him and, in such a way as to put him on an altar to kill him with a knife as a sacrifice. I must admit that after all these years, I still cringe at the thought of this demand of God for an old servant of his called Abraham. It could have been easily discarded if it had been a fairytale, like so many other English stories I have heard. However, my Sunday School teachers never presented this as a fairytale. It is an event that took place within a real family and a long-awaited son named Issacs.

The name of this circle and space, Jehovah-Jireh, is filled with the mystery of the faith in Jehovah God beyond human comprehension. There in the space of a finite human in an infinite God is the secret to understanding the God of that space, Jehovah-Jireh, who provides the sacrifice. The son Isaac and his father participated in an unusual act of faith, with death looking right at them from a dead whom life came. Not death raised its ugly head again to take that miracle life away. Except for the power of God Jehovah, who brought life out of a dead woman who now brought life out of the hand of a believing husband. Where is the sacrifice? (Genesis 22).

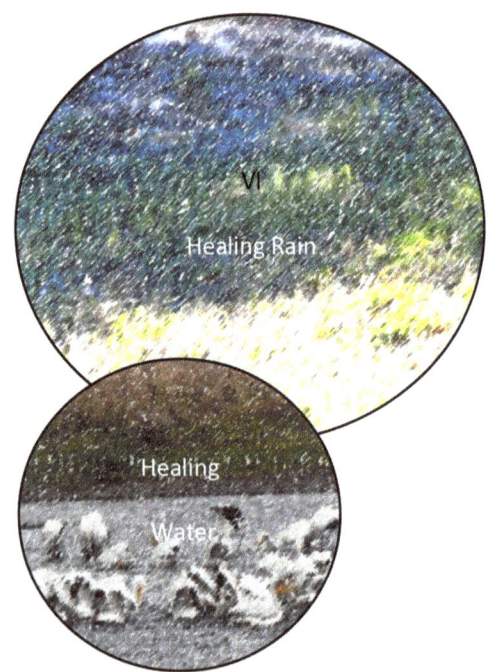

Jehovah-rophe (God the Healer)

In the first compound circle of God's name, we see a difficult and protracted circumstance of Abraham's family waiting for a promised child and then being asked to take that child and sacrifice him to God. It seems like a bridge too far, a space too empty for the human mind. Except it was filled with faith of a man who "believe God, and it was counted to him for righteousness. This space was filled with not only faith but with *God's provision of the sacrifice of a lamb, so Abraham did not have to slay his only son.* Eventually, though, God the Father did have to offer his only Son as a "lamb slain before the foundation of the world." So, in *Jahovah-jireh*, we discovered a space filled with faith and redemption from this event. We now move to another overlapping compound name filled with **healing and sustenance from a parched land.**

As with Jehovah-Jireh, this compound named Jehovah-rope rose out of another trying circumstance in the life of God's people, Israel. It was a time and space recorded in Exodus when Israel journeyed out of Egypt in a great deliverance. They had crossed the Red Sea in triumph. They enjoyed the blessings of deliverance. However, as they journeyed, their joy turned into sadness, and their rejoicing into regrets. Their journey became difficult as they faced what they thought would be a disaster in the wilderness. They thought they had come out of Egypt to die in the wilderness as they ran out of any source of water to sustain them. In Exodus 15, we read a most chilling commentary:

> *"Then Moses led Israel from the Red Sea, and they went into the Desert of Shur. For three days, they traveled in the desert without finding water. When they came to Mirah, they could not drink its water because it was bitter (that is why the place was called Marah."*

That is why the place was called "Mirah, " meaning "bitter." Regrettably, it was more than a description of the place but of God's people whose journey took them there. They also became bitter, like the water they found. It was bitter water in a bitter land.

In the case of Abraham, called after years of waiting to kill his son of promise and offer him as a sacrifice on an altar he built with his own hands. Now, another Patriarch Moses and the Israelites searching desperately for three days to find water to survive did so but could not drink it, for it was bitter water. That space seemed like a cruel joke, but unlike Sarah, no one was laughing. This was not about the birth of a child; this was now about the survival of the people from that child.

Jehovah-rope intervened again, but this time not to provide a sacrifice for redemption (Jehovah-Jireh) but healing for the body and souls of the people who desperately needed it. As Moses cried out to him (Exodus 15:25), God showed him a piece of dead wood. Moses, in obedience, did what God told him to do. He threw it into the water, and the water became fit to drink. The commentary changed from the people's condition to Jehovah's communication. He said to them:

> *"If you listen carefully to the Lord your God and do what is right in his eyes if you pay attention to his commands and keep all his decrees, I will not bring on you any of the diseases I brought on the Egyptians, for I am the Lord [Jehovah-rophe] who heals you."*

It was a new name he introduced. It was a new unique *circle/space* in which to understand God. A space that uniquely captures all his power to heal. In this *Divine space* expressed in this name, Jehovah-rope encircled all the focus on his power, promise, and purpose to provide all the healing we need for body and soul. It is there for all those who cry out to him in the pain of their problems and the crisis of their condition. It is important to understand that this is not simply a description of his identity. That was already established in his name Jehovah. Here, in this combination and overlap, who he is connected to what he will do. It is a space of action. It is a space of his willingness to act in his being on behalf of all those who cry out to him in pain. Not only for Moses but for anyone who would turn to him.

Jehovah-rophe is a combined *circle* and *space* as exemplified in the New Testament through all the healing Jesus did as he came as the expressed image of his Father. It was said of him: "News about him spread all over Syria, and people brought to him all who were ill with various diseases, those suffering severe pain, the demon-possessed, those having seizures, and paralyzed; and he healed them Matthew 4:24). It is not only who he is. It is what he will do to those who come to him. He is a great physician. Insurance already paid. There are no restrictions on pre-existing ailments. It is already assumed that one is coming to him. No appointment and waiting are necessary. No profiling of your identity is based only on who he is, *Jehovah-rophe.* It is a space bursting at the edges of all eternity of Jesus Christ as "living water," as he told the woman at the well who needed healing in body and soul (John 5). It is a space filled with forgiveness from man's rebelliousness against God and his ways, but who would turn to him and find him *Jehovah-rophe?* It is like an open-door space with a large welcome sign that reads, *"And the Spirit and the bride say 'Come!' And let the one who hears say 'Come!' Let the one who is thirsty come and let one who wishes would take the free gift of the water of life"* (Revelation 22:17).

Jehovah-rophe What else can we say? It is an immeasurable space of God's forgiveness and grace. A God of *comfort in crisis* of *provisions in pain.* A God who comes to us as the prophet Malachi declared, "…but for you who revere my name, the sun of righteousness will rise with healing in its rays" (Malachi 4:2). I have known that space in that circle of a healing God. A place where you search for healing water for your body and soul. I was married for 38 years. I planned all those years with the disposition that I am likely to die before my wife. It was arrogant. Although motivated by love, there was also folly, for although next to each other, I could not know how each of our life's rivers would flow. Nevertheless, I relied on statistics that say women live longer than men, particularly in marriages. It did not turn out the way I planned it. Unexpectedly and without warning of any kind, a retune visit to the doctor for slight dizziness turned out to be much worse. Within a week, we were facing a doctor with a grim look as he was taken aback by what he had discovered. Your wife is very sick. Do what you need to do, as she has stage 4 cancer in an almost inoperable location in her brain. Working for the government in the school system in Florida, she had very good health insurance and, for so many years, followed the usual checkup with no sign of malady all those years. She was looking forward to retirement. And the very month it was to begin a period we looked forward to enjoying the diagnostic came with just six months to live. I was a leader and Pastor, and she assisted me in the ministry for most of her years. But she faced this news with a composure I had never known she carried. On the other hand, my world was turned upside down. I cried out to God and asked him if he had to do that the same month she retired. Could you not at least give her a little time to enjoy retirement? I tried to stay strong on the outside during those months of progressing deterioration as her invaded mind was alert while her body began losing ever so slowly its motor skills until, in the last two weeks of an eight-month ordeal, she slipped away into the unconscious just two weeks before she was gone. When she was gone, my own trial began. I entered a dark place hidden from anyone else but God. I cried in secret. The uncontrollable tears would come each day. I became scared that my tears would never stop. I knew God promised someday he would wipe away all tears from our eyes, but I need this now, I told him. I went to the grave of my wife and prayed, looking up for God to stop the tears, if not the pain. From that day, he did not stop the tears, but they came once per week, then about once a month, until the regularity became unnoticeable.

In that space, each day became a challenge to be or not to be. I needed help. I traveled two hours away to talk to my brother about the wasteland and wilderness experience I was going through because of the loss of my wife. He asked me a strange question out of the blue. What were you doing when you met your wife? He asked. I said I was writing a book that the publishing company Moody Press had asked me. They wanted me to rewrite it for a particular audience. But I did not. I got married. As I said that, I noted inside that it was forty years ago that I put that book on the shelf. He said to me to get back to it. I noted it was forty years ago. I had been in the literal wilderness. I got back to it, and writing has been what God used to save me from going under. Forty years in the wilderness, he forgave me for the neglect. I began to write every day for over six years now with one publication, "The Dark Side of the Gospel," and seven other manuscripts.

I am yet haunted by the pain that God took my wife away for all those years, even productive in ministry, starting a church that is still ongoing. I would not have fulfilled this ministry of being a prophet and a writer of his gospel without him getting my attention in such a way. I have often reflected on whether I would have gotten back to writing if God did not take my wife of 38 years home. I do not know for sure. But what I do know it is the *space* and *place* of God as *Jehovah-rophe* the healer of my soul from which I write. I would have never known such healing without walking this wilderness.

Jehovah-Nissi (*The Lord is my Banner*)

It did not take long after Jehovah's deliverance from bitter water in Marah, where he had revealed himself as Jehovah-raphe (a healer), for Rephidim to face bitter warfare with their staunch enemy, the Amalekites.

As the battle was won and victory was gained, "Moses built an altar and called it ***The Lord is my Banner***" (Exodus 17:15)— Jehovah-nissi – my protector. Nevertheless, Israelites again began to complain about these two geographical places. There was no food as they journeyed into the wilderness of sin, but God once again provided for them with manna. It was not enough. The murmuring continued as they outwardly suggested to Moses that they had it better in Egypt.

This complaint was not to be taken lightly. It was not the people's random sayings. It was a direct assault that questioned whether God could truly look out for them. Indeed, they questioned whether he was among them at all (Exodus 17). For in Marah, although the water was bitter, at least there was water. Their journey brought them to a place where there was no water at all.

At Horeb, the answer came to show them that the Lord was among them when he supplied them with water from an unlikely place—a rock. Nevertheless, there were yet doubt and disappointments even after such miraculous blessings and the presence of Christ among them as the Rock (1 Corinthians 10:4). So, they came to a place where their greatest foe was not the elements, but their fiercest enemies, the Amalekites. They came against Israel (Exodus 17:8). Their worst ancient enemies were blocking any progress they desired to make. They fought without mercy. They struck hard where Israel was most vulnerable (Cf. Deuteronomy 25: 17, 18).

Out of this circle of cruelty against Israel's vulnerability came a striking battle victory that depended on God and Moses, the leader, and Aron and Hur, who held their hands up. As long as Moses' hands were held up, there was a success with Joshua and Israel's army. It is out of this mysterious connection between the weakness of humans and lifting up the hands of humans towards God to bring his powerful and victorious easily that we fight our battles and win.

The uniqueness of this space in God's name is symbolic, as Moses applied it as a "banner." It symbolizes both the presence and power of God, reminding each of his followers of his presence with us in battle. We are reminded that he is our "banner," Jehovah-Nissi.

Jehovah M' Kaddesh (Holyness)

Holiness

Jehovah M' Kaddesh is one of the more obscure names for God. But there is no room for obscurity in the circle of the model for understanding God and his person. Let us face it. It is true that the name may be obscure to us, but we must be careful to understand that no name of God is obscure to him. Each speaks to his person and character and is an important means of bringing his person and character to us.

Although God is represented in three Persons and diverse manners (Hebrews 1:1-3), he is yet one God (Deuteronomy 6:4; Mark 12:29). But as we stated the one God represented in the unlimited circle with space without edges in each name represents a dimension of God's person and character and therefore, we must be careful not to ignore that unique *circle/space* that this name for God seeks to focus our attention. The most important reason this name for God should garner more attention is that it represents one of the most important dimensions or characters of God's person that infuses every other.

Jehovah-M' Kaddesh is a name that expresses his holiness. No other name expresses this unique *space* as his holiness. In the eternal space of the throne of God, his special angels sing, *"Day and night they never stop saying: Holy, holy, holy, in the Lord God Almighty. Who was, and is, and is to come"* (Revelation 4:8).

The importance and meaning of this name *Jehovah – M' Kaddesh* can be seen in the event and the larger context of its introduction in Leviticus 20:7-8: "Consecrate yourselves and be holy *because I am the Lord your God. Keep my decrees and follow them.* **I am the Lord, who makes you holy.**"

How Did the story of Bereshith Come to us?

There is only three ways the record of Bereshith—the ancient history of the world recorded by Moses in the book of Genesis could have been transmitted to him:

- The *Written Word* so Moses and the people could read it.
- The *Spoken Word* so the people could hear it
- The *Inspired Word* through Divine revelation from God so the people could know it, believe it, and live by it.

The first means of transmission was for the ancient world to record the story of *Bereshith* was to write it down. In the antediluvian world, when the life of man was so protracted, there was comparatively little need for *writing* of any kind, and no alphabetical writing then existed" (Clark's Commentary, Volume I, Abingdon Press, NY p.26).

25

GOD WANTS TO KNOW WHAT WE THINK OF HIM

"WHO DO THE CROWDS SAY I AM?"

(Luke 9:18)

This title, "Concepts of God," can be misleading because it is more centered on who God reveals Himself to be than on what we mere mortals think He is. Nevertheless, I think it wise to begin here since it was where Jesus began His inquiry of Himself. Jesus, throughout His earthly ministry, revealed Himself astonishingly as a Divine Person yet so inquisitive. For example: (1) He is in a large crowd, and a lady decides to touch "the hem of His garment." Ok, you would think he could let this one go since the lady was healed; after all, we are in the middle of a crowd. Even the disciples thought He should. But not Jesus. He was inquisitive. He wanted to know "who touched me." Zacchaeus about Him coming, and he wanted to see Him. Little did He realize that although he climbed a tree, anyone who wanted to see him, which by his profession as a tax collector, would hardly look up to even notice him. But not Jesus. He not only looked up at the tree but called on him to come down and decided even to visit this tax collector's home. Even as a boy of twelve, His parents could not find Him because of this Divine inquisitiveness.

Now he is with His disciples. Moreover, there is much to talk about. And there is much that could pressure His interest. Like the off-the-mark question "Who touched me?" that startled the disciples, leaving them in wonder as to why He would ask such a question came another with astonishing force, and no less surprising: "Who do the crowds say I am? Here are several important lessons to learn about God asking such a question:

- It is a question of Divine interest. It says to all humankind everywhere that God wants to know what you are saying about Him. It follows that we must be careful what we say about God, for He is listening.
- It is a question of the Divine to His followers. He wanted to know what His followers were being told about Him. He wanted to know what information channel to which they are listening. What newscast are they tuning into? What are they listening to that could corrupt their understanding of who I am?
- God has a Divine interest in not only what various "crowds" are saying about Him but also how His followers are being influenced by what they have been exposed to.

- Jesus's asking this question was not an academic pursuit. His follow-up question, like that of a keen reporter, dispelled any doubt that the question of what people are thinking and saying about God is some philosophical inquiry or academic exercise. This is not a pursuit for meditational material. This is a serious pursuit for which all humankind should seek, as God Himself exemplified: All humankind must seek the knowledge of God.

I contend this is the heart of this pursuit, the heart of the inquiry. What the world thinks about God determines the kind of world in which we live. The disciples and the world are affected by the consciousness of the prevailing winds of the knowledge of God.

"Who Do the Crowds Say I Am? Some Say:

- "Some Say John the Baptist
- "Others Say Elijah"
- "Still Others," one of the Prophets came back to life.

What can we learn from the answers?

- We can learn that the school of public opinion is never a good place to learn about God. I contend Jesus wanted His followers not to look at public opinion or take a pool to learn about Him.
- Who God is cannot be determined by who or what is trending at any given time.
  In Jesus' time, His double were essential people with their historical trends and following. Although they were good people in their time, they were not Jesus. They were not God in the flesh.
- No one would suggest any of these men as messiah if asked. However, there is no doubt that men or women of fame today can be viewed as a Messiah. Indeed, the answer of the First Century disciples would not vary too much from trends we would see flourishing today: There is a rich and growing appetite for godless messiahs. There is a yearning for economic messiahs, social messiahs, political messiahs, and the like. Jesus wanted to know what His followers were hearing. He wanted to know who was attracting their attention, vying for an alternative to Him.
- As Jesus was concerned, what was the popular opinion about Him? It should occupy no less an interest of the Church today. Are we seeing messiahs of money? Are we seeing those who would deliver us do so through deceptions because there is such a messianic craving for deliverance from what plagues us today?
- I contend Jesus inquired about what the world thinks of Him to teach His followers that He is not a God who berries His head like an ostrich in the sand. He is not a God who created the world as a place for human inhabitation and then left town. That is not who He is.

But What About You? He asked, Who Do You Say I am? Peter answered, "You are the Messiah, the Son of the Living God" (Matthew 16:16).

"But What About You?

Jesus, with this question, moves perceptively from a public space to a personal one. Then, he would later move from that personal response to a spiritual one. With this brief encounter, He would lay the foundation of a Divine space. From which space of Peter's confession of Who God is was going to be built a new spiritual as well as visible Body of Christ. The world, with its varied views of Who God is, was going to have an opportunity to know God through His Son, as Peter confessed. The world then cannot be justified in their claims that He is someone else. His Coming in historical space and time is a testimony of who He is. His claims definitively would make Him a liar as to Who He is. His Claims, Communication, Conduct, Cross, and Church are all a living continuum of Who He is.

It is the basis of how every individual would be judged: Who do you say I am?" That is the question.

I cannot overstate the importance of this historical narrative in the life of the Church then and now. When Jesus said, "But what about you? Who do you say I am? He was not engaging in religious hyperbole. When He spoke, He was making it real? He indicated what we need to think, act, and behave concerning our belief in Him. If we do not know Who He is, we cannot confess Who He is. We cannot think of His thoughts or be a communicator of Who He is in this world. The world's ideas as to Whom He clashes like a hurricane against Him. Christ and the world would never be compatible. Moreover, this is so even when associated with such names as John the Baptist, Elisha, or one of the tremendous historical prophets. It is well to note that none of these men ever claim to be the Messiah.

I have found it often helpful to consider three narrative elements in these gospel events. First, look at the context or setting of the story. Sometimes, it is inherent in the story that the Gospel's writer presents. This story has a unique setting, for the story by Jesus is often initiated by a question from the audience, such as in the case of The Good Samaritan, someone from the crowd asked Jesus, "Who is my neighbor?" Nevertheless, this story is unique in that Jesus Himself initiates the setting by asking questions. Second, the setting is best followed by the STATING of the story. This is often given in a straight-faced way by reading the narrative and restating the story to understand the essence of it. In this case, Jesus is engaging His disciples, initiating their testimonies as to what people are saying about Him, and His poignant pursuit as to their own personal view or understanding of Who He is. Third, after there is a full understanding of the Setting and the setting, then comes the third and often most important. What is the MEANING of the story? What is important to grasp is that often the meaning is not left for someone to impose on the story. For in the narrative itself, often the meaning or interpretation comes seamlessly after the setting and the stating. In this story, Jesus Himself clarified the meaning of the story. In His response to Peter, He laid out a view of the story's meaning from a space that they could not fathom or suspect in the setting or the stating. Jesus, in the following, then gave the most important aspect of the story, the meaning of it in His direct response to Peter and all the followers who would come after in His Church. We do not know for sure why Jesus' response to Peter's answer was only recorded by the Gospel writer Matthew. Perhaps because his Gospel was directed to a more Hebrew audience as the Gospel with more emphasis on Jesus as the Messiah. For whatever reason for Matthew's exclusive inclusion of Jesus' extended response to Peter's confession that He was the Christ "the Son of the living God," Jesus left no doubt that His response included the need for the whole world to know. If only from the prophetic perspective that declared like a battle cry the foundation on which the church which would minister to the whole despite any resistance from that world. The foundation would be assured on the rock of Peter's confession. Here then, the Third step, The MEANING of the story, is detailed by Matthew:

Jesus replied:

"Blessed are you, Simon, son of Jonah, for this was not revealed to you by flesh and blood but by my Father in Heaven.

"Now I say to you that you are Peter (which means 'rock'), and upon this rock, I will build my Church, and all the powers of hell will not conquer it (Matthew 16:18 NLT).

What, then, can we learn from Jesus' brief yet penetrating, perceptive, and prophetic proposition to Peter and the world:

- It means Jesus confirms to Peter and the world that He was indeed the Messiah.

After the context, in the story under consideration, Jesus Himself gives the contest. Look at the context of the story or events. Jesus presented it by asking what the social climate of belief about Him was. Then, you want to follow the story by the writers. What is the state of the story? All three Gospel writers, Matthew, Mark, and Luke recorded this narrative. Mark said it occurred while Jesus and His disciples walked to Caesarea. However, each focuses on the substance of the story's starting point, which is centered around two critical questions. Then, at the end of it, one must ask what the story's meaning was. The setting, the stating, or the meaning.

26

CREATOR - A GOD WHO ACTS

For He spoke, and it came to be.
He commanded, and it stood firm.   Psalm 33: 9

Through Him, all things were made.
Without Him, nothing was made
that has been made.   John 1:3

He is a God who Acted to Create the Physical World for Us

"Let there be Light!"

The very first pronouncement about God represented Him as a God of action. This is not an afterthought or an accident of structure. It was not for poetic consumption or literary style. This is the serious business of God through His prophets, letting every human on this planet know that what we behold each day of our lives is because of a God who acted in historical space and time. And more astonishingly He moved on the prophets to let us know he did so on our behalf for our comfort and survival. He made things "good for food and pleasant to the eyes." There can be no doubt that the sky, the trees, and the flowers have no eyes, so they can behold their own beauty. In all their majestic beauty, the oceans, the skies, and the mountains cannot appreciate themselves. They cannot analyze their own structure and conclude for themselves how wonderfully majestic we are. Why? God said he made them for us to appreciate. He declared them *pleasant to our eyes (Geneses 1-3).*

It is easy to think, especially in Christian circles, so much of how God did for us in sending His Son. But Long before His Son he sent the rain, the flowers, the trees, the birds, the fruits, and all the other living things for our survival and pleasure. So that by the time His Son came He was just one of the many things that He did for each of us. Christ did not come to take over the show. He came also to reveal His Father was there all the time throughout the ages, showing us His love, mercy, and grace in the spaces He acted in and created for us.

In the theology of content—in the message of what God said we can so easily lose the message of what He did. For example, all that we can see and behold in this Universe is said of God whom He spoke into existence. It was accomplished through the power of His command. Here we see the important action of words. His words in action created the fishes in the sea, the birds in the sky, and every living thing that crawled upon the earth. In short, He even acted in His commands to create beautifully detailed butterflies.

CREATED TO FLY:

He is a God who Acted to create

When God finished the physical world, including the animals He then uniquely turned His attention to creating us. The universe's ecosystem was self-contained. To this day, it still does not need us to survive. However, we cannot survive a moment without it. I contend that our unique dependence on all the universe offers to survive God's silent way of teaching us who He is. We learn we cannot survive without dependence on Him. We are called to humility because of this reality of complete dependence on what He has made and what He has done for us.

What can it mean that God reached down like a potter reaches for clay from the ground? He took the dust of the earth in his hands and fashioned it into a form like us with all the various structures of humanity. He made bones of various sizes, some as strong as from the earth. Particular tasks involve tissues of various consistencies that are able to stretch and contract and sometimes lie in place, all forming the matter of a man. Cells live in the crevices of bones, some hollowed out to protect certain kinds. Some lay dormant like armies in trenches waiting for any invasion that would threaten life with the innate command to fight any dangerous foreign matter entering their domain. They stand ready to battle for us, and most often, beyond our consciousness, they battle for our survival. They thrive and fight for us.

Lifeless veins and rivers of blood are waiting on God to be set free to roam the full length of the body to do their job with life, giving nourishment to everything in their hidden parts. Lifeless organs, large and small, whose varied tasks are still being studied and discovered to this day. Nerves are like the *blue tooth* of the brain—a vast communication system made to process signals from all the varied stimuli within and without in the world. Warnings, heat, cold, pleasure and pain, and signals for procreation and protective prompts for survival. What a colossal mess of mystery God has made that we take often for granted. Moreover, we give Him no credit for His incredible work. All this and more beyond my humble ability to explain laying lifeless on the earth before Him just like a stone from the earth on the ground. Until God's lips touch that of this lifeless body of clay called a man. The narrative so stated can hide the latent power of this extraordinary Devine act of God: "God breath into man the breath of life, and man became a living soul." As we consider these words, we must be careful not to see them as a poetic statement meant for psychological consumption but as a truth of God's action to create us in historical space and time. It is in that space that we can contain the knowledge of who God is and the full implications of His creative action on our behalf.

I contend we must be careful not to overlook the theology of this act. God did not make humanity raised up from the dust of the earth as a living carcass of a body. God did not create a suffocated machine that can cry, love, or accomplish things born of hope, aspirations, and planning. If this were the case, there would be no need for prayer, forgiveness, or compassion for all the things that make us human and, in some small way, divine. "fearfully and wonderfully made" (Psalm 139:14) because God acted. He breath. Moreover, mankind has become more than a living body. He became a spiritual being with a "living soul" that can never die. Because such a soul can be saved or lost. However, it can never die made in the eternal image of God. So, with the "breath of God," Adam, our human father, became mysteriously much more. He became a "living soul," of which the body he formed was just the space in which this eternal breathing of an individual soul inhabits. Thus, it is that every breath we take is a solemn reminder of His deliberate divine act on our behalf.

We breathe because of His prior action and not ours. He acted to create and nerves. Some respond to heat and cold. Others respond to pressure and even pain. Others respond to love. Others that could stretch and contract long before man developed a simple rubber band. And he made a heart and fashioned it to beat for a lifetime keeping everything going after he would set it in motion. He acted to make an individual brain like a computer before man would make one of their own. And he gave as much thought to the toes and the simple curvature of one's feet to keep the whole upright body for posture and balance without a tail or wings. I contend that according to the narrative of creation, every single part of one of the most complex systems in the universe—the human body was fashioned by the hand of God. The reproductive system he fashioned for not just procreation but also a multitude of pleasures is as much a revelation of God, who He is, and what He thinks of us. It is the reason only a fool will say there is no God, for He is all over us in what He fashioned with His own hands.

Moses Who Made Your Mouth?

Moses, a child of a Jewish mom who placed him in a river and downstream, was discovered by Pharaoh's daughter. Raised as a son of Pharaoh rose to great prominence in Egypt. However, in time, through his conflicting allegiances between his people in slavery and his position in Pharaoh's kingdom, he had to choose for his own survival to flee Egypt. He ended up far from the concerns and conditions of his people in Egypt. However, God said their cries had come up to Him. And God, after many years, decided to Act on behalf of His people. His actions involve meeting Moses to send him on a mission of deliverance for his people. What is important is the nature of Moses' defense for not being the right choice of God for the job and God's counterargument to rebuff that of Moses.

Whether Moses had a physical speech problem or felt he was a good enough speaker to approach Pharaoh to deliver God's message, "Let my people go," we do not know. The fact that God sought him out for the task is, on its face, evidence that God thought he could do it. However, Moses did not see it that way. His argument for the defense was straightforward. He told God, "I am a man of slow speech..." (Exodus 4:10-12) as if God were One, not knowing the abilities of whom He calls. On the other hand, it was more that Moses was ignorant of who God was. So, God had to give him several lessons:

1. He was a God who defied normalcy. He made a bush burn without being consumed by its flames.
2. He was a God who can communicate through any means He chooses. He spoke to Moses through the non-consuming fire.
3. He was a God who could take a dead shepherd's stick in the hands of Moses and turn it into life, much like He took the body of his lifeless ancestor Adam and pored life into Him.
4. He was a God who can make the ground we stand on "holy ground" when we stand in His presence.

It was in that unique space on the mountain that God, who acted to make Moses through Adam, had now to perform before him to make him believe in His power, His people, His purpose, and His promise. He told Moses, with all his perceived deficiencies, "I will put my words in your mouth," even as he reminded him sternly that it was a mouth He fashioned and was so able to use to deliver His people out of bondage.

I contend that the essence of God's response demonstrated the importance of what God thinks of His actions and how He wanted His human creation to think, act, and behave before the visible world. It lies in the question God asked Moses. "Who made your mouth?"

If actions speak louder than words, then look around and note what the creator did. And He did not charge us for His work. It was freely given all the abilities inherent in the universe He created by His words, and us He created by His handy work.

The narrative of the Scriptures reveals not a passive God but One who acted in historical space and time and is engaged in our time and will continue to do so in action.

It is not like God to sit on a lazy throne in the Heavens just waiting to be worshiped. However, He is a God actively engaged with us. A God who notes the passing of the seasons, who "knows our frame" and engages in each person's passage through this life. One who sees the "sparrow falls" considers how "lilies grow" and how many strands of hair each person has. He knows how and when each baby is born, even those unborn, never cloud His notice. He is a God who acts and demands our actions as well.

In the following narrative account, we have a detailed action from a mother's secret place. Even God's continued action in creation is reported. It is found in the account of Jerimiah that as God called him to act on behalf of His people, God reported His action on Jerimiah's behalf. We often begin the journey of someone, at their birth and for many years later after their upbringing and youthful days. However, the faithful day when Jerimiah was called to be a Prophet of God, He was careful to let Jerimiah in on what was to him God's secret action on his behalf and also for our understanding of God's continued action hundreds of years after His action in Creation. He is still at work. Jerimiah's first prophecy to his people recalled:

"The word of the Lord came to me saying,

*Before **I formed you** in the womb*

***I knew you** before you were born*

I set you apart,

I appointed you

A prophet to the nations."

(Jerimiah 1: 4-5)

27

THE CREATOR OF MORALITY

God is light
And in Him, there is no darkness at all -1 John 5:5-12

Freedom and Form

From the beginning, God's dealings with His human creation were clear. He wanted them to know He was a God of absolute standards. His essence was spiritual Light. His moral character was absolute holiness. That holiness was projected in all His dealings with His creation. He was not a God of anything goes. He was not a God who said to His creation, "Do whatever you want" or "Do whatever pleases *you*."

Two essential things God represented from the beginning that, despite all that has occurred, I contend endured to this day. The first is *freedom,* and the second is *form.* These two spiritual parameters inhabit the space of God's first significant instructions to His human creation. It is not my intention to dig deep into the theology of this. We begin at the beginning to show that before humanity did anything, God revealed himself to His creation as a God who created and established creeds. He did so in the spoken words as recorded in Genesis. It is from this point that the Prophets spoke. Each of them said to the people, "Thus sayeth the Lord.." This phase or similar statements are recorded in the Old Testament some 1900 times. The Bible narrative can be viewed from the perspective of these two spiritual parameters—form and freedom. God wanted His human creation to pursue happiness in freedom. However, He also wanted them to follow His holiness in form. Both parameters lavished the landscape of the holy Scriptures. They are essential companions rooted in the character of God. Both exist in the space of humanity as a gift from God. Happiness and joy cannot be found in freedom without form; neither can they be found in Form without freedom. Form without freedom is legalism, which cannot be satisfied. Freedom without form is pure chaos. I contend that the flow of civilization has been a constant revelation of the relationships of adherence to the objection of these parameters.

Form and Freedom: Form for security, freedom to fly.

The Apostle Paul in the New Testament considered these two spiritual parameters. He admonished the early believers to "**stand fast in the liberty wherewith Christ has made us free**. He wrote extensively on this freedom and its corresponding restraints to live in the Spirit of Holiness (Galatians 5: 1-17).

The Apostle Peter also clearly contrasted these two parameters. He wrote of this great freedom to the Early Church: "Live as free people…" he said to them. But he also spoke of the form: "Do not use your freedom as a cover-up for evil …" he admonished (1 Peter 2:16).

These are not the byproduct of a philosophical position. They are not centered in a system for social order, although no social order or happiness can be attained without the freedoms within the forms. I contend they are critical for survival because they are based on something and Someone much more profound than mere words. As I have established from the beginning, the foundation of these connected spiritual principles is based on the moral character of a holy God. He desires our freedom to enjoy all that He has provided. However, in this freedom, He wants us to live to please ourselves and Him in the form he established in the Holy Scriptures.

28

A God Who Cares

I believe one of the greatest secrets among God's people is that we serve a God who cares for everyone on the earth. As a professional fashion and celebrity photographer, I have had the privilege of photographing some of the most famous people in the world, including several presidents. In recent years, I have turned my photographic interest more towards nature, especially our feather friends of all varieties. I have learned more about life on the earth and God in Heaven for doing so. I have never ceased to be fascinated by the details, say in a spider's web, a butterfly's wings, or even in the variety of leaves on trees of every kind. Even a simple stalk growing carelessly along a country path is smothered with details that hardly anyone stops to notice in life in the fast lane. I would take a picture just because I like its apparent shape until I get home and review what I have taken. The conclusion that has bothered me for some time is why God designed so many minutes and beautiful details that one can hardly even see without a close-up study.

After years of doing this, I came across a statement in Genesis that finally gave me a clue as to why all of these fascinating details of life in the ecosystem in which we inhabit. The statement was concerning the care Elohim—the God of Creation gave to his creation: "The Lord God made all kinds of trees to grow out of the ground—trees that were pleasing to the eyes..." (Genesis 2:9)

I contend that God made every detail of this earth and sky in part for our enjoyment—just for us to look at and enjoy the beauty of His details. He cares about what we do. He cares to place in his handiwork something to bring beauty into our lives, something pleasant to look at.

When I was a boy going to Sunday School, I learned over and over How God cares because He sent His Son into the world to die for us. And for sure, He did. As I grew older in the faith, I learned He cared just as much when he sent us butterflies to behold. For His love is there as well. I contend that before His Son came to this earth, mankind found a God that cared when he provided vegetables. He cared when He provided food of every kind to eat (Genesis 2:9). And what a sorry life it would be if He provided all this without the taste buds for us to salivate and enjoy. We live in a world lavished with the demonstration that God cares, not only about how we live to please Him but also about how He provides for us.

29

COUNCILOR

"Come now and let us reason together" (Isaiah 1:18)

When you need someone to talk to, He is there.

There is no greater virtue and no greater expression of wisdom than the humility of Christ. Through every virtue of Christ, His wisdom and humility are supreme. He is the fullest expression of the Torah that is likened to water. Jesus is the Water of Life (Jn 4:13, 14), as although it flows from the highest hills, like Christ, it settles in the lowest places. This cannot be missed from anything that can be said of Christ. This cannot be ignored. This is the essence of Christ's life of wisdom. It should permeate every aspect of evangelical Christian involvement and mission today (Proverbs 18:40).

Look at the book:
"In your relationship with one another, have the same mindset as Christ Jesus:

> *Who, being in the very nature of God,*
> *He did not consider equality with God to be something to be used to His advantage,*
> *Rather, He made himself nothing by taking the very nature of a servant,*
> *Being made in human likeness.*
> *And being found in appearance as a man,*
> *He humbled himself*
> *By becoming obedient to death—even the death of the cross*
> *(Philippians 2: 5-8).*

It is quite easy to take what is fundamentally a historical description of reality—real space and time events; with the spiritual eloquence of the Apostle Paul and turn such vital historical passage into but a poetic expression. One can read such verses in a church reading and respond, "What a beautiful passage." Nevertheless, in its historical significance, it is not a beautiful passage at all. Isaiah saw this reality from a prophetic perspective and concluded that this was no expression of beauty. Beauty was going to be the result.

Nevertheless, we must be careful to see that the Divine process of getting there was not at all a beauty. Humility is not an attractive virtue in process but in production. The Apostle Paul continued his admonition:

> *Therefore, God exalted Him to the highest place,*
> *And gave Him the name that is above every name,*
> *That is the name of Jesus; every knee should bow*
> *In heaven and on earth and under the earth,*
> *And every tongue acknowledges that Jesus Christ is the Lord*
> *To the glory of God, the Father (Philippians 2:9-11).*

Nevertheless, before this, Isaiah the Prophet saw the humble means through which Christ would come and said 53:2:

> *"He grew up before him like a tender shoot,*
> *And like a root out of dry ground.*
> *He had no beauty or majesty to attract us to him,*
> *Nothing in his appearance that we should desire him.*

I have found that reading Isaiah, the gifted prophet's words concerning Christ, soaring with such majestic rhythm and eloquence, makes it so easy to forget what and to whom he is referring. For example, "like a tender shoot" can bring a beautiful "tender" plant to mind. However, it is analogous to Christ in His humility, which comes to us not from majestic heritage but from the humble roots of Jessie. It foreshadowed the question hurled against Him when He did come: "Can anything good come from Nazareth? (Jn 1:43). The prophet's further expands this "root out of the dry ground" that explained the "tender shoot" not of emotional sensibility, but His earthly heritage structure; like a man without an adequate home; like a wanderer in the desert with not much in inheritance; a place with not much substance for anything to grow. This was the mantle of His ministry, how the Prophet described His humble walk among humanity. I contend that anyone who desires to understand the real "root" of the Christian life and movement must begin with the fundamental knowledge of the wisdom of Christ's humility—a place and space where Christ is the example that thwarts all self-promotion and makes such antithesis to the Christian cause in the world. The world might see Him in all His glory, but not from a majestic place, but the humble servant life He lived among us.

Being human comes with a fallen structure of humanity that Jesus Christ had to face. For example, here is one in the mirror:

Spaces in Conflict

I pray often. But at times, I start in earnest and end with a wandering mind. So, I start over just to end up in the same place until my own humanity faces me, and I fall asleep, sometimes on my knees.

I talk—sometimes too much, sometimes too little. Often, I do not know when to do either, especially in casual conversations.

I like to work; and I like doing nothing. And often I am conflicted doing either one. I struggle with my humanity for when I am working, I feel the need to rest; when I rest, and I feel the urging to work.

I love to cook. I like to enjoy what I cook and see others enjoy it as well. It's like a high point. The low point comes when it's time to do the dishes. So, I opt to use paper plates, but my friends want me to help save the planet.

I like to explain often complex things, but dislike being misunderstood, so I remain silent when I should not be.

I love a challenge. I often felt that being white would make things too easy, but being black, over the years, I have experienced things too hard.

Sometimes, I feel like the palmist's human cry: "Oh, that I had the wings of a dove! I would fly away and be at rest. I would flee far away and stay in the desert" (Ps 55:6-7).

So, I call myself a shadow man. In the shadows, most solace. It is like the mythical place Bruce Hornsby sang about in "*Dream Land.*" It is like my shadow land. Despite my limitations, busyness, faults, and pain, I do not feel alone there. I go there often and feel safe in my natural human fears. It is the place where I most experience the presence of God. When my humanness comes face to face with me, I run to that place. It is like what Kim Walker-Smith sang about in "Throne Room." I go there. It is from that space that I understand, as well as fail to understand, why God wanted to take on all this human baggage. *His humanity is divine.* That is my response. Although, I do not know how that could be. These essays attempt to explain what I do not fully grasp. So, we face it together, hoping to find some wisdom in that space.

Wisdom—she began through the disciple Luke using his skills as a historian to set the historical pattern of the life of his Master Jesus Christ (Luke 1:1-4, Acts 1:1). It is noteworthy, then, that in wisdom Luke did not directly turn to the birth of Jesus Christ which wisdom so beautifully narrates through him— the most beautifully written story of his master's birth ever written. Wisdom stirred the historian Luke to begin the story of Jesus Christ by sharing with us the unique, humble, aged family of a Priest and his wife in such a divine-human description: "*Both of them were righteous in the sight of God, observing all the Lord's commands and decrees blamelessly. But they were childless because Elizabeth was not able to conceive and they were both very old* (Luke 1:7).

Folly, in the traditions of her community, had rewarded her barrenness despite her holy living with disgrace and shame. Wisdom found Luke and moved him to begin the historical narrative of the Life of his Master, Jesus, from this humble and humiliating place. Wisdom wanted us to know two mothers' humble stories to introduce His. Wisdom wanted us to know the humble roots of the time and place where His ministry began. Wisdom wanted us to see what humility looks like in its historical roots, how it was framed in the lives of those who knew her, the lives of the forgotten, or those looked down upon. Elizabeth's story was lost in what would be the incredibly famous glow of her relative Mary's story as the mother of Jesus. In the historical narrative, Luke reported both humility and glory.

From Elizabeth's question, wisdom's humility is revealed: "*But why am I <u>so favored</u>, that the mother of my Lord should come to me?*" (Luke 1:43). And from Mary's spontaneous song, wisdom's grace in the song was revealed as well: Mary said, "My soul" glorifies the Lord, *and my spirit rejoices in God my Savior, for he has been mindful of the humble state of his servant*" (Luke 1:46-48). Later, wisdom wanted us to see Jesus and John as if they were the clash of titans in historical time and space, but with wisdom and humility. Wisdom had brought them together before, but in the waters of their mother's wombs. Now, she brought them together again in the waters of the Jordan River as they faced each other when wisdom called out to them from her call to ministry.

In John's words, he had heard through wisdom and humility as he leaped into his mother's womb. He now expressed the same. As Jesus came walking up to him, the edge of his long attire flipping from His strides, John said, "*He is that One who comes after me, the straps of whose sandals I am not worthy to untie*" (John 1:27 cf. Luke 1:25, 43). The theme of "unworthiness" had followed them all through their childhood. Now, as men before God, they still stood humble before Him. Just before, one of the greatest expressions of the Glory of God was about to be revealed to them. John spoke humbly even as he held the Son of God in humble hands and led Him to the water. He stood next to him and then over him in historical time and space as he placed him fully immersed—as entirely humbled as the Jordan filled with the history of wisdom and folly. So, Jesus, who was fully committed to the will of God now, also was symbolically fully submitted to the role of a servant in the Jordan. Both sons—Son of God and Son of man met in total submission and humility to the will of the Father in the river. Both met each other at the river of humility yet saw the glory of God come down.

Let us face it: **Humility is** not considered among humans' top virtues to be selected or encouraged. Left to one's own rationale and reason, it would not even come close to the top. Indeed, resisting the temptation to take the human stage driven by self-importance is difficult. However, it is one of those virtues of wisdom that calls us to love her, esteem her, and exhibit her if we are to live a life of wisdom. It is one of those virtues of the heart that is not often seen or even heard; nevertheless, in the life of the One who was the expression of the wisdom of God, it is the primary virtue expressed in His earthly life. Why? Because it was the virtue most exhibited in the way His journey on earth began and the essence of His conduct throughout his ministry. For example, although His Mother heard the prediction that she would give birth to the Messiah and has been given so much glory through the ages, she found no glory in her. She wisely said to the prophetic angel in response, "I am the Lord's servant … May your word to me be fulfilled" (Lk 1:38). And later, she sang at Elizabeth's home: "***<u>My soul glorifies the Lord</u>***… (Lk 1:46). Jesus echoed the same creed as he explained the arc of his life on earth to His followers. Like a spiritual laser beam, he said to them, ***"For I have come down from heaven, <u>not to do my own will</u>, but the will*** *of Him who sent me* (Jn 6:38). This is astonishing, as all the while He also made the claim to them *"My Father and I are One"* (Jn 10:30). This is what makes humility such an impressive and enduring quality of life. It is the fundamental mystery in the life of Christ that He was both One with the Father yet on earth willingly took on the role of a "Son of man did not come to be served, but to served…" (Mt 20:28) a faithful servant in historical time and space. This was not some mystical extension of the divine but a fundamental role for us in historical times.

This often-overlooked virtue is the key that opens the door to all the other virtues necessary for a life of wisdom. For example: What good is love if one is not humbled enough to express it to the *"lease of these"*? What good is grace to one not humbled enough to see their undeserving soul? What good is salvation if one cannot *"become like little children'* to *'enter the Kingdom of heaven" (cf. Mt 18:2-4)?* Wisdom declared then that the gate to the Kingdom of God was so narrow that no traveler could go in unless they were willing to *bow*.

I must also point out, understandingly, that the virtue of humility is often associated with weakness. Jesus' life demonstrated the abject folly of this position. On the contrary, His servant's life demonstrated the divine power of humility even when facing hostility. His servant's life on earth changed the world from start to finish. He engaged help from no political agency or power. He enlisted no armies. He sought no riches of his own. He once had to take money from a fish to pay his taxes. When he died, He was buried in another man's tomb. However, more books have been written about him than any other historical figure. No single historical person has engaged more followers in every generation. However, He is the one who came into this world in the humblest of ways. The final verdict was left to the Father. Consider the following to grasp the incredible power of humility as exemplified in Christ—Philippians 2: (v. 6) Who being in the very nature God, did not consider equality with God something to be used to His advantage; (7) instead, He made himself nothing by taking **the very nature of a servant**, being made in human likeness. (8) And being found in appearance as a man, **He humbled himself** by becoming obedient to death—even the death of the cross! (9) Therefore, **God exalted Him to the highest place and gave Him a name above every name,** (10) that at the name of Jesus, every knee should bow, in heaven and on earth and under the earth, and every tongue acknowledge that **Jesus is Lord to the glory of God the Father.** Paul made this argument to the believers at Philippi as a paramount example: "Do nothing out of selfish ambition or vain conceit; instead, in humility, *value others above yourselves. He was not looking to your interests but each of you to the interests of the others (v. 3-4).* The only way this can be done is through the wisdom of humility. You climb God's mountains not on your feet but on your knees.

In the entire narrative of Scripture, no event demonstrates this paramount virtue of wisdom as this man of history and faith came into the world. For here is Someone whom the Prophets predicted among His people to come as the Messiah—the Liberator of His people—the King of Kings and Lord of Lords. It was a rational expectation consistent with who He was and what He was predicted to do. He was the Creator of the Universe—maker of everything and all-powerful, yet he chose to come in humility. He was born by choice into a low-income family from the poor side of town. His actual place of birth was among the animals, for in his travels with His parent to Bethlehem, there was no place for Him in the Inn. Born a King among the animals, the family never complained that the Father gave them the wrong address. What greater expression of humility and its value to God than Jesus, His son, to come as a baby as God growing up like everyone else?

PART TWO

THE SPACE OF THE CROSS

30

THE CROSS SPACE

The symbol of the cross stands in the conceptual model of spaces of existence. It bridges the space between God and the rest of us. Here, I attempted to create a model that, in every symbolic way, is consistent with the reality of God's revelation in the narrative of the Holy Scriptures.

Look at the Book:

"For there is one God and One mediator between God and mankind, the man Christ Jesus who gave himself [in His death on the cross] as a ransom for all people…" (1 Timothy 2:5-6, emphasis mine)

When the Apostle Paul said these words to young Pastor Timothy, he was not engaging in hyperbole or what we might call "sweet talk." He said that when we think of God, even in the expression of three persons, we are to think of Him as one. However, he told Thimothy we should think of God in Christ as a mediator to the Father because of the Cross. He is saying what we ought to think and, therefore, act about the divine spaces, as represented in the model's cross. Two significant spaces of God and Mankind stand apart because of mankind's rebellion against his creator. Moreover, because of the Father's great love for us, He sent his son as a bridge between these two universe spaces. Moreover, between Heaven and Earth stands the cross as a bridge space for humanity. So, the cross in the model is a symbol of the reality of this interconnection between ***God and mankind, the man Christ Jesus.***

In this world, we have various ways to travel from one space to the other. If we have one, we can walk, use a bike, or motorbike for short distances. We can use a car, a cab, Uber, or train for long distances. For international travel from one continent to another, we can take to the skies on airplanes. We can even get on a rocket and go to outer space. Nevertheless, nothing here is scheduled to get us to Heaven in the wink of an eye except through Jesus. Moreover, that is because of what Christ did on the cross. Moreover, this is not hyperbole. It is the reality afforded by what the historical Jesus did on a cross just outside Jerusalem on a hill hanging on a cross as a sacrifice for each of us. A cross sunken in the earth. Its top point to heaven. Its arms outstretched as a welcome to anyone who would come in repentance and receive His grace. This is the story from reproach of sin to redemption in Christ.

Jesus the Son of God the Son of Man

From Reproach to Redemption

In Elohim's space of the cross, we come to the most defining distinction as to who Elohim is in regard to humankind. Here is this distinctive space: In all of human history, whether through oral traditions or written records, it is clear that people would give their last drop of blood for their God or gods and their belief in their God or gods. Nevertheless, the opposite remains unrecorded, except in Judo-Christian historical records and traditions.

Many archaeological sites abound of rituals of people even sacrificing their own children to appease their gods. It would be unthinkable that any God or gods would sacrifice themselves for the sins of mankind. This is unheard of except in the Judo-Christian historical culture and records. It would be unthinkable to fathom that the Christian God or any other gods of the people would die for them, and then in such a despicable way on that of an open cross in the countryside. But there lies the uniqueness of Elohim's redemptive space. He came to Earth and died on an "old rugged cross" for the sins of every one of us.

Look at the book:

> <u>Who, being in very nature God</u>, did not consider equality with God something to be used to his own advantage; rather, he made himself nothing by taking the very nature of a servant, <u>being made in human likeness</u>. And being found in appearance as a man, he humbled himself by becoming obedient to death—<u>even the death of the cross</u> (Philippians 2: 6-8 emphasis mine).

It was at this very point of the intersection of Elohim's redemptive space and humankind's sinfulness that the Apostle Paul found incomprehensible. To the Church at Rome, he said in another look at the book:

Oh, the depth of the riches of the wisdom and knowledge of God! How unsearchable his judgments and his paths beyond tracing out!

I stand like one on the ocean shores, looking as far as my eyes can see the horizon beyond me. I look at the sky. I see only blue all the while knowing that more is there. There is more to this unreachable horizon and the unreachable vastness of the universe. I cannot fathom either. And I cannot fathom the God that made it. However, there is a reasonableness about not understanding the physical vastness of the universe. What defies all logic is that any God or anyone who comes close to bearing such an awesome name God would even associate themselves with being a sacrifice on behalf of their people. And even more so as the wrongdoing of the people was against the very God who would then voluntarily—without reservation die for them. Notwithstanding, such is the heart of the Christian story of redemption, scattered like love pebbles on the path of redemption from Genesis in the historical past to a cross outside the city of Jerusalem and all the way to a New Heaven and a New Earth in Revelation.

I have studied this Elohim space for the better part of my life, including years of formal studies and a lifetime alone. With many sermons, essays, and books, I can fathom two words I found in the Holy Scriptures. It is found in the first passage of Scripture I memorized as a boy: John 3:16. Nothing I have studied or read throughout my life has exhausted two words I found there. That verse is the heart of the Bible. Moreover, in the verse, like the head of Elohim, redemptive space. Two words for God: "*So love.*" It could even be narrowed to one word— "so." If anyone could fathom the singular meaning of the word "so," they would have captured the whole nature of Elohim's redemptive space.

What is captured in that article "so" from the Greek translation of that passage from the New Testament is the heart of the Gospel. It has always been elusive to me, and to some measure, it still is. I am still standing on the shoreline of God's redemptive love. It is an unfathomable Elohim space. I can see it in the photos I take as a professional photographer. However, I find it both definitive and illusive. That is the point I am making here in so many ways. Here is how the

Apostle Paul further expressed it:

Very Rarely will anyone die for a righteous person, though for a good person someone might possibly die. But God demonstrates his own love for us in this: <u>While we were still sinners, Christ died for us.</u> (Romans 5:7,8 emphasis mine).

Shakespeare could not have written a more extraordinary universal story. No more excellent plotline could have been devised and put forth. The world is a stage—yes! However, no more excellent characters throughout all history could have occupied this world stage. The drama of redemption. The nemesis of Satan. On the face of it, we are dealing with the most incredible story we have ever told. That a God would come down among humans and give His life in atonement for any people, indeed for the whole world, has never been done.

Confronting the Space of the Cross

More than a Symbol

The cross is one of the most tragic symbols in human history. Nevertheless, it is what an effective symbol does. It references something authentic. It represents –despite its horror the most incredible love space in the universe. I am not attempting to be dramatic. I say this because the narrative of the Holy Scriptures bears it out. For example, the Apostle Paul knew the Law and the Prophets well. He was well-versed in all the traditions of his people. He describes it as "a Hebrew of Hebrews; as to the law, a Pharisee." In addition, he became the most prolific writer of the New Testament in his Epistles. However, in all his wealth of knowledge and traditional values, he concluded, "God forbid **that I should glory save in the cross of our Lord Jesus Christ**" (Galatians:14-18). This is then Paul not attempting to be poetic but precise about what he considered most valuable to him. The Apostle, who accomplished most in the New Testament Church, testified that nothing else took the space of the cross for him.

Paul's understanding of glory is profoundly shaped by his experience and interpretation of the cross. This central Christian symbol, the cross, emerges not as an emblem of suffering or defeat but as a beacon of unparalleled triumph. In Paul's view, the mundane allurements, and accolades of the world pale in significance to the profound, transformative glory found in the cross of Jesus Christ. Through it, the believer gains access to a deep awareness of God's intrinsic virtues - love, mercy, grace, and redemption. Paul encourages a shift in focus from worldly pursuits to a contemplative embrace of the cross, suggesting that therein lies the true essence of divine love and salvation.

The cross is pivotal for many reasons, primarily illustrating the gravity and consequences of sin, while simultaneously heralding God's redemptive plan. Understanding the significance of the cross involves exploring several key themes:

1. **The Cause of the Cross: ** Humanity's fallen state necessitates the cross. Romans 3:23 and 1 Corinthians 15:22 underscore the universality of sin, tracing its origins to Adam's disobedience which introduced a pervasive spiritual malaise into human existence. The cross represents God's intervention, a divine antidote to the sin problem.

2. **Consequence and Condemnation of Sin: ** The scripture portrays sin's outcome as twofold - physical and spiritual death. This severance from God, depicted through Adam and Eve's expulsion from Eden, underscores a universal brokenness, a theme evident in the fractured nature of human relationships and the disharmony within creation itself.

3. **The Cure for Sin: ** The narrative of redemption is a testament to God's relentless pursuit of humanity. From the preordained sacrifice of Christ to the proclamation of the Gospel and the eschatological hope of believers' rapture and Christ's return, the narrative presents a holistic solution to sin's scourge.

4. **Compassion as the Motive: ** God's outreach to humanity is propelled by His boundless love and mercy, as eloquently expressed in Lamentations 3:22-23, and reaffirmed in Ephesians 2:4-5. This divine compassion is the bedrock of the redemption story, manifesting itself in the offering of grace and the promise of new life through Christ.

5. **The Cross and the Gospel: ** The cross is indispensable to the Gospel message. It stands as the pivotal moment in God's redemptive plan, a symbol of sacrifice, and the vehicle through which salvation is achieved. It calls for reflection on the profound sacrifice of Christ and challenges believers to embody the light of this truth, mirroring the transformative power of the cross in their lives.

By re-centering our attention on the cross, Paul invites a reevaluation of its significance, not just as a historical event but as the nexus of Christian faith and practice. The cross symbolizes the ultimate expression of God's love and the definitive answer to humanity's deepest needs.

It is in that space for which Paul's glory enables him not to be influenced by all the glitter in the world that would cause one to glory. They are dead to him because of the cross. The cross renders the shallow glory of the world of no value compared to the glory of the cross. It is in this cross space that we can get an understanding of all the virtues of who Elohim is. Are you looking for love? Are you looking for mercy? Are you looking for grace? Are you looking for redemption? Are you looking for love in all the wrong places? Stop! Moreover, take a look—a long look at the cross of Jesus Christ.

Why is the cross space such that Paul and all God's children want to pause and glory in that space? Here is but a brief outline summary of that space:

1. What is the **CAUSE** of the Cross? Why was the cross necessary?

   The Scriptures in Romans 3:23 explained, "For all have sinned and come short of the glory of God." Moreover, in 1 Corinthians 15:22, the Apostle Paul said, "For as in Adam all die, so in Christ all will be made alive." The "cause," then, in brief, is the sinfulness of humanity. As the human father, Adam also became the father of humanity in its sinfulness. So, the cause is Adam's choice to disregard Elohim's command. This results in the entrance of sin like a spiritual virus into the human stream, contaminating every facet of God's creation. When this occurred, nothing humankind on their own could have done to save humanity. The solution had to be from another place.

2. What was the **CONSEQUENCE AND CONDEMNATION** of sin? What was the effect of sin in the human stream?

   If the answer can be given in one word, it would be "death." God had warned Adam and Eve, "The day you eat of this tree, you will surely die" (Genesis 2:16-17). However, they listened to the temper's lies that it was not so. But it was. This death was two-fold. The first was (1) **physical**. Moreover, each of us lives with that consequence to this day. All humanity, including animals, will succumb to physical death. It is a common experience for us all. It is an appointment each of us must keep. It is an unavoidable consequence of the Adamic nature of death in each of us. The second form of death and most critical for all humanity was (2) **spiritual** death. It meant that the connection between humanity and God or God to humanity was severed. This was represented by angels with flaming swords as Adam and Eve exited the Garden, where they communed with their Creator before the wall of sin was erected between them. That spiritual unity or access to their Creator was severed. It was broken. A keyword of this effect was "brokenness." It is why every human relationship on every level must combat brokenness and separation from families to nations. Humanity has to work on relationships. Even in nature, there is a reason the prediction of a coming time when "the lion will lay down with the lamb" (Isaiah 11:16) because the order of unity in nature was disrupted (the whole creation groans….)

3. Is there a **CURE** for sin? Is there a way out of the darkness of sin and death?

   This is the redemption story of the Bible. That after humankind's sin, all was not lost. The Bible narrative reveals a relentless pursuit of Elohim's love space to call humanity back to Him at every turn. Every dimension of this story is incredible. **(1) Its creation** before the foundation of the world presented us with Jesus Christ as this sacrificial Lamb slain (Revelation 13:8) **(2) Its currier** or agency in Christ the Son of God. **(3)** Its **content is the Gospel, which refers to the "good news" of salvation proclaimed by Christ himself, as well as by** the Apostles and the New Testament Church. **(4)** Its **consummation** in the rapture of all God's children and the Second Coming of Christ at the end of the age.

4. The **COMPASSION.** What so motivated Elohim to reach out to His human creation?

   The narrative of this redemptive story is declared without ambiguity in Lamentations 3:22-23: "Because of the LORD'S great love we are not consumed, for his compassions never fail. They are new every morning; great is your faithfulness. An extended version of this theme is found in Paul's letter to Ephesians 2:4-5 "But because of his great love for us, God, who is rich in mercy, made us alive with Christ even when we were dead in transgressions—it is by grace you have been saved."

5. The **CROSS:** How does the cross fit into the Gospel? What does the symbol of the cross mean to the Gospel? Why is it so crucial to the Christian message?

   As the sun is to the Earth, so is the cross to the Gospel. It shines the light at the core of the Gospel light. As the moon is to the Earth, reflecting the sun's light to the Earth, every believer must reflect the light of the cross to everyone. From the dawn of the Fathers, through the prophetic from Abraham to Christ, the offering of blood sacrifice as a penalty for sin was the law. One day, a young man showed up at the Jordan, and John the Baptist made this astonishing announcement: "Behold the Lamb of God that takes away the sins of the world" (John 1:29). All the traditions of blood sacrifice over and over were nullified. There would be bloodshed once and for all through the perfect sacrifice of Jesus on the cross once and for all. Such is the meaning of the cross in the gospel. There is no Gospel devoid of this cross space. It is the only space in which mankind can find redemption.

The central passage of the holy Scriptures is focused on the cross:

6. The **CONFESSION & CONCESSION** What is required of anyone to receive this salvation? If it is free, how is it obtained?

One of the most explicit passages concerning how one obtains God's salvation is found in the Gospel of John 1: 12: "Yet to all those who did receive Him, to those who believe in His name, he gave the right to become children of God." There is much to unpack here from this powerful statement by the disciple John concerning Jesus Christ. John began his Gospel narrative by giving us the story world—the context. He first laid the foundation of who Jesus was, that he was indeed Elohim, the Creator of the universe. "Through him, all things were made; without him, nothing was made that has been made" (John 1:3). One does not have to agree with John. However, it must be accepted that what John was saying was clear. This historical Jesus was indeed the Creator of the universe. He noted, "He was in the world, and though the world was made through him, the world did not recognize him" (John 1:10). He further expanded the context or story world by stating, "He came to that which was his own, but his own did not receive him (John 1:11). Then john said in our selected passage (and I paraphrase here): Although he was the Creator; although he was the light of life; although he came to his own people that rejected him, that it still remains those among humankind who accepted him and who believe in him he gave them the "right" to this extraordinary relationship called "children of God." The entire Bible is a story of redemption and cannot be fully explained here if it ever could. However, John adequately explains that one must accept Jesus for who He is, the Elohim—creator of the world. Believe in what he came to do to give his life a ransom for all those who would come to him. Furthermore, when they do by faith and believing in Him, He turn gives them the birth certificate to be no longer children of the evil one, but children of God.

7. The **CONVERSION: A NEW BIRTH.** What happens to a person who, by faith, turns to Christ for salvation?

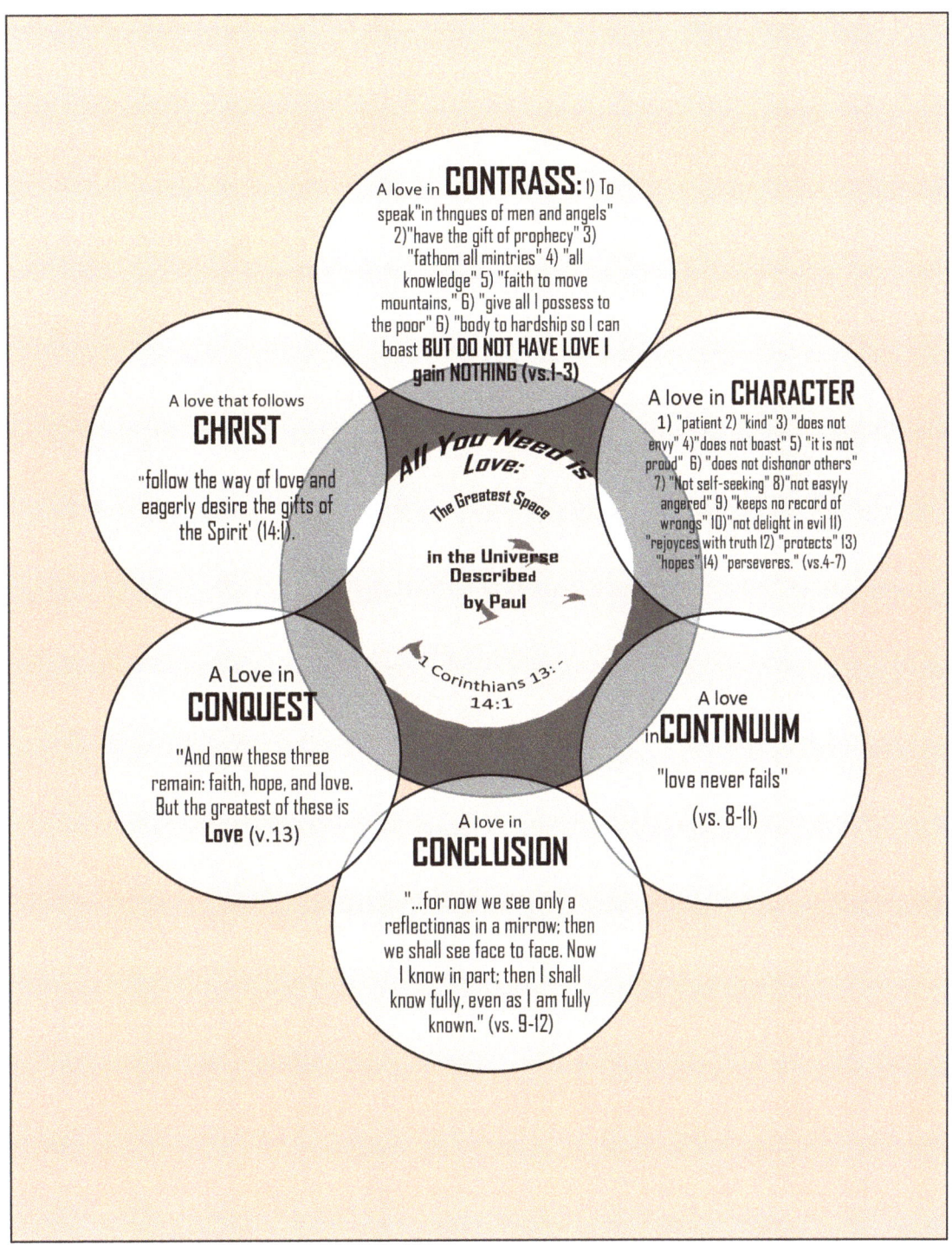

A love in **CONTRASS:** 1) To speak "in thngues of men and angels" 2) "have the gift of prophecy" 3) "fathom all mintries" 4) "all knowledge" 5) "faith to move mountains." 6) "give all I possess to the poor" 6) "body to hardship so I can boast **BUT DO NOT HAVE LOVE I gain NOTHING (vs.1-3)**

A love that follows **CHRIST** "follow the way of love and eagerly desire the gifts of the Spirit' (14:1).

A love in **CHARACTER** 1) "patient 2) "kind" 3) "does not envy" 4)"does not boast" 5) "it is not proud" 6) "does not dishonor others" 7) "Not self-seeking" 8)"not easily angered" 9) "keeps no record of wrongs" 10)"not delight in evil 11) "rejoyces with truth 12) "protects" 13) "hopes" 14) "perseveres." (vs.4-7)

All You Need is Love: The Greatest Space in the Universe Described by Paul 1 Corinthians 13: 14:1

A love in **CONQUEST** "And now these three remain: faith, hope, and love. But the greatest of these is **Love** (v.13)

A love in **CONTINUUM** "love never fails" (vs. 8-11)

A love in **CONCLUSION** "...for now we see only a reflectionas in a mirrow; then we shall see face to face. Now I know in part; then I shall know fully, even as I am fully known." (vs. 9-12)

John, who developed the Gospel story world in chapter one, begins with Christ as the Creator, then moves to see Jesus coming as an ordinary man to be peptized by John. At the time, many were following John the Baptist, but in an extraordinary declaration when Jesus showed up, John declared Jesus to be the "Lamb of God" who takes away the sins of the world. This is a continuation of the context or story world that would be fully developed in Jesus' meeting with Nicodemus, in which He fully explained to him what it means to be "born again." That is to be born not of flesh and blood, but of the Holy Spirit in chapter 3 of his Gospel. It is often overlooked that one of the central passages of the word of God, John 3:16, was said to the teacher of the Law who wanted to know, "How can one be born again when he is old?" (John 3: 4). He completely missed that the new birth was a spiritual pregnancy and a spiritual birth.

8. **CONSUMATION OF SALVATION.** What is the end of salvation? What is the ultimate purpose of salvation?

Salvation is a word that covers all of the above. It covers the cause. It covers the cure. It covers the ultimate consummation of what began before the foundation of the world. It covers past sins. It covers the present condition before God. Paul said, "There is therefore now no condemnation to them that in Christ. On in Crist presently live justified before God. So that no sin is held against the believer as far as their standing before God, for they stand in Christ. There is much that can be said about the future state of all God's children. Someone told me (I do not remember who it was) that salvation here is that we are saved from the guilt or condemnation of sin. But what is yet to come is the salvation from the very presence of sin. No more tears, tragedy, trials, no more wars, and no more death. No need for fire stations, medical facilities, doctors or undertakers, no poverty, no shame—a space where there is nothing resembling sin or its effects. It would take all the imaginative powers one could muster to envision a space without sin.

9. **COMMUNION COMMEMORATION**

The Catholic Church as a whole, throughout its history, has done much to remind us of the importance of this sacrament held in such esteem in its services. The great point of difference between evangelicals and Catholics as to whether the bread and wine become the actual body and blood of Jesus Christ should be left alone. Whether this is so or not, it remains what it was originally intended to be: a symbolic representation of the historical space and time when Jesus hung on a cross and gave his life as a ransom for the sins of the world. It is clear that Jesus intended this one and only ritual to his followers to be just that. He clearly taught, "As often as you do this, you remember the Lord's death till He comes" (1 Corinthians 11:26).

I must confess that this communion ritual became even more personal when COVID-19 came, and many churches closed their doors. I had always participated in this with the rest of my church community. But now that long practice I started as a teenager was no longer available together. I did a little research, wanting to find the wine that best represented the historical wine used for this purpose. The closest I found was a class of wine used among the Jews at their Passover celebration and the brand that best represented the bread as well. I began participating in this holy ritual, focusing, despite the many distractions, on the historical events of the cross. Next to writing about the Gospel message, this was very personal and meaningful. Although COVID requirements are now being relaxed and churches are beginning to open their doors, I continue this event at least on a weekly basis to remember the LORD's death and ultimate sacrifice till he comes. It has been a place of solace, aloneness with God, a most sacred time and space—a place and a space taken out of a busy day, many interruptions but avoiding them to have this protected space with the LORD each week—sometimes several times a week to meet with God in this way.

Look at the Book"

"For I received from the Lord what I also pass on you: The Lord Jesus, on the night He was betrayed, took bread, and when He had given thanks, he broke I and said, 'this is my body, which is for you, do this in remembrance of me.' In the same way, after supper, he took the cup, saying, 'This cup is the new covenant in my blood; do this in remembrance of Me. For whenever you eat this bread and drink this cup, you proclaim the Lod's death until he comes (1 Corinthians 11:24-26). Here is given to each of us access through this ritual to participate in something here on Earth to remember someone, our LORD Jesus Christ, in heaven. In this way, the cross and its messages are being spread worldwide by eating and drinking in that holy communion space until He comes. Then, we do not have to fight to remember. The ritual would have become a part of who we are and what we are becoming.

A Brief History of Sacrifice and the Cross

EXODUS

God created a historical space called Exodus. It was another word for a Great *redemption* or *deliverance.* It would be remembered in Israel from generation to generation, from the Passover ritual to the parting of the waters, through the Ten Commandments, all the various additional sacrificial offerings, extensive in its application to forgiveness of sins, recorded in the book of Leviticus. The Ark of the Covenant, the walls of Jericho falling down to the conquest of Jerusalem, and the building of a House of God there. All spaces that flow out of Egypt and the great promise of God to Abraham. Egypt was a space of great suffering and a space of great sacrifice and deliverance. It gave birth to the redemptive space of the "blood of the Lamb." When I see the blood, I will pass over you." These were words of redemption and hope rooted in the sacrifice of a lamb in every Israelite's home. The sacrifice of a choice lamb, instructions given at a time of great dread and severe suffering in Egypt. Given at a time when the promise of a homeland seemed like a distant dream, and death was like a vast blanket covering the land from house to house. However, salvation seed was planted in the land of slavery. Moreover, a great deliverance was at hand.

Exodus, as a book and a period in Israel's history, presents us with an important symbol of blood. God began to rain down disaster on the Egyptian's physical space in various plagues. Pharoah refused to let Moses lead his people out of Egypt; things then began to get personal. Every first-born male, as Pharoah did to the Hebrew boys some years before, was now turned against every first-born boy of Egypt. The family of Pharoah was exposed to this space of judgment. But in Israel, there was a provision for protection and deliverance in the blood of the lamb they were instructed to put on the door of their homes (Exodus 12). Just like their Father Jacob was instructed to do many years before. There was to be blood--the blood of the lamb, a symbol of Christ's blood. It was to be sprinkled on the doorposts of the Hebrew home. Furthermore, the promise of this placement was that a space of redemption and protection would come to that space. "When I see the blood," said the Lord to his people, "I will pass over you" (Exodus 12:13). This became a space in the heart of Israel to be celebrated in time immemorial named "The Passover." They were to remember the time when Passover Space was created for their protection and deliverance. They were to remember the power of God in His great deliverance.

Exodus revealed Elohim's spaces of Love, grace, and redemption. It revealed the space in Elohim's heart and his willingness to be present among his people. From a burning bush in a holy space on a mountain, through clouds by day and fire by night; through water from a rock, through the ark of the covenant carried by the people, through a space of a temple made according to his designs yet by humans hands, through a brazen serpent in the wilderness created a space where the Israelites can look and live and be delivered from their deadly afflictions. Through Judges, prophets, priests, kings, and his one and only Son, Jesus Christ Son, and by the Holy Spirit in his Church, Elohim has always created welcome spaces for the redemption of His people and all mankind. Through our responses to these historical events and the spaces presented to us today, he created a salvation space long ago in which our choices of these things can make the difference as to who we are and who we are becoming. Like the wind, rain, and all around us, these spaces exist to show us the way home back to the One who created us and brought us here. We cannot be isolated from the spaces of existence in which he allows.

We cannot function at any moment without choosing from the spaces he allows us to inhabit. There is no way out from the challenges of choices of existence every moment of our lives. It is how we are made. It is how the world in which we inherit and inhabit is constructed with spaces of existence. It is how we survive. It is how we thrive in spaces the Creator designed for our good and his purpose. Naked came we into this world, and naked shall we return except for the eternal spaces we chose to inhabit, or shall we be allowed to inhabit our spirit and soul while we journey our brief space here? In Exodus, a special ceremony of the Passover was initiated. The people experienced mighty deliverance from the death angel passing through Egypt. They were spared only because they, in obedience, sacrificed a lamb whose blood was placed on the doorposts of their home. Their deliverance then, and the deliverance of everyone, was to be realized only through blood. They were told of this Passover event: "In days to come when your sons ask you, what does this mean (the celebration of Passover)? Say to him 'with a mighty hand the Lord brought us out of Egypt out of the land of slavery" (Deuteronomy 26:8). Egypt in the mind of God represented a space of slavery. He called it the "land of slavery." It was a designation of a geographical space, but it was more. It was to become in their heart, in their personal space of their soul, a space that represented God's mercy, God's love for his people. It was to represent "his mighty hand" of deliverance. It was to be something they were not to forget. God, even before the Apostle to the Gentiles, wanted the Gentiles to know who he was. When God told Israel that the deliverance was planned. He said he did so not only for them as his covenant people but also that by his mighty hand, "the Egyptians will know that I am the Lord (Exodus 14: 1-4 Cf. Joshua 13:3, Judges 3:3).

God parted the waters. The God of spaces created one of deliverance against the most advanced war machine at the time. He did so by creating a safe space. He created a space for the life of his people to exist in the middle of the raging waters. He did not make them with gills to function in that space. He changed the space to accommodate them. He is a God of spaces. They walked through on dry land because God, in his power, made it so. He makes spaces so his children can exist in safety and salvation (Exodus 14:5). When he is done, He closes back the space in which his children's enemies cannot function. He placed the waters back in their space. When Israel faced their most difficult challenge in the desert, they feared for survival. Instead of turning to God, they turned to grumbling and fear. However, despite this, the narrative revealed in that space and time, "the glory of the Lord appeared in the desert" (Exodus 16:10).

Exodus is an important historical book both for Israel and the foundation of the Christian Church. In Exodus, there is a fuller revelation of God to Moses and the People. God called Moses to come up and meet him. He wanted to give him the moral and spiritual code that he wanted for people to live. God asked him to chisel out two tablets of stone Moses did and held them in his hand. The Scriptural narrative then described how God "came down in the cloud, stood there with him, and proclaimed his name the Lord (Exodus 34:5-6). Here God revealed a new name by which he is to be known among his people. He expressed several singular spaces of his name: (1) Compassionate, (2) Gracious space, (3) Slow to Anger, (4) Abounding in love, (5) Abounding in faithfulness, (6) Maintaining love to thousands, (7) **forgiving wickedness, rebellion, and Sin** (Exodus 34:5-8).

When Elohim spoke to Moses these words concerning who He is what was the point? He could not have been doing so for himself. Elohim has no need to know more of himself. There is no space left in Him to be filled with knowledge of Himself. These descriptions of Elohim spaces are who God is and never who he is becoming. For no one, including Himself can improve upon him. So, for what purpose did He reveal himself to Moses? So, even here, there is such a difference for us. For as He reveals himself to us, there is that Divine pull like spiritual gravity that we would say, "Oh God make us be loving as you love, gracious as you are gracious, slow to anger as you are, abounding in faithfulness towards you…." We become less filled with our own space and are filled with the spaces of Elohim's essence. So, what is this critical point of God revealing himself? As we align ourselves with Him, it is we who become the focus of His revelation. It is "us" who can be affected by knowing who he is and what is His name. It is not Elohim who needs to know more of himself but us. Such knowledge cannot change who He is, but this knowledge can change who we are and how we understand this world. Indeed, not just for Moses but for each of us is this unique opportunity of his Divine purpose: "We shall be like him for we shall see him as he is (1 John 3:2). And the Apostle Paul said for us to "let this mind be in you that was in Christ Jesus…." (Philippians 2:5). All the knowledge of God in the universe is intended to attract us to be of His character of love and truth and wisdom lived out before a watching world.

It is the fundamental reason for part one of this work. It is that we know the unique spaces of God, which Elohim cannot improve. But we can. As we see his space, we can improve ours. To what another end could there be to know of God? We can be certain it could not be for God to know himself more. Such knowledge is meaningless if it does not result in change in us.

JOSHUA

The Symbol of the cross and the redemption it declared were foreshadowed in Joshua's establishment of "the city of refuge" (Joshua 20), which became a place where those who entered could find redemption for their sins.

LIVITICUS

Leviticus is a difficult book to fathom. Whether it is approached as a theological or practical social study makes it no easier. It represented a legalistic complicated roadmap for dealing with all kinds of sins and the various sacrificial offerings for each type of sin. Even who, when, and where these sacrifices were to be made. There were rules governing the **"burnt offering"** of bullocks, sheep, goats, turtle doves, and young pigeons (Leviticus 5). There were strict rules as to how long such an offering was to remain on the fire to be "burnt" but not consumed. Then there was the **"meat-offering,"** which was vegetable in nature, sometimes raw, sometimes baked, and laws governing every aspect of this, depending on the nature of the sin. And no part of the instructions was to be compromised (Leviticus 6). Then there was the "sin offering" of two kinds one for the whole congregation and the other for individuals. A young bullock was brought to the outer court of the Tabernacle, where the elders would lay their hands on its head, and he was killed. The high Priest took the blood of the bullock into the holy place and sprinkled the blood seven times before the veil, putting some of the blood on the horns of the altar of incense, and the rest poured out at the foot of the altar of burnt offering. And this is not even the extent of it. Such details is found in this book. It is easy for many of us to read poetic books like the Psalms, Proverbs, and other books. We meditate on them and linger long there. But not so Leviticus. God's rules for dealing with sin, with its demands of death, sacrifices, and blood, were never intended to be easy, as Leviticus made clear. It is not even easy writing about it, for there remains the **"trespass-offering,"** the" peace-offering," and the great annual offering of "atonement" by the High Priest for the sins of the people. Then there is the range of uncleanness among the people with specific rules and regulations. When one even takes a casual reading—if that is at all possible- of the book of Leviticus, one comes to the question at the heart of the redemption story: What was all this all about? What was this to accomplish? Especially in light of such progressive revelation and conclusion in the New Testament.

Look at the Book:

*"Instead, those sacrifices are an annual reminder of sins because **it is impossible for the blood of bulls and goats to take away sins.** Therefore, when Christ came into the world, He said: 'Sacrifice and offering you did not desire, **but a body You prepared for Me.** In burnt offerings and sin offerings, You took no delight. Then I said, 'Here I am, it is written about Me in the scroll: I have come to do your will, of God'"* (Hebrews 10:4-7 [8-39 BSB).

*Day after day, every priest stands and performs his religious duties; again, and again, he **offers the same sacrifices, which can never take away sins.***

*But when this priest had offered for all time one sacrifice for sins, he sat down at the right hand of God, and since that time, he waits for his enemies to be made his footstool. **For by one sacrifice, he has made perfect forever those who are being made holy** (Hebrews 10: 11-14 emphasis mine).*

So, it is not to be missed, Elohim, the Space Maker, created a unique space of redemption. As Adam was fashioned out of the dust of the Earth, so it was written that Elohim specifically prepared the body of the second Adam, His Son Jesus Christ: "but a body You prepared for Me," in which Jesus was going to come to do the will of Elohim.

Isaiah saw this Divine will working out Long before it did in future historical space and time when he said:

*Yet it was the LORD's will to crush him and cause him to suffer, and though the LORD makes his life an offering for sin, he will see his offspring and prolong his days, and **the will of the LORD will prosper in his hand** (Isaiah 53:10 emphasis mine).*

PROVERBS

In Proverb 30:4, the question is raised, "What is his name, and what is the name of his Son? This is an Old Testament preview of Jesus. So, the Old Testament questioned, and the New Testament answered, "his name shall be called Emanuel which means "God with us."

JESUS AND SACRIFICE

"Therefore, the Lord himself will give you a sign: The virgin will conceive and give birth to a son and will call him Immanuel" (Isaiah 7:14). Here is the prophetic space of Emanuel: God with us. (9:2"The people walking in darkness have seen a great light; on those living in the land of deep darkness a light dawned." "For us a child is born, to us a son is given, and the government will be on his shoulders. And he will be called Wonderful, Councilor, Mighty God Everlasting Father, Prince of Peace" (Isaiah 9:6)

The symbol of the cross represents an exclusive space for Jesus to hang there alone. In the crossfire, it was only him on which the spark and fire of God's wrath fell. It faced it for every person and, in so doing, created an exclusive space where everyone will come. So said the prophet **ISAIAH**

"I, even I, am the Lord, and apart from me there is no Savior" (Isaiah 43:11) ISAIAH 53 "THE SPACE BETEEN HEVEN AND HELL STANDS THE CROSS" Isaiah described it in all its horror. ISAIAH 53: "Who has believed our message, and to whom has the arm of the Lord been revealed? He grew up before him like a tender shoot, and like a root out of dry ground. He had no beauty or majesty to attract us to him, nothing in his appearance that we should desire him. He was despised and rejected by mankind, a man of suffering, and familiar with pain...to be continued...THE SPACE BETWEEN SPIRITUAL LIFE AND DEATH, HEAVEN AND HELL, EARTH AND HEAVEN STANDS THE ROSS IN ALL ITS UGLYNESS, ITS HORROR, AND ITS REDEMPTION...Isaiah saw its lack of beauty even as he saw its necessity for salvation. It was Jesus who stood in the space--the gap between heaven and hell and bridged it with his sacrifice. And that is what the cross represents: The filling of the space between the separation between God and mankind.

It was and is an exclusive space that could only be occupied by Christ himself. It is a world apart, being linked by the Cross. It is the darkest space that only the Light of Christ, the Light of the world was powerful enough to shine--to make a difference. For my rebellion in Adam. For my murder in Cain. For my disobedience in Jonah; For my denial in Peter, and my betrayal in Judas. He went willingly to go to the cross to die in my stead. Gory to God in the highest and on earth peace to men of good will. Not for any righteousness that I have done but according to his mercy he saved us. I contend the toughest part Jesus had to endure was "he was led like a lamb to the slaughter, and like a sheep before it shearers is silent, so he did not open his mouth." If it were me I would have said something. How in this world did he remain silent after all that was done to him? That is worse than any physical suffering. To remain in a silent space to give me a salvation voice beyond what I could comprehend. I would have blown it all because I would have said something. I would have voiced my opinion and opposition. I would have broken the silence in my suffering. I would have yelled out in opposition and pain. I would have said something. ISAIAH 53:9 "He was assigned a grave with the wicked, and with the rich in his death though he had done no violence nor was any deceit in his mouth." WHY? I contend to bridge the space between wickedness at the grave and righteousness at the resurrection. "Yet it was the Lord's will to crush him and cause him to suffer" (v.10) Why? He took on suffering, so I would be saved from it.

JERIMIAH

Jerimiah 16: A day of Disaster is coming...but also a Day of Deliverance. The difference is the choice of mankind. Jerimiah 17 continues the coming days of vengeance... picked up with deliverance in chapter 23 concerning Jesus "the righteous branch" (v.5). "This is the name by which he will be called The Lord the Righteous Savior" cf. 29: v.11 "For I know the plans I have for you, declared the Lord, Plan to prosper you and not to harm you, plans to give you hope and a future. Then you will call on me and pray to me and I will listen..."v.13 "You will seek me and find me when you search for me with all your heart..." Salvation (30:11). (cf. 33:2).

EZEKIEL 22:26

The priests do violence to my law and profane my holy things. They do not distinguish between the unclean and the clean, the holy and the common. The result is that they created a space where choices do not matter because good and evil are the same. One cannot distinguish between the two. But in Christ, one is confronted with the cross. The cross forces every person to make a choice of this One who sacrificed himself for their salvation. It is the greatest news in the world, this heavenly message of the Gospel. Whosoever comes to Christ will never perish but have everlasting life. This is the meaning of the Elohim space of the cross.

MATTHEW

MATTHEW 10:38 said: "Whoever does not take up their cross and follow me is not worthy of me. Whoever finds their life will lose it, and whoever loses their life for my sake will find it…. The line is drawn in the blood of the cross. Jesus looked ahead to the cross in Matthew 26 "As you know, the Passover is two days away--and the Son of Man will be handed over to be crucified." Jesus knew what was coming. It was established in the past way down in Egypt land. And now it had arrived in Jerusalem's sores at his time. Now he was going to be the sacrificially unblemished Lamb. There was going to be blood. Somebody was going to die. And he was the only one who fit the bill. The only one without sin to die for sin. Presented us with the road to the cross as well as the resurrection. Mathew 27-28 gave us the road to the cross.

ACTS

In Acts chapter two, Peter got up to preach: "This man [Jesus] was handed over to you by God's deliberate plan and foreknowledge, and you, with the help of wicked men, put him to death by nailing him to the cross. But God raised him from the dead, freeing him from the agony of death, because it was impossible for death to keep its hold on him.

In Acts 4:12, Peter and John, before the Sanhedrin, were taken to task for healing a lame man at the Temple doors. They asked Peter and John "By what power or in what name [authority] you do this [healing a lame man]"? This gave rise to a very exclusive claim in verse 12: "Salvation," Peter responded, "is found in no one else, for there is no other name [no other space available] under heaven given to mankind by which we must be saved" (4:1-20). He was lame from birth. Everyone who went to the temple knew of the long condition of his life. The religious leaders could not deny the miracle, so they tried to put muzzle the source of it.

ROMANS

In Romans 3:25, "God presented Christ as a sacrifice of atonement through the shedding of blood." The Space of the Cross is one of payment for sin. 4:25 "He was delivered over to death for our sins and was raised to life for our justification" - The Cross.

1 Timothy 2:5 we find the central theme of this section. We touched in a random fashion different book of the Bible, but one theme remains throughout the centrality of Jesus Christ the Son of God who came to be a perfect sacrifice for the sins of the world: to be the bridge space between God and mankind that that whoever chooses to come to him would not perish but receive eternal life. In this passage, Paul, speaking to young Pastor Timothy, speaks of this central truth: "For there is one God [Elohim] and one mediator between God and mankind, the man Christ Jesus, who gave himself as a ransom for all people.

HEBREWS

Hebrews not only 1:1-3 but throughout the whole book, Christ is the representation of the Father and the One who bridges the gap between the world and Heaven through the cross. The writer of Hebrews made it clear: "Without the shedding of blood, there is no remission of sin. There had to be blood, and the Son of God did not shy away from redemption's requirements of the Father (Hebrews 8).

1 John 2:1 "…we have an Advocate with the Father -- Jesus Christ, the Righteous One. He is the atoning sacrifice for our sins and not only for our sins but also for the sins of the whole world" in verse 2. John 4:10: "This is love, not that we love God, but that he loves us and sent his son as an atoning sacrifice for our sins. Since he so loves us we ought to love one another.

This selected narration concerning Jesus as the clear redemptive space by His unique sacrifice from the various prior rituals to reality, symbols to the Savior, types and renditions from the wilderness to Golgotha's Hill just outside the Holy City where a Holy One hung on a cross between heaven and Hell; bridging the divide; completing the task of God's atonement for sin. There is said it. "It is finished." Mankind's redemption was finished. This was what it took for Elohim to create redemption. It was by the will of Elohim to crush His Son for us. No payment short of Him would do.

PART THREE

THE SPACE OF "US"

INTRODUCTION

"Many people become so thoroughly accustomed to the frictions, frustrations, and general floundering of their day-to-day existence, that nothing short of murder or stark insanity strikes them as peculiar. They are so utterly adjusted to maladjustment that it does not even occur to them that human life might be, except by sheer luck, different from what they know it to be. The particular peepholes that define their outlook on the world become too small for them to see its large and exciting horizons."

Wendell Johnson *"People in Quandaries"* (1946).

"There is a flow to history and culture. The flow is rooted and has its wellspring in the thoughts of people. People are unique in the inner life of the mind—what they are in their thought world determines how they act. This is true of their value systems, and it is true of their creativity. It is true of their corporate actions, such as political decisions, and it is true of their personal lives. The result of their thought world flows through their fingers or from their tongues into the external world. This is true of Michelangelo's chisel, and it is true of a dictator's sword."

Francis A. Schaeffer *"How Should We Then Live?"* (1976)

I contend that the wisdom is this: We live in our minds before we live in our world. This is the heart of this unique human space we now consider in part two. Here, we move from the high and lofty Elohim space [part one] to the lowly crevasses of "us," where Elohim's creative rivers come to trickle and settle in the spaces of how we are put together.

As we now face this space of "us," we must do so with humility, if only because we are all strangers here. For we did not make ourselves. It is like a gift that we must learn to apply to understand and to appreciate the complexity of us. It is partly simple in that there is but one world we all exist in. But each of us lives in our own unique DNA space of it; indeed, of the entire Universe. For space however extensive that divides, significantly also connects. We can either explore them or exploit them.

I also contend that the consideration of the varied and complex space of us is no less mysterious than attempting to understand the space of God. Why? As far as understanding is concerned, these spaces cannot be separated from each other. To understand God and mankind, this work's premise is that we must study both. We cannot understand either without the other. Elohim is the space to start. But it cannot end there. It is not a simple task that I am attempting here. But if we face it with openness, humility, and honesty, we will be rewarded with great wisdom for daily living and success.

The Space of "Me" ...

I will start this journey with what I call the inner force of *"general gravity"* – a concept taken from the physical world: This mysterious force called gravity keeps the vase and varied spaces of our universe in their unique, organized orbit. This is no small thing: Gravity in all its forms, internal and external, is all around us. This is why I use the term "general gravity" to identify all the forces around us and in us—forces of influence that determine who we are and who we are becoming. I use this term to call attention to our own unique internal universe—to our own "orbit"—the things we cluster around, and that cluster around us. Spaces act with and against each other like gravity in "us," and to us, that makes us who we are, whom we are becoming, and gives us the ability to choose from that inner space who *we want to be.* We are all abord. Let the space exploration begins—to go to spaces we have not gone before.

31

THE SPACE OF *US* – GENERAL GRAVITY

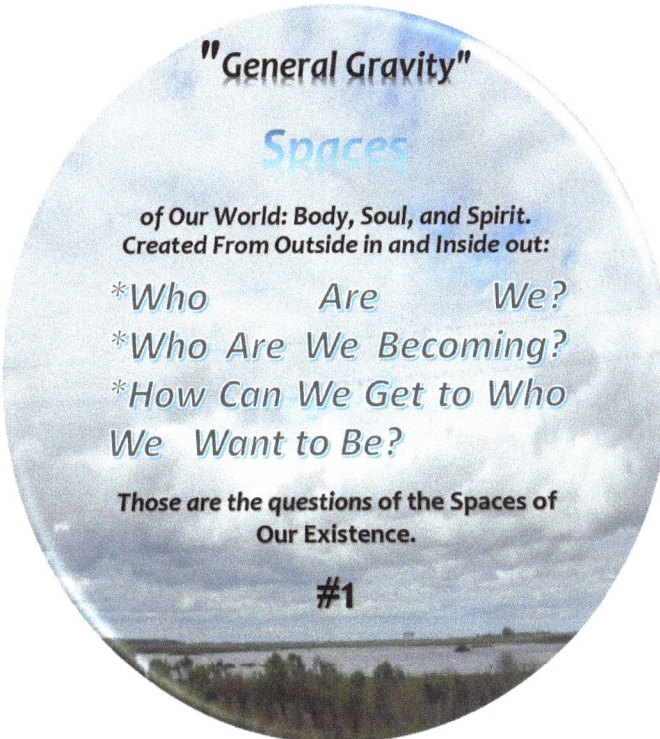

"General Gravity"

Spaces

of Our World: Body, Soul, and Spirit.
Created From Outside in and Inside out:

*Who   Are   We?
*Who Are We Becoming?
*How Can We Get to Who
We   Want to Be?

Those are the questions of the Spaces of
Our Existence.

#1

#1 The Space Inside My Skin"

The primary spaces of personal existence are all inside. Even our awareness of God or any movement towards Him comes from within.

Like a skilled surgeon of the innermost spaces inside our skin, the ancient songwriter David said: "*For it was you who created my inwards parts;* **you knit me** *together in my mother's whom. I will praise You because* **I** *have been fearfully and wonderfully made*" (Psalm139:13-14 CSB Italic mine). Job, one of the most ancient books ever written, said, "You clothe **me with skin and flesh** and **knit me together with** bones and sinews" (Job 10:11 emphasis mine).

It must not be missed Elohim's separation as well as the intersection of flesh and bones from *who we are*: The making of us included "us" as distinct yet mysteriously united with this marvelous body inside our skin. It is distinct from our *personhood* or "*humanness*" beyond the unique individual volume of matter that constitutes *us. It is no small thing for us to understand the "us" of us.* In our Divine physical formation, it is considered as Paul described it: A "*building,*" a "house,"a "*tabernacle*" (2 Corinthians 5:1). So that the "real" us moves beyond the skin in both directions of spaces—inside out, outside in. It is a dynamic and fundamental awareness that we must constantly understand, cultivate, and navigate in our ever-changing gravity spaces of influence. In reference to cultivation, I once as a teenager had the rare opportunity to work as an assistant to a most accomplished leader of a multi-islands religious organization leader. I saw up-close the multi-tasking, the attention to details, the critical decisions as a leader, the tireless energy he brought to his ministry and tasks. I could not understand how he navigate all these challenges and spaces. I muster the courage to ask. How do you keep so alert and energized all day long doing what you do? I asked him. He said, "What you do not see is the many times throughout the day I am flat on my back in my office. For about five minutes I shut down. It takes practice. But during this time, I practice putting every thought of anything out of my mind. I do not fall asleep or even meditate. It is more like purging everything inside. Then, I continued my day without any other baggage that would hinder my ability to function at my peak. I have practiced this for over fifty years. I am still trying to get it right. It is not like a one-time practice. It is more like a rewarding journey. It is one of the many tools I have learned along the way to navigate the constant gravity of influences from spaces of existence. However, the first basic key is to understand the nature of gravity's influence on us.

Job, as well as other ancient writers of the Word of God, move further to illustrate that we are more than the formation of skin and flesh but like an out-of-body perspective looked on as the potter not only formed the clay but brought the clay to life—connected yet separate spaces inside. He separates the person from that which he was— "*cloth **me** with skin*." Moses in his historical works—the Pentateuch in the first book Genesis graphicly demonstrated this reality in his narrative of this Divine space of which he wrote, and David sang: "Then the LORD God formed a man from the dust of the ground [the complete physical body] and breathed into his nostrils [the body] the breath of life, and the man became a living being" (Genesis 2:7).

It is clear that the "*breath of life*" in its mystery was more than life in a singular form that God gave us. For example, the mystery was life in all its individual spaces in each of us. Adam was not Eve. Although all of us were given life, what makes us one is what makes us different as well. Each of us lives within the import of existence with unique spaces within our skin with mysterious living choices that make us individually who we are, who we are becoming, and even choices of who we want to be. We know these things to be true, as the ancient Job spoke. This existence is inside our skin. This mystery of existence is "cloth with skin." We know this self-evident truth that we are all created within our skin, which is truly who we are. This *humanness* of humans: One yet distinct.

I must contend here that this is not a discourse for shallow consideration. Why? That is my point from the biblical perspective of the ancient Prophets. No one exists as a shallow human being, no matter their status, ethnicity, gender, or religion. We are the most advanced and complex in our Universe. It is what the Psalmist expressed in how we were made. "*Fearfully and wonderfully made,*" he sang—made with inexpressible "awe." For example, consider the versatility of a human hand. It is what those who work in robotic spaces marvel at and work for years to emulate to grab with just the wight pressure of various matter, to hurt, to touch, to feel hot and cold, and all the varied temperatures in between, but they fall short on the other side of that space. Those mysterious sensibilities we take for granted. Like the ones contained in a hug or a touch just at the right time that can heal the soul in spaces of loss. Like the touch of love and care which cannot be measured in Fahrenheit but in degrees only the soul knows—inexpressible spaces of existence. Like the will that calls upon the hand to do this or that. I contend, it is why many human relationships fail. It is not because of "big things." It is often because we miss the need to "Catch the foxes for *us*, the little foxes that spoil and ruin the vineyard [vineyard of love] while our vineyards are in blossom" (Song of Solomon 2:15). The wise King Solomon understood and spoke this: A King, a ruler, yet a poet of love. So many relationships fail because we are so *utterly adjusted to maladjustment.* It is the reason we begin at the "us" space. Because it is so easy to routinely begin in some other space.

Soul Gravity

It is said that Einstein's study of gravity led him to his great postulations and conclusions about the nature of space and time, mass or bodies, and their critical relationship to one another in the universe. His contribution to ongoing science is immense.

I would contend, however, that the real mystery of existence in time, space, volume, and matter lies not with what is outside the skin but with what lies deep inside. What lies inside our skin is that which connects us with who we are beyond velocity, mass, space, and time. Not the physical mass of who we are but the result of this mysterious interconnectedness with our humanness—the use of who we are. I would further contend, who are we, who are we becoming, and how can we get to who we want to be, are the questions that do not involve mass, velocity, physical space, and time and their relative theorems and their physical mysteries, but the mysteries of the spirit, mind, and soul. It is the connection to our "humanness" of us. Like nature's gravity outside, humans pull us with their own internal gravity that answers those questions. Questions that the great minds of our scientific civilization and culture have done little to answer. Let me break it down a little bit more.

For example, **what good is the external scientific knowledge of the dangers of global warming if humans, especially the leaders among us, lack the internal "will" to do anything about it?** This is not a rhetorical or hyperbolic question. This is serious. I would contend that the greatest danger of global warming is not the scientific reality of its existence. It is a realistic question as a guide to the relative importance of the danger of not seeing the importance of internal consideration of spaces juxtaposed with our grand genius of external theorems. Put in more philosophical terms but no less true: We cannot save the universe without ignoring the one within. It is the reason it is at this critical space, after considering Elohim's unique space in the universe, where we started. We continue—however difficult, with the universe within. It is like coming to the profound realization that we have found the enemy of continued meaningful existence in our world, and it is us. *I must admit, one can go to school and "master" the great theorem of our universe over time and yet come up short in understanding themselves—enough to save it.* In is understanding the gravity of the soul and not just the gravity of our solo systems.

Look at the book:

There are three things too wonderful for me,
four that I cannot understand:
The way of an eagle in the sky,
the way of a snake on a rock,
the way of a ship at sea,
and the way of a man with a maiden.
(Proverbs 30: 18,19 [or I can add a fifth: The way of a maiden with a man).

For another example. One of the largest nuclear energy plants in Europe now lies vulnerable in the war in Ukraine in real time as I write this. If some mad person finds it in their warped political interest to blow it up in an unimaginable catastrophe, it would not be from the power without but the weakness of human character within.

To study oneself is not easy. Why? The gravity that surrounds us constantly pulls us away from ourselves. The center of gravity from which we face the world should be from within. But for many the center of gravity has shifted away from their center to that of others. It is the state of existence for many where other spaces pull away from us. Everything else outside is deemed more important than our space to us. We tend to live our lives in the spaces of others and neglect our own. However, the reality is that we cannot give others any more than what we have cultivated and developed inside our space. It is the most sacred and important space we have to guard, as well as to guide and, yes, to give. But not in neglect of our own. And the "me" inside has a way of reminding us of neglect. We are conditioned to defer to the outside forces of social and temporal gravity spaces. It is the sentiment expressed in Shakespeare's "Hamlet" by Polonius: "*This: To thine own self be true. And it must follow as the night the day, Thou canst not then be false to any man*" (Act 1, Scene III).

I contend it will demand everything we have to explore our personal spaces. Why? For example, it is like looking into our home, not only in those spaces we find so relaxing and calming but also in those rooms like in the basement, attic, shed, or garage spaces we so often neglect. And those rooms or spaces that trouble us hold us back and hold us down. Spaces we guard and do not allow others to see, and often including ourselves. Spaces from old relationships to present ones that are cramped, stifling, and even confusing. Joy and happiness are there, but for a moment, they are lost, and sadness comes flushing in. Spaces we do not often want to explore like how others treated us in the past, or even now regret how we others.

There, in those hidden spaces, we find pockets of spaces like drawers unchecked, hidden, and forgotten. Even circumstances beyond our control may have built up an internal space of regret and pain. Our childhood spaces that never left our soul but silently grew with us filled a large chunk of who we are—right there within our skin. Such spaces and unmentioned others, we do not care to consider or to know about. And yet are among the spaces that influence us to be less than who we can be or want to be.

But to put our internal house in order, such spaces cannot be neglected. They must be faced with moving forward—these neglected spaces in our skin. The Apostle Paul made the comparison of spaces: *For we know that if our earthly **house** of this **tabernacle** were dissolved, we have a building of God, **a house not made with hands**, eternal in the heavens* (2 Corinthians 5:1 KJV). So, I contend looking first inside "our earthly house" is the only way to change who we are. It is the only way to change who we are becoming. It is the only way to change who we want to be. And, in the end, *where* we want to be—in a house "*not made with hands eternal in the heavens*. But it must be understood that it all starts with the one house we have.

Personal Space – A graphic Essay

SAYINGS ON SPACES

I try to make sense of my world by thinking of spaces. It is what this book is about.

Everything around me what my eyes have seen and not see exist in a space. Like the 37.2 trillion cells said to be in me and each of us.

What is it the common thread in biotic and abiotic elements of the vast universe? It is that each large and small must occupy a space-individualy and shared. And this is so in unfathomable ways to exist. I contend, the pursuit of navigating spaces is to understand who we are, figure out who we are becoming, to get to who we want to be. I acknowledge this is no small task for a mare human. So, we start with humility. We embrace appriciation. For we know little of our own spaces. Yet, spaces are the mysterious gift of existence. I am because of a space given to me to occupy in my life that is but for a moment. It will not last this gift of time and space. Se we must make the best of it. We must be "making the most of every opportunity, because the days are evil" (Ephesians 5:1). The model on which this book is besed is but a conceptual tool towards that end.

There are mystery spaces of body, soul, and spirit. Practical spaces I must deal with everyday. Even spaces intangible yet so real. Objective spaces and imagine spaces, paralel spaces and internected spaces, all contributing, like food and water, and air so we can know who we are and who we are becoming, and who we want to be.

Like a spring emotions rise. Thoughts bloom like Spring flowers. Memories long pass emerge like yesterday's spaces jockeying for control of who I am. Intersecting with who I am becoming and who I wand to be.

I contend, it is in the mix of all these spaces of existance lie boundless possibilities worth exploring inside.

Spaces

One of the most comforting things in these essays, and not to be missed, is to know that no matter what state or space we are in, Elohim, the God of creation, is a "Space Maker." He is the Creator of spaces on the outside, and He can change and create spaces on the inside as well. The following graphic of one of David's psalm prayers would be empty words or poetic folly if God was not a Space Maker.

Look at the book:

Psalm 51: "Create in me a pure heart and renew a steadfast spirit within me." David understood that all the prestige and power of his palace could not save him from his sinfulness to God. So, from that space, we hear the cry of his soul as he confronts his adultery with Bathsheba. Again, the following is a dividing of the Scriptures for understanding and an outline for further study of the space of me:

32

THE SPACE OF *US* – LET'S GET PHYSICAL

"General Gravity"

Spaces

of Our World:
Body, Soul, and Spirit.
Created From Outside in and
Inside out:

Physical Body

I was excited on the first day of my biology class in university. And right away topical selections for term papers were being handed out. Selections had to be made and turned in early in the Semester so assignments could be confirmed, and research could begin. It was going to be a significant percentage of the final grade—no room for error. I had a choice of any organ in the body, and I chose the most often overlooked one. Despite it being the most obvious and largest of the lot we go through, life takes for granted its value to us—our skin.

The skin covers everything on the inside of our body, soul, and spirit while being one of the most critical parts of it. It is a marvelous defense against heat and cold. It is dangerous as well as sensuous. It holds us all together and can prevent us from bleeding out while keeping thousands of other dangerous stuffs from getting in. Without its constant protection and regeneration, we cannot function. And that is only scratching the surface because its outer layer is made up of dead skin. It is part of what makes it so effective in protecting life inside. It is why I titled my research paper "This Coat of Death." As I laid out in the paper, it protects and functions to give us life.

As a boy, I discovered in me a thirst for learning. And it was, for me, no different from the desire for food or water. The more mysterious the subject the more my desire to know about it. But Despite my obvious delight and ecstasy about what I was discovering in my research of the human skin, I knew it was not a religious or even a social study. It was biology. And it was the skin. It was, in reality, biological scientific research on the skin. And that is what I did.

But I made one big "mistake" as far as my professor was concerned. Despite the well-documented biological and scientific data of my paper in my conclusions, I took the liberty and freedom I had to make conclusions based on my research. One of them was the thought that this complex organ of the skin, with all its interconnected sensors and connections to the rest of the body, including the brain and even emotions and procreation, could not be an afterthought. Not so well-designed skin of ours. Because of my conclusions as a logical designer looking at the design of the skin, my ongoing grade of "A," like lead in water, drastically dropped to "C." Because I ventured to believe that a logical design presupposes a designer. Had I said it points to random evolution time plus chance I would have merited an "A."

My mysterious skin was working overtime to keep me from boiling. The Professor was not satisfied in giving me a C but set his sights on attempting to humiliate me in front of biology class, all for my conclusions in my otherwise scientifically based research on the skin. But I took comfort that the conclusion I honestly came to after my research was not far for those knowledgeable ancient Prophets and gifted Palmists of the ages had themselves concluded. They did this even without the marvels of scientific advancements in instruments that can enable us to see into the microscopic marvels, informing us of more mysteries today than they knew.

Look at the book (Job 10:11-12):

You clothe me with skin and flesh
and *knit me together* with bones and sinews"
You have *granted me* life and loving devotion,
and your care has preserved *my spirit*…

These words sound like they came from the pen and heart of an honest man—not taken up with high philosophical jargon like his friends who visited him in his troubles. Despite his body and skin afflictions, he praised God, Who "clothed me with skin and flesh and knit me together."

I must be clear that, as Job said, we are "knit together" of skin, bones, sinews, and spirit. It would be impossible to put asunder what God has joined together. It cannot, in reality, be done. But as we are made with this unique conceptual ability to move our preceptive space like making various dimensions of us objective so we can stand aloft and conceptually look at spaces of us to understand the "us" of who we are. So, we can look as we do here at the "body" to understand more fully that dimension or space of us while knowing it cannot be fully separated from the rest of who we are. So, with this basic understanding, we seek to study the biblical "divisions" of the word towards a more perfect understanding of who we are as a whole.

A Line in the Sand

This is a story that started in the sand. This is not so unusual when one looks at all the array of colorful plants, and varied fruits, from grass that feeds the flocks to massive trees that have provided lumber throughout the ages and not overlooked plants all over the world through their leaves, provide a healthy breath of oxygen we need, as we provide them what they need. My point here to begin with an acknowledgment that our bodies came from the "dust of the earth" to which it will someday return is not a partially "down" story. As we look around, the earth provides an abundance of raw materials, from moles to mountains of abundance, value, and life.

It is to say we can look down upon the earth is not in any way to "look down" upon from which we came. From there, we find the source of all living things, including us. For whatever it is worth in mysterious humility of design God made the earth and the universe by speaking it into existence. But then pause to fashion man and woman with his own hands, then breathe (not spoke as He did the vast universe) His breath into them something called "the breath of life." Then the result together came "a living soul."

I have studied all the Bible story narratives my earliest days Even before I could read, they were read to me. I have many questions more than most about this story and I do not think I would get answered before I ask Elohim in Heaven. The Bible, more than any other book, is filled with symbols, and often it will reveal in detail how they are applied. Why, then, do so many of the details of the making of Adam and Eve leave us with so many little applications of the creation of Adam and Eve?

- What are we to learn of ourselves that we are made from the dust of the Earth?
- What are we to learn of ourselves that with the first man, life began when Elohim breathed into him "the breath of life"?
- What does it mean man became a "living soul?" Is there another kind of soul? Like "non-living" souls?
- Why did Elohim use a rib to form a woman?
- What are we to learn about ourselves because of the rib?
- What are we to understand about ourselves that of all His creation He made us last and then rested?
- What are we to learn about ourselves that Elohim came down in the "cool of the evenings" to talk with us?
- What are we to learn of ourselves that we were banished from the Garden?
- What are we to learn about our bodies that we were naked and not ashamed before sin, but then try to cover up so much so that God asked, "Who told you were naked?"
- What are we to learn about ourselves that we are ashamed of our naked bodies?
- Are we not to love our bodies?
- If Adam was made from the ground, what was the natural color of the first man?
- Why is hate and not love so often associated with the color of one skin?
- Why so much hatred over skin color and not blood color, which is of one-color red?
- What are we to learn of male and female bodies that only the woman by God's design given to carry the physical burden of children and childbirth?
- God breathed into Adam; the *breath of life* fully formed. When are we to conclude that this breath of life is transferred to the child formed in a mother's whom? Would we ever know? Who is qualified to know?
- If Elohim left certain details out of the creation story, what are we to think of ourselves because of this? Can Divine silence about parts of ourselves be golden?

33

THE SPACE OF *US* – SAMSON'S LESSONS

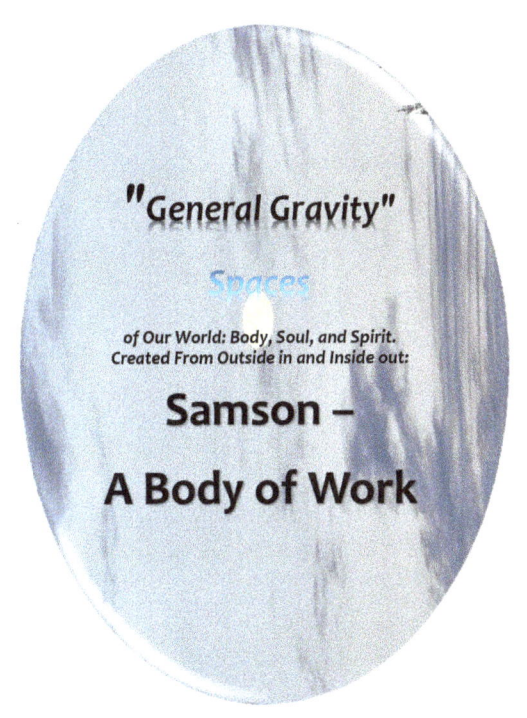

"General Gravity"

Spaces

of Our World: Body, Soul, and Spirit.
Created From Outside in and Inside out:

Samson –

A Body of Work

Before he was born, Samson was special. His mother vowed he would be consecrated to the Lord as a Nazarite. This meant he would practice a certain physical lifestyle of abstinence. This includes a most notable distinction in his community that no hair on his head was to be cut. He was to drink no kind of alcoholic drinks. These and other practices in his body were to be a sign that he was to be loyal to his people Israel's God. He soon discovered within his body, by surprise, it seems, a super strength that was unmatched by any other in the history of his people. And he was going to discover unmatched by the strength of his soul. It was through this very strong body that another beautiful body of an Egyptian woman found an entrance.

One day, he traveled near the Philistines borderland next to his hometown of Zora. He saw a beautiful Egyptian woman from Tinman named Delilah. All he saw initially was her physical beauty, and that was all it took for him to fall in love with her. So much so that he was willing to defy his parent's objections: "Is there not a woman among the daughters of your kinsmen, of among all our people, that you must go to take a wife from the uncircumcised Philistines?" (Judges 14:3). Of course, the ritual of circumcision was something that only the male body endured. However, in representation, this body practice—or lack of it influenced the entire culture of the Philistines, including their women. Circumcised or not, Delilah was an attractive Egyptian woman, and Samson, known to be among the strongest men who ever lived, loved her. And no one could stand against him except a beautiful woman, not in the strength of his body or love. It did not matter for Samson the strength of his body. The vulnerability for him was within his Body.

Unlike other judges of Israel, Samson, because of his great body strength, waged a one-man battle against the Philistines. The period of the Judges was a rough time for Israel, who faced crusades after the crusade of their enemies, disrupting their crops and stealing their goods, making their lives unbearable. God raised up judges in Israel to defend them, but none was as successful as Samson. As a young man, a lion suddenly came at him and he tore the lion apart with his bare hands. With just the jawbone of an ass, he put to fight troupes of Philistines men that came against him. In so many ways, he was unbeatable, and the Philippines had to find the path of weakness to a man who was the "Rocky" of his day. As others have discovered throughout civilization, the beautiful body of a woman is often stronger than that of a man. Because the secret weapon of her attraction and love, however cynical, is often stronger than the power of his body.

Delilah could not tear a lion with her bare hands, but she knew how to make Samson's heart slow down just enough to get in and change its direction. She did not have to power to lift her city gate off its swing, but she knew how to swing Samson's attention from the source of his strength to focus on her beautiful body. When Samson broke his mother's vow to his God, he also broke the link to his strength. Samson was indeed physically strong. However, in some strange way, his strength was connected to his body with its natural hair. So, his loss of strength was connected to his body, which remained the natural way in which God designed him. The body and its natural features are not a small thing to God. It is not an afterthought to Him. The very hair on our heads is numbered. Samson lost his strength. He lost his physical eyes. He lost the freedom of his body when he broke the vow he made of his body to Elohim. He never regained his strength to destroy his enemy and defend his people until his body regained its hair.

As a boy, in my first venture into day school, I had a teacher who constantly repeated a story to us about a crippled boy in a class. She said his mother would keep saying to him, "God has a plan for everyone, and he has one for you." Many of us cannot be strong like Samson or beautiful like the Egyptian Delilah. Nevertheless, Elohim gave us our body space, so no matter its beauty or its blemishes, it is what He gave us. And he has a plan for what He did. That story of the cripple boy, I have never forgotten. It has lifted me up so many times I cannot count the ways. God has a plan for everyone, and he has one for you.

34

THE SPACE OF *US* – LET'S GET SPIRITUAL

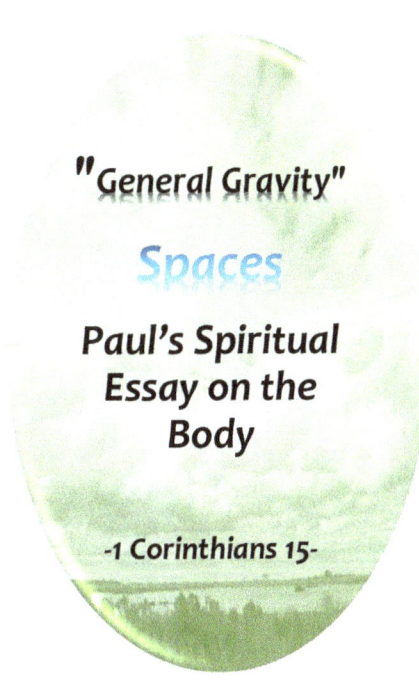

"General Gravity"

Spaces

Paul's Spiritual Essay on the Body

-1 Corinthians 15-

Reverse Reflections on Our Bodies

If there was a church in the New Testament that challenged the Apostle's teaching on about every practical and theological matter, it was the church at Corinth. It was a thriving Gentile city filled with farmers, scholars, intellectuals from Greek great traditions and Jewish communities with their legal and religious traditions. It was like a birthplace of democracy where people worship any god that suite their fancy. Yet It was not a place that made it easy to discuss the Divine nature of the human's body.

The sixth century BC temple of Apollo was located in the middle of the city. The way the church interacted with their bodies was influenced much by the lascivious laxity in the city. Sexual orgy were prevalent in the secular world, and elements of it had crept into acceptance in the local church, along with other practices. In chapter 15 of First Corinthians, the Apostle, versed in the teachings in the Gospel, now had to confront head-on those who looked at the resurrection of the body as folly and felt it should be left out of the Gospel. Paul here argues that without the resurrection of Christ, we have no Gospel. And without our own future resurrection of our bodies, all our preaching and teachings are in vain.

The Apostle, in writing to the congregation on the topic of the resurrection of the Body revealed very important insights into the *body space* we have at present to consider. It is an important flow of understanding that if you know how something will end, like the resurrection, you can then "reverse engineer" back to the beginning and gain insights into who we are in the present. And this is how the Apostle approaches his discussion of the body. In the following graphic, I have laid out in the "Timothy trail," rightly diving the word of truth in the important description of this space in the graphic. Of course, this is not meant to be an intellectual exercise. However, it is meant to be understood as Paul intended from this space.

Look at the Book:

> "Therefore, my dear brothers and sisters, stand firm. Let nothing move you. Always give yourselves fully to the work of the Lord because you know that your labor in the Lord is not in vain."
> (1 Corinthians 15:58)

I must make clear that this Pauline conclusion is meant to be the guiding light as to how the previous discussion of this body of the earth and what will happen to it in the end, in the perspective or space in which we must look at the heart of the discussion. We do so and can understand the importance of this "body space" in how it will be viewed in the future and how we must live with this body today. This is, of course, an unlikely approach and topic. However, it is critical to understand that this was not the case for the Apostle Paul, who confronted the Christian congregation of Corinth in the first century. His teaching is even more relevant today when so much effort is given to the consideration of our body space—even among Christians.

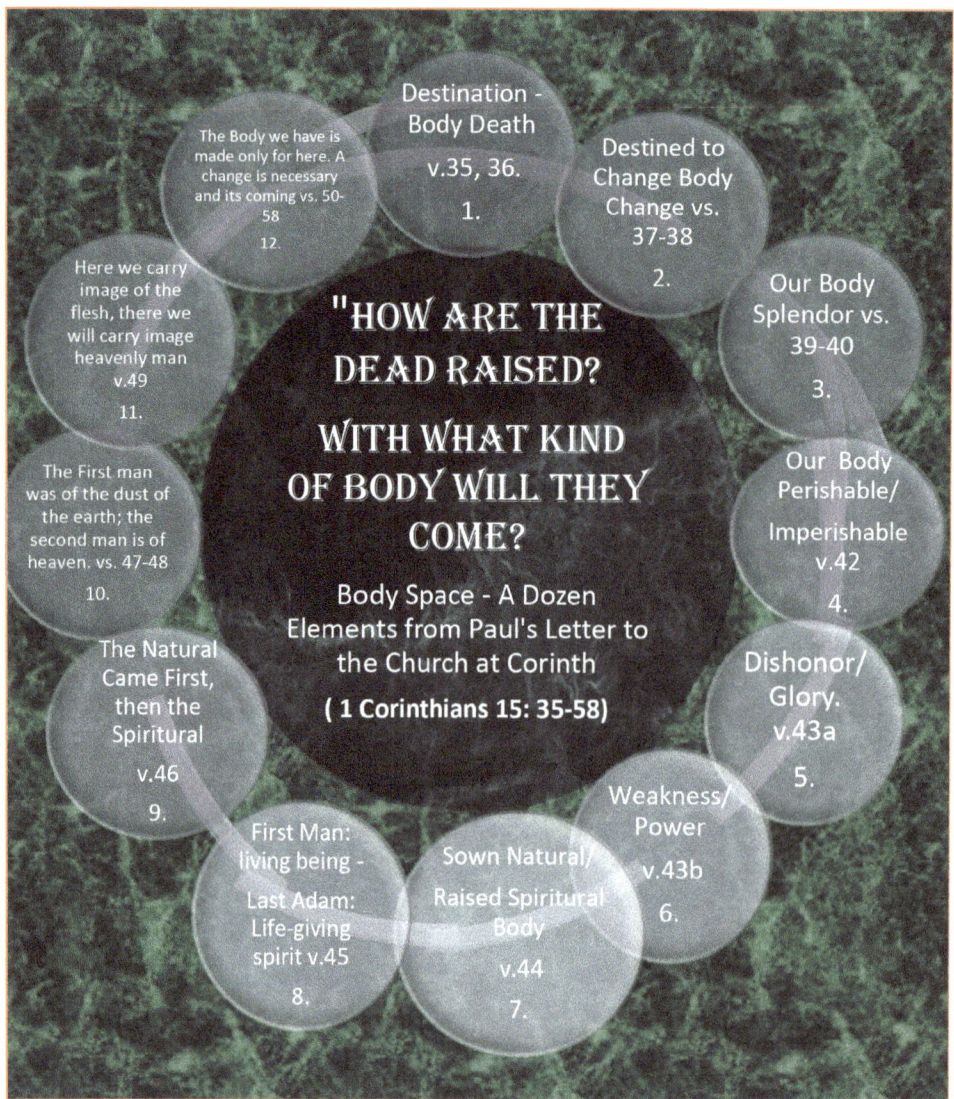

Having set forth his case for the resurrection of Jesus Christ in the opening verses of chapter 15, Paul moved to consider the resurrection of Christ's followers. He faced the issue head-on without equivocation, raising two important questions as I have identified twelve description elements in the graphic: (1) **How are the dead raised**? And (2**) With what kind of body will they come?** His following discourse focused more on the answer, giving more treatment to the second question: *What kind of Body?* The following is a more detailed or deep dive into the Apostle's discourse that clearly describes the future body space while teaching us the nature of the present body space, which is our focus here.

The Present and Future Spaces of the Believer's Body

1. *DEATH*. *How are the dead raised? Furthermore, what kind of body will they come from?* The Apostle did not raise these questions in a frivolous manner. It was not to begin on a negative note. Paul's view of death was never negative for the believer. He said, "For me to live is Christ, and to die is gain" Philippians 1:2). These serious questions created disunity in the Corinthian Christian community. He argues against the faulty premise on which the questions were raised. However insightful the questions, his detailed arguments and strong language labeling such questions as foolish were based on their premise, suggesting the impossibility of "how are the dead raised?" and "with what kind of body will they come? His answer stated that the questions were baseless and even contrary to nature, as demonstrated in the farming community on which so many depended for their livelihood.

    His argument was simple yet profound and centered around twelve elements of this body space. He argues that these questions were foolish because, as everyone in Corinth knew, everything that goes into the ground first dies like a seed. Moreover, what comes out is always something new. *Hence, his very first point of argument about the Christian's physical body is like a seed; it dies, but that is not the end of the process. It is but the start of a new life.*

    It is a sober thought that, on one hand, seems like giving in to a terminal illness. And yet, as they all knew, and we today know, death is not what is on the farmer's mind when he puts a seed in the ground. They think of the mystery of life that will spring up. Their thoughts are not of death but life when with their families and friends, brothers and sisters go out at harvest times as the best of times. The farmer envisions new flowers, trees, fruits, wheat, and life when the seeds are placed into the ground. He or she thinks not of death but of the coming harvest. This is the vision. This is the extended space of this element of the "body space." As Bruce Springfield, in his song "Atlantic City," there is a line he sings "Well, everything dies... that is a fact. But maybe everything that dies someday comes back" (Lyric Find).

    On the other side of a dead seed, all is not lost because it is from that dead seed that a new plant, flower, tree, or forest is born. The believer envisions a new body, not one of this earth. It is because of Paul's first element of the "body space" that it is destined to dissolve back to the dust of the earth that he outlined the position we should take in this very same body space while here: "stand firm," *he concluded,* in this *body space* you have now. It is going to be ok.

2. **CHANGE**: Paul takes this farming of a seed dying and steps back to what proceeded before. The farmer does not plant with the result of the seed: "When you sow you, you do not plant the body that will be, but just the seed, perhaps of wheat or something else (v.37). Paul then does something significant because he introduces a unique space of Elohim that occupies the mysterious space of natural resurrection. It is a space between what happens every time a seed falls to the ground. There is a death of the seed and a resurrection of something new—a new life distinctly different from what is sown.

    God's revelation is seen in nature. Resurrection power is seen every time a seed falls to the ground. God intercepts that determine the destiny of death with His powerful resurrection space so that He gives a new life each time. In my book "The Death of Wisdom: The Rise of Folly," I wrote *that "there is wisdom* in everything, but only the wise notice" (Christian Faith Publishing 2021). Paul wanted the followers of Christ to take note of that powerful space between a seed that dies and the life that follows. And even to note the often-overlooked reality that although to the eyes some plants may look the same as a human's fingerprints, they are unique. Paul said, *"And to each kind of seed He gives its own body"* (Corinthians 15:38). It is but another powerful reason for followers of Christ to know there is a unique body that Elohim "has determined" for each of His children. This is another: powerful reason to *"stand firm and let nothing move you"* because a powerful change is coming in this seed of a body that will someday fall to the ground. It is then that the real story of abundant life begins. Look ahead and use this space to stand firm in the one you have despite all the troubles and challenges it brings you. Stand firm in the body space you now have. It is going to be ok.

3. **SPLANDOR.** Paul, the most prolific writer in the New Testament Church, never hesitated to go deep with the early church believers. He was not hesitant to speak to people who were farmers. From that space of farming too far away galactical spaces. With the same audience, he seamlessly shows the "splendor" and magnificence of Elohim's power to transform seeds into plants and create an astonishing assortment of body space in all of nature.

    His point on body space is the variety we see around us that Elohim has made. He said, *"Not all flesh is the same."* And he began with you and me and the body we have *"people"* he wanted us to understand *"have one kind of flesh, and animals have another, birds another and fish another* (1 Corinthians 15:39). Then he moves to the heavens to draw even a greater variety and contrast; *"There are also heavenly bodies, and there are earthly bodies;"* (v.40a).

    Then he introduced a word to let know what he thinks of the revelational content and his emotions and feelings of it all. He used this word to speak of various bodies—the word "splendor" both referring to *"heavenly bodies"* and earthly ones. Nevertheless, even here, he said, just like the plants, they each have their own splendor. *"The splendor of the heavenly bodies is one kind, and the splendor of the earthly bodies is another"* (v.40b). He wanted his audience to get this point about *body spaces. "The sun has one kind of splendor, the moon another and the stars another,"* and he wanted us also to know that *"star differs from star in splendor"* (v.41). And he explained all of this about different body spaces in the universe just for us to understand ours.

He said, "So will it be with the resurrection of the dead," our body space of the future. The point is if Elohim can create so many majestic splendors of bodies around us, from the fish's body flesh in the seas to the stars in the sky, so will it be in the resurrection. Elohim is going to intercept the death of this seed of body space, and with all His considerable display of His knowledge of creating body space, we see on earth and heaven fashioned a body *"like the glorious, resurrected body of the Lord Jesus Christ for each of us* (Philippians 3:21). This is but another reason for the majestic splendor of it all: *"Therefore brothers and sisters, stand firm. Let nothing move you...."*

4. ***PERISHABLE BODY SPACE TO IMPERISHABLE.*** Using a different language, the Apostle moves back to his original seed illustration to make this continued analogy. When a seed falls into the ground, it perishes. It is swallowed up into the earth just like all of us will weather on land and sea. We go the way of all the earth. However, again, he wants followers of Jesus, many of whom were suffering in the flesh because of persecution. He wanted them to *"stand firm."* That is not the end of the story." For although the outward man perishes, the inward man is renewed day by day," awaiting this new body space on the way. "The body that is sown is perishable; it is raised imperishable...' (v.42b.) Therefore, brothers and sisters *stand firm.* Let nothing move you." A better day is coming when all will be well. Deep spiritual content has practical importance. Here is to take whatever challenges being in this fleshly body space brings us. In our spirit in our lives, cultivate or get to this "stand firm" space that the Apostle commanded us.

5. ***BODY SOWN IN DISHONOR (TO DIE) RAISED IN GLORY (WITH CHRIST).*** Something mysterious occurs. Although Paul is returning to his original analogy of the farming process of what happens to a seed, he is also saying something new. He is expanding on that unique space between the death of a seed (a space large enough for Elohim to occupy) and the mysterious change that occurs.

We are given insights into this space not simply between life and death, but death and life. The space when the body is *"dishonored"* in the same way as Christ the Son of God's body was dishonored by being nailed to a cross as in shame. Nevertheless, that was Friday, but resurrection Sunday was on its way. And that which was sown in dishonor and shame was raised in glory of the resurrection. *"Stand firm"* in the body space you have. It is not what defines you. *"We know that when Christ appears, we will be like Him, for we will see Him as He is"* (1 John 3:2). *Stand firm! It is going to be ok.*

6. ***BODY SOWN IN WEAKNESS RAISED IN POWER.*** We always die in weakness, for it does not take much power to die. A breath here another there. A heat beat now and then there is none. A virus here or there, an accident here or there and we are gone. It does not take much to die. A little loan mosquito flying here and there has taken many humans off the face of this Earth.

Every day we have life is a precious gift given to us. And we never know when it might be taken away. Because it is a space, we are given but only for a moment. "Man, who is born of woman, are of few days and full of trouble" trouble" (Job 14:1). But here again, the Apostle is making a point of contras and the unique space of Elohim's power between the weakness of a dead seed, and a live branch on a Living Vine. Stand Firm! A new day of power is planned.

7. ***SOWN IN A NATURAL BODY RAISED IN A SPIRITURAL ONE.***

The Apostle widens the contrast even as he maintains the simple process of a seed falling to the ground. He extends the space. He calls our body the "natural body." And he returns to the common earth on which we stand and function. Yet, like a seed, this "natural body" in which we go about our daily business comes at a time when it falls like a seed to the ground to the ground. And this natural body ends there. It must be understood that since the seed "dies," there is no inherent power in the seed to raise itself, or the definition of death is mute and meaningless.

There is no power for that natural body to pick itself up and live. Not even Jesus did that. I contend He could have. But he did not. So, the Scriptures tell us, "The same Spirit that raised Jesus from the dead now lives in us" (Romans 8:11). And He who has to power to raise that body up does not do so. He has chosen that this "natural" body, the product of sinful Adam, should stay dead. Its term is up. Its naturalness is no longer needed. What is needed on the other side is supernatural power. What is needed in the space between the natural and the supernatural is the power of God to change the natural into the spiritual. That is what the Apostle is "breaking down" for us. And that is what happens to the body space. God created the natural, and only God can produce the spiritual. It is what Jesus explained to the law teacher: "What must I do to inherit eternal life?" another question is the same answer: "You *must be born again." That which is born of the flesh is flesh. That which is born of the spirit is spirit. You must be born again.* Why? As Paul later also declared, "Flesh *and blood cannot inherit the kingdom of God"* (vs.44, 50).

Since this 'natural" body space cannot exist beyond the grave, do not bet on it. It is a splendorous body, but its splendor only lasts its natural life course. When this life is over so is this body space we now have. So, until then, *'Stand firm, for you know your labor will not be in vain despite the fact that this "labor" was carried out here in this natural body.* We need this body space to do the work of God here (v.58). But it is a body space with a "natural" (or of this life) term limit on it. This body is great. However, it was given to us on consignment. Our parents supplied it. The original was made from dust to dust. A new one is coming not of earthly parents:

Look at the Book:

Now we know that if our earthly tent is dismantled, we have a building from God, an eternal house in heaven, **not built by human hands**" (2 Corinthians 5:1).

8. ***THE FIRST MAN ADAM—A LIVING BEING – THE LAST ADAM A LIFE-GIVING SPIRIT***

The "*first man Adam*"—Hebrew "Adamah" meaning earth. When Elohim gave the first man this name, it meant he was from the earth as Elohim created him. But the "last Adam" was not from the earth but from Heaven through the work of the Holy Spirit in Mary. The last Adam became a *life-giving spirit*. All God's children are born not of the will or work of man but by the Spirit. It is a different *space*. It's a different occupant. The Apostle in Romans 5: 14 that Adam was "a figure of Him that was to come." This body cannot adequately house the splendor and power of the Spirit, like an eagle in the body of a rat. But the time is coming when the rat dies, and the eagle flies. Until then, *Stand firm, abounding in the work of the Lord* (1 Corinthians 15:58).

9. ***THE NATURAL CAME FIRST – THEN THE SPIRITUAL***

Who is first. There is a natural order of things. This body we have is of the first order. It is an order set by Elohim. This order cannot be changed in this life. Nevertheless, we are not to refuse the "splendor" of this first order. It was first. God gave us this body first. It is to be understood that nothing can come after without first experiencing this first body. Therefore, we must "*stand firm*" in this first gift of this earthly body.

If only because we cannot get the new body without having experienced this first one. This is why the Apostle reminded Christ's followers that despite the splendor of the body that is to come, we could not get there without first living in the one we have. And it must not be overlooked that it is the very one that Christ himself occupies. Despite the destiny of this body space we have, it is also the very same space that "Christ lives in us" (Romans 8:11). The Apostle testified, "I live yet not I, *but Christ lives in us and the life I now live I live unto Christ…*" (Galatians 2:20). It is a mystery that Christ must first occupy this natural body so we can get to the next one He has prepared.

10. ***FIRST MAN-DUST OF THE EARTH SECOND MAN OF HEAVEN***

The Apostle was communicating with a congregation with a multicultural and religious background. Although there was a synagogue, there were temples to other gods, forms of worship, and history. Corinth did not have a rich tradition in Hebrew ways and understanding. Paul, as he would in other letters, could not often appeal to the prophetic history and other spiritual writings and literature of the Hebrew side of his life. So, he would come at the same teaching or theme from a different point of illustration in the hope that it would be the one that the Holy Spirit would apply to the hearts of the varied members of the congregation. Here he returns to the earth—the dust of the earth. Again, with the force of contrast in Adamic and Divine spaces.

The first Adam, he once again points out, was of the dust of the earth, just like the seed from which he started his discourse. He began with what was near and all around them, from the dusty trails to family farms to the bustling life of this busy city. The earth was all around them. When there is a burial in any culture in a tomb of rocks for those with means or a hole in the ground on some plot of land, everyone is familiar with the earth and the dust that came from it and to which many return.

Paul's point that the first Adam was from the earth was easy to grasp. So once again, he began here. Then he moves to the more difficult to grasp, except in its recent history of Jesus Christ His life and time yet fresh in the hearts of those who knew Him and many who saw Him go into Heaven with a cloud of angels, this second Man of Heaven could be understood. This resurrected man who came from Heaven—the body seen going into heaven without any known external forces or need for any rocket ship or other protection sailed through all the galaxies of the heavens in a twinkling of an eye. He was gone. It was an earthen revelation of this heavenly glorious body yet to come. Until then, we serve Him in this one and "stand firm." He is made only for here. A change is necessary its coming vs. 50-58

11. ***JUST AS WE HAVE BORNE THE IMAGE OF THE EARTHLY MAN, SO SHALL WE BEAR THE IMAGE OF THE HEAVENLY MAN.v.49***

Sometimes, when one makes an argument from the obvious, it might seem strange or unnecessary on its face. However, some of the most profound truths go unnoticed because they are so common. For example, Paul's analogy that "we," the entire human race, carry around with us a body that bears the image of the earthly man named Adam. However, we yet have images being presented to us of apelike creatures of man walking on all fours before evolution kicks in, and we walk upright in the image of Adam. Paul living closer to the beginning record of Genesis and to the Hebrew scribes who translated to oral and written narratives, said simply, *"Just as we have borne the image of the earthly man* with his strikingly consistent contract, *"so shall we bear the image of the heavenly man"* (1 Corinthians 15: 49). I must confess I do not know what that *image* is like. Nevertheless, as I look at the creative splendor of the variety of human body images he has created, I have no concern, as the apostle said, of the "splendor" of the new resurrected body image he has coming for us. He concluded that we must *stand firm and let nothing move us* (v.58).

12. ***OUR BODY SPACE IS ONLY FOR HERE. ANOTHER BODY IS COMING MADE FOR A DIFFERENT SPACE. (1 Corinthians 15: 50-56).***

As he would often do in his writings, the Apostle seems to get to a space where his thoughts take flight into a different realm. It is introduced with this added greeting in which he would end this discourse. He said, *"I declare to you brothers and sisters,"* making an emphatic statement that summaries all that his illustrations were pointing: *"that flesh and blood cannot inherit the kingdom of God, nor does the perishable inherit the imperishable* (v.50). What follows is what described as:

- ✓ A Mystery
- ✓ A Transformation
- ✓ A Flash,
- ✓ A twinkling of an eye
- ✓ A last trumpet sound.
- ✓ A resurrection of the dead in Christ changed in their new body
- ✓ A new Fashion called Imperishable
- ✓ A new immortal body – it cannot die
- ✓ A new mystery: Death is dead, swallowed up in something called "victory"

✓ A new body song with two new questions (1) "Where, O death, is your victory?" "Where, O death, is your sting?"

✓ The answer to the questions is in Christ alone: *"victory through our Lord Jesus Christ."*

✓ The Conclusion and the application of this body space:

Look at the Book:

35

PERSONAL INSIDE-OUT SPACES

There are spaces in the world, and within each person, there is a world of spaces. When all is said and done, the spaces within matter most. Genesis Six narrates a period before the flood that was particularly evil. I do not want to dwell on the evil of the period but on how God, through Moses the writer, described the sources of such evil. Chapter six of Genesis starts off with a collective and general description of the story world: *"When human beings began to increase in number on the earth..."* Moses recorded (Genesis 6:1).

The Source of the Situation

The narrative by Moses continued in this general vein to describe the various relationships that contributed to the rapid population growth. There was such rapid population growth that God shifted his focus on the individual lifespan to that of 120 years (v.3). The narrative once again became even more personal as God began to observe that they no longer gathered to *"call upon the name of the Lord"* (Genesis 4:26) but in this period before the flood Moses described the people then that God had *seen "how great the wickedness of the human race had become on the earth"* then added a more personal analysis. He saw that every **"inclination of the thoughts of the human heart was only evil all the time"** (Genesis 6:5).

My focus here on the story world was to indicate the source or space of the wickedness emerging at this stage of progressive revelation in the Scriptures was revealing the core values and conditions of the human's existence come from the inner spaces of one's "inclination of the thoughts of the human heart." Moses was not a man of hyperbolic language. He was not engaging in romantic idioms. When he spoke of the source of human behavior, he was specifically saying the wickedness of the behavior of his human creation that "deeply troubled his heart" came from the **"inclination of the thoughts of the human heart."** The "inside space" was the core of their wicked behavior towards Him and everyone else.

Again, I used this narrative not to get into the morality of the behavior described as "evil" but to point out the internal or, as indicated in the model--the INSIDE-OUT space of humankind's behavior. Later, the progressive nature of biblical revelation is revealed more explicitly by "As a man thinks in his heart, so is he" (Proverbs 23:7). It is important to understand what the model illustrates in all its dimensions. The spaces of existence that determine who we are and who we are becoming yes are affected by our outside world. However, the seat or core of our behavior lies within where choices are made, and behavior follows. God comes to his creation from a personal space in this brief story. Moses described God as "regretful" and that he was "deeply troubled" (Genesis 6:6-7).

Mankind made in the image of God comes to these spaces from within. God is described as regretful and deeply troubles all spaces of the spirit and soul, and humankind is seen from the inside-out of their human inclination, thoughts, and heart. These inner spaces is critical to understanding who we are and who we are becoming. Both God and man dealt with matters of the soul and spirit. On the other hand, in the New Testament, Paul says to the ...."let no root of bitterness spring up in you" (Hebrews 12:15). Paul understood, as did Moses, that as much as we try to blame everything on the outside for our behavior, it is from the inside out that life is lived. That is the importance of the #1 Circle of the model spaces of existence.

Before the flood, the narrative of the world in evil disaster ended with one of the important injunctions, "**but**" in the Bible. After a most unusual lament of God concerning the evil condition of the earth came the injunction, "But Noah found favor in the eyes of the Lord" (Genesis 6:8). Here is the space of the loner standing against the tide. The space within is so strong that the pressure of the majority and the popular tide does not crush its character. A space strong enough to speak truth against the popular tide. A space that follows personal character and conviction rather than the crowd. Here is a story world where one man stood up to the tide of evil in a space where favor with God is assured. A space in a man's heart was found where God's favor abounds. A space of grace in the middle of unmerciful evil. A space that represented a break in the flood of evil.

For there stood one who believed in God against all the odds. One willing to speak from that powerful space of God's favor against an evil worldwide mob. Noar epitomized the lone man willing to speak truth no matter how much it stirs up personal rejection. He exemplified the space where one can stand true to the message no matter the cost. Though rare, Noan understood and saw with his own eyes in historical space and time that when the favor of God's goodness is spurned, evil will inhibit that space. When faith is neglected, doubt will be accepted. When love is rejected, hate will grow. When strength is neglected, weakness will fill the space in our lives. It is impossible to be natural in who we are or what we are becoming. Neither nature nor humankind can live without occupying spaces or spaces that occupy us.

At the end of the day the personal space (1) we inhabit is all we have is all we own. Everything else we leave here. In Genesis, there is an important first explicit commentary on the role of one's inner belief of influence. The narrative said in the Old Testament, "Abraham believed the Lord" (Genesis 15:6). A simple descriptive statement but with profound insight into the role of one's belief system. He became the father of the Jewish people, one of the world's most prophetic and consequential people of influence. He began with this simple description of the inner space of his belief. Inside, in a most private and fundamental space beyond which neither the people of his day could fathom or see at the core of who he was, he believed in God. And God credits righteousness to him.

The writer of Hebrews acknowledges the importance of this Abrahamic space of belief when confirming this space in the New Testament space. The writer gave a list of Abraham's actions and achievements; leaving his home, traveling to a city he never knew, and becoming a father of a people that would be as numerous as the sand, and all of this sprang from his core of believe in God when God told him what in anyone mind an impossible achievement. However, it happened as God said it because "Abraham believed, and it was accounted to him as righteousness (Hebrew 11:8-12).

Paul, in arguing the importance of belief for salvation, was not on the basis of works, but belief in God repeated the same: "Abraham believed God and was credited to him as righteousness" (Romans 4:3). Just like Abraham, the same is true of any humankind. The inner space of belief (whatever that belief may be in God or not) determines who we are and who we are becoming. From there, we determine the choices we make in life--choices that can change the course of one life or astronomically more. The space of Abraham's belief in God garnered no more credit for the righteousness of that inner space in which he existed than any other person who takes God by faith in that space of belief in him.

We look at what goes on inside the body. Only death cuts across these divisional spaces. Nevertheless, life moves these spaces in connection with each other. So, it is not necessary to divide up one's person only to the extent of seeing what goes on "in the house," "In the tabernacle," In the body.

Moses' Message to the Heart of the Matter (Inner Spaces)

Moses in his final address to the Israelites, Moses challenges them at the point of their soul. He did not simply ask them to behave in a certain way. Of course, he expected them to do that. What he did do was to speak to the "inside-out" spaces of their heart and soul. You can see it in a certain language he used in his farewell addresses. For example, his use of the language of the heart: (1) "But if from there you seek the Lord your God, you will find him if you seek him with all your heart and with all your soul" (Deuteronomy 4:29) (2) 7:8 he admonished them how they should "regard" (a language of the heart and mind) idols, and their artifacts. They are told "not to FORGET the Lord" (8:1-2). (3) They are told to **REMEMBER"** wilderness space and explain the purpose of God to "know what was in your HEART" (Deuteronomy 8:2).

He told them **to *KNOW THEN IN YOUR HEART* "** (v.5) why God disciplines them. He tried to teach them that God brought them out of Egypt not simply to deliver them from the slavery of their body but also to deliver their soul from the "stake" of Egypt to manner from God. Stake in Egypt was food for the body, but his manner was to teach them to rely on God's supply. The revelation of 40 years in the wilderness was for them to learn the space of their hearts (8:2). Moses used the language of the heart and mind like "observe" (8:6-8).

Moses continually challenges them to "Praise the Lord for the good land" (8:10), not just work the lands with their physical bodies, but praise him from the soul. He warned them that when things change for the better when they eat and are satisfied, build fine houses, and settle down with herds and flocks, the soul can grow forgetful, and the mind can forget how Good God you want to be able in your inner-spaces to count your blessings, so you do not forget God. Moses spoke to Israel and targeted the spaces of their soul, their spirit, and their mind. He knows that is the space that is needed for them to live out the covenant of blessings from God (Deuteronomy (8: 10-14).

Moses wanted to consider the manner. It did not grow from the ground. It did not come from the earth or anything that existed upon it. It came from above. It was a hard lesson for them because they did not like it. Although it did what it was meant to do, that is to sustain them. He did so to cultivate the spaces of the heart and not the body. In Deuteronomy, where we find Moses' final speeches, we hear him singing a song to the soul of Israel. A speech often focuses on the mind, and often Moses appeals along the journey to the understanding and mind of Israel. But here, at the end of his days and leadership of Israel in these final hours, he sings his songs to their hearts. He told them so. If he were speaking to just their minds, he would not repeatedly speak of them, REMEMBERING days gone by and how God delivered them. He would not repeatedly speak to them about God's various promises and covenants to their forefathers. He would not constantly appeal to them to obey the commandments and to seek God with all their hearts. He was singing songs that moved beyond their minds into the place into the human existence where spaces occupy--in spaces of the heart, soul, and spirit. Spaces where choices are made and mature. Spaces of existence from which the expressions of life are birth (Deuteronomy 29). He sang to the soul to show that God's overriding purpose was to deliver them so that out of Egypt, "that you might know I am the Lord your God" (29:6).

That was what remembering, recalling, stating all the covenants and commandments, and appealing to follow was all about. So that deep in your heart, soul, and spirit, "you might know who I am." Paul would echo his appeal: " I might know him and the power of his resurrection.... (Philippians 3:10) Places of the heart. Spaces of the soul. If there was any question that Moses was alone in this, God taught Moses a song just before his death. I told him to "write it down and teach it to the Israelites and have them sing it" (Deuteronomy 31:19). Music, more than any other means of communication, speaks to the heart. It goes to places that mare words often do not. When you want to expand the space of one's soul and heart, it is often the place where music takes up residence. God knows this. He created a song to remind Israel they would still feel their rhythm when they could not hear his words.

I do not know the specific words of this song or its rhyme. However, I know the verses were like spaces of the heart. A song of love when they face the hatred of their enemies. A song of mercy when attacked mercilessly. A song of hope when the Jordan ragged. It is a song of victory when Jericho's wall seems to swell. Even a sone of judgment in their wayward ways and wandering soul. They can sing it and find peace and solace. God taught them a song that would wash the doubt and depression in the places of their soul and let hope arise in their places.

In his final address to the Israelites, Moses challenges them to the point of their soul. He did not simply ask them to behave in a certain way. Of course, he expected them to do that. What he did do was to speak to the "inside-out" spaces of their heart and soul. You can see it in certain language he used in his farewell addresses. For example, his use of the language of the heart: **(1)** "But if from there you seek the Lord your God, you will find him if you seek him with all your heart and with all your soul" (Deuteronomy 4:29) **(2)** In Deuteronomy 7:8 he admonished them how they should "regard" (a language of the heart and mind) idols, and their artifacts. They are told "not to FORGET the Lord" (8:1-2). **(3)** They are told to REMEMBER" wilderness space and explained the purpose of God to "know what was in your HEART" (8:2). He told them to KNOW THEN IN YOUR HEART " (v.5) why God discipline you.

He tried to teach them that God brought them out of Egypt not simply to deliver them from the slavery of their body but also to deliver their soul from the "stake" of Egypt to manner from God. Stake in Egypt was food for the body, but his manner was to teach them to rely on God's supply. The revelation of 40 years in the wilderness was for them to learn the space of their hearts (8:2). Moses used the language of the heart and mind like "observe" (8:6-8). Moses continually challenges them to "Praise the Lord for the good land" (8:10), not just work the lands with their physical bodies, but praise him from the soul. He warned them that when things change for the better, when they eat and are satisfied, build fine houses, and settle down with herds and flocks, they can grow forgetful, and the mind can get forgetful about how Good God is you want to be able in your inner-spaces to count your blessings, so you do not forget God. Moses spoke to Israel and targeted the spaces of their soul, their spirit, and their mind. He knows that is the space needed for them to live out the covenant of blessings from God (Deuteronomy (8: 10-14). Moses wanted to consider the manner. It did not grow from the ground. It did not come from the earth or anything that existed upon it. It came from above. It was a hard lesson for them because they did not like it. Although it did what it was meant to do, that is to sustain them.

The Judgment Of Judges

The period of the Judges was some three thousand years ago, but its spirit still lives on in our times. Just because Israel made it out of Egypt to the Promised Land did not mean their personal trials were over. They had driven out all their enemies except for the one within. The space within their spirit. The space within their soul. They found there a longing, a desire for things forbidden. They found within themselves a desire—a space with gravity pull yet within them towards the things their forefathers warned them not to desire.

It came with the source of alternative culture and lifestyle that was forbidden and foreign to theirs. They found a space within them--a gravitational pull to other nations' gods. The quest for false gods begins from within. "A man is tempted when he is drawn away by his own lusts" (James 1:14). And they fell for their worship. They followed the lifestyle of their enemies and entertained their godless customs, even to the point of sacrificing their own children to these gods made by hands. They did not watch over the righteous spaces of their hearts and souls. What they desired led them astray from their culture and ways established by covenants and commandments given through their leaders from God.

Sometimes spaces collide, as in Samson's case. He was a Nazarite, so no hair on his head was to be cut. Spiritual space of obedience intersects with nature. A natural characteristic - his hair. His physical strength, a unique space of strength, was connected with his hair not being cut. When it was, his strength was gone. So, although it was a physical attribute, it was also a spiritual space (a vow his mother took for him to be separated from God (Judges 14:3-5). So, his power was also of a spiritual nature--a spiritual space. Here the physical - hair, uncut, was connected to the physical space. When his hair was cu, so was his spirit.

Graphic Essays of Inner Spaces

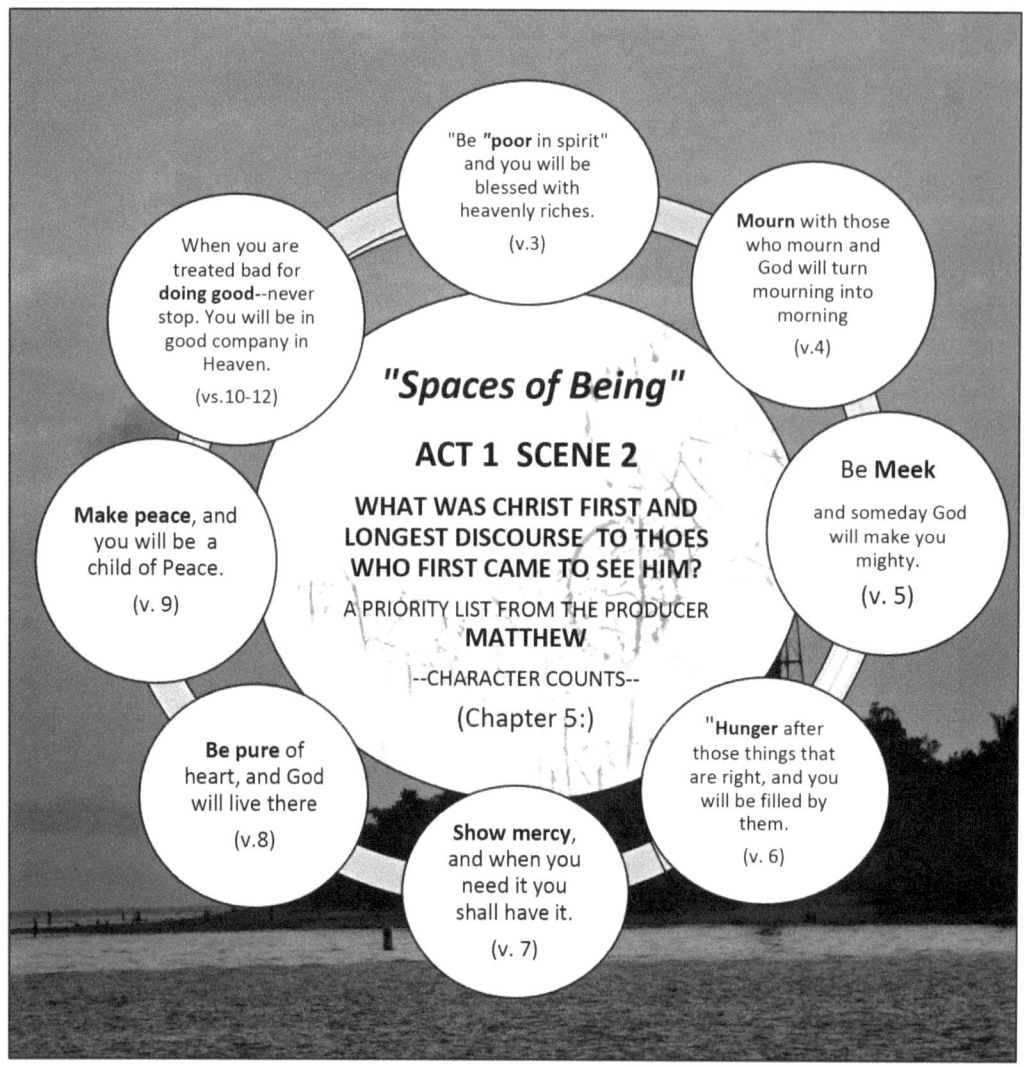

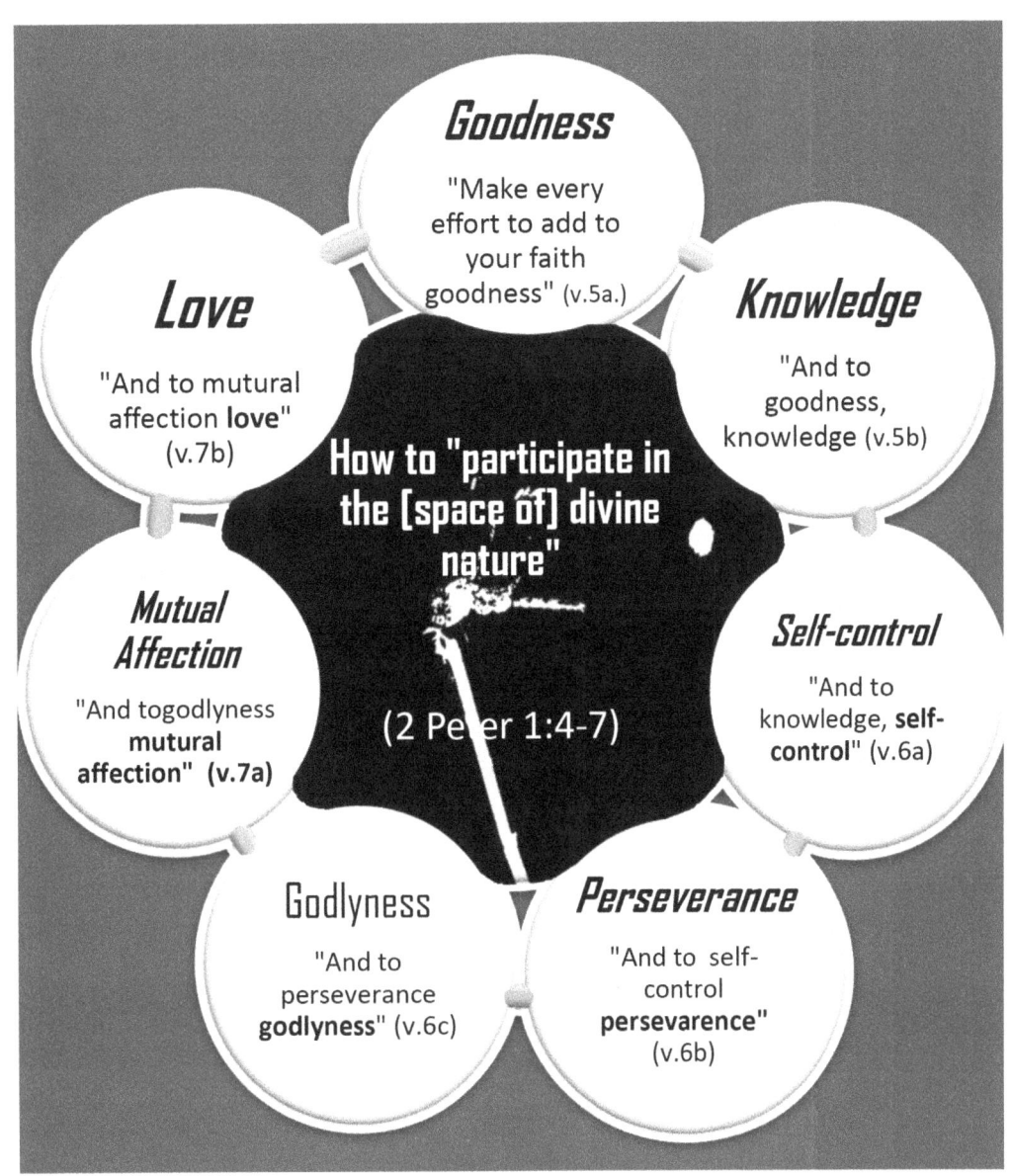

36

THE SPACE OF *US* – CHANGE COMES FROM WITHIN

"General Gravity"

Spaces

of Our World: Body, Soul, and Spirit. Created From Outside in and Inside out:

*Who Are We? *Who Are We Becoming? *How Can We Get to Who We Want to Be?

Those are the questions of the Spaces of Our Existence.

1

Like rain from heavenly places writers from the poetic books of the Bible showered us with revelations of the inner space of us as the focal point of change. It is from the inner space of existence that change is birth, nurtured, and grow. It is from that space the Psalmist cried: "Create **in me** a clean heart and renew a steadfast spirit **within me**" (Psalm 51:10). In the following graphic is an extensive effort to follow Paul instructions "rightly dividing the word of truth" (2 Timothy 3:15) as we look at helpful biblical divisions found in Proverbs; intended for further exploration and learning:

Graphic Essays

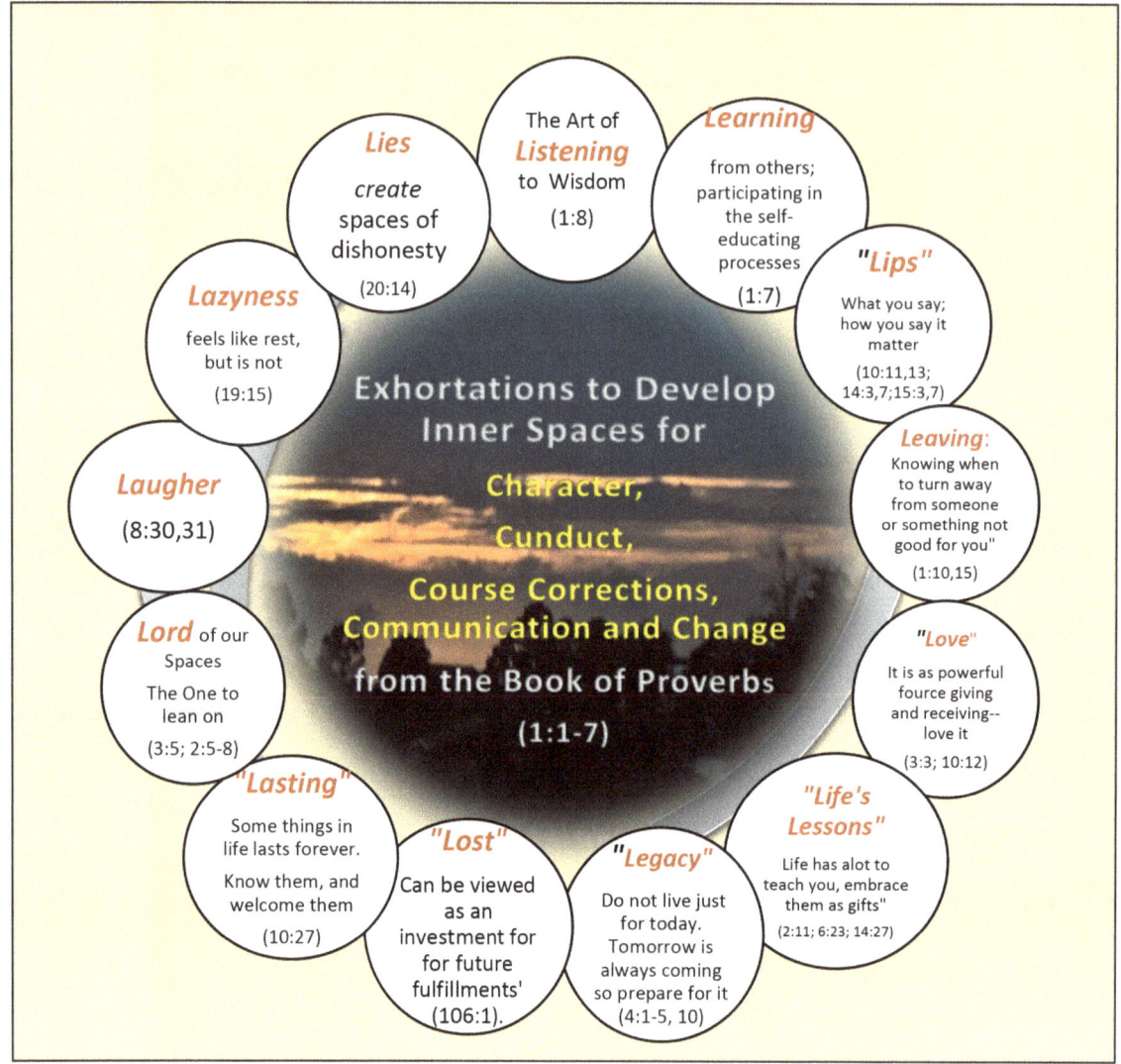

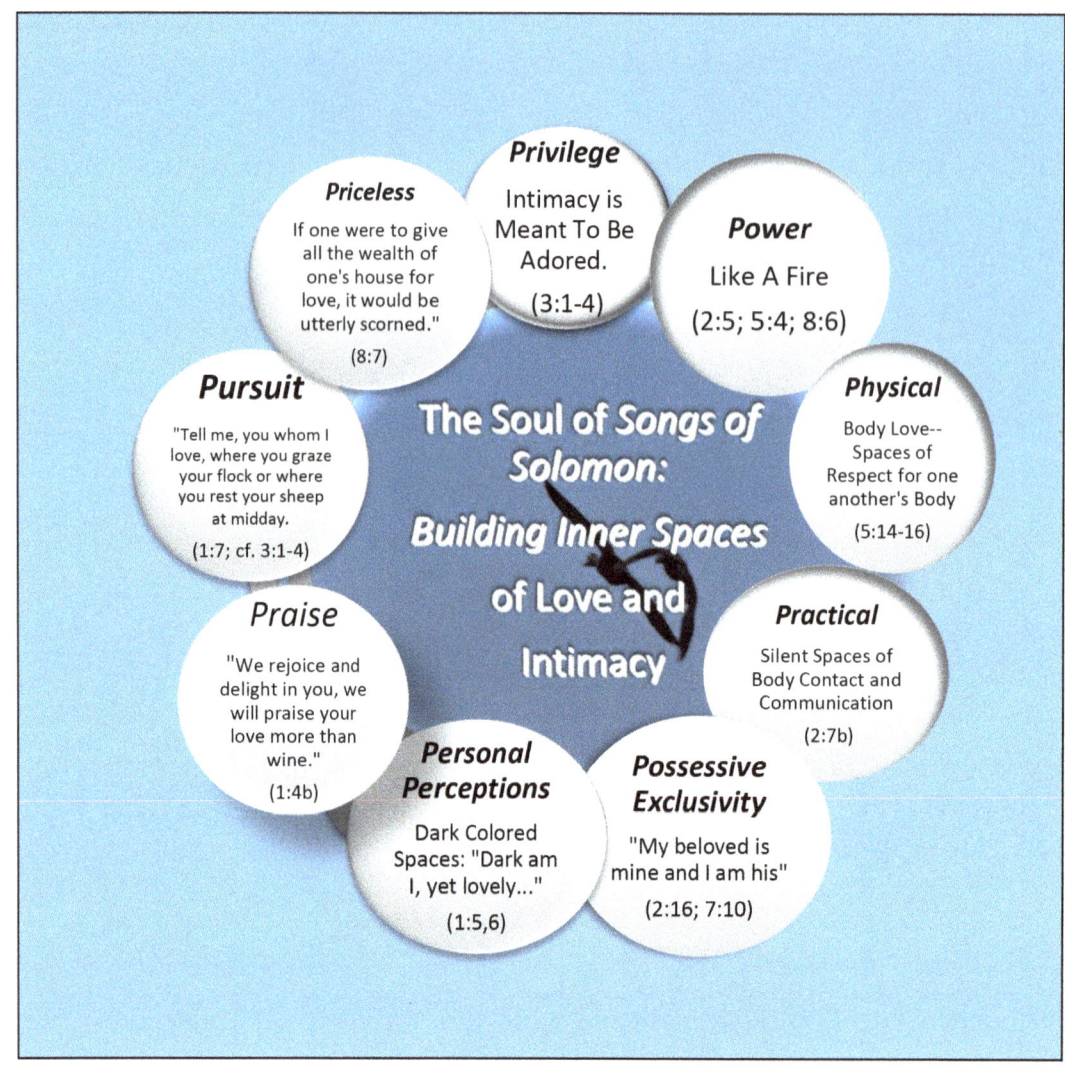

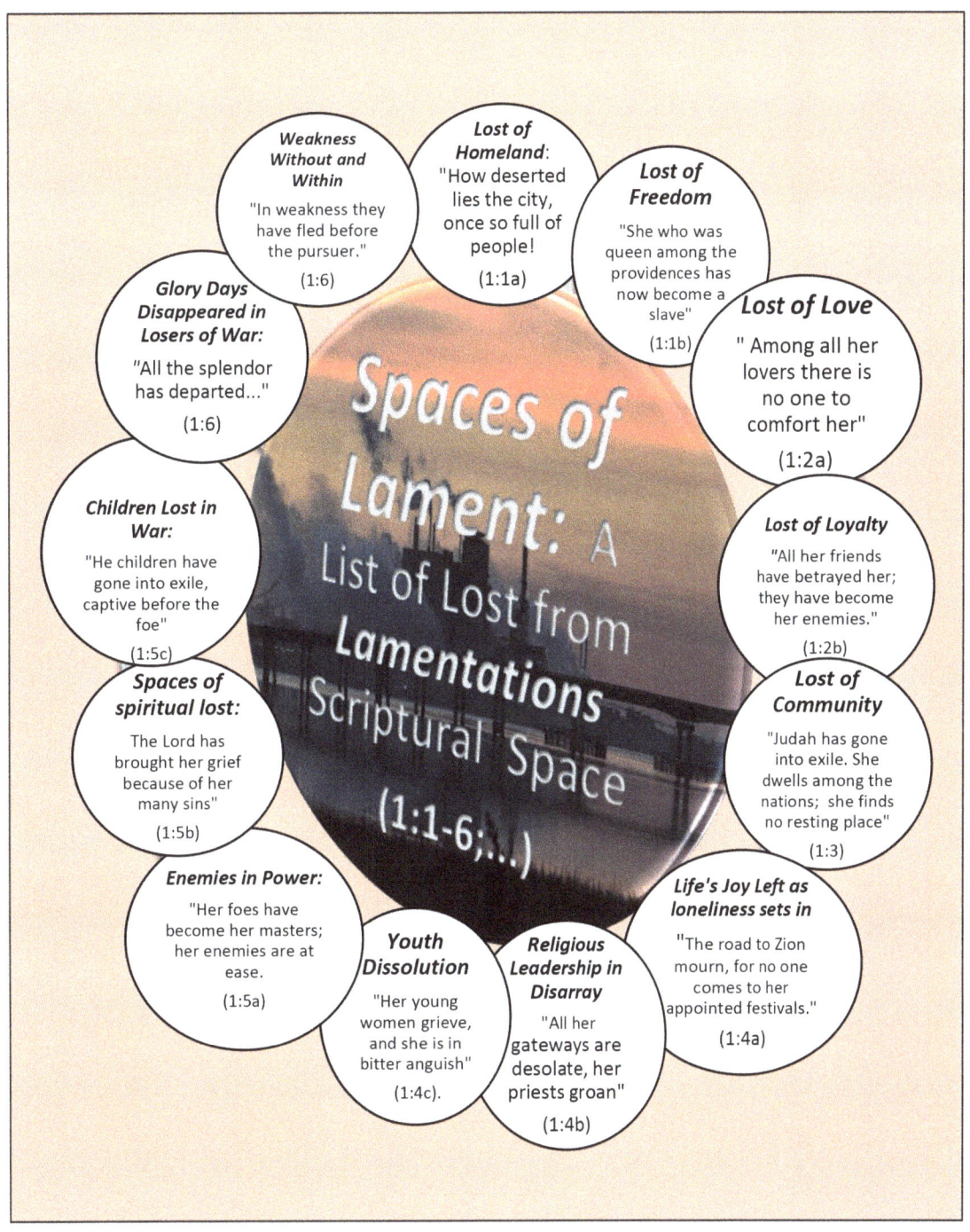

Faith comes from within…. Hebrews 11

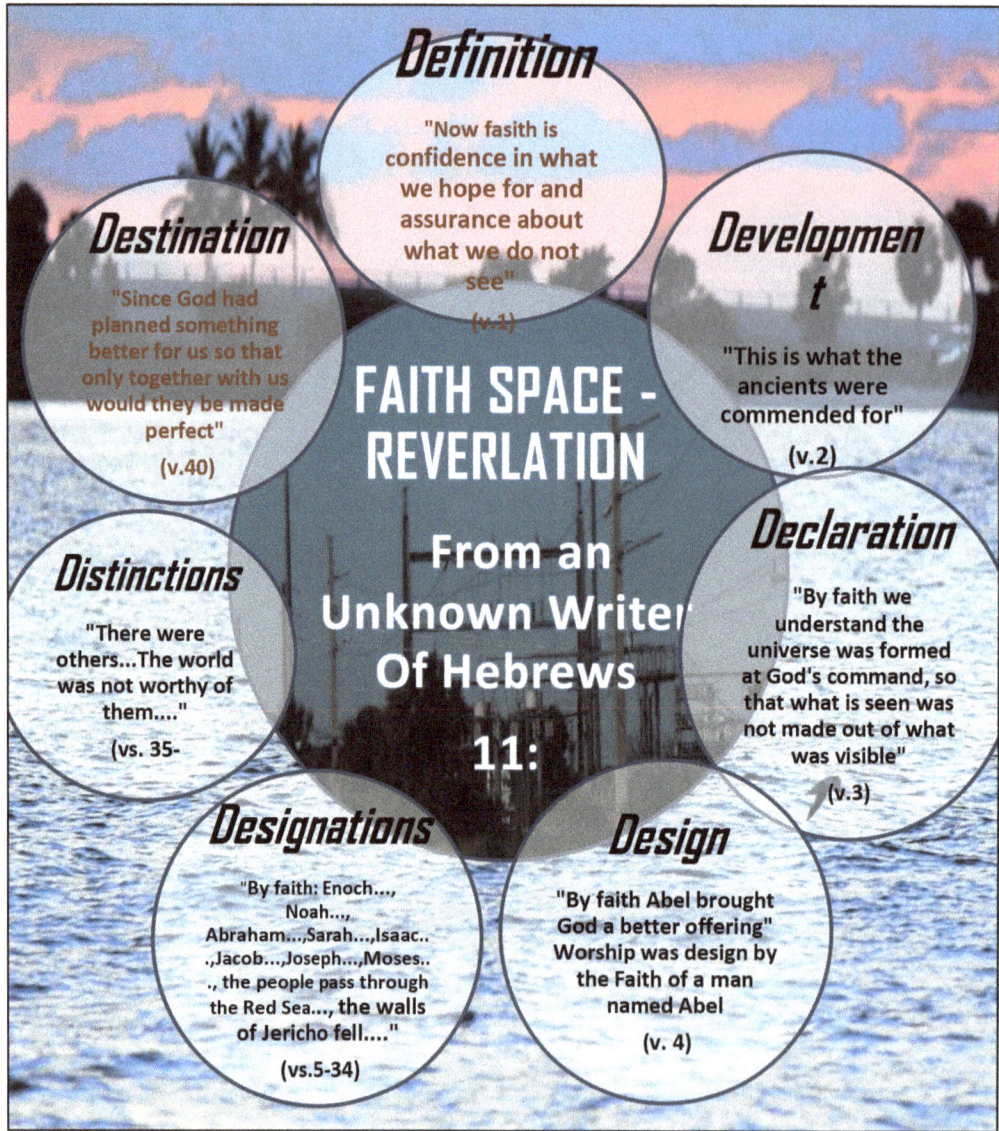

37

The Space of *Us* – Let's Get Practical

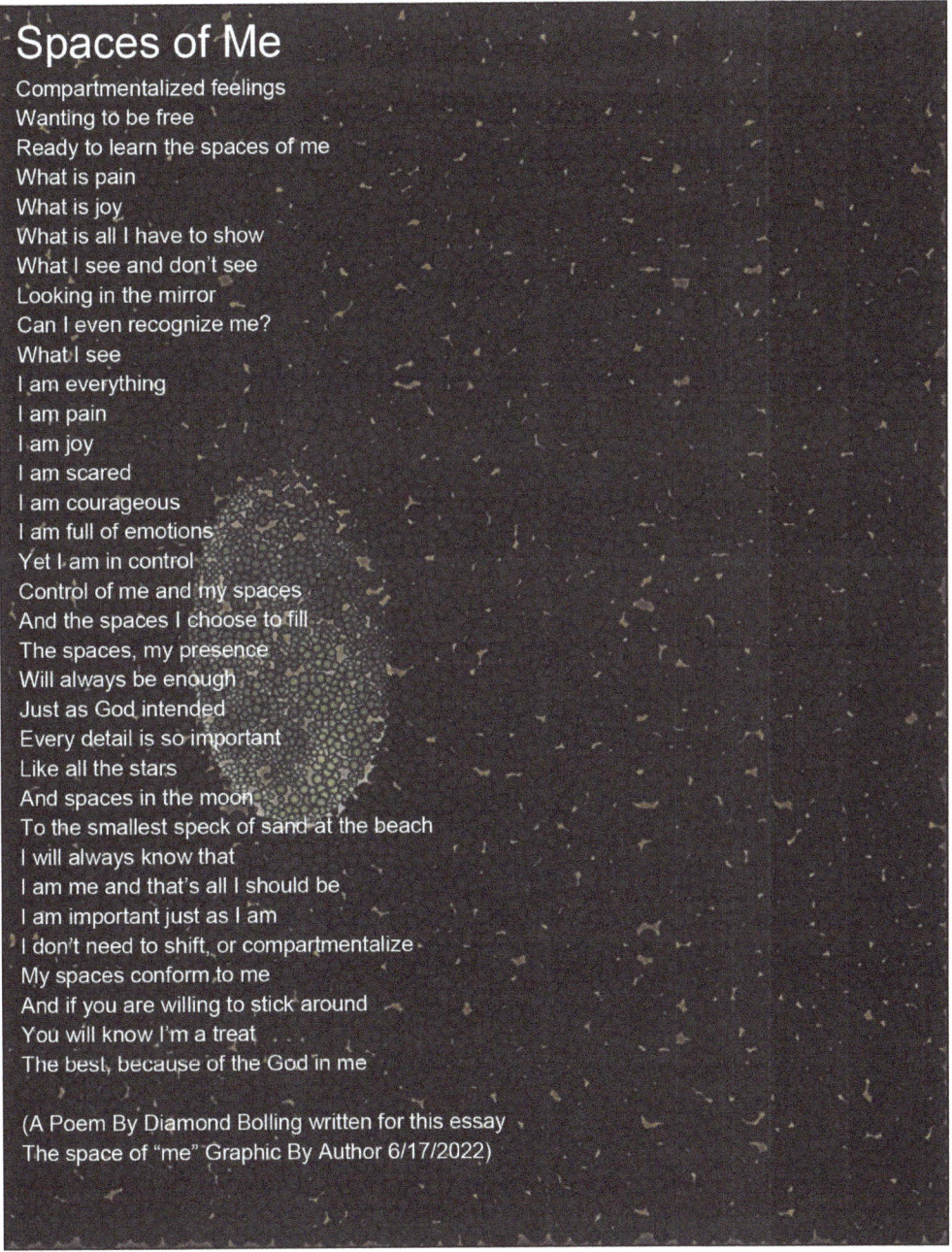

Spaces of Me

Compartmentalized feelings
Wanting to be free
Ready to learn the spaces of me
What is pain
What is joy
What is all I have to show
What I see and don't see
Looking in the mirror
Can I even recognize me?
What I see
I am everything
I am pain
I am joy
I am scared
I am courageous
I am full of emotions
Yet I am in control
Control of me and my spaces
And the spaces I choose to fill
The spaces, my presence
Will always be enough
Just as God intended
Every detail is so important
Like all the stars
And spaces in the moon
To the smallest speck of sand at the beach
I will always know that
I am me and that's all I should be
I am important just as I am
I don't need to shift, or compartmentalize
My spaces conform to me
And if you are willing to stick around
You will know I'm a treat . . .
The best, because of the God in me

(A Poem By Diamond Bolling written for this essay
The space of "me" Graphic By Author 6/17/2022)

James the Apostle –I call him the practical teacher, in his letter holds a mirror up to his readers when he writes:

Anyone who listens to the Word but does not do what it says is like someone who looks at his face in a mirror and, after looking at himself, goes away and immediately forgets what he looks like.

But whoever looks intently into the perfect law that gives freedom and **continues in it**—*not forgetting what he has heard but* **doing it**—*they will be blessed in* **what they do** *(James 1:23-25).*

Years ago, I was a freshman college student in the city of Chicago for the first time. I had to find my way fast. I traveled there from a small island in the Caribbean and had to learn the ways of the big city of Chicago, USA, in a hurry. I had much help from local pastors, teachers, and fellow students, and even before I came here, there were those who took an interest and had lived here to prepare for this new world of American big city life. Admittedly, I was not prepared. There were more things that were "unthinkable" to my West Indian ways that were quite normal in Chicago. It was like what Alvin Toffler described as "Future Shock." It is like a country lady thrust into the big city with big dreams but no map in which to navigate life there. A space where failure does not come with just shattered dreams but with shattered lives.

The varied good instructions prepared me to protect my body. I had little preparation for my soul and my spirit. For example, consider the following:

The year before my college training began at a leading evangelical institution, I was confronted with being among the first black students the few there were to participate in the first year of what was an entirely new word for me. It was called "integration." Integration? What was that? Why was it now happening after a hundred years? Why would that be a "thing" among an institution dedicated to producing Evangelical Christian leaders? They had gone out of their way to prepare me to deal with Chicago police officers to protect my body. No one prepared me for "integration" and how to protect my soul. How was I to deal with this evil space among God's people?

- In the Caribbean, I learned and was trained in electrical technology and how to wire a three-story building. By the age of sixteen, I had accomplished that. They also learned Refrigeration engineering. Through these skills, with many hours after school in practical on-the-job training, I developed quite a positive self-image. It was severely challenging when the job offered to me—the only one offered was to work in an all-White personnel office space cleaning floors and toilets each afternoon after classes. No one prepared me for the combustible turmoil that seems like the eye of a storm winds encircling my soul each day. I grew up on an island where everyone was taught to clean up after themselves. The idea of working at cleaning up after others was too suffocated a concept for me to rap around my head, and more so even my soul. One day, traveling on a Chicago bus that took me to clean toilets, I found solace in a resolution: I resolved that if cleaning other people's toilets would be what helped me complete school and get my degree, then I would do it. I would not let other people define who I am and know myself to be. Furthermore, I am not going to let a task or job selected for me define who I am either.

I must add a high note of this difficult inner struggle. The errand boy side took me to deliver all kinds of design fabric and materials for floors, walls, and ceilings. I refuse just to deliver them. I learned what made them top designers' products. I learned what made their design attractive and what materials were sought after by top Chicago designers. After graduation and becoming a Pastor, I learned the building trade. Now, as a GC, I designed and built homes with a keen eye for interior design development as an errand boy. It is like Joseph sold into slavery out of the difficult situation, learning others may have meant it for evil, for I know that school administration would never send any of their white students to clean the toilets in a black-run office, not even a white one. But, it turned out God used it for Good.

- There were many others who were unprepared to survive the new life. The two seem unusual so that I will mention them. There were the usual not even DWB (driving while black) as I did not have a license to drive. However, that did not stop the White student driver from getting pulled over because they had a black student in the car. And instead of the driver being asked for his ID. I was the one who asked, although I was nowhere close to the wheel. Often, I sat in the back seat to be couscous. Nevertheless, at that time, in that place, not even those precautions worked for a Black man in the big city. The point I am making here is that my Caribbean culture developed a carefree, laidback space inside, unprepared for the unbelievable gravity of spiritual and social forces that came crashing into my space beyond my skin.

- While in the Chicago space, a Black Pastor picked me out and wanted to give me an education not available at the evangelical school I was attending. He took me to a Black like suburban area, which was a significant step up from the project lifestyle. There were wonderful church buildings in the area, but none were of the typical or traditional black churches that have served black communities. He said this is how it goes. An affluent black moved into a White wrote neighborhood. Then the white flight begins. It is an evil process. It includes the wonderful church buildings that are left without financial support. The typical traditional black churches not having the support to purchase or maintain these church buildings built by the white support church members now left. Outside sects with financial resources buy up these buildings. They are left with those coming in with all kinds of teachings. So, white flights were more concerned about the perceived economic threat of a Black family in their suburb than they were about a cult religion taking over the building that the local Black community could not afford. Again, this was just another experience I could never understand. Who would allow their legacy to be so shallow that it would rather sell out their building, what they once considered a cult organization that at least worked out some accommodation with the black church community? If only to save it from heresy.

I am at my worst if I sense I am just drifting along without inner direction. Some people can "roll" like that. I have a friend who can cook, watch TV, and talk to me, and others in her space while talking to me. She calls it multitasking. I am not cut out to be like that. I tend to give or at least try to give my full attention and focus to whatever I am doing. In Chicago, I was like a student without a rudder. My internal space was in disarray. Too many things coming at me in the big city for a small-town guy. I grew up in the less noted space called a "village." My carefully developed isolated center was turned upside down in the big city.

I realize I might crash inside if I did not fix that wanting space inside my skin. I developed a simple model of how I would fix "the space of me." It was the first of many graphic learning models that would come years later, such as what is represented in my work. Nevertheless, the following model of the " me " space was the first I developed to get me through the Chicago big city space. It was my personal inside guide to overcoming both inside and outside challenges as well. I learned often what we humans need are often untapped resources right inside our skin:

Arnold Thompson's "Soul **Spaces for Success Model**"

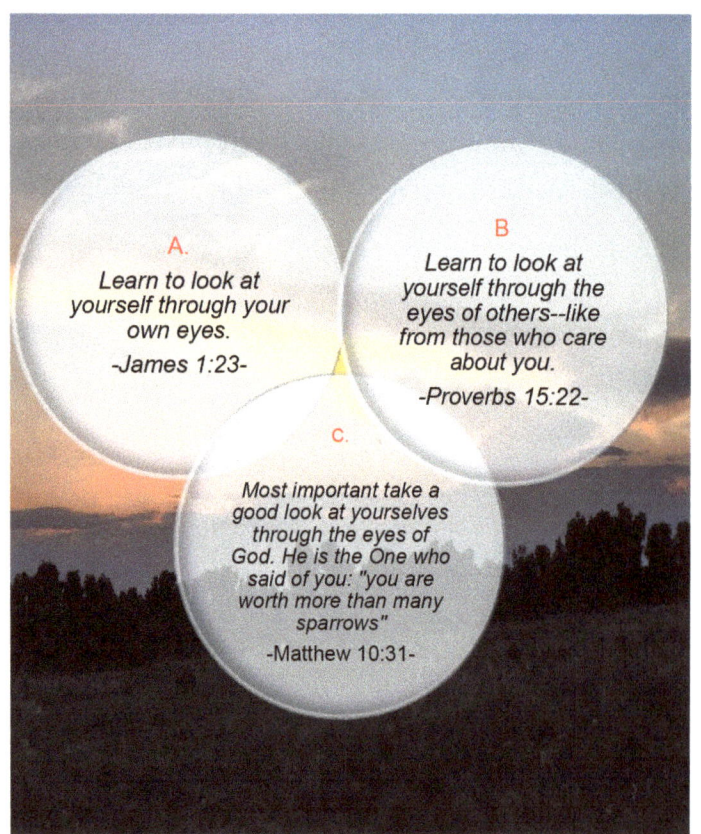

I gave this model this personalized title only because it best describes the heart and source of this system. It came from a space of struggles deep within. And in that space, I found my way out. That is what I am acknowledging here. is being acknowledged here. It worked for me then, both in concept and practice, and continues to do so to this day. It is because it was so personal to me that I never shared it until now. But in researching and presenting essays on personal spaces, I thought it was best after half a century to share it now.

A. PERSONAL SPACE "A": *LEARN TO LOOK AT YOURSELF THROUGH YOUR OWN EYES.*

I once heard about a dog that was walking along with a bone in its mouth and came to a pond on the side of the road. So, the dog paused to look in and saw another dog looking back with a bone in his mouth as well. Unaware that it was his own reflection, the dog dropped the bone he had and dove in to fetch the other. He lost both.

The Apostle James, whom I call the Practical Theologian, gave a more spiritual example of the dog with the bone. He wrote in James 1:23: *Anyone who listens to the word but does not do what it says is like someone who looks at his face in a mirror and, after looking at himself, goes away and immediately forgets what he looks like.*" On the one hand, the dog, not knowing what was seen, was not real but a reflection of what was real. On the other hand, the person with the bible looks in and sees the same thing, which is the reality of who he was, but then goes away and forgets his personal reality. Both ended up with a loss. Why? Is it not because both failed to assess and confront the reality of who they were?

I was from a Caribbean island barely beyond my teens, and I was thrust into the heart of the big city of Chicago. Reflections of America in all its presentations of possibilities and alternatives. How do you know the difference? How do you separate possibilities from a sideshow? How do you separate a convention from a make-believe carnival? How do you know if you are looking at reality or a distortion of it? Sitting in a Chicago bus, a Bible student, a young black man, a highly qualified and experienced technician beyond my pairs, heading to clean a White man's office floors and toilet. How was I going to curb "me"? Everything I faced outside just seemed to make it worse.

From a young age, I have always found that I can be reflective and rely on my reasoning powers to think through a technical problem. So, I turned my attention to "me." I said I must learn to look at myself. I must look not at a reflection, a chlorate of what the City or anyone in it thought of me, but to get a grip of my sum. What do I think of myself as being in this carnival city? I concluded that must be the place to start. I resolved that I could not allow this city to define me. I must see myself first through my own eyes if I am going to survive this city. That was my first redemptive revelation that I stated this way in the first model circle of my redemption. First, look at yourself through your own eyes. Here is what I saw; that was my first step to success. (This success was not defined in grand terms. It was simple to survive the city and its circumstances and complete what I came to do: graduate with my degree).

- I saw inside a kid raised with good values of love, hard work, and accomplishments. One the outside there were things making me feel ashamed, but I had no reason inside to feel that way. So that must go it was not the reality of me. It will crush me if do not.

- The city was not me. The people in the city were not me. The white students who would rather not have Blacks around were not me. And it was not my problem. What possible good it would do to hate others because they hate you? How could hate plus hate equal anything but more hate? I looked inside; I saw no hate or bitterness for any, and I vowed I would keep "me" that way. I was going to 'let no root of bitterness grow in me" (Hebrews 12:15). It was another of those redemptive spaces as I began to explore "me."

- The work I was tasked with, however disruptive to this haughty perception of myself, was still not me. I looked inside, taking a good look at the "me," and saw nothing in cleaning floors and even dirty toilets that made me any different from who I know I am. To survive in this city, I would ensure the city does not define me. It was another of those redemptive spaces I found in me. It freed me to do what I had to do without it being a judgment of me. *It is amazing how, when you determine that something does not matter anymore, it frees up oceans of space for those things that matter.*

- If you look inside and find things that should be there, forgive yourself and move on. I mean, fight the enemies without but make peace with those within. If you do not, the ones within will always win. Whatever I want to fight outside, I must look within and make sure it is not there. For example, it is quite possible that a Black person can become a racist facing structural racism almost every day in school or society at large. It was what I faced in the city in so many ways. The wisdom of this first step to look inside is to ensure that what we fight against is not present in 'me."

I can give many more examples of how important and fundamental this first space is. Every time I come across one of the varied challenges of the city, I reflect on this first rule, and it has led me well in every way. Look at yourself first through your own eyes. who or what do you see when you do? Do you like what you see? I was walking on a sidewalk in Chicago when a friend invited me to a side door. He paid a fee, and we were led into a side door with a seat next to a hole in a wall. I looked, and on the other side, there were nude ladies dancing for a fee. I thought I would see a rassling match. I did, but it was not on the other side of that wall. It was in me. I did not condemn myself. I followed a friend who wanted to show me what the city offered, even to people casually walking by. I was naïve. I learned to be naïve; the city is a dangerous place to be. If you survive a mistake because of ignorance, survive by not making it again.

B. **PERSONAL SPACE "B": *LEARN TO LOOK AT YOURSELF THROUGH THE EYES OF OTHERS.***

It may not seem this way, but this second step is critically important. For example, one of the most important things after my undergraduate degrees was to have the opportunity to be married to someone who enlarged my cultural and spiritual space in understanding the subtleties of the Black American's life and the critical role of both the White church in it. Without learning to look at the Black experience through her eyes and not simply my own, I would be blind to a large dimension of this space and ministry. When I looked into her eyes, telling me of the pain she felt, like being bussed from her own space and friends she had come to know to another school some distance in the name of "integration." You cannot get that from a college history class. In a moment in a flash, you can multiply her pain all across the land despite its worthy goals. You learn there is no substitute for taking the often-ignored space and looking at the world through these close. It is the narrow vision of your own space that is not informed by others who know you. Especially those like family and close friends who are invaluable in being honest with you and letting you know your blind spots.

The advice and counsel of those close to you should be viewed not as a replacement or even a diminishment of your personal space but as an enlargement of your space. It is like education becomes an enlargement of your intellectual space (or it should be), so family and friends, even co-workers who know you, can be a resource for enlarging your social and spiritual space.

My wife and I were invited to a fellowship get-together. When we got there and entered the space, two little white children literally ran away to their parents in the back of the room, shouting and heard by all the other guests, "There are Black people out there!" It was unexpected. It was totally embarrassing. And it was a teachable moment. I soon learned from my wife when we got back home to get with it, for it was also America.

My point is that looking at yourself through your own eyes is a constant effort in the flow of existence. However, you cannot end there. Growing to understand and appreciate also involves looking at yourself through the eyes of others, especially those close to whom you trust and who love you. Those you know have your best interest at heart and can give you an honest view, not what you want to hear, but what you need to hear. When making decisions and judgments in an overly emotional space, who can tell you, "You need to chill." Alternatively, as my mom would say, "Drive some sense into you." Again, it does not mean you abrogate your space. It means you must always be open to enlarging it. I contend that if we are honest, most of the critical, important things we learn in life are from others.

I cannot illustrate here how invaluable it was for 28 years to be a Pastor of a Black American congregation and have a wife—a Black American who guided me into effective church leadership. After we married, we met each week to play a game UNO, and there would be impromptu discussions on marriage life for several years. I cannot imagine how our marriage space would have developed without the benefit of the eyes of those who had been through those early spaces before.

If I had a dollar for each time my wife would tell me, "You have a blind spot," I would be a rich man indeed. The truth is I am rich in that space because of it. Blind spots for automobiles are becoming a thing of the past. Technologies enable us to see 360 degrees while driving the latest ones. Can they develop something to catch all the blind spots within *the space of me?* I contend the answer is no. Furthermore, it is the reason God gave us family and friends. They often have eyes in places we do not. I contend that sometimes, to solve a problem, all that is needed is a little help from a friend.

C. PERSONAL SPACE "C": *LEARN TO LOOK AT YOURSELF THROUGH THE EYES OF GOD.*

Look at the Book:

"The eyes of the LORD are everywhere, keeping watch on the wicked and the good' (Proverbs 1:3)

"For the eyes of the LORD roam t and from over all the earth to show Himself strong on behalf of those whose hearts are fully devoted to Him (2 Chronicles 6:9)

"For a man's ways are before the eyes of the LORD, and the LORD examines all his paths (Proverbs 5:21).

What these selected narratives tell us (and the whole of Scripture reveals the same) is Elohim is omnipresent (no space is beyond him) and His omniscient (no space is beyond His knowledge): He is every place, and He knows everything. We cannot go into any space where He is not. We cannot know anything from which He does not know the end from the beginning. With God, there are no "blind spots" because our ways "are before the eyes of the LORD." He even "perceives my thoughts from afar" (Psalm 139:2).

What, then, is the practical import of this Divine space? Sometimes you look at yourself. You do not like what you see. You look at others, and you end up with the same result. You do not like what even your friends are telling you about you. The "me" of me is down like in a swamp—up to your neck in troubles. If you live long enough, you will acquire friends who will not hesitate to tell you the truth and others who are afraid to do so. You are going to find yourself in that space. It feels like no one understands you. It feels like being alone in the world, even with the best of friends. Even in a marriage relationship, you feel no one cares. It is like a space you wished you had "wings of the morning like a dove you would fly away and be at rest," as the Psalmist cried out (Psalm 55:61). Or, like Job, in the depth of despair, you want to curse the day you were born because of all the seemingly unbearable suffering around you.

I know that space. As a Pastor, I have counseled many from the edge of that space. Many of God's children throughout the ages have known that space. What is important is to look at yourself through the eyes of God. Here are but a few reasons why and how:

- **PRAYER.** Jesus said, "This, then, is how you should pray: "Our Father in heaven, hallowed be our name, your kingdom come that *will be done on earth as it is in heaven. Give us this day our daily bread*...." The space of prayer is always available to anyone. So that their personal space is not restricted but, through prayer, expanded to the throne of heaven. This is no small thing Jesus invites us to participate in with His Father (Luke 11:2-4).

- **PROMISE.** Jesus said, "Do not let your heart be troubled; you believe in God. You believe also in me...." (John 14:1). Jesus fully understands in this world that His follower's heart is not immune from "troubles." And He promised, "I go to prepare a place for you and will come again." One's personal space is expanded by promise."

- **PREVILEDGE.** Jesus said, "Anyone who loves me will obey my *teachings. My Father will love them and will come to them and make our home with them" (Matthew 14:23).* The space of our relationship here can compress. As we grow older, this space can get smaller and smaller. If there are failures, they get small quite quickly. However, if we practice following Jesus, he keeps expanding the small space of our relationship. He expands us with His presence. Moreover, even when we are alone, He fills this space with His presence. For He fills the whole earth with who He is.

- **PROVISION.** Jesus said, *"Peace I leave with you; my peace I give you. I do not give to you as the world give you. Do not let your heart be troubled and do not be afraid"* (Matthew 13:27). Jesus knew while He was here that "peace" will be in short supply. It would, be like a spiritual hurricane caught without the peace of water to sustain us. So, He offered this as something He would leave us in abundance, so it would have been provided when needed. So, when the winds stir up against us, we have this enduring peace. So, when we look at our space, we dare not see this ready expansion of peace available to us. So, when our times fill us with fear, we block it out with the peace of God. They cannot occupy the same space.

PACTICE Jesus said 'Let not your heart be troubled" Jesus wants us to exist in a practice space. A space where we actively seek to do his will. The safest place in the universe is still in the will of God. It is to be where God provided for us. He said, "I am the vine. You are the branches. If you remain in me, you will bear much fruit…" (John 15:51).

PARADICE. "I go to prepare a place for you… (John 14:1)

Although these steps might seem conceptual, as we have said, change must begin inside before it is demonstrated in practice on the outside. To this end, this personal model developed so many years ago was helpful to me with life in the big city of Chicago, from a Caribbean Island. I had to find a way to brave the city and its challenges. There is so much to be gained by these truths. They have worked for me, and I still use them. For they still work.

38

THE SPACE OF *US* – MOSES MEMORIES AND MESSAGE

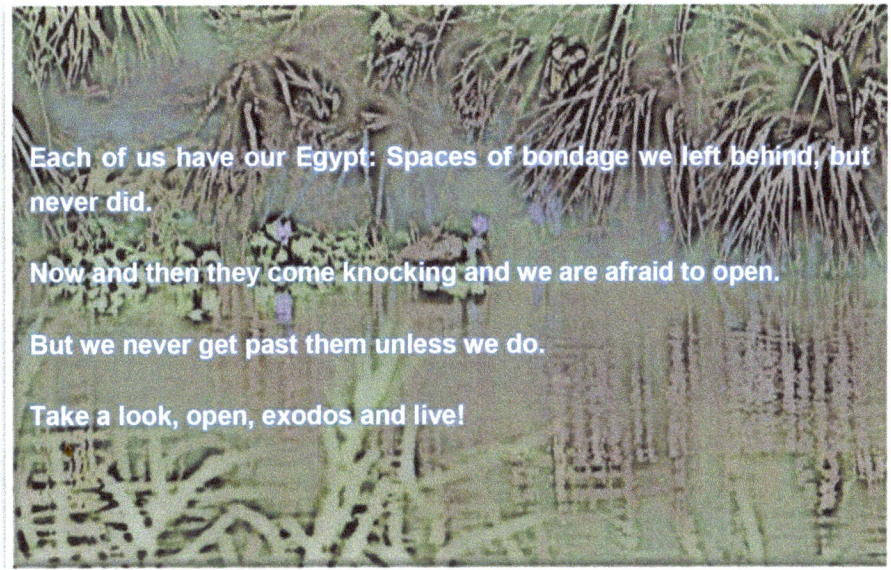

Each of us have our Egypt: Spaces of bondage we left behind, but never did.

Now and then they come knocking and we are afraid to open.

But we never get past them unless we do.

Take a look, open, exodos and live!

The book of Exodus introduces us to gardens of personal spaces in the service of Elohim.

Private Spaces

In the calling of Moses, we see **Private Spaces** of communication. It was no small thing that God spoke to Moses directly. He called him by name. Later we learned what was discussed in the historical record he made. However, in his calling, the discourse was an entirely personal and private affair. The subject was deep as they both traversed the garden of his inner soul. He laid bare his limitations. He exposed all his personal fears before God. He held a strong view of himself. He was good at handling sheep; he would not deny that. People and the power of Pharaoh he knew gave him pause-even before Elohim. He thought he had left Egypt all past and done with. Nevertheless, God was now stirring up memories of Egyptian stew. It was God who was bringing Egypt front and center on the mountain. Although Moses had forgotten his people Elohim did not. And more personally, He did not forget Moses. That is why He called him by name.

Moses was confronted with his past deeds in Egypt. They came flashing back as God wanted to send him there again. He had started a new life, and it pulled him away from any concern in Egypt, although the people that he once ruled yet still suffered in slavery there. It was his own people that made him run away. I did not do it on my own. My people wanted to kill me. Now you want to send me back to Egypt. Yes! You got that right!

Present Spaces

In the historical present, Moses stood before God and was confronted with a miracle of God's presence. God was present to him in a burning bush that was not consumed. Moses needed to know he was in the presence space of miracles because he was going to need miracles in his life if his commission was going to be successful. To clarify this point, God told him to "take off your shoes, because where you stand is holy ground" (Exodus 3:5). He was confronted with the reality every child of God must face inside their skin; it is to know ***they function in the space of God's presence.*** What was critical in Moses' present spaces was to confront his weaknesses. To Moses' credit, he did not hesitate to let God know. So much so to the point of making God angry at him, to let God know how unfit he was for the tasks which God was calling him. His personal fears within crimpled him in understanding the power of God from without. He has yet to learn, "greater is He that is within you than he that is in the world, as represented in Pharoah and Egypt.

Moses needed to be able to navigate his present space if he wanted to navigate the space of his future successfully. He had to face Egypt within on the mountain with God if he was going to face Egypt in which he was raised. For wherever he was going, he could not go without taking who he was and who he was becoming with him. It was no small thing; it was important for Moses to know where he was in real-time and in whose presence, he existed, or Egypt would swallow him whole. I contend that the most critical part of Moses' mission occurred right there on the mountain, dealing with his fears within. The battle is won or lost in that critical space within one's skin. That was the most critical part of the mission. He must understand his present space and be in the right space if he will succeed in another. When Moses understood this, then God introduced another important personal space,

Purpose Space

The inner purpose space of our life forms our "north star" to get us home. As a boy, I remember my teacher constantly talking about how a crippled boy learned to live in the crippled space in which he was born. His mother would constantly repeat to him that a space of purpose was created in her son. Each time she senses in him spaces of fear and doubt, she would say to him, " God has a plan for everyone, and God has one for you." It is a powerful space we can cultivate through choices driven by our "north star" purpose. We cannot live a worthy life if we do not have a worthy purpose. God introduced Moses to his purpose. His purpose was big. It confronted him with everything he ran away from—everything he left behind. It was summed up in Egypt, which represented the dark side, the forgotten side, the place he never wanted to see again. However, his grand purpose was going to change the world, and civilization led through that very place, Egypt. Everyone who ever accomplished anything of the grand purpose of their lives must first face their *Egypt*.

I heard a saying, the source of which I do not know: Anything you set out to accomplish, there are always certain things you must do first. For Moses, it was confronting the Egypt he thought he left behind. But his "purpose space," like the Egyptian Nile River, ran right through there.

Practical Spaces

Practical Spaces developed in the narrative of Moses when God asked him a simple question: That ran down from Moses mountain to all God's followers: "What do you have in your hand?" (Exodus 4:2). Moses answered truthfully, "A rod." What Moses did not know was who owned the space of the rod. He did not know in historical space and time that the rod would lead the way of his people out of Pharoah's land. Moses would enlarge his understanding of the space that the rod would occupy in his life and God's purpose. He was going to see a simple practical shepherd rod transform into a space that became "the rod [or staff] of God" (Exodus 4:2KJV).

Right there in the mountain Moses was going to learn of a God who is a Space Maker. He can transform spaces like fire from a tree, like a rod, into a snake and back again. That is what happened when God told him to "cast the rod to the ground…" Moses, in obedience, did so and saw and experienced a transformation of a dead piece of stick that came to life in the form of a serpent, and as he picked it up again, it was transformed back into a stick. However, it was no longer just a stick or a rod. It was transformed into an unlikely space, just like us, for the power of God to occupy. And it was going to be so for all God's children that whatever they have in the hand of God, a transformation space emerged from it.

The power and meaning of this transformation from a stick to a snake from the act of obedience to God must not be missed. It is a "spiritualization process" whereby God can take one's natural abilities and turn them into a spiritual force (Acts 1:8). It is a process of sanctification or consecration where a "thing" like a vessel in the Temple, or clay in the potter's hand is transformed into a Divine or holy form and use. It becomes a space with all the power necessary to fulfill God's purpose.

This available transforming power of that which we have in our hands is, regrettably, one of the most neglected power spaces in the church today. We relentlessly use the practical rods in our lives that were never cast down before the Lord for His empowerment. The space of such empowerment comes from within that river space that flows with humility and obedience. It is an inner space that resists selfish desires. As the Apostle Paul said, it is a space to present your body a "living sacrifice holy and acceptable to God which is our reasonable service (Romans 12:1). In its simplest and most profound act is what Moses did on the mountain before God. Cast whatever you believe you have in your hand, cast it down before the Lord. Give it all to Him and let Him bring all you have alive in His power. Without His anointing, all we have is a dead stick. However, in the hand of God, a stick given to Him comes alive, Egypt bows, and mighty rivers turn into thoroughfares. This is not a romantic statement for emotional content. This is a transforming power to face the Egyptian challenges of our lives. It is a space that determines who we are and who we are becoming. It determines how we fight our battles through the spaces of choices in our lives.

Privilege Spaces

Another important personal space that Exodus's story world presented us with is a space of privilege. From the time Moses was saved from the genocide ordered at the hands of the Egyptian government leaders to crack down on the population of the Israelites, the boy saved by Pharoah's daughter lived a life of power and privilege in Egypt. Until one day, in defense of one of his people, he killed an Egyptian. When he realized he was discovered he fled for his life. Even then, he lived a peaceful family life away from the privilege and power he had in Egypt. However, here on the mountain, God presented him with a new space of privilege, honor, and power. On the mountain Moses had known the privilege of being discovered by Pharoah's daughter in the river and raised as a son of Egypt. Nevertheless, way in the desert, far from all the prestige and honor that this world's kingdom offers, he was going to learn of a new space in building the Kingdom of God.

He was going to look inside the mountain and confront several volatile spaces inside his soul. Here are but a few that yet plague many of God's servants:

- ➢ FEAR. How can God send him back to a place he ran from to save his life? God was now going to give him the privilege of being His representative to deliver His people, but fear stood like a solid roadblock on that path. If this servant of God were ever going to occupy this space of privilege to be God's Prophet, he could not get there without looking deep inside and confronting the fear of dealing with Egypt.

- ➢ FOGETFULNESS. It is understandable to run away to survive. But how could you then forget the people you left behind? Now God shows up in a burning bush, and your soul is sparked with all the painful memories you thought you left behind—forgotten spaces in your soul come rushing back? Memories of your mother's love who risked everything to save you. So forcefully, do you want to forget all you argue with God? But it is what we do. We forget the traumatic spaces of our lives that shape who we are. And we cannot move ahead without looking into those forgotten spaces of our lives. We cannot move forward on the outside without looking inward to a clean house filled with painful memories of lost relationships, lost power, and lost center. However, God was going to do good work in you, but first, you have to do good work in yourself and remember from whence you came.

- ➢ FORMER TROUBLES. Yes, the very things that trouble you in Egypt, you must confront them. Even the violence in your past must be confronted. Even the fact that you once came to the aid of your own countryman, and they did not credit you with it. Your motive and action were misunderstood by your own. Now God does not seem to understand what He is doing to pick you out of the "good life" you had developed with the skills of Egypt but now not its sanctuary.

- ➢ FORCED LABOR – SPACES OF SLAVERY. I was born a free man. My race was enslaved in Egypt land. But I was never a slave. I look inside of me, and there is no slavery there. The slave whip never touched me. But now, before the Lord, I feel inside the whip landing on my brothers and sisters enslaved. The pain and suffering of my people never come close to me until now as God invites me to look inside those hidden crevasses of my life. Egypt protected me from that space. Nevertheless, now, the fire in the bush confronts me with its message of deliverance. Tell Pharoah of Egypt of my past now, "Let my people go." It is a message so weighty inside I could not carry it without pain. "By faith Moses chose to **suffer affliction** with the people of God than to enjoy the pleasures of sin for a season (Hebrews 11:24). Forced labor redeemed by unforced service.

➢ FREE AT LAST. So, Moses in pursuit of grappling with the space of his soul ask his Lord, "When I go to Pharaoh, who shall I say sent me? Moses yearned as we all do, to find a space of solace in the unsettled sanctuary of our souls. And just like that, God obliged him. Moses is presented with a new name for God. He Is the existing One. He is presented with a new revelation of God's space. It is a name that applies to all those who seek freedom from their past to learn who God is in their present space: Tell them the "I am" sent to you. What a revelation. A you. At the space of abandonment to God and his service, the healing of our soul begins. He may not take away all your fears. Nevertheless, He will give you the courage to confront them. He lets you know you can succeed despite your fears. He will not guarantee that the road will be easy. Nevertheless, He will always make way for you. He will even use what you have in your hand. You may not be held high in the eyes; you are your enemies. However, as you endure in the service of God, He will call you up to the mountain. He will call you by his name. He will help you to see how important you are to him. When you look inside and see all those things you would rather not face, he would say from that space to look up to His. He will let you know that he lives in the same rotten space you do. "I came not to call the righteous but sinners" (Luke 5:22). Be free to let God define who you are, who you are becoming, and who you want to be.

➢ **FRAGMENTED SPACES**. Mender of fragments. Moses gave all the fragmented spaces of his life to God. On the mountain where God called Him to go Back to Egypt. He laid down his concerns piece by piece. And God mended Moses' brokenness together so he can say that before he went home to God's heavenly space, he once again took him to a mountain so he can say "I have seen the promised land" in more spaces than one.

➢ **FAITH AND FACTS SPACES**. There was another important space that Moses needed to learn to function. This was difficult because we as humans tend to discard or not know the importance of godly facts, which is what we call truth or God's "revelation." In brief, as humans, we tend to see things the way we want to see them and not see them as they are. And it cuts both ways. On the other hand, we can often deny what is before our eyes. This is often true in church. In some 30 years in Christian counseling, I have often found it a great challenge to give people "the Word of God." As I often do in my writing, I give a directive to the reader to introduce a biblical quotation: "Look at the book." I want to let the reader know that what I say is not based on my opinion but on the narrative and authority of the Holy Scripture. You would expect Christian to have not much difficulty believing the Holy Scriptures. They read it for themselves but find it difficult to accept. So, there is this "Lord I believe, help thou my unbelief" (Mark 9:23). disposition even in the Church. Nevertheless, this sentiment in the lives of Christians is not that unusual.

Moses, one of the greatest leaders of all time, faced this. This strange ability to deny the reality of what we know to be true. For example, Moses is confronted with a burning bush that is not consumed. It is right before his eyes. He is confronted with the voice of God speaking from the bush. On God's command from the bush, he saw a dead piece of wood turned into a live serpent, then turned back into a piece of wood again. Yet he still wanted to know what power God had to send him back to Egypt or even to help him with his stuttering tongue. God had to appeal to him on the basis that He was the one who made his mouth. He could not get the facts on the ground because his heart was not ready on the inside, no matter what the facts showed on the outside.

That is how powerful the inner space is. Even when confronted with the demonstrated power of God, the heart inside creates its own "facts," faith inside gets lost, and trust in God gets pushed aside. It is not an unusual space for believers to find themselves in along the journey. Many Christians cultivate a faith as if it cannot be based on facts. However, look at the book: "Faith comes by hearing and hearing the word of God" (Romans 10:17). "you shall know the truth, and the truth shall set you free" (John 8:32), out of his perception space into Powerful spaces of God's reality. Moses on the mountain had truss issues. He has not yet learned or heard the encouraging space of living in Good's space of trust: "Trust in the Lord with all your heart. Lean not on your own understanding. In all your ways, acknowledge him, and he will direct your path (Proverbs 3:5-6).

39

THE SPACE OF "ME"

The Space of "me" follows every place I go. My joys, tears, fears, sorrows, and everything I can never leave me behind. For it is who I am. However, there is the rub; to be who I want to be, I must often leave who I am behind:

"I have been crucified with Christ, and I no longer live, but Christ lives in me. And the life I live in the body, I live by faith in the Son of God, who loved me and gave himself for me" (The Apostle Paul—Galatians 2:20 emphasis mine).

The Space of Me" appears in the center of my model. It is a deliberate position for understanding spaces. I contend that the individual is more than the product of environmental forces. Everyone who may be subject to all kinds of outside influences acts like general gravity yet has an individual mind, a certain will, and a powerful choice. I must admit that many individuals do not often represent this existential reality. In the early seventies, the popular thinking of the "hippy movement" was to downplay the individual. The popular chant was, "We are just a speck in this vast universe." I never believed this. My sense of history and understanding say otherwise.

The world has been moved and changed today by people who believe—and rightly so- that they were more than a speck in this vast universe. However, this "speck" mentality of people whose worldview never gets past their front door still abounds in our world today. It is why this book is to encourage and enlighten each person to the reality that they are more than the sum total of the world around them. The circle is the largest circle in the model and at the center because the "me" it represents is symbolically and literally at the center. The world of "me" is at the center of who we are, who we are becoming, and determined by our innate choice of who we want to be. Look at the Book—one of the most profound statements on human existence and personal power: "As a man thinketh in his heart, so is he…" (Proverbs 23:7 KJV).

Who Are We?

I shall attempt to trace the flow of biblical history throughout this work as an aid to determining who we are. This stems from a very basic presupposition of being a conservative Christian. Here, I set forth the view of this book. It is not an attempt to have the reader believe as I do. It attempts to let the reader know the basic tenets on which the model of existence here is based.

1. A believer in the God of the Bible as revealed in their original texts.

2. A God who made the universe and everything in it, and specially made all humanity equally to dwell in it.

3. Who made all humankind in his image, and they all have value and divine purpose (not any will perish…) although they may not live out that purpose because of their own personal choice.

4. And fundamentally, if anyone wants to understand who they are, they must first "search the Scriptures…" as we are told to do, for in them, we gain eternal life. "These things are written that we might believe, and that believing we might have life…"

5. I have studied science. It is why I have a state license to install and repair mechanical air conditioning systems. At the age of thirteen, I already had years of after-school workshop study and training in electrical work. As a designer and builder of custom homes for years, I could not do that without relying on all the science that goes into building a modern home. I am a photographer. All the photos in my books feature my work. One of those professions, like building a home or commercial building, relies on art and science. Nevertheless, I have spent over forty years regularly researching Scriptures. I have studied every verse and considered its context and history. I have been a founder and Pastor of a church for 28 years.

6. So, I have much experience in science and the scientific method. In the middle of a deadly pandemic, I know there is a call to "rely on the science." I heard of a church congregation who never stayed home during the worst of the pandemic. The Pastor led them to put their mask on and come to church and praise God just like before the pandemic. The pastor told me they know of no one who came has fallen by this virus. I responded that is what real Christian living is about. That is what it means: "Faith without work is dead" (James 2:14). That is what I believe survival on this planet is about. It means "do not forsake the assembly of yourselves together" to follow the science, but now, when it says to stop following the Savior,

7. We bow only to science, and we lose our souls. We lose what following the Savior is all about. Now I must quickly add. When Daniel decided he was not staying home, knowing the power that he would have him thrown in the lion's den, he fully understood one of those lions could have torn him to pieces. However, he kept on going to the place of prayer anyway. Because he was committed to relying on God no matter what. Daniel lived in a space where he was first a servant of God. It was who he was. His choice, despite the lion, determines who he becomes. A man who faced down his giants and lived to encourage others to do so.

8. This is the fundamental reason what is written here is not based on science, social or otherwise. It is based on God's science in the Scriptures. Because it is the only holistic source of understanding the human condition. So here we have the science and the Scriptures intersecting so we fully understand who we are.

9. Science is good, but it does not take us deep enough to understand who we are. The Scriptures do. I invite you to follow me on this journey to understanding humanity.

The "me" of understanding

Perhaps no one in ancient times understood human nature like Moses. He wrote the first five books called the Pentateuch. However, most of all, he was called to lead Israel out of Egypt and had to deal with every human disposition there was. He had seen it all. It is to someone like this you want to learn from. You want to listen keenly to their choice of words. You want to gather up the space from which they come to you. So, Moses comes to the end of his massive ministry. What does he have to say to his fellow countrymen?

1. DEUTERONOMY: in his final address to the Israelites, Moses challenged them at the point of their soul. He did not simply ask them to behave in a certain way. Of course, he expected them to do that. What he did do was to speak to the "inside-out" spaces of their heart and soul.

2. You can see it in a certain language he used in his farewell addresses. For example, his use of the language of the heart: **(1)** "But if from there you seek the Lord your God, you will find him if you seek him *with all your heart* and with all your soul" (Deuteronomy 4:29). **(2)** 7:8, he admonished them how they should "regard" (a language of the heart and mind) idols and their artifacts. They are told "not to FORGET the Lord" (8:1-2). (3) They are told to REMEMBER" wilderness space and explained the purpose of God to "know what was in your HEART" (8:2). He told them to KNOW THEN IN YOUR HEART " (v. 5) why God discipline you. He tried to teach them that God brought them out of Egypt not simply to deliver them from the slavery of their body but also to deliver their soul from the "stake" of Egypt to manner from God. Stake in Egypt was food for the body, but his manner was to teach them to rely on God's supply. The revelation of 40 years in the wilderness was for them to learn the space of their hearts (8:2). Moses used the language of the heart and mind like "observe" (8:6-8). Moses continually challenges them to "Praise the Lord for the good land" (8:10), not just work the lands with their physical bodies but praise him from the soul. He warned them that when things change for the better, when they eat and are satisfied, build fine houses, settle down with heard and flocks crew forgetful, and the mind can get forgetful how Good God is you want to be able in your inner spaces to count your blessings, so you do not forget God. Moses spoke to Israel and targeted the spaces of their soul, their spirit, and their mind. He knows that is the space that is needed for them to live out the covenant of blessings from God (Deuteronomy 8:10-14). Moses wanted to consider the manner. It did not grow from the ground. It did not come from the earth or anything that existed upon it. It came from above. It was a hard lesson because they did not like it. Although it did what it was

meant to do, that is to sustain them. He did so to cultivate the spaces of the heart and not the body. In Deuteronomy where we find Moses final speeches, we hear him singing song to the should of Israel. A speech often focus on the mind and often Moses appealed along the journey to the understanding and mind of Israel. But here at the end of his days and leadership of Israel in these final hours he is like singing his songs to their hearts. He told them so. If he were speaking to just their minds, he would not repeatedly spoke of them REMEMBERING days gone by and how God delivered them. He would not repeatedly spoke to them about the various promises and covenants made by God to their forefathers. He would not constantly appeal to them to obey the commandments, and to seek God with all their hearts. He was singing songs that moved beyond their minds into the place into the human existence where spaces occupy--in spaces of the heart and soul, and spirit. Spaces where choices are made and mature. Spaces of existence from which the expressions of life are birth (Deuteronomy 29). He sang to the soul to show that God overriding purpose to deliver them so that out of Egypt "that you might know I Am the Lord your God" (29:6). That was what the remembering, the recalling, the stating of all the covenant, and commandments, and appeal to follow was all about. So that deep in your heart, soul, and spirit, "you might know who I am." Paul would record his appeal "That I might know him and the power of his resurrection.... (Philippians 3:10). Places of the heart. Spaces of the soul. If there was any question that Moses was alone in this, just before his death, God taught Moses a song. I told him to "write it down and teach it to the Israelites and have them sing it" (Deuteronomy 31:19). Music, more than any other means of communication, speaks to the heart. It goes to places that mare words often do not reach. When you want to expand the space of one's soul and heart, it is often the place where music takes up residence. God knows this. He created a song that would remind Israel that they would still feel their rhythm when they were not disposed to hear his words. I do not know the specific words of this song or its rhythm. But I know the verses were like spaces of the heart. A song of love when they faced the hatred of their enemies. A song of mercy when attacked mercilessly. A song of hope when the Jordan ragged. It is a song of victory when Jerica's wall seems to swell. Even a sone of judgment in their wayward ways and wandering soul. They can sing it and find peace and solace. God taught them a song that would wash the doubt and depression in the places of their soul and let hope arise in their places. DEUTERONOMY: Moses, in his final address to the Israelites, challenges them at the point of their soul. He did not simply ask them to behave in a certain way. Of course, he expected them to do that. What he did do was to speak to the "inside-out" spaces of their heart and soul. You can see it in certain language he used in his farewell addresses. For example, his use of language of the heart: "But if from there you seek the Lord your God, you will find him if you seek him with all your heart and with all your soul" (Deuteronomy 4:29) (2) 7:8 he admonished them how they should "regard" (a language of the heart and mind) idols, and their artifacts. They are told "**not to FORGET** the Lord" (8:1-2). They are told to **REMEMBER"** wilderness space and explained the purpose of God to "know what was in your HEART" (8:2). He told them **KNOW THEN IN YOUR HEART** " (V.5) why God discipline you. He tried to teach them that God brough them out of Egypt not simple to deliver them from slavery of their body, but also to deliver their soul from the "stake" of Egypt to manner from God. Stake in Egypt was food for the body but his manner was to teach them to rely on God's supply. The revelation of 40 years in the wilderness was for them to learn the space of their hearts (8:2). Moses used language of the heart and mind like "**observe**" (8:6-8).

3. Moses continually challenge them to "Praise the Lord for the good land" (Deuteronomy 8:10) not just work the lands with their physical bodies but praise him from the soul. He warned them when things change for the better, when they eat and are satisfied, build fine houses, settle down with hurds and flocks their souls and grow forgetful and the mind can get forgetful how Good God is you want to be able in your inner spaces to count your blessings, so you do not forget God. Moses spoke to Israel and targeted the spaces of their soul, their spirit, their mind. He know that is the space that is needed for them to live out the covenant of blessings from God (Deuteronomy (8: 10-14) Moses wanted to consider the manner. It did not grow from the ground. It did not come from the earth or anything that exist upon it. It came from above. It was a hard lesson because they did not like it. Although it did what it was meant to do that is to sustain them.

Just because Israel made it out of Egypt to the Promise Land did not mean their trials were over. They had driven out all their enemies except for the one withing. The space within their spirit. The space within their soul. They found there a longing, a desire for things forbidden. They found withing themselves a desire--a space with a gravity pull yet within them towards the very things their forefather's warned them not to desire. It came with the force of alternative culture and lifestyle that was forbidden; that was foreign to theirs. They found a space within them--a gravitational pull to gods of the nations around them, they never knew and did not do anything for them. And they fell for their worship. They followed the lifestyle of their enemies, and entertained their godless customs, even to the point of sacrificing their own children to these gods made by hands. They did not keep watch over the righteous spaces of their heart and soul. What they desired led them astray from their own culture and ways established by covenants and commandments given through their leaders from God.

Sometimes spaces collide, as in Samson's case. He was a Nazarite, and as such, no hair on his head was to be cut. A space intersecting with nature. A natural characteristic - his hair. His physical strength, a unique space of strength, was connected with his hair not being cut. When it was his strength was gone. So, although it was a physical attribute, it was also a spiritual space (a vow his mother took for him to be separated from God (Judges 14:3-5). So, his power was also of a spiritual nature--a spiritual space. Here, the physical - hair, uncut, was connected to the physical space. When his hair was cut 1 Kings introduced us to the building of the Temple of Worship on God's instructions and details the contributions of Nature 1 Kings 6, one can see the contribution of wood, stones, metal, like bronze and gold...to build a place that reminds us not only of God but all that he had made including animal life used in sacrifices to him...foreshadowing the role of blood space in redemption.

No narrative exemplifies the significance of inner spaces that motivate the lives of existence, as does the life of Elisha, the protege of Elijah. He moved steadily from an obscured farmer in his father's field to being a motivating Prophet of Israel (1 KINGS 19:19). Here is an alliterated outline of this Prophet's life that showed the difference between who he was inside and the impact it made on his choices of the spaces within. 1. HE was a lad that one. **WANTED MORE**: He was not satisfied with working in his father's field. He wanted to be more than a field hand. So, when the call to be a Prophet of God came to take up the mantle of a student or assistant to be a disciple of the great prophet of Elijah. There was no hesitation because, Inside-out, he wanted more. 2. **WORKED MORE.** His mentor, Elijah, often told him to take a break and stay back. He told him he did not have to follow his Master every place. Elisha refused. He wanted to be everywhere his Master wanted to go. He was there. He wanted to work harder than any other. Elijah said to him, "Go back," and take a break. You can stay home sometimes. However, his inner soul said no. Go with your master every place he goes. See everything. Learn everything. Work more and work harder. Stay the course with your master. He listened to his inner voice and WORKED MORE. 3. HE **WILLED MORE:** When asked what he wanted from pursuing his master Elijah. He answered, "Give me a double portion" (2 Kings 2:9-14). That was the choice he made. And his master told him. If you see me go--taken up into Heaven, you will have that which you willed. That was who he was, and it determined who he was becoming. He willed more than he had. He was an unsatisfied soul with a purpose of being more good and godly and a goal to be much more than what he had. So, he never let up moving forward in the available spaces worthy of Heaven. Then four. HE **WITHNESS MORE**. He believed in the prophetic promise. It had happened just once before with a man named Enoch. Why would he believe it would happen in his time? This country farmer believed the prophetic promise that he would have what he desired if he were present when his Master was taken up to Heaven. He believed it in his heart and saw it with his eyes. He saw where his master's tunic fell, and he picked it up and had within his soul a double portion of his Master's power space. He soon saw some men working, and one of them lost his ax head in the river. He called for it and saw the iron ax head swim and faith that works (2 Kings 61-7). It was about the powerful divine space in which he function. He wanted more. He worked more, he willed more, and as a result, he witnessed more in his life, from farmland to being a leader of Israel

In 2 KINGS 22:7, Hilkiah - the High Priest, is said did not have to account for the money paid to the contractors and workers for "they are honest in their dealing" (2 Kings 22:7). Here is a situation where the reputation of the high priest and his staff were of such that no one had to watch over them. Character matters. He Hilkiah found the book of the law in the temple as they were working there. It was lost in the house. A geographical location where the written Word of God was silent in the house (2 Kings 22:11,17).

In Proverbs, along with the Psalms, the reader of proverbs is introduced to "us" in different spaces of our lives. The focus is from the inside out. It seeks to build character and well-being from inner spaces that, internally, become the behavior expression of others- the outer spaces. Here is but a sample of the character spaces that the writer of Proverbs exhausted his readers to develop: INSIDE-OUT "Each heart knows its own bitterness, and no one else can share its joy" (14;10). Private spaces are the hallmark of the soul. "who can know it?" It is a statement of the overwhelming importance of inner space. Proverbs 18:14 is A critical statement of the relative differences between the physical space, as in sickness, and the spiritual space, as in a "crushed spirit." The biblical validation of the inner space Psalm 20:27 "The human spirit is the lamp of the Lord that sheds light on one's inmost being" v. 30 "Blows and wounds scrub away evil, and beatings purge the inmost being" 22:1 "A good name is more desirable than great riches; to be esteemed is better than silver or gold." Character Counts. 27:19 "As water reflects the face so one's life reflects the heart.

SOLOMON/ECCLEASSIAS. Then I saw all that God has done. No one can comprehend what goes on under the sun. Despite all their efforts to search it out, no one can discover its meaning. Even if the wise claim they know, they cannot really comprehend it. Then he goes on to make a devastating argument that cannot be denied: The common destiny of everyone: "All share a common destiny-- the righteous and the wise and what they do are in God's hands, but no one knows whether love or hate awaits them. All share a common destiny--the righteous and the wicked, the good and the bad, the clean and the unclean, those who offer sacrifices and those who do not" (9:1-2). Ecclesiastes is like an intellectual journey into the abyss of life. It is filled with darkness and borderline delusional, yet here and there are like lampstand lights in the maze of the tunnels to find the way out so that all is not lost. It shows the difficult spaces of the mind as it raced with life in the intellectual quandary of life and its common issues. Yet, it is what makes his conclusion of the fear of God and obedience to Him so worthy of consideration. It is because it is understandable the conclusion of one who had taken a lifetime considering all the alternative spaces on this planet to Him and found none (this section or thoughts could be considered as the conclusion or summary of this Book. After all the spaces considered, such spaces are all meaningless without God, who alone gives all of life on every level: Righteous and Wicken, good and bad spaces, heaven and hell, and everything and everyone in between. There is no meaning in anything without God. This is the point of the Book. It is a point that every human being should at least consider from the wisest human who ever lives.

ECCLESIASTES. See commentary on the book in line #1. It is a deep dive into Solomon's personal spaces over his lifetime and what he learned from the apparent "meaninglessness" of it all. His journey outside-in and teach each person the values of what is important in life. It can teach us who we are in the choices and values we place on the things in this world and who we are becoming in the values we embrace in this life. The entire discourse of this book is a dive into the ocean of everyone's personal spaces and the value we place on each of them. The writer asked and gave his answer to the ultimate question of life: "What do people gain from all their labors at which they toil under the sun? The modern world is no different at its core from the old. "There is nothing new under the sun." That, which has been one the most valuable things of life since humankind was created on this planet, is still the same despite any advancement. The needed spaces of the mind and heart have not changed. Its longings remain the same, and so are what is valued most. Nothing in modern life can replace the needed space and soul satisfaction. And nothing but the unique space and spaces that God fills can ever be substituted. It will all end up "all is vanity." It is, however, the constant effort of humankind from generation to generation to find the big alternative answer to a unique space the Creator carved out for Himself in every human's heart. It can never be filled either by doing evil or Good. He alone can fill that inner space. He alone can settle the issue of value. Those who claim they alone can fix it as a lie. Only God can is the argument of this book. To consider this book as simple as poetry is to miss its Divine purpose--dealing with who we are and who we are becoming.

JEREMIAH: Jerimiah was called to be a Prophet space to be a spokesperson for God in a climate and culture that had become anti-God. It's tough enough to be a Prophet in these countries, made even worse for a prophet who did not want to take up this task. On his call by God, he told him he was too young and did not know how to speak. He had to ability to speak to God to tell him he did not know how to speak. That was quite a feat to pull off. He did not. This was a call that no one could refuse. Not Moses, who tried the same scheme of excuses. He was afraid he was not up to the task. And the message he had to speak to his people and the nations was no piece of cake. He was given a hard message of judgment, the kind of message that he risked his life to proclaim. Nevertheless, the message created a space in his heart that he could not despise. Jerimiah 39 recorded the fall of Jerusalem. He was among those who were captured.

EZEKIEL: "I came to the exiles who lived in Tel Aviv near the Kbar River. And there, where they were living, I sat among them for seven days--deeply distressed. He had a unique calling and a deep sense of community. So, he lamented and felt the pain of his people as he sat among them (3:15). God was now going to define his ministry further. He was a spokesperson--to tell forth what God said. But now, a new space was being opened up for him to occupy. So we read (v.16), "At the end of seven days the word of the Lord came to me: Son of man, I have made you a watchman for the people of Israel; so hear the word I speak and give them warning for me. Accountability to warn so that you would not be held accountable. As a watchman on the wall, you would see in the distance when the enemy is be able to give fair warning of impending war. The people then can take cover and be prepared. The watchman would not be responsible for those whom the enemy overruns because they had a warning. God changed the space in which Ezekiel would not function. A new role, responsibility, and relationship with his God.

DANIEL: He is an example of personal resolution in the Bible. A hostile King Nebuchadnezzar came to Jerusalem and besieged it. He took some of the best of the city and took them back to for his service. Among them were Daniel and his friends Shadrack, Meshack, and Abennego. The chief official was put in charge of them. They were given a direct native to their enemy, which was inconsistent with Daniel and his friend's religious culture and ways. The report said, "Daniel resolved not to defile himself with the royal food and wine and asked to be omitted from it. He is a strange land. He has no power or standing. However, he took a stand not to defile himself and was willing to bear the consequences. They resolve to honor their God in a strange land. Later they would be tested. Daniel is tested in the Lion's den and his friends in the Nebuchadnezzar furnace. Nevertheless, each stood firm and won the victory in the fire and the lions' home. In the face of crisis, he kept his prayer life up. He discovered there was a space between the lion and life. A wall of unseen protected space. (6:12-22) Daniel interprets the dreams of others, and now he is experiencing his own. Daniel 7:

A friend of mine told me a story that turned her world upside down. It was the week she buried her husband of many decades. So that was traumatic enough. He had gone to his funeral, and while there, she met three young ladies and discovered they were the adult children of her late husband. She had never known he had all these years. I tell this story of long ago not to take sides or to pass or solicit any judgment but to give a real-life example of how one can live years in a space close to another without truly knowing who they are. There were financial clues from the outside (he had ensured the girls were well taken care of), but she had ignored them. People in such traumatic relationship circumstances can fall apart. Sometimes, spaces shift at times when, in your own skin or space, you are the least prepared for them. I contend that people who independently do not know who they are and live on that secure foundation will indeed fall apart. David expressed it when he sang, "Even though I walk to the valley of death, I will fear no evil for you are with me" (Psalm 23).

There is a young man I know who also had a similar experience. He discovered he had brothers and sisters by his dad beyond his immediate family. He would then often introduce them to others as his "half-brother" or "half-sister" until one day, a friend asked him, "Which half was your brother or sister: the top half or the bottom half? That day, he had a change in basic assumptions how he viewed himself and his extended family. He began to see his extended family as a whole family. It changed how he saw himself and in turn, how he saw his extended family, which made for a fuller experience of love caring, and personal growth. "As a man thinks in his heart, so is he" (Proverbs 23:7). I contend that if you cannot see who you are and change those things that need to be, there can be no meaningful growth. Sometimes, before you can change your purpose, you need to change your personal perceptions and often that of others as well.

Shape Shifters

"To thine own self be true, and it must follow as the night the day thou cannot then be false to any man" (Shakespeare in Hamlet, Soliloquy by Polonius). "A double-minded man is unstable in all his ways" (James 1:8). Let your yes be yes, and your no be no (Matthew 5:37). Perhaps not knowing who another person in this world (whoever they are) can be forgiven. However, as you confront the challenges of spaces of your world, it is essential to know who you are. Know not only your strengths but your weaknesses as well. Know you before you do you. You cannot do it if you do not know yourself. People can change like the weather. It is because they know only who they think they are. That is not enough to face your world's challenges. Other people think of knowing how you are. You are the only one besides God who truly can know. A picture of you is not you. Your presentation on social media is no substitute for who you are. Why? Because who you are is beyond the skin that you show others.

The Apostle James spoke of one who "looks at himself in a mirror then goes out and forgot what he sees "(James 1:24). He shifted the shape of what he saw in the morrow. You not only need to know who you are, but you need not let the world outside shift your presentation of who you know you are.

Sometimes, I feel I do not deserve to be me, for so many people have contributed to making me who I am. It is unthinkable that I could survive the many trying experiences I have overcome without the constant stability poured into me by my significant others, friends, and family in my life. So, I come to this subject of my space with a certain humility and complexity of understanding. For there can hardly be any claim of who I am without the contribution of others. Nevertheless, knowing that despite such contribution, the former president observed, "the buck stops here." It stops with me against the world. "passage that deals with this…." I come only to do the will of my Father…. At the end of the day, you are who you are because of who you allow yourself to be. At the end of the day, it is still the "me" space that is the responsible source of who you are.

In his song "Champion," Dante Bowe testified, "I know who I am, I know whose I am."

40

THE SPACE OF ME – ALONENESS

What is loneliness? What is this space that hugs us even in a crowd? What is the scale between loneliness and being alone? Where does loneliness live? Is loneliness just a feeling of being alone? Is it a choice or reaction to experience? Can the space of loneliness be described? If so, how? Is it a crisis or a process? Are there stages of loneliness like they are stages of grief? How do you get into the space of loneliness? How do you get out?

I grew up as the last of eleven. I was raised in a church community in a village where everyone knows everyone. I went to college as a part of a large "student body." After graduation, a pastor of a congregation for three decades and married for almost four. Then cancer came suddenly calling. Our daughter had to leave college during her third year to come help take care of her in those slow, painful leaving of not just a marriage but a very close friend. She was gone. Then my daughter left as she must, to pursue her own dreams.

Suddenly, for the very first time, facing what I never experienced before, living with no one around—not even a pet. From day one, I had to learn about this new, lonely space in my life step by step. One more question: If one has a space in their heart and soul found there after the loss of someone that filled it—can that space ever be filled again? If so, how?

I am not being dramatic. I raised these questions to myself and feel at a loss to find answers for my own soul. So, this essay is without answers yet a quest to find them. It is an important part of my search. When I search for answers, I first begin by asking hard questions. The reader can also find inspiration and answers in their own quest if they desire to know this space or help someone else.

The Mystery of Loneliness.

Loneliness moves in a space of mystery. It is like the wind, not knowing from whence it comes or goes. Sometimes loneliness brings sadness, and other times sweet solace. It's a battle sometimes to "have your own space" and yet want to share it. It is like seeing a beautiful bird pouched alone when countless birds are somewhere, just not there. It is like how we are created from the beginning to navigate this space—to know ourselves in that space.

God described loneliness as being physically incompatible with one's surroundings. It is like in the beginning being enveloped by everything and compatible with nothing. God described it as something amiss—something missing in his creation of man. Man as man was not whole. And if God did not do anything about it all man would ever know was loneliness, for no one compatible with him would be around. Even with the connection of the soul, there would be no connections. He would always be unconnected. Like broken wires inside unable to connect to the flow of life beaming around him. Like the unconnected seeking connections, so He said:

- "It is not good for the man to be alone, but I will make a helper suitable for him" (Genesis 2:18). This was only the beginning. He continued the discourse:
- "One who has unreliable friends soon comes to ruin, but there is a friend who sticks closer than a brother" (Proverbs 18: 24).
- "Do not urge me to leave you or to turn back from you. Where you go I will go and where you stay I will stay. Your people will be my people and your God my God" (Ruth 1:16).
- And let us not neglect our meeting together, as some people do, but encourage one another, especially now that the day of his return is drawing near" (Hebrews 10:25 NLT).
  - o JESUS:
  - o *"I was a stranger, and you did not invite me in*
  - o *I needed clothes, and you did not clothe me*
  - o *I was sick and in prison, and you did not look after me*

So, On my journey to understand the mystery of this space of loneliness, I found Jesus himself confronting this space. He openly shared His prophetic grief of being alone because others rejected him. Nevertheless, the extraordinary application concerned how we treat our fellow humans alone in their nakedness and wantonness.

They were alone in their medical condition and needed help, and no one came to help. They were isolated and alone, like in prison, and were left there without anyone coming to look after them—a spiritual journey in earth-space. Jesus is the ultimate cure for any loneliness. And Heaven is the ultimate cure for forever being alone.

These words of Jesus were not given as poetic expressions. They were not given for emotional comfort. These are heartfelt words from the Divine space to ours, revealing God's own expression of experiencing this space of loneliness. He was showing us in real-time in our lives here those who among us are left lonely (Matthew 25). Each of his identifiable conditions in our world can be substituted with the word or real-time condition of destitute loneliness. For example:

> I was *lonely,* and you did not invite me in.
> I was *lonely,* and you did not clothe me.
> I was *lonely,* sick, and in prison, and you did not look after me.

It must not be missed that the consistent spaces unattended by the part of the religious culture that thought they had gained an all-access pass to heaven were those who overlooked the destitute loneliness of others in desperate need spaces in this world.

There is much left to explore in this space. Most essays I write from much research. This is not one of them. I did not know where to begin. So, I just started to write the questions that led me to consider how I now see Jesus in a new way. I journeyed into a space of loneliness and found Jesus there. Then, thinking back, how could I have missed how lonely Jesus was in this world? He who said he came because His Father so loved this world, then said, "He came to His own and his own did not receive Him (John 1:11). He said, "Foxes have holes…..the son of man had no place…." (Matthew 8:20). There was a scene together in a garden where he went aside to pray as he faced the cross. And as soon as he stepped aside, He returned and found his disciples "sleeping." And his question was an expression of his loneliness on this earth: "Could you not have watched with me …? Then He stood before Pilot alone. No one spoke for him. He hung on the cross alone.

This journey led me to see Jesus as the loneliest man ever. I now understand just a little more of this space. My loneliness is of little value. It is the loneliness of others in need and my attempt to make a difference that takes care of mine.

"I go to prepare a place for you that where I am, you will also be" (John 14):

EPILOGUE

I have often opened the Holy Bible when I am prompted out of a need to hear from God. I have done this often throughout my Christian life as a teenager. God has never failed to give me directions or calm my concerns about whatever was on my mind and heart. Nevertheless, I do not recommend this practice to others. David said, "Thy word is a lamp unto my feet and a light unto my path" (Psalm 119:105). As a boy, I took this literally and so I started to open the Bible to find that light. I now know that although this is true in principle, in practice God's Holy Spirit has a variety of ways in which he guides his followers. That is but one way among many. So, he can use a burning bush for Moses, a vision for Daniel, a friend as in John and David, a storm as in the case of the disciples, and even a big fish as in the case of Jonah. "In the council of many, there is wisdom" (Proverbs 15:22). So, when I speak of this as I have throughout this work, I am not advocating for this, but only to share how I came to be aware of a particular truth or guidance—moreover, the desire to share what I learned with the reader.

So, for example, as I completed this volume after some three years of writing, I found myself with a blank mind, not knowing what to say in conclusion. So, I prayed to God and was prompted to open the Scriptures and read where my eyes were directed on the pages. In so doing, I opened "randomly," without any specific place in mind, and it was to the first words of Luke's gospel. I began to see Luke in a space I had not seen before. Luke was sharing his approach to writing the book by his name. What he said caught my attention and calmed my apprehension about my writings of these three volumes. He humbly acknowledged how his work was based on so many others who were themselves "eyewitnesses." As he put his book together, he relied on their record for things he was not present. He was grateful to them. I was moved by the description of Luke of those who recorded what they saw. He called them *"servants of the word."* And so was I.

This work I shared was simple. I was a "servant of the word," as did Luke. Luke said he was careful in his narrative of his Lord's life since he relied on others. He was careful that his record of their report was correct. In this, I rely on nothing I can write about God and His work in the Old Testament and the New. I was not in any way an "eyewitness." Thus, I became just a "servant of the word." Moreover, Luke added more. He explained how his reliance guided his purpose in writing his book. He said it made him even more careful to collect the eyewitness record and ensure its accuracy in recording those he called "servants of the word" because they were "eyewitnesses" to the holy record of the Word of Life. So was I.

I had to rely entirely on the narrative of other writers in the Holy Scriptures, which was more reliant as Luke added more. He said that because he relied on the "servants of the word, " he was cautious in his research to see that what he wrote was consistent with what was handed down. And so, I was. I was careful to vet every writing.

Then Luke recorded, as is often the case, not just to identify the content and how he approached it but also to mention to whom it was addressed. Here, Luke did an extraordinary thing that could easily be missed in this early Christian movement. He was an Israelite who, along with his people, existed like slaves under the Roman government space. However, he had no hesitancy in addressing his book to one Theophilus, an official in the Roman government. He moves across cultural lines, racial lines, status, and religious divides to address the Gospel of Jesus Christ narrative.

I cannot express the joy and peace that this Gospel writer expressed in his reliance on others and that he can write on matters with authority without having been present because he relied on those who were "servants to the word." Then, he spoke of himself as having "carefully investigated everything from the beginning." I felt assured I was in good company, having carefully investigated every subject matter in these volumes.

After hearing from Elohim's servants, Creators of worlds and universes, my blank mind led me to this excellent writer. In writing the Gospel, he thought of all those not of his race, with information on which he was not an eyewitness, as are so many of the followers of Jesus, but he gave us confidence that we can rely on those who were servants *of the word*.

Thank you for reading these essays, which deal with three significant categories of Space in the Universe: the God Space, the Cross of Jesus Christ Space, and the personal space of "Us"—outside-in, inside-out. The other two volumes cover the vast spaces beyond the edge of our skin, how we can influence these spaces, how they influence who we are, who we are becoming, and how we can navigate who we desire to be.

INTRODUCTION TO VOLUMES 2 AND 3

THE SPACE OF ME AGAINST SPACES OF THE UNIVERSE

Spaces

I am sometimes so alone. Then, I look around and see I am never alone. There are always spaces around me. I exist in a space that is not me. It's me against my world.

I am alone. Then my thoughts rage far and wide filling me with past times and events; present responsibilities and a future calling filled with spaces of possibilities.

How could I be alone when my body, soul and spirit constantly being tugged, pushed, bombarded with blessings of existence all around me?

From birth to death, I could not be alone. There are too many spaces that vouch for my care and attention-like gravity forces pulling me in every direction

while I am here.

How do I know who I am? How do I know who I am becoming? How do I navigate who I desire to be?

JESUS: "My prayer is not that you take them out of the world but that you keep them safe..." (John 17:15).

ACKNOWLEDGMENTS

To my brothers: Kelvin, Kenneth, Leonard, Neville, Ronald, and Conrad.

To my sisters: Mary, Rachel, Beryl, Margaret, Pamela, and Kendra.

They nurtured me as among the last of this good lot; in life and memory, spaces contributed richly to my existence.

To Representative Terry Scott, who invited me to start a Sabbath morning Bible Study at his home in Deerfield Beach, Florida, over two decades ago. The study focused on understanding "the grid", which refers to the invisible frames through which we interpret the world and the way the world perceives us. These weekly Bible lessons led to the development of a model that forms the basis for understanding the spaces of our existence.

I want to share some thoughts on the impactful work of TV host and author Rachel Meadows. As a graduate in communication, I have gained valuable insights from her approach to various issues. Her masterful contextual elements have helped me understand different subjects in a way that's truly enlightening. It is akin to attending a class led by an expert teacher who knows how to create a compelling "story world" that draws you in. Rachel's ability to explain complex topics with such excitement highlights their often-hidden, explosive aspects.

In particular, her repeated invitation on her show to "Watch this Space!" has had a profound impact on my work. For years, I've been developing a model of "Spaces of the Universe," and Rachel's consistent and insightful invitation to "watch this space" made me feel supported in my journey of researching and writing about viewing all our worlds as "spaces" to be understood and navigated. Her encouragement has been an invaluable source of motivation and inspiration for me.

Permissions and Credits

Special Acknowledgments and credits

Page 45: Courtesy of Kady Gracia Photographer 13 yr. "The Rhythm of Time"

Page 86: Courtesy of Konia Gracia, A Portrait of Prayer – Photographer by Author

Page 163: Courtesy of Freddericka Thompson, Photographer, The Eclipse – North Texas, 3-8-24

Page 271: Courtesy of Diamond Bolling, Poet "Spaces of Me"

Content Photography/Graphics Illustrations by Author

Page viii: Courtesy of the Author "Model Spaces of the Universe"

Page ix: Courtesy of the Author, Graphic "Biblical Language of Spaces"

Page 1: "Beginning Spaces"

Page 4: "Fearfully and Wonderfully Made"

Page 9: "Imagination"

Page 25: "Rain Space":

Page 11: "No Fear"

Page 12: "Worth More than Sparrows"

Page 13: "Where Can I Go From Your Spirit"

Page 15: "Shared Spaces"

Page 17: "Spaces of Existence for Existence"

Page 19: "Elohim, Jehovah, Yahweh, *A Space Above All the Rest*"

Page 22: "Saint Augustine, You Have Made Us For Yourself"

Page 24: "Revelation"

Page 25: "Who is Worthy to Opel the Scroll?"

Page 26, 47: "The Potter and the Clay"

Page 29: "Oh, the Depth"

Page 33: "Rainbow Space"

Page 34: "Details, Details!"

Page 35: "Nothing from Nothing is Nothing"

Page 42: "Alpha and Omega"

Page 44: "So High"

Pages 45,46,47: Creator of Time-Space"

Page 55: "Mercy Space"

Poetry, Courtesy Of the Author

The Timoty Trail: "Rightly Dividing the Word of Truth"

Graphic /Model Outlines For Further Study by Author

Dr. Arnold Thompson's academic training includes graduating from Moody Bible Institute, Chicago, in Bible and Evangelism (BA); Florida Atlantic University: Communication Theory and Rhetoric (BA); Evangelical Bible Collège and Seminary: Master of Divinity, and Doctor of Theology.

Dr. Thompson was the founder and senior pastor of Agape Bible Church in Florida for twenty-eight years. As a pastor, he wrote articles on various Christian topics in "Agape Times," a church newsletter, each month for 10 ten years. He has organized and spoken at interfaith conferences at two adult and two youth retreats each year for 20 twenty years and spoken/preaching each Sunday for over 30 thirty years.

The author's other published books include The Dark Side of the Gospel, Deliver Us From Evil—A Prayer for Our Times, The Death of Wisdom: the Rise of Folly, The Evangelical Church at the Crossroads of Secular Culture and Change, Why Do Birds Fly, and three volumes of Spaces of Existence—Understanding Life and Living it.